Freedom of Analysis?

Studies in Generative Grammar 95

Editors

Harry van der Hulst
Jan Koster
Henk van Riemsdijk

Mouton de Gruyter
Berlin · New York

Freedom of Analysis?

Edited by

Sylvia Blaho
Patrik Bye
Martin Krämer

Mouton de Gruyter
Berlin · New York

Mouton de Gruyter (formerly Mouton, The Hague)
is a Division of Walter de Gruyter GmbH & Co. KG, Berlin.

The series Studies in Generative Grammar was formerly published by
Foris Publications Holland.

⊚ Printed on acid-free paper which falls within the guidelines
of the ANSI to ensure permanence and durability.

Library of Congress Cataloging-in-Publication Data

> Freedom of analysis? / edited by Sylvia Blaho, Patrik Bye, Martin Krämer.
>   p. cm. − (Studies in generative grammar ; 95)
>   Includes bibliographical references and index.
>   ISBN 978-3-11-019359-6 (cloth : alk. paper)
>   1. Grammar, Comparative and general − Phonology.   2. Generative grammar.   3. Optimality theory (Linguistics)   I. Blaho, Sylvia, 1979−   II. Bye, Patrik.   III. Krämer, Martin, 1969−
>   P217.6.F74   2007
>   414−dc22
>   2007039606

Bibliographic information published by the Deutsche Nationalbibliothek

The Deutsche Nationalbibliothek lists this publication in the Deutsche Nationalbibliografie;
detailed bibliographic data are available in the Internet at http://dnb.d-nb.de.

ISBN 978-3-11-019359-6
ISSN 0167-4331

© Copyright 2007 by Walter de Gruyter GmbH & Co. KG, D-10785 Berlin.
All rights reserved, including those of translation into foreign languages. No part of this
book may be reproduced in any form or by any means, electronic or mechanical, including
photocopy, recording, or any information storage and retrieval system, without permission
in writing from the publisher.
Cover design: Christopher Schneider, Berlin.
Printed in Germany.

Contents

1	Freedom of Analysis? *Sylvia Blaho, Patrik Bye and Martin Krämer*	1
2	Laryngeal Underspecification and Richness of the Base *Daniel Currie Hall*	11
3	Underlying representations that do not minimize grammatical violations *Andrew Nevins and Bert Vaux*	35
4	Allomorphy – selection, not optimization *Patrik Bye*	63
5	A freer input: Yowlumne opacity and the Enriched Input Model *Orhan Orgun and Ronald Sprouse*	93
6	Derived Environment Effects and Consistency of Exponence *Marc van Oostendorp*	123
7	Colored turbid accents and containment: A case study from lexical stress *Anthi Revithiadou*	149
8	Freedom, Interpretability, and the Loop *Paul de Lacy*	175
9	Restraint of Analysis *John J. McCarthy*	203
10	The roles of GEN and CON in modeling ternary rhythm *Curt Rice*	233
11	Representational complexity in syllable structure and its consequences for GEN and CON *Jennifer L. Smith*	257
12	Restricting GEN *Christian Uffmann*	281
13	The division of labor between segment-internal structure and violable constraints *Bruce Morén*	313

| 14 | Variables in Optimality Theory
Chris Golston | 345 |

	Subject index	373
	Language index	378
	Author index	381
	List of contributors	387

Chapter 1
Freedom of Analysis?*

Sylvia Blaho, Patrik Bye and Martin Krämer

In Classical (Parallelist) Optimality Theory (OT), the burden of description and explanation is made to fall exclusively on universal constraints on output well-formedness. This is enforced through two related principles known as 'Richness of the Base' (McCarthy 2002: 70–71, Prince & Smolensky 2004: 205, 225) and 'Freedom of Analysis'. The first is the idea that there are no restrictions on the *input* to the grammar; the second is the idea that there are no restrictions on the *processes* that map input to output.[1] The present volume addresses what restrictions it might be appropriate to impose on these two types of freedom.

Richness of the Base may be understood as a methodological injunction against assuming the existence of linguistically significant generalizations ouside the system of violable constraints. It entails the set of inputs to the grammar is universal. McCarthy (2002: 70) spells out more specifically what this means:

> [Richness of the Base] says that there are no language-particular restrictions on the input, no linguistically significant generalizations about the lexicon, no principled lexical gaps, no lexical redundancy rules, morpheme structure constraints, or similar devices.

Richness of the Base is part of OT's antidote to the problem of duplication that dogged approaches based on context-sensitive rewrite rules. OT's initial critique of these approaches is that rules had to be complemented by parochial morpheme structure conditions (MSCs) that constrained the underlying form directly. This resulted in a situation where what is intuitively the same generalization might be encoded in the grammar more than once.

OT's second major departure from rule-based derivational theory is its stance on processes. In rule-based approaches, the structural description and structural change are specified on a language-particular basis. In OT, however, processes are also universal and apply blindly.

[GEN] defines for any given input a large space of candidate analyses by freely exercising the basic structural resources of the representational theory. The idea is that the desired output lies somewhere in this space.

(Prince & Smolensky 2004: 7)

Rule-based derivational approaches might be characterized as 'input/process-oriented'. Together, Richness of the Base and Freedom of Analysis direct focus away from the input and processes and encourage reduction to output-constraint interaction in H-EVAL.

Fifteen years after the inception of the OT research programme the time is right to reassess these principles. Are there aspects of phonological knowledge of language that cannot or should not be reduced to output-constraint interaction? To the best understanding of the contributors to this volume, there is such a residue of irreducible properties.

Attention to Richness of the Base has played an important role in exposing pathologies in the analysis. A common analytical error in OT is 'hidden' restrictions on the input. These come to light when the predictions of the grammar are tested against a wider range of inputs and the grammar turns out to generate outputs that are inconsistent with the observed patterns. Despite the heuristic usefulness of Richness of the Base in concentrating attention on the output constraint system, it is still an issue whether it is possible to recognize linguistically significant generalizations outside the OT constraint system without becoming vulnerable to the charge of duplication.

Freedom of Analysis has not received anything like the same attention as Richness of the Base. How much freedom Freedom of Analysis should entail is nonetheless an important issue. There are two parts to this question: (i) how (internally) restricting is GEN, (ii) how (externally) restricted is GEN? The first concerns limits (or lack of such) on GEN's computational power. The second concerns limitations imposed on GEN by other principled domains outside GEN itself. These principled domains may be other aspects of phonology, narrowly conceived, or other modules of language. The most obvious, but not the only, such external restriction is the theory of phonological representations.

In the following paragraphs, we introduce the contributions to this volume in three blocks according to whether they address: (i) restrictions on the underlying form, (ii) internal restrictions in GEN, (iii) external restrictions on GEN.

Let us begin by introducing those articles addressing the possibility of linguistically significant generalizations beyond EVAL.

Daniel Currie Hall argues that, in contrast the the requirements of the Richness of the Base, there are cases where inputs have to be assumed to be crucially underspecified and investigates the consequences of this for Lexicon Optimization. He reviews some cases that empirically support Inkelas's extension of Lexicon Optimization, Alternant Optimization (2004), but shows that the principle does not produce the desired results for the case of Czech voicing assimilation. He argues the data also speaks for allowing underspecified segments to surface, and this in turn has far-reaching consequences for formulating faithfulness constraints.

Lexicon Optimization is also the point of departure in the paper by Andrew Nevins and Bert Vaux. Lexicon Optimization says that the choice of underlying form is governed by the goal of minimizing faithfulness violations in a candidate. It is this that Nevins and Vaux take issue with. Reviewing a large body of experimental evidence, they show that the desire to minimize disparities between the output and the underlying form is consistently outweighed by factors such as morphological knowledge, statistical information about the frequencies of lexical items and phonological structures, and even orthographic knowledge.

Patrik Bye proposes that, in addition to EVAL, there is a parallel system of more or less functionally arbitrary *morpholexical* constraints, one of whose functions is to encode idiosyncratic combinatorial restrictions pertaining to particular affixes. In constrast to OT constraints, morpholexical constraints are declarative *filters*, and any output form that violates them is absolutely ungrammatical. Bye exploits this declarative property to relate the phenomenon of gaps to cases where the distribution of suppletive allomorphs cannot be determined by H-EVAL, because the factual distribution given the constraints in CON is phonologically neutral or even the inverse of the distribution favoured by the constraints. The approach also has consequences for GEN: since absolute ungrammaticality is dealt with outside the system of optimality, the need for GEN to supply the null parse candidate (McCarthy & Prince 2001; McCarthy & Wolf 2005) is rendered unnecessary.

Orhan Orgun and Ronald Sprouse apply the Enriched Input Model (EIM) to opacity, taking up the classic challenge of the interaction of vowel lowering, backness harmony and shortening in Yowlumne (Yawelmani). The enriched input encodes systematic properties that cannot be derived from the output directly. EVAL on this view operates on pairs of enriched input and output, with some constraints relativized to the enriched input, others to the output.

Our second block of contributions addresses internal restrictions on GEN. The question of computational limits on GEN's activity itself consists of two parts. The first concerns the set of *processes* available to GEN. Specifically, is GEN limited to building structure (insertion), or does it have the power to change representations by deletion and substitution of nodes, features, association lines, and so on? The second part of the formal question concerns limitations on the way the available processes *apply*. Are they restricted to applying one at a time, or may they apply in parallel as in Classical OT?[2]

In earlier work in OT (Prince & Smolensky 2004; McCarthy & Prince 2001),[3] Freedom of Analysis was radically restricted by the principle of Containment, according to which "no element may literally be removed from the input form". GEN operations were at that time conceived as exclusively structure-building, and so Freedom of Analysis was essentially Freedom of Insertion: "GEN may supply candidates with syllabic, moraic, or other prosodic structure, with association lines, and with additional segmental material, ranging from empty root nodes through fully specified vowels or consonants" (McCarthy & Prince 2001: 21). With the advent of Correspondence Theory (McCarthy & Prince 1995, 1999), the mapping from input to output was reconstrued as also encompassing structure-changing processes, such as feature change and segment deletion.

Marc van Oostendorp's paper urges a return to the Principle of Containment, and shows how Containment may bring us closer to solving a long-standing issue in OT, that of phonological opacity. Van Oostendorp focuses on a subtype of opacity known as non-derived environment blocking. The key to understanding blocking, he argues, lies in the sensitivity of the phonology to morphological affiliation, or 'colour', which in his approach is explicitly present in the phonological representation. Assuming that epenthetic material (meaning any non-underlying nodes, features and association lines) has a different colour to underlying material allows him to capture non-derived environment blocking in the following way. Autosegmental spreading is only permitted onto a structure with different colour. Spreading within the same morpheme, which entails connecting structures of the same colour with an inserted association line of a *different* colour, crucially violates a constraint, INTEGRITY, that is not violated in derived environments.

The paper by Anthi Revithiadou illustrates some of the potential of the Containment-based approach by extending it to pre- and post-accentuation in Modern Greek. The problem of 'dominant' affixes that induce alternations on the stem has figured prominently in Transderivational Anti-Faithfulness

Theory (TAFT; Alderete 2001). Revithiadou's solution is to propose that, in cases of pre-/post-accentuation, a morpheme comes with a floating accent of the same colour as its sponsor. Since this floating accent is not underlyingly associated with the segmental portion of the morpheme, it has to associate to an adjacent morpheme due to exactly the same kind of INTEGRITY constraint as in Van Oostendorp's paper.

The papers by John McCarthy and Paul de Lacy, which address the second aspect of GEN's computational power, complement one another in interesting ways. They explore some of the architectural consequences for the grammar as a whole depending on initial assumptions about GEN's computational power. Both of them start out by tackling the problem of overgeneration and end up proposing mechanisms for loops between EVAL and another component. De Lacy focuses on the overgeneration of phonetically uninterpretable candidates, while McCarthy focuses on the overgeneration of interpretable candidates that are never attested. McCarthy proposes that there is a loop between EVAL and GEN, while in de Lacy's case the loop is between EVAL and Phonetic Interpretation.

Paul de Lacy shows that, given true Freedom of Analysis, and under standard assumptions about the nature of representations and CON, the grammar overgenerates by routinely returning *phonetically uninterpretable* candidates as optimal. Such structures are ruled out neither by GEN (restrictions on representations or processes) nor constraints in EVAL. There are several imaginable solutions, e.g. additional limitations of the representational theory, hardwiring GEN so as to generate only phonetically interpretable candidates, introducing additional universally undominated constraints to rule out the undesired structures.[4] The solution, argues de Lacy, is not to impose restrictions on Freedom of Analysis or to enrich CON with constraints that are not freely permutable (which would run counter to the spirit of OT), but what he calls the 'interpretative looploop'. If the most harmonic candidate is unpronounceable, the search iterates down the harmonic ordering of forms until a phonetically interpretable representation is found.

While de Lacy explores the consequences of accepting Freedom of Analysis, John McCarthy revisits a possibility first raised by Prince & Smolensky (2004: 94–95). He argues that Freedom of Analysis is restricted to implementing a single edit at a time, and each edit must be harmonically improving in that language. Initially, this restrictive move raises the spectre of undergeneration since, obviously, the output may depart from the input in multiple ways. In order to compensate for its inhibition, therefore, GEN must be *persistent*. The most harmonic candidate returned by EVAL is passed back to GEN, which elaborates the candidate pool further. The loop iterates until no further harmonic improvements can be made. McCarthy shows that Persistent OT usefully reigns in the typological predictions by offering a solution to the forbidden repair problem (Wilson 2001, Steriade 2002). Forbidden repairs are forbidden precisely because they entail non-monotonically improving series of edits.

Our third and last block of papers deals with external restrictions on the working of GEN. These include at least the representational theory, which is the focus of most of the contributions in this block. Prince & Smolensky (2004: 5) propose that the representational theory is housed in GEN: "GEN contains information about the representational primitives and their universally irrevocable relations". As is well known, OT does not commit to any particular theory of representations itself. Much research carried out within the framework of OT tacitly relies in practise on a representational *lingua franca* deriving from SPE work on segmental features and prosodic phonology. In this representational synthesis, the work on Feature Geometry (e.g. Clements & Hume 1995) especially has taken a back seat. It is conceivable that the properties of the representational theory itself fall out entirely from constraint interaction in EVAL, in which case Freedom of Analysis would be limited only by conceptual necessity. Certain directions within OT take this line of reasoning to its logical conclusion, and argue that even discrete phonological categories emerge from the interaction of phonetically detailed constraints (Boersma 1998). The contributions dealing with this question in this volume, on the other hand, assume that phonological representations are irreducibly discrete and that their nature has ramifications for both CON/EVAL and GEN. Perhaps the most important question is whether features should be seen as unary or binary, or even multivalent in some cases. The unary/binary issue has consequences for the formulation of faithfulness constraints on featural identity. Another issue with important ramifications for both CON/EVAL and GEN has to do with phonological structures should be restricted to maximally binary branching (either globally, or on particular levels). The representational theory directly constrains the workings of GEN and, with it, the candidate set for any given input.

It is also imaginable, although hardly desirable, that GEN might be a repository for 'hard' constraints that fall outside both whatever representational theory is assumed and the theory of CON/EVAL. As McCarthy (2002: 8) comments, "Hardwiring universals into GEN is inevitably a matter of brute force stipulation, with no hope of explanation or connection to other matters – it is the end of discussion rather than the beginning".

The issue of what a trade-off between GEN and CON with respect to prosodic representations should look like is the primary issue discussed by Curt Rice. Considering the role of universally allowed foot structures in the light of ternary stress systems Rice weighs the pros and cons of incorporating a requirement on foot binarity either into GEN or CON and the consequences each move would have.

Jen Smith, in her chapter, also considers the division of labour between GEN and CON, this time in relation to syllable structure. She argues that glides that linearly precede the nucleus may be either structurally part of the onset or part of the nucleus, and that GEN must therefore be able to generate both. This entails that constraints must be able to differentiate between structural descriptions with essentially the same phonetic interpretation. Smith nevertheless shows that there is a payoff: constraints can be defined on firmer ground than those that would be necessary if GEN did not permit this representational distinction.

Christian Uffmann provides a critical discussion of various approaches to representations in OT, and elaborates on the consequences of choosing a particular representational theory on the constraint set focussing on the privative vs. binary nature of features and autosegmental representations. He argues that OT approaches embracing autosegmental representations can successfully deal with non-local segmental interactions that correspondence accounts cannot fully account for. He then goes on to outline a proposal for integrating autosegmental representations into OT, and claims that representational restrictions are best placed in GEN.

Bruce Morén explores the general architecture of an OT grammar, with special emphasis on the division of labour between representations and constraints. He argues that making explicit claims about phonological representations is not only inevitable, but also beneficial for the theory, since it limits the shape and number of possible constraints. Segmental representations are constructed not so much on the basis of their phonetic realization but on the basis of where they figure in the system of contrast. Representational primitives are accordingly few in number and phonetically highly abstract: the pronunciation of the 'same' representation in different languages may vary widely compared with more mainstream approaches. This variation lies beyond the control of the constraints, which only make reference to symbolic units of phonology. GEN is limited to generating possibly occurring structures of the language. He illustrates the benefits of such a model by analysing the sound inventory of Hawaiian, and shows that it can account for some puzzles that more phonetically based models are unable to deal with.

Language-specific restrictions on the candidate set is also a feature of Chris Golston's paper, the lynchpin of which is the role of short-term memory (STM) in a psychologically realistic theory of the grammar. Making a connection to work on representations in other areas of cognitive science, he argues that the entire *raison d'être* of phonological structure, prosody and feature geometry, is to organize information into manageable chunks that may be processed easily by STM. Constraints on short-term memory ultimately determine how information is stored in long-term memory and this implies that underlying forms are very largely already prosodified. He argues that GEN is a mapping between stored lexical forms and surface forms. This vastly reduces the burden on GEN, which is restricted to filling in those parts of the representation that are not underlyingly prosodified, which imposes limitations on the number of candidates.

It is apparent that the issues addressed in this volume have occupied the thinking of phonologists for a considerable time. This volume sets out to articulate what these issues are and make visible some of the fruits of our attempts as a community to address them. Although the proposals in this volume don't amount to a uniform model of grammar, they all have in common the view that many of the biggest challenges to OT may be overcome by restricting in one way or another some of the freedoms that have guarded the emphasis on output constraints since the programmes's inception.

Notes
* A number of people and organizations have provided support and assistance of various kind. The idea of hosting a conference on this topic first took shape in discussions with Marc van Oostendorp, Tobias Scheer, Christian Uffmann and Jeroen van de Weijer at the Second Old World Conference in Phonology (OCP) in Tromsø in January 2005. We'd like to thank our editor Harry van der Hulst for taking this project on board, Ursula Kleinhenz for helping us see it to completion, Ståle Berglund and Philipp Conzett for administrative support at various stages, and our three external reviewers for their thorough and thoughtful feedback on the papers in the volume. We gratefully acknowledge the financial support of the Center for Advanced Study in Theoretical Linguistics (CASTL) and the Norwegian Research Council (grant no. 179409/V20). Above all, though, we'd like to thank all those who responded by contributing papers.
1. Mention should also be made of approaches to OT incorporating serialism. In Kiparsky's (2000) implementation of Lexical Phonology and Morphology in OT, morphological stem- and word-formation processes feed into phonological strata, each of which is a

separate ordering of the constraint set CON. On this approach, the input to stratum n is the output of stratum $n-1$ and Richness of the Base is only applicable to the very first level.
2. Some have also proposed that there may be language-specific restrictions on GEN (McCarthy 1993, Blevins 1997). This possibility is not addressed here.
3. Both of these were originally circulated as unpublished manuscripts in 1993.
4. This possibility might be worth exploring in future work. It would presuppose some traffic between GEN and the module that encodes phonetic knowledge. That there is interaction between phonetic knowledge and EVAL has been proposed by Steriade (2002).

References

Alderete, John
 2001 Dominance effects as transderivational anti-faithfulness. *Phonology* 18: 201–253.
Blevins, Juliette
 1997 Rules in Optimality Theory: two case studies. In *Derivations and Constraints in Phonology*, Iggy Roca (ed.), 227–260. Oxford: Clarendon Press.
Boersma, Paul
 1998 *Functional Phonology*. The Hague: Holland Academic Graphics.
Clements, G. N. and Elizabeth Hume
 2005 The internal organization of speech sounds. In *Handbook of Phonological Theory*, John Goldsmith (ed.), 245–306. Oxford: Basil Blackwell.
Inkelas, Sharon
 1994 The consequences of optimization for underspecification. In *Proceedings of the 25th Annual Meeting of the North East Linguistic Society 25*, Jill Beckman (ed.), 287–301. GSLA: Amherst, Mass.
Kiparsky, Paul
 2000 Opacity and cyclicity. *Linguistic Review* 17: 351–365.
McCarthy, John J.
 1993 A case of surface constraint violation. *Canadian Journal of Linguistics* 38: 169–195.
 2002 *Thematic Guide to Optimality Theory*. Cambridge: Cambridge University Press.

McCarthy, John J. and Alan S. Prince
 1995 Faithfulness and reduplicative identity. In *Papers in Optimality Theory*, Jill Beckman, Laura Walsh Dickey, and Suzanne Urbanczyk (eds.), 250–384. (University of Massachusetts Occasional Papers 18.) Amherst, Mass.: GLSA.
 1999 Faithfulness and identity in Prosodic Morphology. In *The Prosody-Morphology Interface*, René Kager, Harry van der Hulst, and Wim Zonneveld (eds.), 218–309. Cambridge: Cambridge University Press.
 2001 Prosodic Morphology: Constraint Interaction and Satisfaction. Revised and updated version of original 1993 manuscript. ROA 482.
McCarthy, John J. and Matthew Wolf
 2005 Less than zero: Correspondence and the null output. ROA 722.

Prince, Alan S., and Paul Smolensky
   1993   Optimality theory. Constraint interaction in generative grammar. Technical Report #2, Rutgers University Center for Cognitive Science. ROA 537; published in 2004 by Blackwell Publishers.

Steriade, Donca
   2002   The phonology of perceptibility effects: The P-map and its conse-quences for constraint organization. Ms., UCLA and MIT. http://web.mit.edu/linguistics/www/bibliography/steriade.html

Wilson, Colin
   2001   Consonant cluster neutralisation and targeted constraints. *Phonology* 18: 147–197.

Chapter 2
Laryngeal Underspecification and Richness of the Base*

Daniel Currie Hall

1. Introduction

There are two aspects of Optimality Theory that pose serious difficulties for any theory that seeks to exclude some amount of information from underlying phonological representations. These are Lexicon Optimization, which Prince & Smolensky (1993: §9.3) propose as a procedure for selecting a single underlying form from among several that yield the same output, and Richness of the Base, which states that the constraint grammar of a language should produce phonotactically well-formed outputs for all conceivable inputs, including those which are not – and could not be – present in that language's lexicon.

The principle of Richness of the Base is motivated by the Optimality Theoretic hypothesis that phonological alternations are generated by the same constraints responsible for static phonotactic generalizations. A successful constraint hierarchy must therefore meet two criteria: for each actual input form in the language, it must produce the correct corresponding output, and for all other inputs, it must produce outputs that are possible, if unattested, surface forms. The contrast between systematic and accidental gaps in the set of surface forms is sharply defined: an unattested surface form represents a systematic gap if and only if there is no possible input form for which it is the optimal output; otherwise, its absence is accidental. According to Richness of the Base, all language-specific systematic gaps must be due to the constraint hierarchy; there can be no language-specific restrictions on inputs, nor on the set of candidates from which the output is selected.[1] In the case of systematic gaps, it is frequently impossible to say, for a given input that cannot surface faithfully, specifically what the output should be, although evidence from loanword adaptations is instructive in some cases.[2]

The difficulty for theories of underspecification arises not from Richness of the Base alone, but from Richness of the Base taken in combination with Lexicon Optimization, which (like Kiparsky's 1968 Alternation Condition) militates in favour of resemblance between input and output forms. When a single attested surface form is the optimal output for more than one possible input, Lexicon Optimization states that the learner will posit as the actual underlying form the one of these for which the output form incurs the least serious constraint violations. Because the output form is the same for each input, surface markedness constraints are irrelevant for Lexicon Optimization; it is the input–output faithfulness constraints in the grammar, and their ranking relative to one another, that determine which input is chosen. The selected input form will therefore resemble the surface form as closely as possible; in fact, in the absence of alternations that would provide evidence to the contrary, and setting aside the possibility of opaque input–output relations introduced by non-standard sorts of constraints, the two forms will be identical. One consequence of this is that it is difficult for underlying representations to be underspecified for any features that are present in their corresponding surface forms: the filling in of unspecified feature values introduces a putatively unnecessary mismatch between input and output.

Prince and Smolensky (1993) do not provide an explicit mechanism for incorporating data from alternations into the computation of inputs. Inkelas (1995, 1996), however, does provide such a mechanism, which she calls Alternant Optimization, and shows how it can yield underspecified input forms in a rather narrowly circumscribed set of cases. Some anomalous voicing patterns in Czech, which have previously been treated in a derivational framework using underspecification (Hall 2003, 2004) and in OT using biaspectual representations (Blaho and Bye 2005), initially look amenable to an OT underspecification treatment similar to what Inkelas proposes for a different but potentially analogous set of facts in Turkish. However, as applied to the Czech facts, Alternant Optimization yields an apparently paradoxical situation in which underspecification is possible if and only if it is unnecessary. Section 2 of this paper describes Inkelas's Alternant Optimization; section 3 introduces the relevant Czech data; section 4 shows how Alternant Optimization might be applied to the Czech case; and sections 5 and 6 discuss the resulting problems and their implications.

2. Alternant Optimization

Alternant Optimization is a refinement of Lexicon Optimization that compares candidate input forms that all yield the same attested set of surface forms in all relevant contexts. Inkelas defines Alternant Optimization as follows:

(1) ALTERNANT OPTIMIZATION (Inkelas 1994: 6–7):
Given a grammar G and a set $S = \{S_1, S_2, \ldots S_i\}$ of surface phonetic forms for a morpheme M, suppose that there is a set of inputs $I = \{I_1, I_2, \ldots I_j\}$, each of whose members has a set of surface realizations equivalent to S. There is some $I_i \in I$ such that the mapping between I_i and the members of S is the most harmonic with respect to G, i.e. incurs the fewest marks for the highest ranked constraints. The learner should choose I_i as the underlying representation for M.

This is a straightforward extension of Lexicon Optimization, the original version of which, though its central claim is the same, does not explicitly address the case in which the set S of output forms has more than one member. As Inkelas demonstrates, Alternant Optimization allows for the underspecification of phonological material that is both alternating and predictable. Unpredictable information must be stored because it cannot otherwise be recovered; non-alternating material is stored because optimization never introduces unnecessary discrepancies between input and output.[3]

2.1. Turkish voicing alternations

Among the examples Inkelas (1995) uses to show how underspecified inputs can arise is the voicing behaviour of root-final stops in Turkish (Inkelas and Orgun 1994). The examples in (2) and (3) suggest a straightforward pattern of coda devoicing: some stops are consistently voiceless, while others are voiced prevocalically but voiceless word-finally and before consonants.

(2) a. [sanat+ɯ]   'art+ACC.'
     b. [sanat+ɯm]   'my art'
     c. [sanat]   'art'
     d. [sanat+lar]   'arts'

(3) a. [kanad+ɯ] 'wing+ACC.'
 b. [kanad+ɯm] 'my wing'
 c. [kanat] 'wing'
 d. [kanat+lar] 'wings'

However, there are also a few Turkish roots, borrowed from French, that end in non-alternating voiced stops, as in (4).

(4) a. [etyd+y] 'étude+ACC.'
 b. [etyd+ym] 'my étude'
 c. [etyd] 'étude'
 d. [etyd+ler] 'études'

Inkelas (1995), following Inkelas and Orgun (1994), argues that the three-way distinction in voicing behaviour can and should be attributed to a ternary distinction in underlying values for voicing features. The non-alternating stops at the ends of /sanat/ and /etyd/ are specified as [−voice] and [+voice], respectively, while the alternating stop at the end of /kanaD/ has no underlying value for [±voice]. The alternations in (3) then arise from the constraints in (5):

(5) a. MAX[VOICE] Input values of [±voice] are present in the output.
 b. CODACOND Stops in coda position are [−voice].
 c. VOICE Stops are [+voice].
 d. DEP[VOICE] Output values of [±voice] are present in the input.

If the constraints in (5) are ranked in the order in which they are listed, underspecified stops such as the one at the end of /kanaD/ will have voicing values filled in to comply with the preferred surface pattern (voiceless in codas, voiced elsewhere), but specifications for [±voice] that are present underlyingly will never be overwritten; the alternations are generated in a purely structure-filling way. In the tableaux in (6)–(8), the winning candidates never violate the top-ranked constraint MAX[VOICE]; alternations therefore arise only in the case of /kanaD/, where the underspecification of the final segment makes MAX[VOICE] vacuous.

(6) a.

/sanat+ɯ/	MAX [VOICE]	CODA COND	VOICE	DEP [VOICE]
☞ [sanatɯ]			*	
[sanadɯ]	*!			*

b.

/sanat/	MAX [VOICE]	CODA COND	VOICE	DEP [VOICE]
☞ [sanat]			*	
[sanad]	*!	*		*

(7) a.

/kanaD+ɯ/	MAX [VOICE]	CODA COND	VOICE	DEP [VOICE]
[kanatɯ]			**!	*
☞ [kanadɯ]			*	*

b.

/kanaD/	MAX [VOICE]	CODA COND	VOICE	DEP [VOICE]
☞ [kanat]			**	*
[kanad]		*!	*	*

(8) a.

/etyd+y/	MAX [VOICE]	CODA COND	VOICE	DEP [VOICE]
[etyty]	*!		**	*
☞ [etydy]			*	

b.

/etyd/	MAX [VOICE]	CODA COND	VOICE	DEP [VOICE]
[etyt]	*!		**	*
☞ [etyd]		*	*	

The underspecification of the /D/ in /kanaD/, which Inkelas (1994, 1996) refers to as archiphonemic underspecification, involves the use of a binary feature to make a ternary distinction. This places Inkelas's analysis into apparent conflict with Halle's (1959) Distinctness Condition:

(9) DISTINCTNESS CONDITION (Halle 1959: 32):
Segment-type {A} will be said to be different from segment-type {B}, if and only if at least one feature which is phonemic in both, has a

different value in {A} than in {B}; i.e., plus in the former and minus in the latter, or *vice versa*.

However, Inkelas's analysis of the Turkish data does not rely on the claim that /D/ is phonemically distinct from /d/ or from /t/. Rather than suggesting that Turkish has three phonemically distinct coronal plosives, one of which is unspecified for [±voice], Inkelas appears to be saying instead that there are only two phonemic coronal plosives, /t/ and /d/, and that the morpheme /kanaD/ is underspecified as to which of these its final segment is.[4]

At any rate, the conclusion is inescapable that the three different patterns of voicing behaviour in (2)–(4) must correspond to three different underlying representations – if their representations do not differ in phonological feature specifications *sensu stricto*, then they must instead be differentiated by some diacritic feature or features that would identify them as belonging to different cophonologies. Inkelas (1994, 1996) and Inkelas, Orgun, and Zoll (1997) argue against the use of cophonologies both on general conceptual grounds and on the basis of specific empirical problems in Turkish. For example, Inkelas (1996: 8) points out the existence of the Turkish morpheme /edʒdaD/ ('ancestor'). The final segment of this morpheme alternates, being voiced prevocalically and voiceless elsewhere, but the /dʒ/ at the end of the first syllable is consistently voiced, even though it is in a coda. If the difference between /kanaD/ and /etyd/ is that the former belongs to a cophonology with coda devoicing and the latter to one without it, then, Inkelas asks, to which of these cophonologies does /edʒdaD/ belong? Each makes a wrong prediction about the behaviour of one of the two segments at issue. In light of such problems, archiphonemic underspecification appears to be the better approach.

In a grammar that includes the constraint ranking in (5), the underlying representation of /kanaD/ will necessarily be underspecified as to the voicing of the final segment, because this is the only input form that produces the attested range of output forms in (3). If the segment in question is specified either as [+voice] or as [−voice], it will fail to alternate. Alternant Optimization is not required here, because there is no choice to be made among possible input forms.

2.2. Yoruba ATR harmony

Inkelas (1994) uses Yoruba ATR harmony to demonstrate that Alternant Optimization can produce underspecified inputs when there is a choice to be made. The Yoruba nominalizing prefix /O-/ predictably takes on the [±ATR] value of the first vowel to its right, as illustrated in (10).[5]

(10)   a.   [dẹ]   'to hunt'
       b.   [ọ+dẹ]   'hunter'
       c.   [kú]   'to die'
       d.   [ò+kú]   'corpse'

The pattern in (10) can obviously be quite straightforwardly derived if the prefix /O-/ is underlyingly unspecified for [±ATR]. Unlike the Turkish case, however, such archiphonemic underspecification here is not a matter of descriptive necessity. Data such as those in (11) indicate that Yoruba tongue root harmony is not a purely structure-filling process.

(11)   a.   [àwọ̀]   'colour'
       b.   [ejò]   'snake'
       c.   [àwò ejò]   'colour of a snake'
       d.   [owó]   'money'
       e.   [ọmọ]   'child'
       f.   [owó ọmọ]   'child's money'

The data in (11) suggest that the constraint or constraints responsible for driving harmony (Inkelas (1996) uses the name ATR.HARMONY as an abbreviation for whatever set of constraints is involved) must outrank not only DEP[ATR] but also MAX[ATR]: underlying specifications for [±ATR] can be overwritten in order to produce a harmonic surface form. Because of this ranking, the prefix /O-/ will surface with the appropriate values for [±ATR] in all contexts regardless of whether it is underlyingly specified as [+ATR], [−ATR], or neither. The choice of underlying representation is now a matter for Alternant Optimization, shown in the tableau in (12).

Inkelas assumes that harmony involves the sharing of a [±ATR] feature between two segments. If the target segment is specified for [±ATR] in the input, then it will incur a violation of MAX[ATR] in the output, because the underlying instance of the feature must be deleted to enable the target to share the feature associated with the trigger (even if the two instances of

(12)

A.	O.	MAX[ATR]	DEP[ATR]
/o-/	[o̧+dȩ]	*!	
	[ò+kú]	*	
/o̧-/	[o̧+dȩ]	*!	
	[ò+kú]	*	
☞/O-/	[o̧+dȩ]		
	[ò+kú]		

the feature have the same value in the input). Underlying /O-/, on the other hand, incurs no relevant faithfulness violations: since there is no underlying instance of [±ATR] in the way, there is no need to violate MAX[ATR], and since the surface specification for [±ATR] was already present on the trigger of harmony, there is no violation of DEP[ATR]. The underspecified input form is therefore chosen as optimal.

Taken together, the Turkish and Yoruba examples illustrate the two ways in which underspecified inputs can arise in Inkelas's system. An underspecified input must either be the only possible input that gives rise to the attested range of output forms, as in the Turkish case, or else it must be preferred by Alternant Optimization in the competition among several possible inputs. In the case of the anomalous Czech segments discussed in the following section, however, neither of these conditions consistently applies.

3. The Czech data

In Czech, as in Turkish, obstruents appear to fall into (at least) three distinct voicing classes. Most voiced and voiceless obstruents both trigger and undergo a process of regressive voicing assimilation, illustrated below by the surface forms of the prepositions *s* /s/ 'with' and *z* /z/ 'from'. The underlying forms of the prepositions can be inferred from their realization in presonorant position, shown in (13).

(13) Prepositions *s* and *z* before sonorants
    a. *s lesem*   [slesem]   'with a forest'
    b. *z lesa*   [zlesa]   'from a forest'
    c. *s mužem*   [smuʒem]   'with a man'
    d. *z muže*   [zmuʒe]   'from a man'

When followed by a voiced obstruent, both surface as [z], as in (14).

(14) Prepositions *s* and *z* before voiced obstruents
    a. *s domem* [zdomem] 'with a house'
    b. *z domu* [zdomu] 'from a house'
    c. *s hradem* [zɦradem] 'with a castle'
    d. *z hradu* [zɦradu] 'from a castle'

Before voiceless obstruents, both surface as [s] (15).

(15) Prepositions *s* and *z* before voiceless obstruents
    a. *s polem* [spolem] 'with a field'
    b. *z pole* [spole] 'from a field'
    c. *s chybou* [sxibou] 'with a mistake'
    d. *z chyby* [sxibi] 'from a mistake'

Word-final obstruents and obstruent clusters are consistently voiceless, including those that can be seen from alternations to be underlyingly voiced (16).

(16) Final obstruent devoicing
    a. *muž* [muʃ] 'man' (NOM. SG.)
    b. *mužem* [muʒem] 'man' (INSTR. SG.)
    c. *myš* [miʃ] 'mouse' (NOM. SG.)
    d. *myši* [miʃi] 'mouse' (inst.sg.)
    e. *hrad* [ɦrat] 'castle' (NOM. SG.)
    f. *hradem* [ɦradem] 'castle' (INSTR. SG.)
    g. *robot* [robot] 'robot' (NOM. SG.)
    h. *robotem* [robotem] 'robot' (INSTR. SG.)
    i. *hvozd* [ɦvost] 'deep forest' (NOM. SG.)
    j. *hvozdem* [ɦvozdem] 'deep forest' (INSTR. SG.)
    k. *host* [ɦost] 'guest' (NOM. SG.)
    l. *hostem* [ɦostem] 'guest' (INSTR. SG.)

Two exceptional segments, the labiodental fricative /v/ and the postalveolar fricative trill /r̝/, undergo but fail to trigger regressive assimilation. When preceded by a voiceless obstruent, /r̝/ instead undergoes progressive assimilatory devoicing. In some varieties of Czech, this happens to /v/, too; in others, /v/ remains voiced after voiceless obstruents.

Here, I will focus on the varieties in which /v/ and /r̝/ pattern identically.[6] In these varieties, there are three categories of obstruents: voiceless ones,

(17) Voicing behaviour of /v/
    a. *v lese*   [vlese]   'in a forest'
    b. *v pole*   [fpole]   'in a field'
    c. *květ*   [kfjet] ∼ [kvjet]   'flower'
    d. *tvůj*   [tfuːj] ∼ [tvuːj]   'your'
    e. *vrána*   [vraːna]   'crow'
    f. *s vránou*   [sfraːnoʊ] ∼ [svraːnoʊ]   'with a crow'

(18) Voicing behaviour of /r̝/
    a. *nářek*   [naːr̝ek]   'lamentation' (NOM. SG.)
    b. *nářky*   [naːr̝̊ki]   'lamentations' (NOM. PL.)
    c. *při*   [pr̝̊i]   'near'
    d. *středa*   [str̝̊eda]   'Wednesday'

voiced ones capable of triggering assimilation, and voiced ones that do not trigger assimilation (but which are still distinguishable from sonorants by the fact that they undergo assimilation).

4. Archiphonemic underspecification in Czech?

From a diachronic perspective, the anomalous behaviour of /v/ and /r̝/ is easily understood: they are former sonorants, historically descended from /*w/ and /*rʲ/, respectively. However, their status in the synchronic phonology of modern Czech must still be accounted for. This appears to call for the same kind of underspecification Inkelas and Orgun (1994) use for Turkish: we ought to be able to say that ordinary voiced obstruents are [+voice], ordinary voiceless obstruents are [−voice], and /V/ and /R̝/ are unspecified for [±voice].[7]

Assuming these specifications, we can generate the Czech pattern using the constraints in (19). Hall (2003, 2004) offers a derivational analysis using monovalent features; here, for the sake of comparison with Inkelas (1996), I follow her in assuming that featural faithfulness is evaluated by MAX and DEP (or PARSE and FILL, in the pre-Correspondence Theory formulation of Inkelas (1994) constraints that apply to values of binary features. As Krämer (2005) points out, these assumptions have consequences for the extent to which underspecification is preferred or permitted by Lexicon Optimization. However, any Optimality Theoretic approach to the Czech data that relies on underspecification is vulnerable to problems of essentially the same sort as those discussed below in §5.

(19) a. MAX[SON]
Underlying values of [±sonorant] are preserved in the output.
b. *[+SON, −VOI]
All sonorants are voiced.
c. MAX[VOI] /___ [+SON]
The rightmost underlying instance of [±voice] to the left of each vowel or sonorant consonant is preserved in the output.[8]
d. *[+VOI]/___ #
Word-final consonants are voiceless.
e. AGREE[VOI]
Adjacent obstruents have identical values for [±voice].
f. MAX[VOI]
Underlying values of [±voice] are preserved in the output.
g. VOICE
Segments are voiced.
h. DEP[VOI]
Output values of [±voice] are present in the input.

The crucial rankings of these constraints are as follows:

− MAX[SON], *[+SON, −VOI] ≫ *[+VOI]/___ #:
Sonorants will always be voiced, even word-finally. (This will be true even if sonorants are not underlyingly specified as [+voice].)

− *[+VOI]/___ # ≫ MAX[VOI], VOICE, DEP[VOI]:
All obstruents are subject to final devoicing.

− MAX[VOI] /___ [+SON] ≫ AGREE[VOI] ≫ MAX[VOI], DEP[VOI]:
In a non-final obstruent cluster, the rightmost obstruent that is underlyingly specified for [±voice] will retain its specification, and the other obstruents in the cluster will assimilate to it.

− AGREE[VOI] ≫ VOICE ≫ DEP[VOI]:
An obstruent that is unspecified for [±voice] will assimilate to another obstruent on either side, but if there is no adjacent obstruent to assimilate to, it will be voiced by default.

- MAX[VOI] ≫ VOICE ≫ DEP[VOI]:
  Default voicing applies only to segments with no underlying specification for [±voice].

The tableaux in (20)–(22) illustrate the interactions of these constraints in various relevant contexts. In (20), underlying /V tom/ yields surface [ftom], illustrating the application of regressive assimilation to underspecified /V/:[9]

(20)   Tableau for *v tom* /V tom/ [ftom] 'in that'

/V tom/	MAX[VOI] / ___ [+SON]	*[+VOI] / ___ #	AGREE [VOI]	MAX [VOI]	VOICE	DEP [VOI]
☞ [ftom]		*			**	*
[vtom]		*	*!		*	*
[vdom]	*!	*		*		**

In (20), AGREE[VOI] ensures that the /Vt/ cluster will undergo assimilation, and MAX[VOI] / ___ [+SON] preserves the underlying voicelessness of the /t/ (at the cost of violating VOICE).

The next example illustrates both word-final obstruent cluster devoicing and progressive assimilation of underspecified /V/:

(21)   Tableau for *hvozd* /ɦVozd/ [ɦvost] 'deep forest'

/ɦVozd/	MAX[VOI] / ___ [+SON]	*[+VOI] / ___ #	AGREE [VOI]	MAX [VOI]	VOICE	DEP [VOI]
☞ [ɦvost]				**	**	***
[ɦvozd]		*!				*
[ɦvozt]			*!	*	*	**
[xfost]	*!			***	****	****
[ɦifost]			*!	**	***	***

In the word-initial /ɦV/ cluster, faithfulness mandates that the /ɦ/ be voiced, and AGREE ensures that the /V/ will follow suit; here, there is no conflict with the default constraint VOICE, and the only faithfulness violation incurred is the necessary violation of DEP[VOI] incurred by inserting any value at all for [±voice] on the /V/.[10] At the opposite end of the word, *[+VOI]/ ___ # requires that the final /d/ surface as [−voice], and AGREE ensures that the /z/ follows suit.

Laryngeal Underspecification and Richness of the Base   23

In (22), we can see both regressive assimilation affecting a regular obstruent and progressive devoicing affecting /R̞/.

(22)   Tableau for *od tří* /od tR̞i:/ [ot tr̞i:] 'from three'

/od tR̞i:/	MAX[VOI] /___ [+SON]	*[+VOI] /___ #	AGREE [VOI]	MAX [VOI]	VOICE	DEP [VOI]
☞ [ot tr̞̊i:]				*	***	**
[od tr̞̊i:]			*!		**	*
[od tr̞i:]			*!		*	*
[od dr̞i:]	*!				*	**

In (22), AGREE again enforces assimilation. Since the /R̞/ has no underlying specification for [±voice], MAX[VOI] /___ [+SON] chooses the voicing feature of the /t/ – the rightmost specified segment in the cluster – as the one that must be preserved.

5. The problem

5.1. The empirical difficulty

Given underspecified representations for underlying /V/ and /R̞/, the constraint hierarchy in (19) produces the right outputs. But there is no way of guaranteeing that /V/ and /R̞/ will consistently be underspecified; Richness of the Base tells us that we should also be able to deal with input forms that include fully specified /f/, /v/, /r̞̊/, and /r̞/, which will behave exactly like regular obstruents. Czech does have an /f/, although only marginally (it occurs only in loanwords and onomatopoeia), but the other three predicted segments do not exist.

This is the crucial difference between the Czech situation and the Turkish one: Turkish has all three of /t/, /D/, and /d/. In Turkish, Richness of the Base makes the right prediction; fully specified, non-alternating forms do exist parallel to the underspecified ones, and if some particular morpheme containing /D/ does not happen to have counterparts containing /t/ and /d/, the gap is merely accidental. In Czech, however, the underspecification is crucially at the level of the segment, rather than the morpheme: in order to account for the surface distribution of [f], [v], [r̞̊], and [r̞], the underlying segments /V/ and /R̥/ must lack voicing specifications wherever they occur; the absence of underlying specified counterparts is systematic. Given standard OT assumptions, there is no way of barring the fully specified segments from the input. The input cannot be constrained directly, and the unwanted segments cannot be banned by output well-formedness constraints, because they do appear in surface forms.

One initially plausible though unorthodox approach might be to suggest that Richness of the Base is relativized to phonemic inventories. Under this view, a constraint grammar must produce phonotactically well-formed outputs for any input sequence of segments drawn from the phonemic inventory of the language, but need not cope with feature combinations that do not correspond to such segments. However, even this drastic measure is of no avail, because Lexicon Optimization ensures that fully specified /v/, /r/, and /r̥/ will in fact be part of the phonemic inventory of Czech. In non-alternating contexts, such as *dva* [dva] 'two', Lexicon Optimization selects an input form that is identical to the output, as illustrated in (23).

(23)

L. O.	MAX[SON]	MAX[VOI] / ___ [+SON]	MAX[VOI]	DEP[VOI]
☞/dva/ [dva]				
/dVa/ [dva]				*!

If /v/ freely occurs in inputs, as predicted by Richness of the Base, then we should expect to find such forms as */vraːn-/ alongside /Vraːn-/ ('crow'); there would be no difference between the forms in isolation, but when preceded by *s* ('with'), the former would produce *[zvraːnou̯] instead of the attested [sfraːnou̯] of (17f).

5.2. The theoretical paradox

The only orthodox way out is to ensure that even fully specified inputs will produce the correct range of surface forms – that is, we need to make sure that /v/, /r/, and /r̥/ will act just like /V/ and /R̥/. We can do this in a very simple and unprincipled way by replacing the constraints MAX[VOICE] / ___ [+SON] and MAX[VOICE] in the hierarchy in (19) with constraints that apply only to segments other than /V/ and /R̥/, and demoting the more general MAX[VOICE] constraint to below VOICE, as in (24).

(24) a. MAX[SON]
      b. *[+SON, −VOI]
      c. MAX[VOI] /___ [+SON], EXCEPT FOR /V/ AND /R̯/
      d. *[+VOI]/___ #
      e. AGREE[VOI]
      f. MAX[VOI], EXCEPT FOR /V/ AND /R̯/
      g. VOICE
      h. MAX[VOI]
      i. DEP[VOI]

Given this new constraint hierarchy, both the fully specified /vraːn-/ and the underspecified /Vraːn-/ will alternate as desired. And, now that the underspecified form is no longer crucial to the analysis, Alternant Optimization selects it as the optimal input, as shown in (25).

(25)

	Alternant Optimization	MAX[VOI] /___ [+SON] (NOT V OR R̯)	MAX[VOI] (NOT V OR R̯)	MAX [VOI]	DEP [VOI]
/vraːn-/	[vraːn+a] [s+fraːn+oʊ]			*!	*
☞/Vraːn-/	[vraːn+a] [s+fraːn+oʊ]				* *

This would be an entirely satisfactory result if there were a principled way of producing the effect of (24). In order for the formulation of constraints like (24c) and (24f) to be justified, the following conditions would have to apply:

- that /V/ and /R̯/ form a natural class, and
- that this natural class might reasonably be expected to have its own MAX[VOICE] constraints.

An initially promising approach would be to try to relate the un–obstruent-like phonological properties of /V/ and /R̯/ to some un–obstruent-like phonetic property, as Padgett (2002) does for Russian /v/, which he argues is really a "narrow approximant" /υ̞/. In Padgett's treatment of Russian, some constraints apply to a natural class encompassing /υ̞/ and obstruents, others to a natural class encompassing /υ̞/ and sonorants, and the narrow approximant's anomalous voicing behaviour falls out accordingly. A similar case might be made for the trilled fricative /R̝/, which clearly has ambivalent phonetic properties, the frication being characteristically obstruent and the vibrancy characteristically sonorant. Czech /V/, however, as argued by Hall (2004, 2007), seems to be quite clearly an obstruent in all respects apart from its voicing behaviour. Phonetically, Czech /V/ is much more removed than Russian /v̞/ from their Common Slavic ancestor /*w/; far from being a narrow approximant (or even a wide fricative), it is described by Kučera (1961) and Palková (1994) as short and close, almost to the point of being a stop. As the spectrograms in figures 1 and 2 illustrate, it does not appear to be any more acoustically sonorous than the well-behaved obstruent stop /b/.[11]

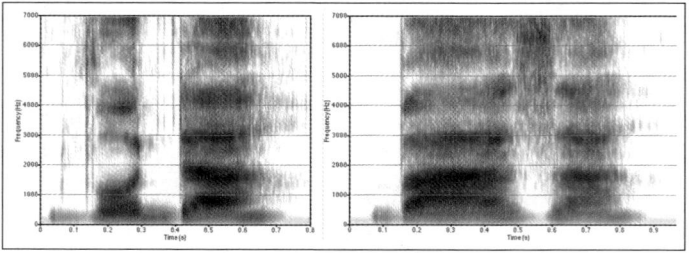

Figure 1. Spectrograms of *voda* /voda/ 'water' and *váza* /vaːza/ 'vase'

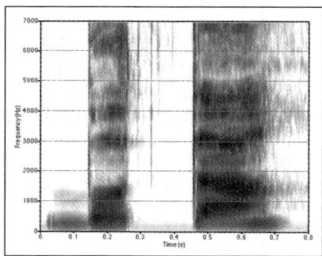

Figure 2. Spectrogram of *bota* /bota/ 'shoe'

Even if /R̝/ can be described on independent grounds as intermediate between a sonorant and an obstruent, there is no obvious independent basis for saying the same of /V/, nor for grouping these segments together as a natural class to the exclusion of other highly sonorous (but phonologically regular) obstruents, such as /ɦ/.

If /V/ and /R̝/ cannot be characterized synchronically as a natural class, then another possibility would be to postulate the existence of a larger and more fine-grained family of MAX[VOICE] constraints – say, one for each segment. Such an approach would have ample precedent in OT; for example, Prince and Smolensky (1993: §8.1.2) explode the constraint HNUC (26) into a hierarchy of more specific constraints (27) penalizing the parsing of particular segments as syllabic peaks.

(26) The Nuclear Harmony Constraint (HNUC): A higher sonority nucleus is more harmonic than one of lower sonority. I.e., if $|x| > |y|$ then Nuc/$x \succ$ Nuc/y.
(Prince and Smolensky 1993: 17)

(27) Peak Hierarchy: *P/$t \gg \ldots \gg$ *P/$i \gg$ *P/a
(Prince and Smolensky 1993: 147)

If each segment has its own MAX[VOICE] and MAX[VOICE] / ___ [+SON] constraints, then an appropriate ranking of these constraints, such as the one shown in (28), can produce the effects of the hierarchy in (24) without any need to say that /V/ and /R̞/ comprise a natural class.

(28) a. MAX[SONORANT]
      b. *[+SON, −VOICE]
      c.
              Z
              |
          MAX[VOICE] / ___ [+SON],
              T
              |
          MAX[VOICE] / ___ [+SON], et cetera
      d. *[+VOICE]/___#
      e. AGREE[VOICE]
      f. MAX[VOICE]/Z, MAX[VOICE]/T, MAX[VOICE]/X, et cetera
      g. VOICE
      h. MAX[VOICE]/V, MAX[VOICE]/R̞
      i. DEP[VOICE]

This approach, however, introduces some new difficulties. First, the constraints in (28c, f, h), unlike Prince & Smolensky's peak hierarchy, have no obvious intrinsic ranking. In the peak hierarchy, a constraint against parsing a less sonorous segment as a peak will in every language outrank a constraint against parsing a more sonorous segment as a peak; this is how the constraints in (27) replicate the effects of the single constraint HNUC. Although other constraints can be freely interleaved with the ones in the peak hierarchy, the *P constraints themselves have a universally fixed ranking that enforces surface well-formedness. The MAX[VOICE] constraints, however, are faithfulness constraints, and there is no analogous basis for assigning them a consistent cross-linguistic ranking. The more general constraint from which they are expanded, unlike HNUC, makes no comparison between segments; it merely states that all underlying instances of [±voice] should be preserved in the output. Nor is there any other clear rationale for imposing a fixed ranking on the MAX[VOICE] constraints. Cross-linguistically, there are many processes that change the voicing features of some segments and not others, but no property of segments appears to correlate universally with susceptibility or resistance to voicing or devoicing in the way that sonority correlates with acceptability in syllable peaks. Sonority is frequently relevant to voicing and devoicing processes, but some of these processes target less sonorous segments (e.g., final obstruent devoicing in many languages), while others target more sonorous ones (e.g., high vowel devoicing in Japanese and in Québécois French). One fruitful approach to this variation has been to say that sonorants and obstruents have different kinds of voicing feature specifications underlyingly (see, e.g., Rice and Avery 1989); it is not clear how any fixed ranking of the MAX[VOICE] family could achieve similar results. And if these constraints must be freely rankable with respect to one another, then the typological consequences of exploding MAX[VOICE] are much more drastic than the consequences of exploding HNUC; the new constraints allow for much more variation between possible grammars.

A second and graver problem is that the exploded MAX[VOICE] constraints themselves are not so easy to formulate as they at first appear. The proposed constraints are relativized to segments, but segments are not representational primitives. A properly formalized version of a constraint such as MAX[VOICE]/D cannot simply refer to the segment /d/, but must instead specify a set of feature values. But what set of feature values will reliably identify /d/ in all languages, which, if we assume that constraints are universal, is what MAX[VOICE]/D must be able to do? A full set of specifications might include [−sonorant], [+coronal], [−continuant], [+anterior], [−nasal], and perhaps others. However, Alternant Optimization predicts that any of these features can be unspecified in an input form if its value is both variable and predictable – for example, if there is a /d/ that predictably surfaces as [n] in some environments, it may be underspecified for [±sonorant] and [±nasal]; a /d/ that alternates predictably with [ð] may be underspecified for [±continuant]; and so on.[12] Furthermore, since Alternant Optimization applies to individual morphemes, rather than to segments or inventories, a single segment /d/ may have multiple representations even within a single language. There is no set of features that will reliably and uniquely identify the segment /d/ (or any other segment) in all contexts in all languages, and so the constraint MAX[VOICE]/D (or any other faithfulness constraint referring to a particular input segment) cannot be formulated in a language-independent way.

If it is not possible for the necessary constraints to be formulated in terms of input segments, an alternative might be to formulate them in terms of output segments. Rather than penalizing the deletion of [±voice] specifications from particular underlying segments, the new constraints would penalize particular surface segments when they do not retain the [±voice] specifications of their input correspondents. For example, MAX[VOICE]/D would be replaced by a local conjunction of the more general faithfulness constraint MAX[VOICE] with the markedness constraint *[t]. However, Moreton and Smolensky (2002) argue that MAX constraints cannot be conjoined with markedness constraints, because the domain of the conjunction's application cannot be specified: MAX applies to input domains, and markedness constraints to surface domains. The exploded version of the MAX[VOICE] constraints therefore cannot be reformulated along these lines.

6. Conclusions

It seems that the anomalous behaviour of Czech /V/ and /R̯/ must be stipulated, one way or another. One way of doing this would be to put the stipulation into the constraint hierarchy, by means of constraints like the ones in (28c) and (28f). This approach would seem to weaken the Optimality Theoretic hypothesis that constraints are universal, in a dangerously unfalsifiable way; including constraints such as MAX[VOI] /___ [+SON], EXCEPT FOR /V/ AND /R̯/ in the universal inventory of constraints makes no testable predictions about languages other than Czech, because the effects of these constraints can always be masked by other constraints.

An alternative approach would be to retreat from the predictions of Richness of the Base and Lexicon Optimization, and put the stipulation into the phonemic inventory. This would require us to say that there can be language-specific restrictions on the underlying representations of segments, and it would mean elevating the phonemic inventory to the status of something other than an epiphenomenon. Richness of the Base could still permit all sequences of phonemes as potential inputs – the only phonotactic properties that would no longer be in the jurisdiction of CON would be gaps in the phonemic inventory. There are two obvious objections to this approach, each of which is, however, answerable. The first objection is that the constraint grammar would no longer be either responsible for, or equipped to deal with, non-native input forms; an alternative account would therefore be needed for various loanword adaptation phenomena. One possible answer to this would be to account for such phenomena from the perspective of perception rather than of production, by means of a theory of how acoustic stimuli are mapped onto phonological representations (see, e.g., Boersma 1998 and Lahiri and Reetz 2002). The second objection is that the possibility of constraining inputs adds a new source of power to the theory. However, this power can be constrained by a sufficiently restrictive set of principles for generating inventories of feature combinations (see, e.g., the Successive Division Algorithm of Dresher 2003).

Even assuming that these objections can be overcome, restrictions on input forms represent a fairly drastic departure from orthodox OT. In light of this, it is worthwhile to keep in mind that the problems posed by the Czech data do not necessarily apply only to languages in which, as in Czech, underspecification appears to be crucial. If Richness of the Base does indeed allow all possible combinations of features to appear in input segments, then it predicts not only the appearance of fully specified underlying /v/, /r̯/, and /r̥/ in Czech, but also the appearance of underspecified segments like the Turkish /D/ in Czech and, for that matter, in all other languages. If features may be freely present or absent in input forms, then unattested alternating segments may in fact be predicted by grammars that have been constructed on the tacit assumption that all input segments are fully specified. The hypothetical universality of constraints such as the ones that drive voicing assimilation in Czech and final devoicing in Czech and Turkish suggests that even in languages that do not ordinarily exhibit these phenomena, they should show up as Emergence of the Unmarked effects when Richness of the Base supplies an input segment that is underspecified enough to make higher-ranking faithfulness constraints irrelevant. The problem that shows up so clearly in the Czech case may therefore be lurking undetected in many apparently well-behaved systems as well.

Notes

* I am grateful to Elan Dresher, Keren Rice, Elizabeth Cowper, Veronika Ambros, members of the phonology group at the University of Toronto, the participants at the Workshop on Freedom of Analysis at the University of Tromsø, and two anonymous reviewers for their helpful input, and to Sharon Inkelas for providing me with a copy of the newer version of her paper on Alternant Optimization (Inkelas 1996). Any errors, omissions, or other deficiencies are, of course, entirely my fault.
1. Universal restrictions on these aspects of the grammar, however, may account for systematic gaps that hold cross-linguistically.
2. On this point, Mackenzie and Dresher (2003) offer a relevant discussion of Baković's 2000 analysis of the Nez Perce vowel system. The surface vowel inventory of Nez Perce is [i, æ, ɑ, ɔ, u], and Baković argues for a constraint ranking that will, among other things, ensure that an input /o/ will be mapped to an output [ɔ], and not to any other vowel in or out of this attested set. However, as Mackenzie and Dresher observe, "no evidence is adduced that an input /o/ does in fact surface as [ɔ] and not, say, as [u]." Indeed, no evidence from the phonological behaviour of native Nez Perce morphemes *can* be adduced that would shed light on the question; in the absence of evidence about loanwords, we know that /o/ must surface as one of [i, æ, ɑ, ɔ, u], but we cannot know which one.
3. But cf. Krämer (2005), who argues that the underlying forms of predictable material are indeterminable, or, at best, contingent upon theory-internal choices about the formalization of features and faithfulness constraints.
4. Archiphonemic underspecification as Inkelas uses it is not limited to the underspecification of features on segments; for example, Inkelas (1996: §5.1) proposes that certain Hausa morphemes that surface with predictably alternating high and low tones in different contexts are archiphonemically underspecified for tone. See also Inkelas (1994: §6.2) for arguments that Stanley's 1967 objections to ternarity do not apply in the present case, and Reiss (2003) for further discussion.
5. For the sake of explicitness, all [−ATR] vowels in the data are transcribed here with the diacritic [̣], including the low vowel [ạ], which has no [+ATR] counterpart. [+ATR] vowels are unmarked. The data are from Pulleyblank (1988) and Archangeli and Pulleyblank (1989), cited in Inkelas (1994).
6. See Hall (2003, 2004, 2007) for a fuller discussion of the more complicated case in which the two exceptional segments behave differently.
7. An analysis involving underspecification for [±sonorant] might also be possible, along lines suggested by Blaho (2002) for /v/ in Hungarian.
8. The somewhat ungainly formulation of this constraint is designed to ensure that an underlying [±voice] specification need not be in immediately pre-sonorant position to be preserved; rather, it will be preserved so long as no other [±voice] specification intevenes between it and the next vowel or sonorant consonant to its right. This is for the sake of clusters such as the one at the beginning of the word *tří* /tRiː/ [tr̝iː] ('three'), in which the /t/, although it is not adjacent to the vowel, nonetheless determines the voicing of the whole cluster because the /R̥/ has no [±voice] feature.
9. In order to save space, the top-ranked constraints, MAX[SON] and *[+SON, −VOI], are not shown in these tableaux, as no relevant candidates violate them.
10. The possibility of underspecification in the output (see, e.g., Itô, Mester, and Padgett

1995) is not contemplated in the tableaux in (20)–(22). In the cases Itô et al. consider, the phonetic realization of the underspecified segments is not at issue; here, to permit the underspecified segments /V/ and /R̥/ to occur in the output would simply pass the problem of their realization over to another component of the grammar.
11. The spectrograms, from Hall (2004), were produced using the speech analysis program Praat (Boersma and Weenink 1992) from recordings of a female native speaker of Czech. The recordings are part of a set of sound files designed to accompany the IPA *Handbook* (International Phonetic Association 1999).
12. See also Morén's discussion, in this volume, of vowel features in Yiddish and Italian.

References

Archangeli, Diana, and Douglas Pulleyblank
    1989   Yoruba vowel harmony. *Linguistic Inquiry* 20:173–218.

Baković, Eric
    2000   Harmony, dominance, and control. Doctoral dissertation, Rutgers University.

Blaho, Sylvia
    2002   The behaviour of /j/, /v/ and /h/ in Hungarian voice assimilation: An OT analysis. In *Proceedings of the 10th Conference of the Student Organisation of Linguistics in Europe*, Marjo van Koppen, Joanna Sio, and Mark de Vos (eds.), 17–31. Leiden: Student Organization of Linguistics in Europe.

Blaho, Sylvia, and Patrik Bye
    2005   Cryptosonorants and the misapplication of voicing assimilation in Biaspectual Phonology. To appear in *The Proceedings of the 31st Meeting of the Berkeley Linguistics Society*, Yuni Kim (ed.). ROA 759.

Boersma, Paul
    1998   *Functional phonology: Formalizing the Interactions Between Articulatory And Perceptual Drives*. The Hague: Holland Academic Graphics.

Boersma, Paul, and David Weenink
    1992   Praat: Doing phonetics by computer. Computer program. Available online at www.praat.org.

Dresher, B. Elan
    2003   The contrastive hierarchy in phonology. *Toronto Working Papers in Linguistics* 20:47–62.

Hall, Daniel Currie
    2003   Laryngeal feature specifications in West Slavic languages. *Toronto Working Papers in Linguistics* 20:93–114.
    2004   A formal approach to /v/: Evidence from Czech and Slovak. In *Formal approaches to Slavic linguistics: The Ottawa meeting 2003*, Olga Arnaudova, Wayles Browne, María Luisa Rivero, and Danijela Stojanović (eds.), 187–205. Ann Arbor, Mich.: Michigan Slavic Publications.
    2007   The role and representation of contrast in phonological theory. Ph. D. diss., University of Toronto.

Halle, Morris
1959   *The Sound Pattern of Russian: A Linguistic and Acoustical Investigation.* The Hague: Mouton.

Inkelas, Sharon
1995   The consequences of optimization for underspecification. In *Proceedings of the 26th Annual Meeting of the North East Linguistic Society*, Jill N. Beckman (ed.), 287–302. Amherst, Mass.: GLSA.

1996   Archiphonemic underspecification: An optimization approach to the phonological description of morphemes. Ms., University of California, Berkeley.

Inkelas, Sharon, Cemil Orhan Orgun, and Cheryl Zoll
1997   Implications of lexical exceptions for the nature of grammar. In *Constraints And Derivations in Phonology*, Iggy Roca (ed.), 393–418. Oxford: Clarendon Press.

Inkelas, Sharon, and Cemil Orhan Orgun
1994   Level economy, derived environment effects, and the treatment of exceptions. In *Proceedings of a workshop on recent developments in lexical phonology*, Richard Wiese (ed.), 63–90. Düsseldorf: Heinrich-Heine Universität.

International Phonetic Association
1999   *Handbook of the International Phonetic Association: A guide to the use of the International Phonetic Alphabet.* Cambridge: Cambridge University Press.

Itô, Junko, Armin Mester, and Jaye Padgett
1995   Licensing and underspecification in Optimality Theory. *Linguistic Inquiry* 26: 571–613. ROA 38.

Kiparsky, Paul
1982[1968] How abstract is phonology? In *Explanation in Phonology*, Paul Kiparsky (ed.), 119–163. Dordrecht: Foris.

Krämer, Martin
2005   Optimal underlying representations. In *Proceedings of the 35th Annual Meeting of the North East Linguistic Society*, ed. Leah Bateman and Cherlon Ussery. Amherst, Mass.: GLSA Publications.

Kučera, Henry
1961   *The Phonology of Czech.* The Hague: Mouton.

Lahiri, Aditi, and Henning Reetz
2002   Underspecified recognition. In *Laboratory Phonology 7*, Carlos Gussenhoven and Natasha Warner (eds.), 637–676. Berlin: Mouton.

Mackenzie, Sara, and B. Elan Dresher
2003   Contrast and phonological activity in the Nez Perce vowel system. In *Proceedings of the 29th Meeting of the Berkeley Linguistics Society*, Pawel M. Nowak, Corey Yoquelet, and David Mortensen (eds.), 283–294. Berkeley, Cal.: Berkeley Linguistics Society.

Morén, Bruce
2007   The division of labor between segment-internal structure and violable constraints. This volume.

Moreton, Elliott, and Paul Smolensky
    2002   Typological consequences of local constraint conjunction. In *WCCFL 21: Proceedings of the 21st West Coast Conference on Formal Linguistics*, Line Mikkelsen and Christopher Potts (eds.), 306–319. Cambridge, Mass.: Cascadilla Press.

Padgett, Jaye
    2002   Russian voicing assimilation, final devoicing, and the problem of [v] (*or,* the mouse that squeaked). Ms., University of California, Santa Cruz. ROA 528.

Palková, Zdena
    1994   *Fonetika a fonologie češtiny s obecním úvodem do problematiky oboru* [The phonetics and phonology of Czech, with an introduction to the issues of the field]. Prague: Státní pedagogické nakladatelství.

Prince, Alan S., and Paul Smolensky
    1993   Optimality theory. Constraint interaction in generative grammar. Technical Report #2, Rutgers University Center for Cognitive Science. ROA 537; Published in 2004 by Blackwell Publishers).

Pulleyblank, Douglas
    1988   Feature hierarchy and Tiv vowels. *Phonology* 5:299–326.

Reiss, Charles
    2003   Deriving the feature-filling/feature-changing contrast: An application to Hungarian vowel harmony. *Linguistic Inquiry* 34:199–224.

Rice, Keren D., and J. Peter Avery
    1989   On the interaction between sonorancy and voicing. *Toronto Working Papers in Linguistics* 10:65–82.

Stanley, Richard
    1967   Redundancy rules in phonology. *Language* 43:393–436.

Chapter 3
Underlying representations that do not minimize grammatical violations*

Andrew Nevins and Bert Vaux

1. Overview

In this paper we review evidence from a variety of sources, including deneutralization studies, that indicate that the choice of underlying representations is governed by causal reasoning, statistical inference, orthographic know-ledge, and hypercorrection, but rarely, if ever, by a principle of minimizing faithfulness violations.

2. What kinds of knowledge are used in inferring URs?

There is a well-known principle in OT which goes by the name of Lexicon Optimization. The classic definition, from Prince and Smolensky (1993), is reproduced in (1). Sharon Inkelas' adoption of the principle and definition are reproduced in (2).

(1) Lexicon Optimization.
"Suppose that several different inputs I_-, I_2, ..., I_n when parsed by a grammar G lead to corresponding outputs O_1, O_2,...,O_n, all of which are realized as the same phonetic form P – these inputs are all phonetically equivalent with respect to G. Now one of these outputs must be the most harmonic, by virtue of incurring the least significant violation marks: suppose this optimal one is labelled O_k. Then the learner should choose, as the underlying form for P, the input I_k." (Inkelas 1994: 209)

(2) "Given a grammar G and a set S = {S_1, S_2, ..., S_i} of surface phonetic forms for a morpheme M, suppose that there is a set of inputs I = {I_1, I_2, ...,Ij}, each of whose members has a set of surface realizations equivalent to S. There is some $I_i \in$ I such that the mapping between

I_i and the members of S is the most harmonic with respect to G, i.e. incurs the fewest marks for the highest ranked constraints. The learner should choose I_i as the underlying representation for M." (Inkelas 1994)

Inkelas' idea is that, in the absence of any alternations to the contrary, a phonological form is stored identically to its surface form. The intuition here is one that many researchers consider to be the null hypothesis: that there is maximum transparency in the mapping of input to output forms, whenever possible.

Of course, in the face of alternations, such as Turkish [tat∼tadɨ] (meaning "taste", in the nominative and in the accusative), there *is* no way to store an underlying form that is *maximally* transparent to both the nominative and accusative form. Storing the underlying form *tat* would be transparent for the nominative *tat* but unfair to the accusative *tadɨ*, while storing the underlying form *tad* would of course be transparent for the sake of *tadɨ* but would not lead to a transparent mapping for *tat*. In this case, Lexicon Optimization steps in, and says that the UR that will be chosen will be the one that minimizes the number of constraint violations that would be incurred. This is illustrated in the Tableau in (3).

(3) Comparative tableau, evaluated in parallel, to select most harmonic input

/tat/+/I/	*VOICED-CODA	IDENT-VOICE
Wrong output: [tatɨ]		
Right output: [tadɨ]		!*
/tad/+/I/	*VOICED-CODA	IDENT-VOICE
Wrong output: [tatɨ]		!*
Right output: [tadɨ]		

Result: **/tad/ chosen.**

Given the existence of final devoicing in Turkish, we know that *VOICED-CODA must outrank IDENT-IO-VOICE. Otherwise, there wouldn't be any devoicing at all. Hence, given that ranking, which any learner establishes based on hearing coda devoicing, we can compare how different possible URs would fare. As it turns out, storing the word as /tat/ leads to a completely gratuitous violation of Faithfulness in the output [tadɨ], so instead, /tad/ will be stored. The story is thus that URs are chosen so as to minimize grammatical violations. If Lexicon Optimization is right, learners will never store something like /tat/ as an underlying form for [tadɨ], because the choice of URs is governed by avoiding faithfulness violations.

The purpose of this paper is to show that learners do not respect Lexicon Optimization in a wide range of cases; rather, they seem to be going for underlying forms that flagrantly violate faithfulness constraints, when they could easily choose otherwise. After examining this behavior in detail, it becomes apparent that morphophonological knowledge, lexical statistics, segmental frequencies, and orthographic representations all play a role in constructing underlying representations, and that these factors *consistently* outweigh the desire to maintain maximal input-output transparency.

One of the best testing grounds for what kinds of underlying forms speakers come up with involves "deneutralization" phenomena. When learners hear a single output form, without hearing alternations, the expectation of Lexicon Optimization is that they will store that input form as faithfully as possible. Lexicon Optimization thus presents a new face on the intuition that was expressed by Paul Kiparsky's Alternation Condition (Kiparsky 1973): morphemes that don't alternate are stored in the maximally simple form. Kiparsky's Alternation Condition provided a guideline for what kinds of underlying representations could be assumed. After the seemingly heady days of SPE, where *nightingale* was stored with an abstract consonant in order to capture the fact that it resisted vowel shortening, Kiparsky's alternation represented a move towards anti-abstraction: why store phonological forms as any different from their surface form, if there is no alternation-based evidence to the contrary?

Our paper can thus be seen as not only a demonstration that Lexicon Optimization is empirically inadequate, but also that Kiparsky's Alternation Condition is too strong. Learners *do* go out of their way to construct "abstract" underlying forms in the absence of alternations, in the sense of "abstract" where it means "not identical to the surface". UR construction turns out to be a much more complicated procedure than can be computed by a Tableaudes-Tableaux. This finding may speak to Stig Eliasson's conclusion that not everything should be accounted for with the same grammatical machinery, and that some of the core acquisition mechanisms, in this case, the creation of inputs to the phonological computation, may lie outside the grammar proper.

3. Lexicostatistic influences on UR construction

One of the easiest examples to demonstrate this with at the outset occurs in Turkish. Consider a learner encountering a new word in Turkish in the nominative, a "wug" word, or nonce word, or novel form, as they are variously called. Suppose that the learner hears the word *nühüp*. Since Turkish has final devoicing, there are two choices for what the underlying form could be: *nühüp* or *nühüb*. Lexicon Optimization says, "Stop wasting my time! It will be *nühüp*! Why would anyone possibly choose otherwise?". The tableau for a lexicon-optimization based prediction for this scenario is given in (4).

(4)   Comparative tableau, evaluated in parallel, to select most harmonic input

/nüüp/	*Voiced-Coda	Ident-Voice
Right output: [nühüp]		
Wrong output: [nühüb]	*	*
/nüüb/	*Voiced-Coda	Ident-Voice
Right output: [nühüp]		*
Wrong output: [nühüb]	*	

Result: **/nühüp/ chosen.**

Together with Beste Yolcu, a graduate student at Harvard University, we were able to ask 6 linguistically naive residents of Istanbul what the accusative form would be for this word (Nevins and Yolcu-Kamali 2005). Actually, we didn't ask them what the accusative would be. We asked them to fill in the blank in a sentence where the syntactic context demanded accusative case. As it turned out, 5 out of 6 of these speakers wrote down *nühübü*. This constituted a case of de-neutralization: since final devoicing *neutralizes* the contrast between voiced and voiceless stops, when a speaker *only* hears the voiceless form, he has to guess what the underlying representation actually is. By producing the accusative, we get direct access to what he chose for the underlying form, because the vowel ending of the accusative allows the underlying form to surface intact, it no longer being in the environment for final devoicing. Technically speaking, this is deneutralization because the UR could be either a /p/ or a /b/, and by producing the accusative, we get to see what the real underlying form is, outside of the neutralized environment in which the learner first encountered it.

A metaphor might help here. This is akin to the "blicket detector" task of Sobel, Tenenbaum, and Gopnik (2004). Children were introduced to a blicket-detecting machine that lights up and plays music when certain objects (blickets) are placed on it and were told that "blickets make the machine go". Sobel *et al.* studied 3- and 4-year old children's abilities to make a *backwards blocking* inference with the machine. In studies on backwards blocking, participants observe an outcome occurring in the presence of two potential causes (A and B). Participants then observe that event A independently causes the outcome. Participants are less likely to judge B as the cause of the outcome. In the task at hand, A and B are two blocks placed on the blicket detector together, which results in the machine activating. Subsequently object A is put on the detector alone, again resulting in activation of the machine. Children were then asked whether B was a blicket. 3-year old children's average percentage of responses that B was a blicket was 50%, while 3-year old children's average percentage of responses that B was a blicket was 12.5%.

Importantly the A and B backwards-blocking task is highly similar in structure to the coda deneutralization task we performed with nonce words in Turkish. Participants observed an outcome (e.g. [p] in final position) which occurs in the presence of two potential causes: the rule of coda-devoicing, or the existence of an underlying /p/. Much like the 3-year olds in Sobel et.al's experiment, once it is known that the presence of A alone is sufficient to trigger the outcome (in this case, that coda devoicing exists as a regular process in Turkish), then the likelihood that B is playing any role in the outcome plummets to 50%. Under the logic of rational parameter estimation models, such as the "Power PC" model of Cheng (1997), a blocked object in the backwards blocking paradigm has a strength parameter that is undefined, leading to complete uncertainty about the blickethood (or /p/-hood) of B.

In effect, in the backwards blocking condition of Sobel *et al.*, the blickethood of B is *neutralized* when it is placed on the blicket detector in the presence of A, a known blicket. When participants have to decide whether B is a blicket or not, they are forced to make a guess about the deneutralized likelihood of B's blickethood. This is entirely parallel to asking Turkish volunteers to form the accusative of nonce words they have only heard in the nominative.

We note briefly here that, for proponents of a theory in which there *are* no underlying forms, only Output-to-Output faithfulness relations with privileged bases, the lesson learned by these forms is the same. Thus, suppose that one wanted to deny underlying forms existed altogether, but claim that there is an Asymmetric Faithfulness relation required in the Accusative-to-Nominative mapping. The point is, in such a theory, freely choosing the Accusative *nühübü* when presented with the Nominative *nühüp* still flies in the face of grammatical pressure to minimize faithfulness violations. We will thus not consider such alternative models in further discussion, as the point remains the same: by choosing a voiced obstruent in the Accusative, speakers are demonstrating choice of a "base" of derivation that brings them away from a faithful mapping between forms.

In fact, the nonce word situation is not altogether different from the fate of loanwords. When the word *group* is imported to Turkish, it first undergoes epenthesis, yielding *gurup*. But for seemingly inexplicable reasons, its accusative form is *gurubu*. (Interested participants may wish to know that Google reveals 20,000 times more hits for *gurubu* than *gurupu*, although the latter does come up a handful of times, for reasons to become clear shortly.) Lewis (1967), in his grammar of Turkish, comments on the fact that polysyllabic loanwords are quite commonly adapted with underlyingly voiced final obstruents. This is thus a productive generalization, one which Lewis and subsequent scholars have characterized in terms of a morpheme-structure constraint: a constraint on what underlying forms can or should look like. Loanwords, however, as we know, enter the language in a variety of ways, and become "fixed" in their behavior relatively quickly. It is thus interesting to observe speakers' on-line behavior when immediately confronted with the task of deducing an underlying form.

Some of the results of our preliminary nonce-word study are included in the table in (5). In addition to these words, we randomly intermixed additional filler words, words with a seemingly exceptional voiced stop in the nominative, words which ended in sonorants, and monosyllabic words, to which we will turn in just a moment. (Note that Turkish velar stops are deleted between vowels, so we couldn't include those.) Here are the results for the number of speakers out of 6 who picked an underlying form that was voiced:

(5)

Voiceless Isolation form	Voiced UR, as shown by Acc	#/6
nühüp	nühübü	5
adɨp	adɨbɨ	4
gelep	gelebi	3
gotut	gotudu	3
rikep	rikebi	3
torsot	torsodu	3
ɨpanč	ɨpandʒɨ	3
sɨsap	sɨsabɨ	3
rutunk	rutungu	2
ongup	ongubu	2
südörp	südörbu	2
köbüt	köbüdü	0

One of the most obvious conclusions is that speakers do not behave uniformly. (Analysis of individual subjects reveals this as well; a single person is not "consistent" with respect to choosing all voiced or voiceless stops). Lexicon Optimization predicts that all of these should be stored as voiceless.

We are able to conclude based on this example that the driving force behind UR construction is *not* minimization of faithfulness violations.

Of course, there are alternatives to Lexicon Optimization that can be imagined and discussed here. In fact, Kiparsky's Alternation Condition, when dealing with Vowel Harmony, made the assumption that all alternating morphemes are stored with the *Marked* Value of the alternating feature. The idea was that neutralizing rules could delete structure, but not add structure. Now, we know that this is not generally true, due to the existence of neutralizing rules that yield the marked value, such as final *voicing*, even of underlyingly voiceless obstruents, as discussed for the Caucasian language Lezgian by Yu (2004). But suppose that it may be true on a language-particular basis. In that case, when faced with neutralized codas, learners might initially, in the absence of evidence to the contrary, store *all* such codas as underlyingly voiced, perhaps due to the evidence from existing alternations. In a recent paper by McCarthy (2004) on "free rides"[1], this intuition is echoed: in some situations, learners will adjust all of their underlying representations to be divergent from the surface form, based on more general evidence from morphophonemic alternations.

However, there are varying rates here as to how many speakers chose a voiced UR: none of them completely went for the Lexicon Optimization solution, and none of them completely went for the Store-as-Marked +Voice-solution. They seem eager to guess that *nühüp* comes from an underlying /nühüb/, but very hesitant to conclude that *köbüt* could come from underlying /köbüd/. What kinds of factors might play a role here?

Ernestus and Baayen (2003) in their study of nonce word production in Dutch deneutralization of coda devoicing note the role of sub-lexical factors in biasing learners towards postulating one or the other underlying representation.

One of the factors that Ernestus & Baayen (henceforth, "E&B") note that plays a role in whether an obstruent will be underlyingly voiced or not is its place of articulation. One model, for example, starts with the assumption that speakers know that there is neutralization in a certain position, and that they base their choice on whether an obstruent is underlyingly voiced (in a certain position) or not through their knowledge of the phonology of the language, so may decide to assign underlying [+voice] to those obstruents which are more robustly voiced *elsewhere*. For example, in Dutch, bilabial stops are more "robust" than alveolar stops, in the sense that they never undergo postlexical devoicing assimilation in function words. Crosslinguistically, bilabial stops are the most favored voiced obstruent, due to the following aerodynamic factors. Sustaining voicing requires that the oral pressure be lower than subglottal pressure. On the other hand, making an obstruent increases the oral pressure. So what to do in order to keep the subglottal-to-oral pressure ratio high enough to allow voicing? One option is to increase the volume of the oral cavity. A bilabial place of articulation allows this, and allows the cheeks to expand enough, allowing increased volume, which decreases the oral pressure. Ohala, Kingston, and others have thus reasoned that bilabial stops are more "eligible" for a [+voice] specification to begin with. Indeed, a brief inspection of our Turkish data does reveal that speakers as a pooled whole do prefer assigning [+voice] to the bilabial stop, so this type of explanation may play a role.

In Dutch, however, speakers showed a very different pattern, which turns out to be inconsistent with a "robustness" of [+voice] explanation. For nonce verbs such as *ik mip*, they overwhelmingly preferred the past-tense *mipte*. For nonce verbs with a final coronal stop, such as *ik nort*, they preferred the past tense *nortte*, with an underlying voiceless stop, though not to the degree of preference for underlyingly voicelessness observed for labial stops. Most surprising were the results for nonce verbs with a velar fricative, such as *ik teeg* (in which the <g> is pronounced as voiceless [x]), for which subjects overwhelmingly preferred the voiced past-tense *teegde*.

E&B concluded that the most relevant factor in whether speakers will assign an underlying voiced or voiceless representation to a final obstruent for a given place of articulation is lexical statistics, and not the robustness of voicing or any phonological-strength-related factors. The velar fricative is not known for its robust compatibility with voicing. But in the Dutch lexicon, 97% of stem-final velar fricatives are underlyingly voiced.

E & B performed a database count, and found the following (6).

(6) Dutch obstruents in CELEX database

Place	Underlying [+voice]	Underlying [−voice]	Percent
Bilabial Stop	210	20	91% voiceless
Coronal stop	177	542	75% voiceless
Velar fricative	127	4	97% voiced

They conclude that "Speakers tend to choose that phoneme as the underlying representation that makes the morpheme resemble similar morphemes in the lexicon. That is, they are more likely to choose a given underlying representation when there are more similar words in the lexicon sharing this underlying representation. Speakers recognize that there is neutralization and base their choice for the underlying representation on the distribution of the underlying representations among existing morphemes, serving as exemplars." (E&B, p.7)

It is interesting to return to the Turkish pattern we have observed in our preliminary study, in which bilabials are the place of articulation with the greatest tendency for an underlying [+voice] specification in final position. If E&B are on the right track, perhaps the Dutch/Turkish difference in nonce-word formation is correlated with a difference in the lexical statistics of voicing specification in word-final position. A quick glance at an electronic Turkish database reveals that this is the case.

(7) Turkish obstruents in TELL database

Place	Underlying [+voice]	Underlying [−voice]	Percent
Bilabial Stop	431	56	85% voiced
Coronal stop	391	1224	75% voiceless

E&B note that the simple lexicostatistic of a predominance of underlying voiced vs. voiceless is one source of knowledge that speakers draw on in postulating the underlying representation for a novel word. We would like to point out here that this simple lexicostatistic *alone* cannot be the *whole* model for explaining our nonce word data, since speakers do not, on the whole, pick [b] exactly 85% of the time for nonce words. E& B point out other that factors can provide useful information about what to predict for the UR of an obstruent as well. For example, the quality of the vowel in the final syllable turns out to have an important information gain as to whether the final obstruent will be underlyingly voiced or not when a database is consulted, and indeed, E & B found that experimental performance correlated with this as well.

One of the factors that E & B note has very little predictive significance in Dutch as to whether a word will have an underlyingly voiced or voiceless obstruent is the length of the word. However, in Turkish, this factor turns out to be crucial. Monosyllabic loanwords such as *tube* are overwhelmingly adapted as underlyingly voiceless, yielding non-alternating nominative-accusative pairs, such as *tüp~tüpü*. So there is a syllable-based generalization for Turkish; according to Inkelas, Pycha, and Sprouse (2004), while over half of Turkish polysyllabic obstruent-final words undergo voicing alterations, only one-fifth of monosyllabic obstruent-final words show alternation. In our nonce word study, we found a similar trend. The rates of adopting a UR with an underlying voiced stop were significantly lower for monosyllabic nonce words than in (5).

(8)

Voiceless Isolation form	Voiced UR, as shown by Acc	#/6
čɨč	čɨdʒɨ	0
rat	rat	0
münk	münk	0
šüt	šüt	0
sep	sep	1
üp	üp	1

As for why the monosyllabic vs. polysyllabic generalization should hold for Turkish, there are a variety of functionally-based speculations, but none are completely solid. Wedel (2002) suggested that monosyllabic words do not alternate – i.e, tend to be underlyingly voiceless – because they have a high neighborhood density. Neighborhood density measures the number of existing words in the lexicon that are one segment away. Wedel's idea is that CVC words are shorter, and have many more lexical neighbors. He notes that high neighborhood density slows down lexical access, which has been found by Luce and Pison (1998). His idea is that high neighborhood density makes lexical access tough especially when it is coupled with alternations, which he supposes make lexical access harder. (This latter fact, as far as we know, has never been demonstrated experimentally.) In any event, Inkelas, Pycha & Sprouse show that there *is* no such correlation in Turkish between lexical neighborhood size and whether or not a final obstruent alternates:

(9)

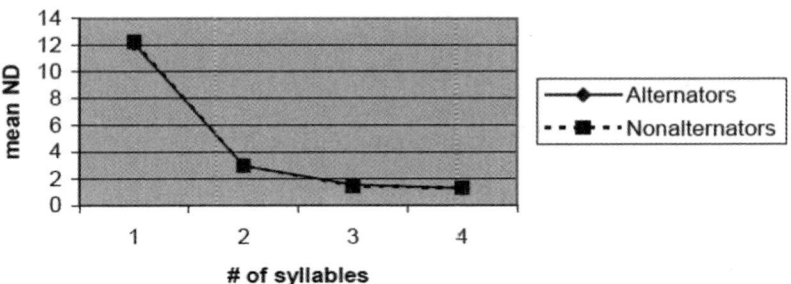

Perhaps the lexical neighborhood factor became grammaticalized, and perhaps not. Perhaps there is no principled reason why the voiceless tendency holds in monosyllables, and perhaps there is. Turkish speakers, however, have access to this lexical knowledge, and when constructing underlying representations, they make use of the fact that there is a monosyllabic vs. polysyllabic generalization: monosyllabic roots have final obstruents that tend to be underlyingly voiceless, and polysyllabic roots have final obstruents that tend to be underlyingly voiced. This productive generalization yields, oddly enough, loanword adaptations of *tube* and *group* as having the URs /tüp/ and /gurub/, completely the opposite of what a transparent surface mapping of the input would predict.

Why would natural language have such semi-productive tendencies to begin with? In other words, why should it be the case that the underlying voice specification of a final obstruent has some statistical correlation with unrelated phonological cues, such as the quality of the preceding vowel in Dutch, or the syllabicity of the word in Turkish? E&B make the suggestion that if the speaker forgets the underlying [voice] specification of a final obstruent (for an existing word in a neutralized context), he or she can deduce it from other morphemes in the lexicon and other sublexical cues. In other words, redundancy helps!

There are a variety of computational procedures that can model the experimental results we have been talking about, given knowledge of the lexicon and the statistical tendencies for voiced vs. voiceless specification, and our goal here is not to demonstrate which of the many computational models of analogy and nearest neighbor computations can best fit the experimental data. It seems when there are morpheme-structure-generalizations that act as cues, one of the more promising models for cases such as these, involves choosing URs based on an "exemplar set" of existing URs in the lexicon. One specific implementation involves the Analogy-Based modeling of Skousen (1989), where the analogical set contains words that share subsets of identical feature-values with the target word. A frequent argument against models of this type is the one embodied in the OT slogan "Knowledge is in the Constraints, not in the Lexicon", with the presupposition that it is computationally implausible to consult an analogical set of existing URs in the lexicon when deciding what the UR is for a newly-presented output form. However, a wide range of psycholinguistic evidence suggests that there *is* co-activation of similar-looking lexical candidates during lexical access.

We have thus considered the role of various grammatical pressures that contribute to construction of the UR for outputs that are neutralized due to coda devoicing. It turns out that the role of statistical frequency, and the desire to build URs that look the most like already existing URs in the Lexicon, plays a decisive role, and leaves little-to-no room for faithfulness-based optimization.

A similar situation, involving an altogether different process, involves Korean coronal fortition. This case is particularly interesting:

(10)   a.   Korean underlying /t t^h t' s s' c c^h c' h/ all neutralize to [t] word-finally (Ahn 1998; Iverson 1989)

           b.   Korean underlying /t/ is extremely rare (Sohn 2001; Kang 2003)

(11)   a.   English *internet* → [intʰənɛt],[intʰənɛsil]
       b.   English *Hamlet* → [hɛmnit],[hɛmnisil]

The suffixed object forms reveal the underlying form that Korean speakers have assigned to these words: both of them have an underlying /s/ as the final consonant. Since there are no constraints on underlying representations under Richness-of-the-Base, this fact is impossible to explain in terms of Lexicon Optimization. Why not just assign underlying /t/ for *internet*? McCarthy's Free Ride paper proposes a solution to this problem, within OT, one which was already anticipated in Harrison and Kaun (2000) which suggested the possibility of "Pattern-Responsive" Lexicon Optimization.

(12)   "I will propose a learning principle according to which learners who have discovered the /A/ → [B] unfaithful map from alternations will attempt to generalize it, projecting /A/ inputs for *all* surface [B]s, whether they alternate or not. In other words, the nonalternating [B]s attempt to take a free ride on the independently motivated /A/ → [B] map."

The problem for this Pattern-Responsive generalization of unfaithful mappings for Korean, as pointed out by Idsardi (2005), is the following. Since all of the underlying phonemes in (10) exhibit unfaithful alternations, there is no way to know *which* underlying /A/ to pick. In other words, the Free Ride principle does not add anything new to the solution. It gives no way of knowing which of many possible URs a learner will choose; it merely re-describes the problem. However, lexical statistics go a long way towards understanding what Korean learners are doing. In a study of the SEJONG corpus performed by Albright (2005), it turns out that 56% of the morpheme-final coronals are /s/. Thus, rather than going for a maximally faithful underlying form, learners are using lexical statistics in constructing URs. This should not be overly surprising when viewed from a broader perspective on cognition. Randy Gallistel, a researcher on animal cognition, points out that when animals have to solve problems with incomplete knowledge, they frequently employ frequency matching as a strategy (Gallistel 1990).

Returning to the discussion of the blicket detector task of Sobel, Tenenbaum, and (Gopnik 2004), we turn to a discussion of their Experiment 3. In this experiment, they exposed kids to lots of objects before introducing them to the blicket detector. There were two conditions. In the "rare blicket" condition, 1 out of 10 of the objects they were exposed to beforehand were blickets. In the "common blicket" condition, 9 out of 10 objects were blickets. The children were then presented with the exact same task as before: seeing two objects, A and B, seeing that A lights up the blicket detector, and seeing that A and B together light up the blicket detector. The children were then asked if B was a blicket or not.

The children were remarkably sensitive to the *base rates* of whether something was a blicket or not as an independent fact about the world. The 4-year olds categorized B as a blicket on average 25% of the time in the rare blicket setup, but 81% of the time in the common blicket setup. Children's causal inferences about whether B was a blicket — which is logically indeterminate, given the backwards blocking scenario – depended on base rates. This is remarkably similar to the facts noted above: language users may be remarkably sensitive to the lexical statistics – the base rates – of underlying forms. Turkish speakers thus use the base-rate information of whether a word is likely to have an underlying /b/ or /p/ in making the decision of whether nonce words come from one or the other.

It is worth briefly noting here that Sobel *et al.* were not surprised that the children's outcomes – 81% response that B was a blicket given a 90% base rate, and 25% response that B was a blicket given a 10% response rate – did not match exactly the base rate. Bayesian inference models often recognize that individuals may use the base rates more conservatively than others, and do not expect a perfect match. The point is that the base rates make a difference, and that they make a difference in the right direction, with statistically reliable effects.

In more recent work, Inkelas (2000) has recognized the fact that lexicon optimization does not explain the behavior of speakers when they encounter new words and construct underlying representations for them. She tentatively suggests that learners "Sort underlying representations of lexemes by phonological specification and use analogy to come up with lexical representations for new lexemes for which the observed data doesn't yet force a particular underlying representation." (Inkelas: 2000).

This amounts to abandoning Lexicon Optimization, which says that when observed data doesn't force a particular underlying representation, the most transparent one is chosen. At this point we note, extremely briefly, that abandoning Lexicon Optimization will necessitate a reassessment of the widely-adopted RIP/CD algorithm for acquiring the order of constraints.

There remains the interesting question about what happens when there are inputs, say A and B, that both map to the output C, and the frequencies of A and B are completely equal. Such a case is unknown to us, if attested at all in natural language. However, in his study of pigeon conditioning, G. S. Reynolds (1961) found that when both a triangle and a red circle were perfect predictors of the food response, certain pigeons would subsequently peck at equal rates for triangles alone and certain others for red circles alone. Both stimulus cues had 100% mapping to the desired output, and both stimulus cues had completely identical presentation rates during the conditioning process, so it seems natural to peck for either of them in subsequent trials. However, some of Reynolds' pigeons simply went for one of these stimulus cues and stuck with it, ignoring the other subsequently. In the figure below, Pigeon 105 consistently pecked at the triangle, ignoring the red circle as a predictor when presented alone. Pigeon 107, on the other hand, consistently pecked at the red circle, ignoring the triangle as a predictor.

(13)

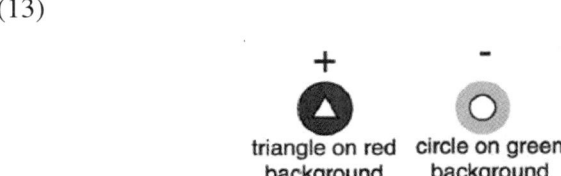

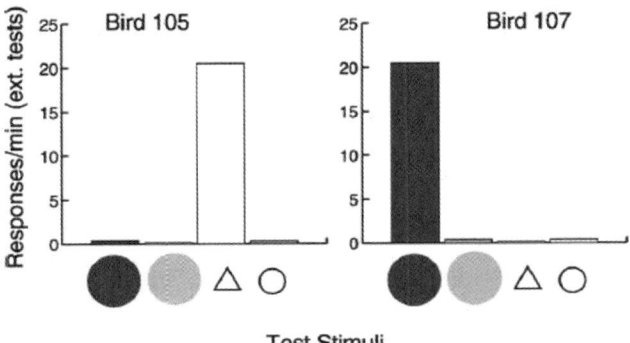

Gallistel (2003) interprets these outcomes as the result of redundancy reduction strategy: "Bandwidth reduction, a. k. a. parsimony applies: letting one of them do all the work maximizes the information conveyed per signal". It remains to be seen whether artificial language experiments can be designed which present two non-native phonemes in equal proportion, both of which neutralize to the same output. If so, such experiments would yield important insights into whether humans opt for deterministic behavior even in cases of perfect random choice.

A final case of interest that demonstrates the importance of segmental frequency trumping the principle of transparent URs comes from the study of Spanish rhotics. As pointed out in a series of papers by Jim Harris, Spanish neutralizes the contrast between the flap ⟨r⟩ and the trill ⟨rr⟩ in initial position: only the trill is possible in initial position. However, these two rhotics contrast intervocalically. (As a brief reminder, Spanish orthography uses one 'r' for the tap, and two 'rr's for the trill, while the IPA uses one 'r' for the trill.)

(14)   Spanish trill contrastive intervocalically.
   a.   *pero* [pero] 'but' (flap)
   b.   *perro* [pero] 'dog' (trill)

An immediate question arises as to the representation of r-initial words, such as *rosa*, which have a surface trill. A completely transparent underlying form would be with the trill, of course. A much more abstract representation would be one with the flap underlying.

(15)   Representation of [rosa] (surface trill)
   a.   /rosa/ (underlying trill)
   b.   /rosa/ (underlying flap) plus rule of initial trilling: ɾ → [r] in the environment: # _

The second analysis is of course much more complicated. Nonetheless, the rule of initial trilling (or its constraint-based equivalent) does represent a valid generalization about the language. This second analysis is ruled out, of course, by Kiparsky's alternation condition: there is no reason to specify /rosa/ as underlyingly [ɾosa] if there are no alternations to support this. However, we can begin to examine the lexical statistics of /r/, the trill, vs. /ɾ/, the flap. These can only be compared in intervocalic position, the position where they both are allowed. Harris (2001), examining the *Vox* Spanish dictionary, estimated 80% of intervocalic, morpheme-internal rhotics are the flap, while only 20% are the trill. If the preference to adhere to lexicostatistics for one segment versus another plays such a dominant role in UR construction, we might expect the drastic result that lexicostatistical preference overrides lexicon optimization here too. Note that there *is* no "free ride" to be taken here, as there are no alternations, morphological, postlexical, or otherwise, which turn an underlying flap into a trill in word-initial context. There are no morphological or phrasal concatenations that would suddenly make a non-initial rhotic into the initial segment of a word and thus trigger the context of the rule of initial trilling.

There is, however, one marginal process in Spanish, which does just what we are looking for: it moves an initial rhotic into a non-initial segment of the word. There is a language game that inverts the order of syllables, just like French *Verlan*. Thus, *casa* becomes *saca*, *gato* becomes *toga*, and so forth. What is important for our purposes is the output of the game for words like *rosa* (with an initial trill) and *reto* (meaning "challenge", also with an initial trill): it surfaces with an intervocalic flap.

(16) a. [rosa] → [saɾo] (surface transformation)
      b. /rosa/ → [saɾo] (uderlying derivation to game output)

On the account in which *rosa* really is stored with a UR that contains an underlying flap in initial position, the game's result is expected. The flap is transposed to non-initial position: in other words, the game-transposition "bleeds" otherwise regular application of initial trilling.

However, on the account in which *rosa* is stored with an underlying trill, the output of the game is puzzling. Trills *are* allowed in intervocalic position. Learners are certainly not inventing a rule like "Trills become flaps in intervocalic position only when that results from Verlan-transposition". This rule is counter to the phonotactics of the language and therefore, without any evidence on which the learner could base it. The rule also requires access to the derivational history of its input, a "no-no" in all rule-based frameworks that ban "looking back", as well as in all existing versions of OT.

This language game, then, is a controlled experiment: it creates an environment in which we can see the "naked" underlying form of a rhotic, when it is transposed to a position where the rule of absolute neutralization can no longer apply. The result of the experiment shows that *rosa*, a non-alternating surface form with a trill in the output, is stored with an underlying flap instead. The explanation for this fact lies in the strong influence of segmental frequencies on UR construction, coupled with context-sensitive phonotactic knowledge.

4. Hypercorrection

In this next section, however, we will consider two additional considerations which can bias the choice of a UR in one direction or the other.

The first is hypercorrection. English flapping presents a case in which the two coronal stops /d/ and /t/ are neutralized to the flap [ɾ]. Nonetheless, since flapping is considered to be a casual speech rule, speakers are sometimes aware of the fact that an underlying /t/ should not be flapped in careful speech, and attempt to correct this mapping by pronouncing [t] where flapping otherwise yields [ɾ]. Speakers know that surface flaps may come from underlying /t/. Sometimes, they may "overdo" the application of this knowledge. It is interesting to observe that some speakers exhibit hypercorrection when it comes to "undoing" flapping. The second author's wife has yielded the following forms in careful speech (to be read in a slow "baby talk" register)

(17)   enchilat^{h}a, chet^{h}ar cheese, somebot^{h}y

Interestingly, this speaker is systematic in producing no flaps in careful speech. And this tendency is not unique. Internet research reveals 25,000 Google hits for the spelling *sporatic*. An experimental study of repetition priming by McLennan, Luce, and Charles-Luce (2003) found that, in an experiment where subjects were exposed to both careful and casual speech, a casually-pronounced stimulus such as [koɾər] facilitated reaction time in repetition of both *coder* and *coater*, even though the latter is a highly infrequent word. They took the results to show that flapped stimuli are ambiguous and always activate both possible underlying representations. Lexicon Optimization, if it is the kind of thing that would make predictions about which underlying form is primed in lexical access, predicts that only the more harmonic *coader* will be activated. The Pattern-Responsive/Free-Ride theory, in its literal form (i.e. with the italicized universal quantification in (12)), predicts that only the unfaithful *coater* will be activated. Hypercorrective inferences about conversion from casual-to-careful speech, however, involve "undoing" phonological rules, however, and will choose the /t/ as a possibility in both perception and production.

In production sometimes, then, the desire to produce "careful speech" overrides even frequency biases for the input word, and has the effect of blocking the application of the optional rule of flapping, and when this happens, it reveals the true UR that speakers have adopted. On the assumption that the /d/-to-flap mapping is more faithful than the /t/-to-flap mapping by virtue of not changing [+voice] specifications, speakers who follow the hypercorrective impulse reveal a UR created at the expense of ignoring lexicon optimization.

5. Spelling

One of the most informative choices of a UR in the case of ambiguous neutralized input can come from orthographic knowledge. This follows a general theme we have been establishing: when speakers come across a neutralized output, they will use any information they can get their hands on in order to come up with a UR. They won't simply fall back on Lexicon Optimization. In fact, in any case in which they have any amount of knowledge to base a decision on, such as knowledge of alternations, segmental frequency and analogical exemplars, they'll use it. The same goes for knowing how a word is spelled. Orthographic knowledge plays an important role in phonological representations, particularly because in many writing systems, such as for English vowels, a morpheme retains the same spelling even when it undergoes drastic phonological alternations. Thus, it becomes a natural fallback of cognition to associate two distinct types of representations: the underlying form, which provides the same input to phonological derivations in a variety of alternating environments, and the orthographic representation (to be abbreviated "OR"), which retains the same representation in a variety of alternating environments.

Of course, mismatches exist in both directions, due to the fact that phonological systems change much faster than orthographic systems. But the association exerts a strong tendency in both directions. Sapir's informants, in his famous paper "The Psychological Reality of the Phoneme" (Sapir 1949) have their first experiences with writing systems. Sapir, who expected them to shape the OR based on the surface representations of morphemes, was surprised when he found that they decide to shape the OR based on their pre-existing knowledge of the UR. In the cases we turn to now, subjects decide to base the UR, otherwise indeterminate, on their existing knowledge of the OR.

An initial example comes from vowel reduction in English. As noted by Michaels (1980), English orthography maintains distinct ways of writing unstressed vowels that are pronounced with identical surface form, such as the second vowel in *Néwton, Vénus, mámmal, Rússell*.

(18) a. Newton, Venus, mammal, Russell
 b. [nuwtən, vijnəs, mæməl, rʌsəl]
 c. *-ian* affixation

Michaels points out the effects of *-ian* affixation, which shifts stress to the immediately preceding syllable, even if it was a reduced vowel. The prediction of LO is that the underlying vowel is stored for these proper names as a central vowel, so under stress, the second vowel of *Newton* should become something like *Newtʌnian* – if speakers are using a "violation optimization" strategy for constructing URs, or even a "faithfulness maximization among affixed forms" strategy, they should be able to produce an affixed form with a stressed central vowel (the "caret"), no problem. However, speakers of English who know the orthographic representation for these words will tell you that the affixed forms are as follows:

(19) a. [nutonijən, vənuwšən, məmejlijən, rəsijlijən]
 b. /nuton, vijnus, mæmejl, rʌsijl/

When speakers encounter an unstressed vowel and have no evidence for its underlying form, they thus use the following strategy: a vowel that is spelled ⟨o⟩" has the UR /o/, a vowel that is spelled ⟨u⟩ has the UR /u/, a vowel that is spelled ⟨a⟩ has the UR /ej/, and a vowel that is spelled ⟨e⟩ has the UR /ij/. (Michaels also notes that speakers know that a vowel that is spelled ⟨i⟩ has the UR /ɪ/, based on evidence from Dárwin-Darwínian.). Michaels notes the result of an experiment with adults asked to say the derived form of the name *Zinken*. They had no idea what to pronounce. He then showed them the spelling of the name, with the variant spellings and found their results were of course consistent with what the spelling told them.

(20) a. Zinken, Zinkan, Zinkun, Zinkon
 b. ziŋkijnijən, ziŋkejnijən, ziŋkunijən, ziŋkonijən

Orthographic knowledge is further likely to play a similar role in UR construction for speakers of non-rhotic dialects. This may be of interest in light of the conclusions of Krämer (2005), who suggests that speakers may import an /r/ to follow the underlying representation of all non-high vowels, yielding an explanation for the so-called "intrusive r" that yields identity for the following two sentences ((a) and (b) as in (c)).

(21) a. The tuna is here
 b. The tuner is here
 c. ðə tunəɹ ɪz hijə

We wish to bring into consideration some suggestive evidence from McCarthy (1992) on r-insertion. This evidence suggests that *-ic* affixation can reveal the underlying forms of words with final non-high vowels in non-rhotic dialects. Specifically, McCarthy notes that in his own Eastern Massachusetts English, the words *algebra* and *Homer* are produced with an identical final rime: they both end with a schwa. However, they behave differently under *-ic* affixation, yielding *algebraic* vs. *Homeric*.

(22) a. URs under Lexicon Optimization: /ældʒəbrə, homə/
 b. URs under Free-Ride Extension of [r] to after non-high vowels: /ældʒəbrər, homər/
 c. URs under orthographic knowledge of pre-neutralization source: /ældʒəbrej, homijɹ/
 d. algebraic, Homeric

In accordance with Michaels' proposal, speakers will resort to the orthography when they cannot deduce a UR from the neutralized phonological output[2]. Of course, they can use knowledge from alternations they have heard from other speakers as well. This accounts for the lexical knowledge that accounts for the "linking" r found in the word *tuner*. As for the intrusive [r] in the word *tuna*, it may be possible that this word has been listed with an /r/ in its UR, as there are few alternations involving *tuna*. However, the fact that intrusive [r] shows up even in L2 pronunciations, as noted by Jespersen (1909) who cites example of nonrhotic English speakers' attempts at German yielding *hatte[r] ich* and *sagte[r] er*, it is tempting to explain intrusive [r] as the output of an active phonological rule operating in URs constructed with the help of orthographic knowledge.

We end this paper with a discussion of the results of a study we are carrying out on European Portuguese (henceforth "EP"), with the help of Salvador Mascarenhas, a student at the University of Lisboa (Nevins, Mascarenhas, and Kilimangalam 2005). EP is known for its massive vowel reduction, which, esentially, turns all unstressed round vowels to [u], as discussed in the book the *The Phonology of Portuguese*, by Mateus and d'Andrade (2000).

(23)   Eur. Port.: Unstressed /ɔ,o,u/ → [u]

Of additional interest is the process of vowel harmony that occurs in the third conjugation. In the first person singular and in the subjunctive, stems with an underlying mid vowel show up with a high vowel:

(24)   a.   /dormír/ 'to sleep'
        b.   [dormímos] 'we sleep'
        c.   [dúrmu] 'I sleep'
        d.   [dúrma] 'sleep 3SG. SUBJUNCTIVE'

The traditional wisdom, which we follow here, is that the stem vowel shows up as [u] in those contexts (e. g. 1. SG.)where the theme vowel is deleted for morphophonological reasons. We can call this harmony process "mid-vowel raising", since this is its effect, factoring out the triggering cause.

These two processes, unstressed vowel reduction, and mid-vowel raising, may combine to yield ambiguity for third conjugation stems. Consider the hypothetical verb stems 'gomir' and 'gumir'.

(25)   a.   /gomir/, /gumir/ → [gumír], by unstressed vowel reduction
        b.   /gumir/ → [gúmu] (1. SG.) inflection as usual
        c.   /gomir/ → [gúmu] (1. SG.) by mid-vowel raising

These verbs will have an identical infinitive pronunciation, and an identical first person singular pronunciation. They will diverge, of course, on the 2nd person singular, where mid-vowel raising can no longer apply:

(26)   a.   /gumir/ → [gúməs] (2. SG.) inflection as usual
        b.   /gomir/ → [góməs] (2. SG.) inflection as usual

We have conducted a wug-test survey of European Portuguese speakers, in which we present them with the infinitive *gumir* and the first person singular *Eu gumu*, and asked them to produce the second person singular. Our results thus far show fifty-fifty choice (27).

(27)   No orthographic information. Subject hears *gumir. Eu gumu, Tu ...*"
        a.   [goməs] 3/6 speakers
        b.   [guməs] 3/6 speakers

In this experiment, we have an additional twist: after presenting each subject with 40 nonce verbs of this sort (suitably randomized and balanced with distractors), we then go back and ask them to go through the procedure again, but this time we show them the orthography. For 3 of the speakers, we have showed them the infinitive written as *gumir*, and for 3 of the speakers, we have showed them the infinitive written as *gomir*.

(28) a. *gomir* → Tu [goməs] 3/3 speakers
 b. *gumir* → Tu [guməs] 3/3 speakers

It is striking to note the unanimity in responses among speakers when an orthographic form is shown, despite the fact that the same speaker may have produced the opposite result in the first half of the task with the same verb.

This experiment again shows that European Portuguese speakers rely on orthographic cues when they can, and when they can't, they go for probabilistic guessing of what the underlying form of the stem vowel is. If minimizing grammatical violations were all there was to the story, all 6 of the speakers should be choosing [guməs] when they hear *gumir* and *gumu*. As for what the exact factors are that bias them for choosing [o] or [u] for a given verb, we are awaiting the consultation of an electronic Portuguese lexicon to perform analyses of whether certain vowels are more probable between certain consonant clusters.

In closing, these results should not be too surprising, from a broader point of view. A long psycholinguistic literature has revealed the effects of orthographic knowledge in phonological tasks. Seidenberg and Tanenhaus (1979) found that speakers take longer to decide whether *pie* and *rye* rhyme than *pie* and *tie*, even though these tasks require only a phonetic judgement and are presented entirely auditorally.

Hallé, Chéreau, and Segui (2000) found that French speakers detect the phoneme /b/ more easily than the phoneme /p/ when they hear tokens like French word *absurde*, which is pronounced with a [p], due to voiceless assimilation, but not when they heard tokens like *rhapsodie*. This effect held up in a subsequent experiment even with non-words, so that *apsorie* yielded a high rate of /b/ detection, while *rapselg* did not. Hallé *et al.* concluded that French subjects perceived a [b] in *apsorie* but not in *rapselg* due to the similarity of the former to existing words in the French lexicon which are known to be morphologically and orthographically derived from the prefix *ab-*, with a [b]. They point out that a variety of models of real-time lexical access activate lexical neighbors, and that this sort of effect can overshadow the simplistic mechanism of isormorphism between the phonetic signal and the phonological representation. Yes, these speakers are using "higher-level, top-down" knowledge in making their automatic decision, but as we have seen throughout this paper, perhaps *everybody* is: it may be that reliance on lexical neighbors and orthographic cues is an inescapable urge for Man, the problem solver.

6. Conclusion

The ideal outcome of this paper would be that practising phonologists would simply stop believing that speakers ever use a principle like Lexicon Optimization, as there is no empirical evidence for its existence. It remains an interesting research challenge to see if there are *ever* any cases where the desire to minimize faithfulness violations takes precedence over the set of heuristics described here for UR construction.

Notes

* We are grateful to Adam Albright, William Idsardi and Timothy O'Donnell for valuable discussion leading to the development of this paper, and to Klaus Abels for delivering the paper in Tromsø.
1. The term, incidentally, is originally due to Morris Halle, as acknowledged by Zwicky (1970) in a CLS paper on rule-ordering.
2. Note that *Homeric* is subject to trisyllabic laxing, of the form *serene–serenity*, so Michaels also correctly predicts the quality of its medial vowel given an underlying /ij/.

References

Ahn, Sang-Cheol
    1998   *An Introduction to Korean Phonology*. Seoul: Hanshin.
Albright, Adam
    2005   Explaining universal tendencies and language particulars in analogical change. Paper presented at Explaining Linguistic Universals Workshop, Berkeley, Cal.
Cheng, P.W.
    1997   From Covariation to Causation: A causal power theory. *Psychological Review* 104:367–405.
Ernestus, Miriam, and Harald Baayen
    2003   Predicting the Unpredictable: Interpreting Neutralized Segments in Dutch. *Language* 79.1:5–38.
Gallistel, Randy
    1990   *The Organization of Learning*. Cambridge, Mass.: MIT Press.

2003	Conditioning from an information processing perspective. *Behavioural Processes* 61(1): 89–101.

Hallé, Pierre, Céline Chéreau, and Juan Segui
2000 Where is the /b/ in "absurde" [apsyrd]? It is in French Listeners' Minds. *Journal of Memory and Language* 43:618–639.

Harris, James
2001 Flaps, trills, and syllable structure in Spanish. In *MIT Working Papers in Linguistics 42*. Cambridge, Mass: MITWPL.

Harrison, K. David, and Abigail Kaun
2000 Pattern-Responsive Lexicon Optimization. In *Proceedings of the 30th Meeting of the North East Linguistics Society*, Ji-Yung Kim and Masako Hirotani (eds.), 327–340. Amherst, Mass.: GLSA.

Idsardi, William
2005 A Bayesian Account of Loanword Adaptation. Paper presented at Harvard International Symposium on Korean Linguistics.

Inkelas, Sharon
1994 The consequences of lexicon optimization for underspecification. ROA 40.
2000 Phonotactic blocking through structural immunity. ROA 366.

Inkelas, Sharon, Anne Pycha, and Ronald Sprouse
2004 Morphophonemics and the Lexicon: A case study from Turkish. In *Experimental Approaches to Phonology*, Maria-Josep Solé, Patrice Beddor, and Manjari Ohala (eds.), 369–385. Oxford: Oxford University Press.

Iverson, Gregory
1989 On the category Supralaryngeal. *Phonology* 6:285–303.

Jespersen, Otto
1909 *A Modern English Grammar on Historical Principles Part I: Sounds and Spellings*. Heidelberg: Carl Winter.

Kang, Yoonjung
2003 Perceptual similarity in loanword phonology: English postvocalic word-final stops in Korean. *Phonology* 10:243–279.

Kiparsky, Paul
1973 Phonological representations. In *Three Dimensions of Linguistic Theory*, Omoko Fujimura (ed.), 5–56. Tokyo: TEC.

Krämer, Martin
2005 Optimal Underlying Representations. In *The Proceedings of the 35th Meeting of the North East Linguistic Society*, Leah Bateman and Cherlon Ussery, (eds.). Amherst, MA: GLSA.

Lewis, Geoffrey L.
1967 *Turkish Grammar*. Oxford: Clarendon.

Luce, Paul, and David Pisoni
1998 Recognizing spoken words: The neighborhood activation model. *Ear and Hearing* 19: 1–38.

McCarthy, John J.
1992 Synchronic Rule Inversion. In *Proceedings of the 17th Meeting of the Berkeley Linguistics Society*, 192–207.
2004 Taking a free ride in morphophonemic learning. ROA 683.

McLennan, Conor, Paul Luce, and Jan Charles-Luce
    2003   Representation of Lexical form. *Journal of Experimental Psychology: Learning, Memory, and Cognition* 29(4): 539–553.

Michaels, David
    1980   Spelling and the phonology of tense vowels. *Language and Speech* 23:197–225.

Nevins, Andrew, Salvador Mascarenhas, and Ashtamurty Kilimangalam
    2005   Exceptions as Reanalysis in Portuguese Vowel Height Alternations. Paper Presented at the XXI Encontro Nacional da Associação Portuguesa de Linguística, Porto.

Nevins, Andrew, and Beste Yolcu-Kamali
    2005   Constructing Underlying Representations based on Informed Guesses: Turkish Evidence. Paper presented at the Central Eurasian Studies Society Conference, Boston, Mass.

Prince, Alan S., and Paul Smolensky
    1993   Optimality theory. Constraint interaction in generative grammar. Technical Report #2, Rutgers University Center for Cognitive Science. ROA 537; published in 2004 by Blackwell Publishers.

Mateus, Maria Helena and Ernesto d'Andrade
    2000   *The Phonology of Portuguese*. Oxford: OUP.

Reynolds, George S.
    1961   Attention in the pigeon. *Journal of the Experimental Analysis of Behavior* 4: 203–208.

Sapir, Edward
    1949   The Psychological Reality of the Phoneme. In *Selected Writings of Edward Sapir*, D.G. Mandelbaum (ed.), 46–51. Berkeley, Cal.: University of California Press.

Seidenberg, M. S., and M. K. Tanenhaus
    1979   Orthographic effects on rhyme monitoring. *Journal of Experimental Psychology: Human Learning and Memory* 5:546–554.

Skousen, Royal
    1989   *Analogical Modeling of Language*. Dordrecht: Kluwer.

Sobel, David, Joshua Tenenbaum, and Alison Gopnik
    2004   Children's causal inferences from indirect evidence: Backwards blocking and Bayesian reasoning in preschoolers. *Cognitive Science* 28:303–333.

Sohn, Hyang-Sook
    2001   Optimization of Word-final coronals in Korean. In *Proceedings of HILP 5*, 159–177. University of Potsdam.

Wedel, Andrew
    2002   Phonological alternation, lexical neighborhood density and markedness in processing. Handout from presentation at LabPhon 8, Yale University.

Yu, Alan
    2004   Explaining final obstruent voicing in Lezgian: Phonetics and history. *Language* 80.1:73–97.

Zwicky, Arnold
   1970   The free-ride principle and two rules of complete assimilation in English. In *Papers from the Sixth Chicago Linguistic Society*, 579–588.

Chapter 4
Allomorphy – selection, not optimization*

Patrik Bye

> "[E]verything language-specific is allocated to the lexicon"
> (Green 2005: vi)

1. Preliminary considerations

The distribution of suppletive allomorphs may be governed by a variety of contextual factors, including the semantics, phonology, and exact identity of the selecting lexical item. Where the choice is determined on the basis of the phonological context, it is very often the case that the choice is driven by euphony: the environment and the form of the allomorph are related in some phonologically natural way.[1] The advent of Optimality Theory (OT; Prince & Smolensky 1993; McCarthy & Prince 2001) has not only brought euphonic considerations in allomorph choice into sharper focus, but fostered the idea that universal markedness constraints are the engine of all phonologically conditioned allomorphy. The view that has come to prevail is succinctly summed up by Rubach and Booij's dictum (2001) that '[w]hile the allomorphs themselves are arbitrary, their distribution is not'. In this paper I challenge this view and review a number of cases where, assuming a reasonable interpretation of what constraints there are in CON, optimization either fails to make a prediction, or makes the wrong prediction about the distribution of the allomorphs. I argue instead that allomorph distribution reflects language-specific combinatorial requirements (subcategorization frames). Being arbitrary, these requirements are housed the lexicon.[2]

The idea that allomorph distribution reflects phonological subcategorization is not new. The same point has recently been argued by Paster (2005). The present paper strengthens the empirical case for phonological subcategorization in allomorphy and includes a proposal for how language-particular constraints on phonological subcategorization articulate with the OT constraint system. Adopting terminology first introduced by Lieber (1980, 1982), I will refer to language-specific regularities as **morpholexical**. The recognition of a division of labour between non-arbitrary ('true') phonology and arbitrary (morpholexical) phonology allows us to be stricter about the kind of constraints we admit to H-EVAL. I will adopt the most conservative view on this point, adumbrated in Kager (2008), that constraints in H-EVAL are limited to the *universal* set made available by CON. Ejecting language-specific information from H-EVAL has one desirable consequence for OT, which is that it brings the tasks of describing particular languages and developing factorial typologies more into line, a desideratum encoded into Smolensky's claim that grammars possess 'inherent typology'.

The formal principles governing the interaction of properly phonological constraints and morpholexical constraints differ in fundamental ways. Properly phonological constraints in H-EVAL are extrinsically ranked and violable. Differential priority between morpholexical constraints, on the other hand, is determined intrinsically by appeal to the Elsewhere Principle. Specifically, a morpholexical constraint $\mathcal{M}$ is only violable if a more specific morpholexical constraint is applicable. If there is no such constraint, $\mathcal{M}$ will be inviolable. The property of inviolability, *modulo* intrinsic relations of precedence, allows us to treat allomorphy under the same rubric as ineffability (a.k.a. 'gaps'; for recent OT proposals to deal with gaps, see McCarthy & Wolf 2005, and Rice 2005). Both are instantiations of absolute ungrammaticality, which we can understand as a failure of the lexicon to supply a morpholexically consistent form f for a syntactically parsed lemma $\mathcal{L}$.[3] On this view, the definition of allomorphy between two affixes A and B, where A and B encode the same morphosyntactic features, is that the form f_A with allomorph A is absolutely ungrammatical in contexts where form f_B with allomorph B is grammatical, and *vice versa*. Other things being equal, $\mathcal{L}$ will be expressible either through f_A or f_B. In situations of ineffability, on the other hand, the form f_A with allomorph A is absolutely ungrammatical, but the lexicon does not supply any allomorph B to fill the cell in the paradigm. In this case, $\mathcal{L}$ is unpronounceable – a gap.

The structure of the remainder of the paper is as follows. The theory of morpholexical constraints is described in more detail in section 2 and applied to the description of gaps in section 3. Section 4 extends the approach to suppletive allomorphy and ties it to the conception of absolute ungrammaticality. Section 5 addresses alternative ways in which morpholexical and phonological constraints might interlock and section 6 concludes by placing morpholexical constraints within a broader philosophical context and offers a few thoughts on directions for future development.

2. The declarative component: MORPHOLEXICAL CONTROL

Phonological regularities may derive from two sources: (i) phonetic knowledge, (ii) lexical knowledge. The constraints from these sources form separate modules, each with its own formal principles. Constraints deriving from phonetic knowledge (properly phonological constraints) are universal, extrinsically ranked, violable, and they produce a harmonic ordering of forms. Constraints deriving from lexical knowledge (morpholexical constraints) are parochial, intrinsically ranked, and essentially inviolable. Morpholexical constraints are declarative and, as such, they are surface-true (non-defeasible), irreparable (structure-checking, so inputs can only be accepted or rejected as inconsistent), and non-interacting – except (in some versions of Declarative Phonology) by Elsewhere Principle (Scobbie 1993). I will assume that a morpholexical constraint $\mathcal{M}$ is only violable if there is a more specific morpholexical constraint $\mathcal{M}'$ that is applicable. The violation of a general morpholexical constraint thus does not result in absolute ungrammaticality as long as it permits the satisfaction of a morpholexical constraint with higher intrinsic precedence.

One way of conceptualizing the interaction between the two modules takes its lead from CONTROL Theory (Orgun & Sprouse 1999). In this scheme, the output of H-EVAL is fed into a declarative component (cf. Scobbie 1993), MORPHOLEXICAL CONTROL. MORPHOLEXICAL CONTROL checks to see whether the relevant language-specific combinatorial restrictions are satisfied or not. If all such restrictions are obeyed in the output of H-EVAL, it is allowed to pass to phonetic implementation. If any restriction is violated, the form is rejected as absolutely ungrammatical, and is not pronounced at all (marked by ⊥). The scheme is shown in (1).

The content of MORPHOLEXICAL CONTROL and the original version of CONTROL is crucially different. In the proposal of Orgun & Sprouse (1999), constraints of CONTROL are members of the universal constraint set CON. As pointed out by McCarthy (2003), McCarthy & Wolf (2005), and Raffelsiefen (2004), this leaves CONTROL Theory vulnerable to the charge of duplication. As Raffelsiefen writes (p. 118), '[E]very phonological markedness constraint

(1) H-EVAL and MORPHOLEXICAL CONTROL

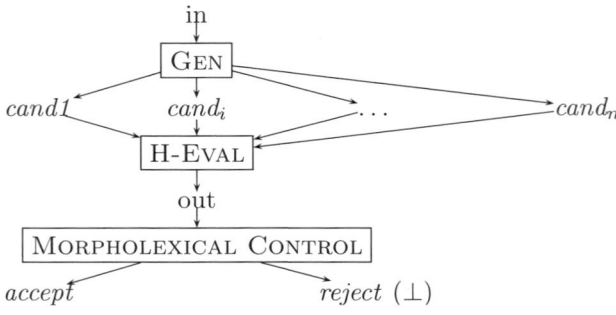

associated with gaps, would have to be assigned to both H-EVAL and CONTROL, clearly an undesirable outcome.' Morpholexical constraints, on the other hand, represent *post hoc* generalizations over a static lexicon. As such, they are unabashedly language-specific. Since the morpholexical constraints are different to universal phonological constraints in content and origin, duplication is not an objection that can be martialled against the approach.

At this point it is necessary to ask how subcategorization should be encoded. One of the anonymous reviewers points out that subcategorization, as generally used in the literature, presupposes that affixes themselves have lexical entries, and affixes select their hosts. This is a highly controversial assumption, and it distinguishes what Stump (2001: 1) calls 'lexical' from 'inferential' theories of inflection. The theory of morpholexical constraints is compatible with both of these approaches, but it I will adopt an inferential implementation here. Let us clarify what this conception entails. To begin, we may note that subcategorization is used ambiguously in the literature. In the first sense, subcategorization is used to refer to the relationship between morphologically distinct chunks of the representation, most obviously the edge orientation and linear arrangement of specific bits of affixal material. The first sense of the term may be illustrated by statements such as 'the English plural suffix subcategorizes for the right edge of the word'. In the second sense, subcategorization is used to refer to a relation between certain lexemes or lexeme classes and morphological realizations. Illustrations of this second sense (stated inferentially) are '*ox* in the plural subcategorizes for the suffix -*en*', and 'plural nouns subcategorize for the suffix -*s*'. Both of these statements are idiosyncratic facts about English plurals, and therefore it is appropriate to see them as being housed in the lexicon. I will distinguish the two senses of subcategorization by using **anchoring** for the first sense, and

selection for the second. For the purposes of the present paper, I will assume that both are properties of lexemes or lexeme classes (i.e. in inferential terms), which may be implemented as **attribute value matrices (AVMs)**. AVMs for 'cat' and the abstract type 'plural noun' in English are illustrated in (2).

(2) a. $\begin{bmatrix} \text{SEMANTICS} & \text{'cat'} \\ \text{SYNTAX} & [\text{CATEGORY N}] \\ \text{PHONOLOGY} & /\text{kæt}/ \end{bmatrix}$

b. $\begin{bmatrix} \text{SYNTAX} & \begin{bmatrix} \text{CATEGORY} & \text{N} \\ \text{INFLECTION} & \text{plural} \end{bmatrix} \\ \text{SELECT} & /-z/ \\ \text{ANCHOR} &]_N \quad \text{stem}\_\_ \end{bmatrix}$

In forming the plural of 'cat', the contents of (2a) and (2b) is combined. In this way, all English nouns inherit the property of selecting -s in the plural unless, that is, some more specific plural is applicable.

3. Gaps in Norwegian imperatives

CONTROL Theory was developed as a theory of absolute ungrammaticality. As in CONTROL Theory, absolute ungrammaticality arises when the optimal candidate output by H-EVAL is rejected as inconsistent ($\bot$) with some constraint in MORPHOLEXICAL CONTROL. Unlike CONTROL, morpholexical constraints have language-specific content. Consider as an example a case from Norwegian, which has figured in recent discussions of gaps (Rice 2005). In Norwegian, rising-sonority clusters are precluded from surfacing in coda position by *SONSEQ in (3).

(3) *SONSEQ (Clements 1990)
Sonority must decrease monotonically from the nucleus to the coda.

In conformity with this restriction, noun and adjective stems that end underlyingly in a rising-sonority cluster undergo epenthesis, as shown in (4).

(4) /oːpn-/ oːpn-e 'open-INF' oːpen 'open (A)'
/sykl-/ sykl-e 'cycle-INF' sykel 'bicycle (N)'

The data is readily accounted for by ranking *SONSEQ above DEP-V, as shown in (5).

(5)

/sykl_N/	SONSEQ	DEP-V
a. ☞ sykel		*
b. sykl	*	

It is an entailment of the conservative line sketched above that the ranking *SONSEQ≫DEP-V should have universal jurisdiction in the language, independent of lexical and morphological factors. However, when we look at the imperative forms of verbs, we find that epenthesis does not apply. The forms in (6a) show that, where there is an imperative form, it corresponds to the bare stem. The forms on the left bearing the suffix -e represent the infinitive. For the verbs in (6b), whose stems end in a rising-sonority cluster, there is no corresponding imperative form at all. In these cases, the bare stem is phonologically ill-formed, but any attempt to repair by epenthesis is also deemed unacceptable. In short, nothing is good enough.

(6) a. skriːv-e   skriːv!   'write!'
       jøːr-e   jøːr!   'do!'
    b. oːp.n-e   *oːpn!   *oːpen!   'open!'
       syk.l-e   *sykl!   *sykel!   'cycle!'

There is no good phonological reason for the imperative gap in Norwegian. The fact that epenthesis fails in this morphosyntactically circumscribed environment should be understood as an unpredictable (and hence lexical) fact about imperatives in Norwegian. The relevant morpholexical constraint would seem to require that the imperative form of the verb only contain material that stands in a relation of exponence to the lexical item. The proposed lexical specification of the imperative is given in (7).

(7) $\text{SUBCAT}_{\text{IMP}}$

$$\begin{bmatrix} \text{SYNTAX} & \begin{bmatrix} \text{CATEGORY} & \text{N} \\ \text{INFLECTION} & \text{IMPERATIVE} \end{bmatrix} \\ \text{SELECT} & [\ ] \\ \text{ATTACH} & \text{stem } S, \text{ where } \forall x \in S, x \sqsubset S \\ & x \text{ is an exponent of } S; \text{ non-underlying material} \\ & \text{in the host is disallowed)} \end{bmatrix}$$

In line with (1), the tableau in (8) represents the evaluation of the imperative verb /sykl$_{\text{V}_{\text{IMP}}}$/ in two consecutive computations: harmonic ordering by

H-EVAL, followed by declarative assessment. Within the optimizing component of the grammar, epenthesis follows inexorably from the ranking of *SONSEQ above DEP-V established by the behaviour of nouns. The input is thus mapped onto an output form that is phonologically fully interpretable: *sykel*. The output of H-EVAL is subsequently checked against the constraints in MORPHOLOGICAL CONTROL and found to violate SUBCAT$_{IMP}$ in (7). Following Orgun & Sprouse (1999), I use the symbol ⚔ to mark a form rejected as inconsistent with the most specific applicable morpholexical constraint.

(8)

		/sykl$_{V_{IMP}}$/	SONSEQ	DEP-V
H-EVAL	a. ☞ sykel			*
	b. sykl		*!	
MCONTROL			SUBCAT$_{IMP}$	
	⚔ sykel		⊥	

The Norwegian imperative represents a case where a particular morphosyntactic category, in this case [imperative] only has a single exponent: there are no alternative ways to form an imperative given that this one crashes. Since the only available strategy is rejected as absolutely ungrammatical by MORPHOLEXICAL CONTROL, imperative force is ineffable for these verbs. Speakers have to rely instead on alternative strategies to realize their communicative intentions, e.g. by using forms that are semantically closely related to the imperative (e.g. 'you must/will open...') and by exploiting non-linguistic resources to convey imperative force. In the next section we will look at cases in which absolute ungrammaticality does not result in ineffability thanks to the existence of more than one exponent, i.e. allomorphy.

4. Allomorphy: optimization or subcategorization?

Section 4.1 reviews OT approaches to the problem of allomorph distribution, and sketches the morpholexical alternative. 4.2 is a review of the kind of case that has been taken as supporting the OT approach to allomorph distribution, while 4.3 examines non-optimal allomorph distribution in detail and argues for the necessity of morpholexical constraints in grammar.

4.1. Three approaches

The forms of suppletive allomorphs must be lexically specified by definition. Nevertheless, allomorph distribution is widely seen as a problem of optimizat ion. There are two optimization-based approaches to allomorph distribution on the market today, (i) what I will call the Markedness-driven approach (Kager 1996; Mascaró 1996; McCarthy 2002; Rubach & Booij 2001; Green 2005; Wolf 2005, and many others), and (ii) MPARSE Theory (McCarthy & Prince 2001; McCarthy & Wolf 2005).

According to the Markedness-driven approach, allomorph distribution is an instance of the Emergence of the Unmarked (McCarthy & Prince 1994). Construing it in this way means that allomorphs $\{A, B, \ldots\}$ standing as exponents to some morphosyntactic feature structure ϕ must compete directly for attachment to the host: all allomorphs must therefore crucially be present in the input as a disjunction $/\{A, B, \ldots\}/$ and H-EVAL produces a harmonic ordering on $\{f_A, f_B, \ldots\}$, where $f_\aleph$ is a candidate form of the grammatical word ω_ϕ in which ϕ is exponed by allomorph $\aleph$. The second crucial property of the Markedness-driven approach is that allomorphs must differ inherently in complexity (e.g. number of segments). Suppose that A is more complex than B in some sense, e.g. by being longer. Other things being equal, f_B should be selected because f_A will violate more structural well-formedness constraints.[4] The form with the more complex allomorph (f_A) will only emerge when selecting the form with the less complex allomorph (f_B) would entail the violation of a crucially highly ranked markedness constraint *PHONO.

MPARSE theory differs from the Markedness-driven approach in that allomorphs $\{A, B, \ldots\}$ do *not* compete directly but are input to separate evaluations. This is a property MPARSE Theory shares with the current proposal. Suppose, as before, that f_B violates *PHONO and f_A satisfies *PHONO. The constraint MPARSE$_\phi$ requires that the morphosyntactic category ϕ be morphologically parsed. A morphologically unparsed expression, known as the 'null parse' (represented by $\odot$), is unpronounceable. If, in a given language, it is more important to avoid violations of *PHONO than it is to enforce morphological parsing of ϕ, then f_B will be bested by the null parse. Since f_A does not violate *PHONO, f_A will be more harmonic than $\odot$. If f_A and f_B fare equally on *PHONO, however, other things being equal we predict free variation. We return to this issue in 4.3.

In the morpholexical theory of allomorphy, allomorphs $\{A, B, \ldots\}$ also do not compete directly, as in MPARSE Theory. Where f_A is accepted, f_B is rejected as absolutely ungrammatical, and *vice versa* (because of complementary combinatorial requirements). A key prediction of this approach is that we should find cases in which an allomorph is banned from an environment for reasons that are phonologically arbitrary, i.e. nothing to do with markedness or complexity. In particular, we should find cases in which the distribution of allomorphs either cannot be predicted on phonological grounds or is *counter* to what one would predict on phonological grounds. This prediction contrasts with those made by the two current theories of allomorph distribution as optimization.

4.2. Phonologically 'optimal' allomorphy

To clarify the optimization-based view a bit more, let us examine a putative case of phonologically natural allomorph distribution. In Djabugay[5], a Pama-Nyungan language in Queensland, Australia, the genitive has the allomorphs -*n* after vowel-final stems, and -*ŋun* after consonant-final stems (Patz 1991; Kager 1996; Rubach & Booij 2001). This is shown in (9).

(9) *Djabugay genitive*
    a. *Vowel-final*
        guludu-n   *guludu-ŋun   'dove'
    b. *Consonant-final*
        gaɲal-ŋun   *gaɲal-n   'goanna'

An account of this data must capture two facts: (i) -*n* does not occur after consonant-final stems, (ii) -*ŋun* does not occur after vowel-final stems. It is a fact about Djabugay phonotactics that complex codas never occur, diagnosing top-ranked *COMPLEX CODA in (10). The fact that -*n* does not attach to consonant-final stems appears to be no accident.

(10) *COMPLEX CODA (*CXCODA)
      Complex codas are disallowed.

The tableau in (11) shows how the Markedness-driven approach deals with the selection of the -*n* allomorph following a consonant-final stem. Since Djabugay allows codas, MAX must outrank NOCODA.

The fact that -*ŋun* does not attach to vowel-final stems, however, cannot be explained in the same way. Since Djabugay permits codas, non-occurring

(11) *gaɲalŋun≻gaɲaln on syllabic well-formedness*

/gaɲal+ { ŋun / n } /	*CxCoda	Max	NoCoda
a. ☞ gaɲalŋun			**
b. gaɲaln	*!		*

guluduŋun is phonotactically fine, and so both candidates (a) and (b) in (12) fare equally well. For (b), this is an undesirable result, as indicated by the 'frownie' ☹.

(12) *guluduŋun≈guludun* (harmonic ordering indeterminate)

/guludu+ { ŋun / n } /	*CxCoda	Max	NoCoda
a. ☞ guluduŋun			*
b. ☞,☹ guludun			*

It is at this point we have to field the notion of relative complexity. Since -*ŋun* has more structure than its competitor -*n*, -*ŋun* will violate more markedness constraints, and its less complex rival -*n* will win. This is shown in (13).

(13) *Eliminating a phonotactically legitimate allomorph*

/guludu+ { ŋun / n } /	*CxCoda	Max	NoCoda	*ŋ	*n
a. guluduŋun			*	*!	*
b. ☞ guludun			*		*

In (13), the two allomorphs are comparable in the sense that the set of markedness violations pertaining to the one allomorph is a subset of the set of markedness violations of the other. In fact, candidate (a) is harmonically bounded by candidate (b).

In other cases the allomorphs are not strictly comparable in this way. For example, in Udihe (Nikolaeva & Tolskaya 2001), a Southern Tungus language of the Siberian Far East, the perfective is marked in one of two ways. Stems ending in a high vowel take the suffix -*ge*, e.g. *dogdi-ge-*, 'hear (perf.)'; *bu-ge-*, 'give'. Elsewhere the perfective is marked by laryngealization of the stem final vowel, e.g. *etetḛ-*, 'work'; *zawa̰-*, 'take, grab'; *olokto̰-*, 'cook'. The distribution of morphological laryngealization and -*ge* appears partially motivated by the fact that Udihe lacks laryngealized high vowels (undominated *[+high, +constricted glottis]), ruling out forms such as *dogdḭ-. Wherever it is possible to mark the perfective through laryngealization of the final vowel, suffixation of -ge is *not* possible, even though it's phonotactically unimpeachable, e.g. *etete-ge-, *tukæ:-ge-. The distribution of the allomorphs apparently requires us to rank some markedness constraint (*g, *e, or *σ) above the constraint that bans laryngealized vowels, *V_{Lar}. This is suspicious for two reasons, though. First, it seems completely arbitrary which of the markedness constraints should play the role of blocker in this case. Second, because *V_{Lar} is not obviously in conflict with any of the candidate blocker constraints, none of the rankings we might choose (*g≫*V_{Lar}, or *e≫*V_{Lar}, or *σ≫*V_{Lar}) would do any other phonotactic work: the distribution of the perfective allomorphs is the only evidence for the ranking. This kind of consideration tends to erode the appeal of Markedness-driven approach.

4.3. Non-optimal allomorphy

The Markedness-driven approach only works (at all) when the undesired allomorph is inferior to the desired allomorph in either of two ways: either it gives rise to a form with worse phonotactics or prosody than the desired allomorph, or it is more complex than the desired allomorph. Nonetheless, there is a residue of cases where the undesired allomorph actually has the edge over its competitor in terms of complexity or markedness, or both.

One frequently cited problematic case comes from Dyirbal (Dixon 1972), a Pama-Nyungan language spoken in Queensland, Australia. The pattern we are interested in here involves sensitivity to the location of the main stress foot, so before we address the details, a brief note on stress assignment is in order. As (14) shows, stress is essentially trochaic.

(14) *Stress assignment in Dyirbal* (Dixon 1972: 274–5)
 (ɲí.nay) 'sit'
 (wáyɲ.d̪i).ŋu 'motion uphill REL'

The allomorphy concerns the ergative marker, which has two variants, -*gu* and -*ŋgu*. The -*ŋgu* allomorph may only attach to the head foot, which in Dyirbal is the first foot of the word; -*gu* attaches elsewhere. Representative examples are shown in (15) (Dixon 1972; cf. McCarthy & Prince 2001).

(15) *Dyirbal ergative allomorphy*
    a. *Head-foot*
        (ya.ɾa-ŋ).gu   'man'
    b. *Outside head-foot*
        (ya.ma).(ni.-gu)   'rainbow'
        (ba.la).(ga.ra).-gu   'they'

McCarthy & Prince (2001) attempt to capture the distribution of *-ŋgu* by proposing the morpheme-specific Alignment constraint in (16).

(16) AFX-TO-FT
The base to which /-ŋgu/ is affixed is the head foot.

Obviously, the content of (16) is language-specific, but let us set this aside and consider how each of the optimization-based approaches fare in capturing the distribution of each allomorph. The Markedness-driven approach is especially ill-equipped for dealing with this case. The least complex allomorph *-gu* is destined to win in both the specific environment (after the head foot) and elsewhere, since *-ŋgu* is both longer and entails a violation of NOCODA. The right result can therefore only be obtained for stems that exceed two syllables, as in (17a). For bisyllabic stems, the wrong result is predicted (17b).

(17) *Markedness-driven approach: elsewhere allomorph wins in either case*

a.

/yamani+ { ŋgu / gu }/	AFX-TO-FT	NOCODA	*ŋ
a. (ya.ma).(ni.|ŋgu)	*!	*	*
b. ☞ (ya.ma).(ni.|gu)			

b.

/yaɾa+ { ŋgu / gu }/	AFX-TO-FT	NOCODA	*ŋ
a. ☺ (ya.ɾa|ŋ).gu		¡*!	*
b. ☞ (ya.ɾa)|.gu			

MPARSE Theory fares only slightly better, but descriptive success comes at a cost. As McCarthy & Wolf (2005: 28) themselves admit, 'A key property of this analysis is the need for a stipulated priority relationship among allomorphs'. According to their implementation, this means that *-ŋgu* must be 'tried' before *-gu*, so that if *-ŋgu* is successful, *-gu* isn't even attempted. This plainly goes against the Richness of the Base, which says that "there are no language-particular restrictions on the input, no linguistically significant generalizations about the lexicon, no principled lexical gaps, no lexical redundancy rules, morpheme structure constraints, or similar devices" (McCarthy 2002: 70). Granting the stipulated ordering, let us see what it is possible to achieve using the MPARSE approach. AFX-TO-FT must outrank MPARSE$_{erg}$. In (18), -ŋgu is attempted first and returns the null parse (18a). On attempting -gu in (18b), AFX-TO-FT is silent, and the job of deciding between the candidates falls to MPARSE$_{erg}$, which favours the pronounced candidate (a).

(18) a.

/yamani+ŋgu/		AFX-TO-FT	MPARSE$_{erg}$
a.	(ya.ma).(niŋ.gu)	*!	
b. ☞	⊙		*

b.

/yamani+gu/		AFX-TO-FT	MPARSE$_{erg}$
a. ☞	(ya.ma).(ni.gu)		
b.	⊙		*!

For stems exceeding two syllables, it does not matter whether the stipulated priority relationship between the allomorphs is in force or not. For bisyllabic stems, however, the stipulation is crucial. The effect of lifting it is to allow both allomorphs to survive in the output (19).

(19) a.

/yaɽa+ŋgu/		AFX-TO-FT	MPARSE$_{erg}$
a. ☞	(ya.ɽaŋ).gu		
b.	⊙		*!

b.

/yaɽa+gu/		AFX-TO-FT	MPARSE$_{erg}$
a. ☞,☹	(ya.ɽa).gu		
b.	⊙		*!

In sum, the facts of the distribution of the ergative allomorphs -ŋgu and -gu in Dyirbal cannot be stated relying on output constraints and their interaction alone. There is a vital language-specific contribution, and this needs to be forced out into the open. The distribution is specified in the morpholexical constraints in (20).

Since the phonological condition in (20a) is a superset of that in (20b), (20a) takes intrinsic precedence over (20b) as dictated by the Elsewhere Principle. Tableaux (21) to (24) provide full analysis for each possible combination of affix and environment.

(20) a. $\begin{bmatrix} \text{SYNTAX} & \begin{bmatrix} \text{CATEGORY} & \text{N} \\ \text{INFLECTION} & \text{ergative} \end{bmatrix} \\ \text{PHONOLOGY} & \text{Ft}']_{\text{stem}} \\ \text{SELECT} & \text{ŋgu} \\ \text{ANCHOR} &]_{\text{stem}\text{—}} \end{bmatrix}$

b. $\begin{bmatrix} \text{SYNTAX} & \begin{bmatrix} \text{CATEGORY} & \text{N} \\ \text{INFLECTION} & \text{ergative} \end{bmatrix} \\ \text{PHONOLOGY} &]_{\text{stem}} \\ \text{SELECT} & \text{gu} \\ \text{ANCHOR} &]_{\text{stem}\text{—}} \end{bmatrix}$

(21)

		/yamani+ŋgu/	MAX	NOCODA
H-EVAL	a. ☞	(yama)niŋgu		*
	b.	(yama)nigu	*!	
MCONTROL			SUBCAT: *-ŋgu*	
	✂	(yama)niŋgu	⊥	

(22)

		/yamani+gu/	MAX	NOCODA
H-EVAL	a.	(yama)niŋgu		*!
	b. ☞	(yama)nigu		
MCONTROL			SUBCAT: *-gu*	
		(yama)nigu	✓	

(23)

		/yaɻa+ŋgu/	MAX	NOCODA
H-EVAL	a.	(yaɻaŋ)gu		*
	b. ☞	(yaɻa)gu	*!	
MCONTROL			SUBCAT: *-ŋgu*	
		(yaɻaŋ)gu	✓	

(24)

		/yaɻa+gu/	MAX	NOCODA
H-EVAL	a.	(yaɻaŋ)gu		*!
	b. ☞	(yaɻa)gu		
MCONTROL			SUBCAT: *-gu*	
	✂	(yaɻa)gu	*blocked by EP*	

Let us look at some additional cases illustrating the point that suppletive allomorph distribution may be arbitrary from the point of view of markedness. From here on, complete analyses will not be provided.

Ndyuka, an English-lexified creole spoken in Suriname (Huttar 1996) has a transitive marker that varies between -*mi* and ∅. There are two restrictions on the occurrence of -*mi*: (i) it must be followed by a monosyllable, (ii) it must be preceded immediately by a nucleus bearing a high tone, (iii) if the high-tone nucleus is the only mora, it cannot be a high vowel. Examples illustrating (i) are: *a fómi en*, 'he hit him' vs. *a fón ála*, 'he hit everyone'; *a fón sama*, 'he hit someone'. Examples illustrating (ii) are: *a boó-mi en*, 'he blew it' vs. *a bóo en*, 'he bored it' (*a *bóo-mi en*); *a fií-mi en*, 'he freed it' vs. *a fíi en*. Examples of condition (iii): *a hó-mi en*, 'he hoed it' vs. *a dú en*, 'he did (troubled) him' (*a *dú-mi en*), *a sá-mi en*, 'he sawed it' vs. *a sí en*, 'he saw it' (*a *sí-mi en*).

In Korean (Martin & Lee 1969; Lapointe 1999), the conjunctive 'and' varies in shape between -*wa* and -*kwa*. The -*wa* variant attaches to stems ending in a vowel while -*kwa* attaches to stems that end in a consonant, e.g. *nay c^{h}iŋkwu-wa*, 'and my friend'; *coŋi-wa*, 'and paper'; *ay-wa*, 'and child'; *c^{h}ayk-kwa*, 'and a book'; *sensayŋ-kwa*, 'and the teacher'; *pap-kwa*, 'and rice'. As in the Dyirbal case, the Markedness-driven approach would lead us to expect -*wa* across the board. It is particularly unexpected to find -*kwa* selecting for consonant-final stems, since this results in a violation of *COMPLEX ONSET, which choosing -*wa* would avoid.

In Standard Italian (Lepschy & Lepschy 1988), the form of the definite article in the masculine plural varies in shape between *ʎi* and *i*. The variation in shape does not stand in any phonologically natural relationship to the environment. The *ʎi* allomorph is used when the following word begins with a cluster or geminate, e.g. *ʎi spuntini*, 'the snacks'; *ʎi studi*, 'the studies'; *ʎi ttsii*, 'the uncles'; *ʎi ɲɲɔkki*, 'the gnocchi', or if the following word begins with a vowel, e.g. *ʎi albergi*, 'the hotels'; *ʎi ambienti*, 'the surroundings'; *ʎi iŋgleːzi*, 'the English'. These two environments cannot be unified into any natural class. The *i* allomorph is used elsewhere, e.g. *i padri*, 'the fathers'; *i ragattsi*, 'the boys'; *i vini*, 'the wines'. Although *ʎi* has the virtue of having an onset, there is no sense in which *ʎi* represents a harmonic improvement over *i* in those environments in which it appears.

Burushaski, a language isolate of Northern Pakistan (Berger 1974) evinces extraordinarily rich allomorphy in plural formation. In animates, vowel-final stems take -*mu* and consonant-final stems take -*išu* by default. This much appears phonologically sensible. However, stems ending in certain consonants idiosyncratically select other suffixes. For example, Stems ending in -*n* take -*yu* rather than -*išu*, but there are no obvious markedness-based considerations that would motivate this.

Many languages evince allomorphy that is conditioned by syllable or mora count. This kind of allomorphy has been the object of a recent survey by Paster (2005), who also argues that allomorph distribution is best handled as an instance of subcategorization. Let us consider a few examples.

In Turkana (Nilo-Saharan, Kenya), concrete nouns form their plurals by prefixation of *ŋa-/ŋI-* (where I is a high front vowel whose [ATR] value varies depending on the [ATR] specification of the root) and adding a suffix, whose shape is arbitrarily dependent on the prosody of the root (Dimmendaal 1983: 226, 2000: 44, 235). If the stem is consonant-final and contains two nuclear moras, the suffix is -*a*, e.g. *ŋa-kiɲàŋ-a*, 'crocodile' (sg. *a-kɪɲaŋ*); *ŋa-ŋàsɛ̀p-a*, 'placenta' (sg. *a-ŋasɛp`*); *ŋɪ-kààl-a*, 'camel' (sg. *ɛ-kàal*). If the stem is consonant-final and contains a single nuclear mora, the suffix is -*In*, e.g. *ŋa-kwap-ɪn`*, 'land' (sg. *a-kwap`*); *ŋi-rot-in`*, 'road' (sg. *e-rot`*). *ŋa-muɲ-ɪn*, 'snake' (sg. *a-muɲ*). If the stem is vowel-final and contains two nuclear moras, the suffix is -*I*, e.g. *ŋi-wɔrʊ-ɪ`*, 'cloth' (sg. *e-wɔ̀rʊ̀*); *ŋi-suro-i`*, 'dik-dik' (sg. *e-suro`*); *ŋa-pɔɔ-ɪ`*, 'hare' (sg. *a-pɔ̀ɔ*). We do indeed see that vowel-final and consonant-final stems take different allomorphs, but where we might expect a vowel-final stem to select a consonant-initial allomorph, we simply find variation in vowel quality instead.

In Axininca Campa (Arawakan, Peru; Payne 1981), an alienable noun must bear a 'genitive' marker -*ni* or -*ti* whenever prefixed by a personal possessive marker. The choice of allomorph depends on the bimoraicity or otherwise of the stem. The suffix -*ni* attaches to a stem with two nuclear moras; -*ti* attaches elsewhere. Examples (from Payne 1981: 50, 77–78, 244–9) are: *no-yor^{y}a-ni*, 'my manioc worm' (non-possessed *kor^{y}a*); *i-çaa-ni*, 'his anteater' (np. *çaa*); *a-sari-ni*, 'our macaw' (np. *sari*); *i-wisiro-ti*, 'his small toucan' (np. *pisiro*); *no-yairo-ti* 'my termite' (np. *kairo*); *a-yaarato-ti*, 'our black bee' (np. *yaarato*). Again, the variation here is phonologically neutral, and doesn't seem to correlate with any known dimension of markedness.

In Kimatuumbi (Bantu, Tanzania; Odden 1996: 51–3), the perfective is marked with the suffix -*i̧te* on polysyllabic stems whose final syllable contains a long vowel and monosyllabic verb stems, but an -*i̧*- infix elsewhere, e.g. *ni̧-chól-i̧te*, 'I have drawn' (infinitive *chóla*); *ni̧-ti̧n-i̧te*, 'I have chopped' (inf. *ti̧na*); *ni̧-káat-i̧te*, 'I have cut' (inf. *káata*); *ni̧-bálaang-i̧te*, 'I have counted' (inf. *bálaanga*); *nį-chéleew-įte*, 'I have been late' (inf. *chéleewa*); *nį-áandįįke*, 'I have written' (inf. *áandįka*); *ni-bélįįke*, 'I have borne' (inf. *béleka*); *ni-chíilįįye*, 'I have been late' (inf. *chíiliya*). In addition, infixation is accompanied by mutation of the indicative marker *-a* to *-e*. There doesn't appear to be any property that would allow us to group the monosyllables and the polysyllables with long final nucleus together as a natural class. Two separate phonological structures are idiosyncratically simply selecting the same marker, as in the case of Standard Italian. The elsewhere allomorph *-į-*, although briefer than the specific allomorph, would seem to imply a worsening of phonological structure, since infixation entails a violation of CONTIGUITY.

Paster (2005) cites additional cases from Kaititj, Zuni and Nakanai in which choice of allomorph is determined by stem size, although not in any natural way. We will briefly review the Kaititj and Nakanai cases here. In Kaititj (Pama-Nyungan, Northern Territory, Australia; Koch 1980), the ergative-instrumental-locative is marked by *-ŋ* on disyllabic stems, but *-l~-ḷ* in larger stems, e.g. *aki-ŋ*, 'head'; *a^{d}nmi-ŋ*, 'red ochre'; *ilt^{y}i-ŋ*, 'hand'; *aṭuyi-l*, 'man'; *ayirki-l*, 'sun'; *ḷu^{d}npiriḷ*, 'forehead'.

Nakanai (Austronesian, New Britain; Johnson 1980) is a nice example of allomorphy in both shape and attachment site. Nominalization is done by prefixing *-il-* to the penultimate nucleus of the word, which bears the stress, e.g. *il-áu*, 'steering' (verb *áu*); *p-il-ého*, 'death' (v. *pého*, 'die'); *t-il-ága*, 'fear' (v. *tága*). The *-il-* affix is subject to the requirement that it be contained within the word-initial syllable, and so it may only affix to bimoraic stems. Elsewhere, the nominalizer is the suffix *-la*, e.g. *vigilemulí-la*, 'story' (v. *vigilemúli*, 'tell a story'); *vikuéla*, 'fight (n.)' (v. *vikúe*); *goilóla*, 'entrance' (v. *goílo*, 'go in'). See McCarthy (2003: 101-2) for an attempted analysis in terms of ranked constraints and Paster (2005) for critique.

A similar, although less impressive example comes from Kentakbong (Austro-Asiatic, Malaysia; Omar 1975: 292f.; Yu 2004: 215ff.). In this language, the imperfect is marked by prefixing *ʔən-* to a monosyllabic stem, but *infixing* *-ən-* in a disyllabic stem, e.g. *ʔən-co*, 'is speaking' (< *co*); *ʔən-cãs*, 'is excreting' (< *cãs*); *s-ən-apoh*, 'is sweeping' (< *sapoh*); *t-ən-anɛm*, 'is planting' (< *tanɛm*); *k-ən-ayiʔ*, 'is making' (< *kayiʔ*).

In most of the examples cited in this section, the choice of suppletive allomorph would seem to be phonologically neutral. In the Axininca Campa case, the choice of *-ti* or *-ni* is neither optimal nor pessimal. The choice cannot be made by appeal to phonotactic or prosodic well-formedness, or even brevity. In some cases, the choice of a particular allomorph *does* result in more marked phonological structure compared with the structure that would result if the other allomorph were chosen. An example is Korean, where -*kwa* specifically attaches to consonant-final stems and -*wa* elsewhere. The present theory would lead us to expect cases in which the distribution of *both* allomorphs is the opposite of what one would expect on phonological grounds. One possible case comes from the French-lexified Antillean creole spoken in Haiti (Klein 2003). In Haitian the postposed determiner is -*a* following a stem ending in a [−ATR] vowel, but -*la* following a stem ending in consonant. Examples are *papa-a* 'the father'; *vɛ-a* 'the glass'; *bɔkɔ-a* 'the sorcerer', vs. *malad-la* 'the sick (person)'; *ʃat-la* 'the cat'; *liv-la* 'the book'. If this pattern genuinely represents suppletive allomorphy then, under the assumptions of the markedness-driven approach, both -*a* and -*la* would have to be disjunctively present in the input. In either case, the desired winner would be harmonically bounded: *papa-a* by *papa-la on ONSET, and *ʃat-la* by *ʃat-a on NOCODA. Even worse, potentially, is the fact that stems ending in a [+ATR] vowel suffix -*a* but avoid hiatus through glide insertion, e.g. *papjeja* 'the paper'; *batowa*, 'the boat'; *laplija* 'rain'; *tuwa* 'the hole'. Glide insertion is blocked when the stem ends in a [−ATR] vowel, as in *papa*, *vɛ*, or *bɔkɔ*, apparently to avoid a sequence of a [−ATR] vowel followed by a [+ATR] glide. The glide insertion facts are incompatible with the notion that both allomorphs are disjunctively present in the input. If this were so, hiatus could be evaded simply by selecting -*la* at no cost to faithfulness. Instead, what we find is glide insertion, which violates DEP-C.[6]

5. Alternative conceptions

The question still remains why the overall architecture of the grammar should be as in (1). There are three logical points at which morpholexical constraints might be evaluated relative to properly phonological constraints: before, after, or simultaneously. I shall argue below that morpholexical constraints cannot be assessed *before* H-EVAL. However, it turns out not to matter whether morpholexical constraints are evaluated at the same time as or after the properly phonological constraints. What is important is that morpholexical constraints are declarative and phonological constraints are violable.

5.1. Prosodic anchoring

One consideration that speaks against assessing morpholexical constraint satisfaction *before* H-EVAL is that there are cases where the affix is prosodically rather than morphologically anchored. Since the richness of the base entails that prosodic structure may be absent in the input, morpholexical constraint evaluation would have nothing to go on until prosodic structure is fleshed out. A case in point is Ulwa (Hale & Lacayo Blanco 1989; McCarthy & Prince 2001). Ulwa has a set of possessive infixes that attach following the head foot of the noun stem. Ulwa is left-to-right iambic, so infixation of possessive *-ka-* gives forms like *(ki:)-ka* 'his stone', *(su:)-ka-lu* 'his stone', *(ana:)-(ka-la:)ka* 'his chin'.

5.2. Opacity

The possibility of opacity is a countervailing consideration that might favour evaluating morpholexical constraints *before* H-EVAL. Opacity may effect both selection and anchoring, and we will review each type in turn.

5.2.1. *Opaque anchoring*

In this paper, anchoring is seen as a morpholexical attribute. In most of the OT literature, anchoring is conceived as a relation between domain edges (the left/right edge of the affix and the right/left edge of the stem), a conception I will call 'hard anchoring'. Given that the constraints that assess this relation are inviolable on this approach (abstracting away from the Elsewhere Principle), there is no way of modelling phonologically motivated misalignment as long as we remain faithful to this conception of anchoring. The OT literature is nonetheless replete with examples of affix displacement. As a result, it has become routine to describe the patterns using affix-specific alignment constraints which, despite being language-specific, figure in the analyses as violable. Parochial alignment constraints compromise OT's explanatory goals, and it would surely be good for the theory if the language-specific contribution was distilled out and dealt with separately. Obviously, dealing with anchoring morpholexically has to be achieved without loss of empirical coverage if it is to be worthwhile pursuing, but it is impossible to reconcile hard anchoring with the facts.

In one of OT's most famous test cases, McCarthy & Prince (2001: 11–14) deal with infixation in Tagalog as a case of 'displaced' prefixation motivated by highly ranked syllable structure constraints. As Yu (2004) shows, however, a surprising number of languages have affixes that are *inherently* infixing. He furnishes examples in which infixation results in forms that are either no better, or worse compared with the hypothetical prefixed or suffixed forms, offering a striking parallel to the claims set forth here with regard to allomorphy. In Leti (Blevins 1999), for example, the nominalizer -*ni*- is invariably infixing, even at the cost of introducing complex onsets, e.g. /ni+kaati/→*k-ni-aati*, 'carving'; /ni+polu/→*p-ni-olu*, 'calling'. Similarly, in the Pingding dialect of Mandarin Chinese, the diminutive infix -*l*- directly precedes the rhyme of the syllable, leading to the creation of onset clusters that are otherwise unattested in the language. These findings invite a non-phonological interpretation of the facts of Tagalog. In his survey of 101 languages, Yu found that the subcategorization requirements of infixes were never violated, which leads him to stipulate that affix-specific alignment constraints constitute an undominated block in H-EVAL. This, however, is tantamount to conceding that affix placement is governed by declarative constraints.

Unfortunately, this still doesn't quite square with the fact that the anchoring of affixes may be opacified by phonological processes such as epenthesis or metathesis. The Haitian case discussed earlier provided an illustration of the former, e.g. [stem bato] w [afx a] 'the boat'. In this example, glide insertion drives a wedge between the stem and the affix, making anchoring of the left edge of the suffix with the right edge of the stem non-surface-true. An example of metathesis is furnished by Kui, a South-Central Dravidian language with speakers in Orissa, Madhya Pradesh, Andhra Pradesh and Tamil Nadu (Winfield 1928). In this language, the infinitive and present participle of verbs in the second conjugation are marked by -*pa* and -*pi* respectively, e.g. *ih-pa* 'stab', *ih-pi* 'stabbing'; *mus-pa* 'immerse', *mus-pi* 'immersing'. With stems ending in a velar stop, the initial *p* of the suffix and the final *k* of the verb stem metathesize resulting in imbrication of stem and affix, e.g. /mraak+pa/→*mraapka* 'to obliterate' (pres.part. *mraapki*; cf. future *mraak-i*); /slik+pi/→*slipki* 'plucking' (inf. *slipka*; cf. fut. *slik-i*).

A partial strategy for dealing with phenomena of this kind is what we might call 'soft anchoring'. Soft anchoring defines the edge-orientation of an affix in terms of linear precedence relations between the phonological material of the affix and the host. A suffix, on this conception, is an affix for which it is the case that at least some substring follows the last string element of the host. A definition along these lines would still leave purely phonological processes like epenthesis and metathesis free to operate at morpheme boundaries. One of the anonymous reviewers nevertheless points out that opacity involving the anchoring of a *prosodic* affix (as in Ulwa) could not be expedited in the same way. To see this, consider a hypothetical language with a suffix -*aa*- that attaches to a disyllabic head foot. Suppose this feeds epenthesis so that /pataka+aa/ is realized as *(pá.ta).t̯-aa-.ka*. Even if we invoke soft anchoring, the categorical nature of morpholexical constraints would leave us no way of distinguishing the desired form *pa.ta.t̯-aa-.ka* from **pa.ta.k-aa-.ta* or **pa.ta.ka.t̯-aa*. All three forms will be ruled absolutely ungrammatical by the morpholexical constraint requiring anchoring of -*aa* after the head foot. Before considering a possible solution, let us address the problem of opaque allomorph selection. Both problems yield to very similar solutions.

5.2.2. Opaque selection

In Burushaski (Berger 1974) animate nouns ending in -*n* take the suffix -*yu*. The sequence *ny*, however, is disallowed by the rules of Burushaski phonotactics and the stem-final nasal does not surface, e.g. /dušmán+yu/ → *dušmáyu* 'enemy (pl)'. In the pronounced form, the suffix directly follows a vowel, but vowel-final animate stems condition a different allomorph of the plural, -*mu*, e.g. *dus̯tá-mu* 'seedling (pl)'. In Correspondence Theory (McCarthy & Prince 1999), which countenances literal deletion of information present in the input, information relevant to allomorph selection may be unrecoverably lost in the output. Taken together with Correspondence, evaluating morpholexical constraints after H-EVAL rules out the possibility that subcategorization requirements be satisfied opaquely, to the detriment of empirical coverage. Classical OT, on the other hand, assumes the Containment Principle, according to which no information may be removed in the output form (Prince & Smolensky 2004: 5; McCarthy & Prince 2001: 21). Today there is a renewed interest in Containment-based approaches to OT, especially in connection with opacity. In Oostendorp's (2007) Coloured Containment model, phonological representations make explicit reference to the morphological affiliation ('colour') of phonological material. Integrating the theory of morpholexical constraints with a model along these lines would eliminate the contradictory pressure to place morpholexical constraint evaluation before H-EVAL, which, as we have seen, is incompatible with the existence of transparent prosodic affixation. Given Containment, the stem-final -*n* in our Burushaski case would be covertly present in the output, and thus in principle available for the purposes of selecting the correct allomorph. For our hypothetical case involving opaque anchoring of a prosodic affix, it will be possible to exploit Oostendorp's notion of morphological colour. Suppose that the stem /pataka/ is assigned the 'colour' α, the affix /aa/ the colour β, and the epenthetic /t/ the colour γ. We can parse then each of our three forms into 'colour domains' as follows: $\{(pa.ta)\}_\alpha.\{t\}_\gamma\{aa\}_\beta.\{ka\}_\alpha$ (the desired output), $*\{(pa.ta).k\}_\alpha\{aa\}_\beta.\{t\}_\gamma\{a\}_\alpha$, and $*\{(pa.ta).ka\}_\alpha.\{t\}_\gamma\{aa\}_\beta$. Assuming colour is explicitly represented, it should be possible in principle to define the placement of -*aa* so as to discount epenthetic material, e.g. by requiring that no α-coloured material intervene between the head foot and the affix.

6. Conclusions

Several cases of phonologically conditioned suppletive allomorphy turn out to be impossible to square with the standard assumption that allomorph distribution falls out from markedness considerations. In the kind of cases we've considered, appeal to markedness either fails to distinguish between the available allomorphs, or it makes the wrong choice in one or both environments. MPARSE Theory fails to account completely for the distribution without stipulating priority of allomorphs in the input, which goes against the Richness of the Base. Ultimately it seems there is no way around sacrificing the Richness of the Base in order to account for functionally arbitrary allomorph distribution. This is acknowledged explicitly here and implemented through language-specific declarative constraints in the morpholexicon. Modeling allomorph selection declaratively allows us to forge a link between allomorph selection and gaps: both entail absolute ungrammaticality. This notion is notoriously difficult to square with any notion of optimization (although see McCarthy & Wolf 2005 for an attempt), but is a trivial matter for declarative approaches. In cases of allomorphy, the one allomorph is absolutely ungrammatical in contexts where the other is grammatical, and *vice versa*. A growing number of researchers are warming to the idea that there may be a declarative component to phonology. Paster (2005), as we have seen, invokes subcategorization to deal with syllable-counting allomorphy and Bermúdez-Otero (forthcoming) appeals to categorical constraints to capture defectiveness in morphological paradigms in Spanish.

There is nevertheless a large number of cases where the choice of allomorph seems to coincide with the predictions of markedness. It might be possible to retain an optimization-based approach to these cases, but it is obviously more economical to unify allomorph selection under a single mechanism. Since some cases are arbitrary, we would have the option of saying that allomorph selection is arbitrary in principle, even where it happens to coincide with naturalness considerations (cf. Blevins 2004).

The strongest potential objection to the current proposal is that it implies a hybrid vision of grammar. Conceding a need to complement OT with declarative constraints might be criticized as being 'tantamount to giving up on the entire enterprise' of Optimality Theory (cf. Halle & Idsardi 1997 on approaches combining OT and rules). In debate it is often assumed that phonological constraints/rules are *either* universal and functionally grounded *or* language-specific and essentially functionally arbitrary. There is a widespread sentiment among practitioners and opponents of OT alike, that the theory is really only worth pursuing if it succeeds in reducing all phonological patterns to the interaction of universal violable constraints. Neo-structuralists (e.g. Hale & Reiss 2000) and evolutionary phonologists (Blevins 2004) are united in claiming that constraints/rules are essentially arbitrary, arguing that the incorporation of substantive considerations of naturalness into the grammar, e.g. by restricting CON to the set of functionally grounded constraints, serves only to duplicate the patterns that emerge independently as a result of diachronic processes. On the other hand, recent work by Hayes (1999), Boersma (1998), and others suggests that "Children are not arbitrary inductive sponges" (to use Hayes' own words from his talk at the 13th Manchester Phonology Meeting, 28th May 2005). Wilson (2003) provides experimental evidence that suggests human beings are unable to acquire unnatural phonological patterns (or find them very difficult to learn), and work by Fleischhacker (2002) and Zuraw (2005) suggests that speakers have access to constraints which could not possibly be the result of induction over the lexicon, but must reflect phonetic knowledge.

The polarization of this debate betrays an unspoken and ungrounded assumption that the kind of things phonologists spend their professional lives worrying about ('phonological phenomena') neatly corresponds to a unique principled cognitive domain, or module of language, with a theory of its own. In reality, there is as much reason for assuming this as there is for assuming that 'things with stripes' or 'things you might find in someone's garage' constitute principled domains. Made fully explicit, though, the assumption that those phenomena we *call* phonological are a natural class is a useful heuristic, which leads us to try and apply our theories as widely as possible. Sustained empirical engagement and sensitivity to the differential success or failure of these attempts will help us discern how many principled cognitive domains we are actually dealing with and what their natures are. For this reason, the appeal of a hybrid model such as this one cannot be settled by appeal to Occam's Razor. At this stage in our knowledge it seems most reasonable to suppose that a particular language is an alloy of both universal phonetically natural constraints and arbitrary parochial (morpholexical) constraints.

By way of conclusion, I'll mention two ways in which I envision this line of research may be extended. First, by countenancing the possibility of non-concatenative allomorphy, many unnatural alternations ('crazy rules'; Bach & Harms 1972) may turn out to be cases of featural affixation. The theory of morpholexical constraints may thus be expected to provide an alternative theory of morphophonogical processes. Second, it has been recognized since J. R. Firth (see Ogden 1993) that there are subgrammatical regularities in language and that different classes may pattern differently phonologically, as is the case with stress assignment in English nouns and verbs. On further development, morpholexical constraints provide us with a way of characterizing this kind of **polysystematicity**. It is hoped that future work will provide more robust evidence of a distinctly morpholexical contribution to phonological patterning. Once we have a clearer picture of the two domains, the next step will be to set out to discover the mechanisms that underlie the emergence of the computational principles governing each domain.

Notes

* In addition to the Workshop on the Freedom of Analysis, this work has benefited from being presented to audiences at the University of Chicago and Northwestern University. For helpful discussion I'd like to thank Sylvia Blaho, Suzanne van der Feest, Paula Fikkert, Matt Goldrick, Chris Golston, Dafna Graf, Daniel Currie Hall, Chris Kennedy, Martin Krämer, Paul de Lacy, Ove Lorentz, Jason Merchant, Bruce Morén, Salikoko Mufwene, Marc van Oostendorp, Janet Pierrehumbert, Anthi Revithiadou, Curt Rice, Jason Riggle, Jen Smith, Dragana Šurkalović, Christian Uffman, Ilya Yakubovich, Alan Yu, as well as two anonymous reviewers.
1. The *locus classicus* for phonologically conditioned suppletion is Carstairs (1988). In this paper I restrict my attention to suppletive allomorphs of affixes and ignore stem alternations, which I will address in future research.
2. What counts as suppletion may sometimes be difficult to determine. Since there is nothing to prevent allomorphs with distinct underlying forms from displaying a more or less close family resemblance, we must be open to the possibility that suppletion may hold

between similar allomorphs as well. Whether variation is best ascribed to the interaction of grounded constraints or the lexicon is often only something that may be determined after prolonged study of a particular language. As the Austronesian scholar Ken Rehg (2001:218) also comments, "one of the imperatives of generative phonology – that allomorphy must be minimised – is sometimes at odds with the data, typically in very subtle ways".

3. The term **lemma** refers to the non-phonological part of a lexical item (Levelt 1989).
4. Alternatively, if we want to invoke the 'nihilistic' markedness constraint against all structure, *STRUC, f_A will incur a greater number of violations on *STRUC than f_B.
5. *Ethnologue* (http://www.ethnologue.com/) gives the name of this language as 'Dyaabugay'.
6. Martin Krämer (p.c.) suggests that the Haitian facts may reflect fully phonological intervocalic deletion of *l*. Reported cases of intervocalic *l*-deletion do not seem to be thick on the ground, however. Welmers (1976) describes Vai (Niger-Congo; Liberia) as having *optional* deletion of *l* between vowels in what seems to be a language change in progress. Acoustically, *l* can be difficult to distinguish from the surrounding vowels and this will especially be the case where *l* tends to a more resonant pronunciation (as when both sides of the tongue are significantly lowered). The effect of the change is that, at the second stage, /l/ can only appear in word-initial position. The question is what kind of constraint this distributional fact might reflect. The choices for post-deletion Vai would seem to be a licensing constraint requiring all instances of *l* to coincide with the left edge of a word, or a constraint penalizing intervocalic laterals. Since *l* never appears between vowels at the second stage, we might assume that a learner exposed only to Stage 2 forms posits the licensing constraint. In Haitian Creole *l* occurs word medially after both consonants (*lapli*) and vowels (*malad*), at least in morphologically underived environments. A *VlV constraint would have to be better substantiated typologically as well as by appeal to the phonetics of laterals in Haitian.

References

Bach, Emmon, and Robert Harms
    1972   How do languages get crazy rules? In *Linguistic Change and Generative Theory*, Robert P. Stockwell and Ronald K. S. Macaulay, (eds.), 1–21. Bloomington, Ind.: Indiana University Press.

Berger, Hermann
    1974   *Das Yasin-Burushaski (Werchikwar). Grammatik, Texte, Wörterbuch.* (= *Neuindische Studien 3.*) Wiesbaden: Otto Harrasowitz.

Bermúdez-Otero, Ricardo
    forthcoming   Spanish pseudoplurals: Phonological cues in the acquisition of a syntax-morphology mismatch. In *Deponency And Morphological Mismatches*, Matthew Baerman, Greville Corbett, Dunstan Brown and Andrew Hippisley (eds.). Oxford: Oxford University Press.

Blevins, Juliette
    1999   Untangling Leti infixation. *Oceanic Linguistics* 38:383–403.

2004 *Evolutionary Phonology. The Emergence of Sound Systems.* Cambridge: Cambridge University Press.
Boersma, Paul
1998 *Functional Phonology.* The Hague: Holland Academic Graphics.
Carstairs, Andrew
1988 Some implications of phonologically conditioned suppletion. In *Yearbook of morphology 1988*, Geert Booij and Jaap van Marle (eds.), 67–94. Dordrecht: Kluwer. Reprinted in Charles W. Kreidler (ed.), 2001. *Phonology – Critical Concepts. Volume 5: The Interface with Morphology and Syntax*, 111–139. London: Routledge.
Clements, G. N.
1990 The role of the sonority cycle in core syllabification. In *Papers in Laboratory Phonology I: Between the Grammar and Physics of Speech*, John Kingston and Mary Beckman (eds.), 283–333. Cambridge: Cambridge University Press.
Dimmendaal, Gerrit J.
1983 *The Turkana Language.* Dordrecht: Foris.
2000 Number marking and noun categorization in Nilo-Saharan languages. *Anthropological Linguistics* 42: 214–261.
Dixon, Robert M. W.
1972 *The Dyirbal Language of North Queensland.* Cambridge: Cambridge University Press.
Fleischhacker, Heidi
2002 Cluster-dependent epenthesis asymmetries. In *UCLA Working Papers in Linguistics 7*, Adam Albright and Taehong Cho (eds.), 71–116. Los Angeles: UCLA Department of Linguistics.
Green, Anthony Dubach
2005 Phonology Limited. ROA 745.
Hale, Kenneth, and Abanel Lacayo Blanco
1989 *Diccionario elemental del ulwa (sumu meridional).* Cambridge, Mass.: Center for Cognitive Science, MIT.
Hale, Mark, and Charles Reiss
2000 Phonology as Cognition. In *Phonological Knowledge*, Noel Burton-Roberts, Philip Carr, and Gerry Docherty (eds.), 161–184. Oxford: Oxford University Press.
Halle, Morris, and William J. Idsardi
1997 r, hypercorrection, and the Elsewhere Condition. In *Derivations and Constraints in Phonology*, Iggy Roca (ed.), 331–348. Oxford: Clarendon Press.
Hayes, Bruce P.
1999 Phonetically-Driven Phonology: The Role of Optimality Theory and Inductive Grounding. In *Functionalism and Formalism in Linguistics. Vol. 1: General Papers*, Michael Darnell, Frederick J. Newmeyer, Michael Noonan, Edith Moravcsik, and Kathleen Wheatley (eds.), 243–284. Amsterdam: John Benjamins.
Huttar, George L.
1996 Epenthetic *-mi* in Ndyuka: A transitive marker? *SIL Electronic Working Papers* 1996-003. http://www.sil.org/silewp.

Johnston, Raymond Leslie
1980   *Nakanai of New Britain: The Grammar of an Oceanic Language*. Canberra: Australian National University.

Kager, René
1996   On affix allomorphy and syllable counting. In *Interfaces in Phonology*, Ursula Kleinhenz (ed.), 155–171. *Studia Grammatica 41.*) Berlin: Akademie Verlag.
2008   Lexical irregularity and the typology of contrast. In *The Structure of Words*, Kristin Hanson and Sharon Inkelas (eds.). Cambridge, Mass.: The MIT Press.

Klein, Thomas B.
2003   Syllable structure and lexical markedness in creole morphophonology: Determiner allomorphy in Haitian and elsewhere. In *The Phonology and Morphology of Creole Languages*, Ingo Plag (ed.), 209–228. Tübingen: Max Niemeyer.

Koch, Harold J.
1980   Kaititj nominal inflection: Some comparative notes. In *Papers in Australian Linguistics 13: Contributions to Australian Linguistics*, Bruce Rigsby and Peter Sutton (eds.), 259–274. (= *Pacific Linguistics Series A, 59.*) Canberra: Australian National University.

Lapointe, Steven G.
1999   Stem selection and OT. In *Yearbook of morphology 1999*, Geert Booij and Jaap van Marle (eds.), 263–297. Dordrecht: Kluwer.

Lepschy, Anna Laura, and Giulio Lepschy
1988   *The Italian Language Today.* 2nd edition. London: Hutchinson.

Levelt, Willem J. M.
1989   *Speaking. From Intention to Articulation*. Cambridge, Mass.: The MIT Press.

Lieber, Rochelle
1980   The Organization of the Lexicon. Ph. D. diss., MIT.
1982   Allomorphy. *Linguistic Analysis* 10: 27–52.

Martin, Samuel E., and Young-Sook C. Lee
1964   *Beginning Korean*. New Haven, CT: Yale University Press.

Mascaró, Joan
1996   External allomorphy as emergence of the unmarked. In *Current Trends in Phonology: Models and Methods*, Jacques Durand and Bernard Laks (eds.), 473–483. Salford: European Studies Research Institute.

McCarthy, John J.
2002   *Thematic Guide to Optimality Theory*. Cambridge: Cambridge University Press.
2003   Richness of the base and the determination of underlying representations. ROA 616.

McCarthy, John J., and Alan S. Prince
1993   Prosodic Morphology I. Ms., University of Massachusetts at Amherst and Rutgers University. Updated and enlarged 2001. ROA 482.
1994   The Emergence of the Unmarked. In *NELS 24. Vol. 2*, Mercè Gonzàlez (ed.), 333–379.
1999   Faithfulness identity in Prosodic Morphology. In *The Prosody-Morphology Interface*, René Kager, Harry van der Hulst, and Wim Zonneveld (eds.), 218–309. Cambridge: Cambridge University Press.

McCarthy, John J., and Matthew Wolf
    2005   Less than zero: Correspondence and the null output. ROA 722.
Nikolaeva, Irina, and Maria Tolskaya
    2001   *A Grammar of Udihe*. Berlin: Mouton de Gruyter.
Odden, David
    1996   *The Phonology and Morphology of Kimatuumbi*. Oxford: Clarendon Press.
Ogden, Richard
    1993   What Firthian Prosodic Analysis has to say to us. In *Computational Phonology (Edinburgh Working Papers in Cognitive Science 8)*, T. Mark Ellison and James M. Scobbie (ed.), 107–127. Edinburgh: Edinburgh University.
Omar, Asmah Haji
    1975   *Essays on Malaysian Linguistics*. Kuala Lumpur: Dewan Bahsa dan Pustaka.
Oostendorp, Marc van
    2007   Derived environment effects and Consistency of Exponence. This volume.
Orgun, Cemil Orhan, and Ronald L. Sprouse
    1999   From MPARSE to CONTROL: deriving ungrammaticality. *Phonology* 16:191–224.
Paster, Mary
    2005   Subcategorization vs. output optimization in syllable-counting allomorphy. In *Proceedings of the 24th West Coast Conference on Formal Linguistics*.
Patz, Elizabeth
    1991   Djabugay. In *The Handbook of Australian Languages*, Robert M. W. Dixon and Barry J. Blake (eds.), 245–347. Melbourne: Oxford University Press.
Payne, David L.
    1981   *The Phonology and Morphology of Axininca Campa*. Arlington, TX: Summer Institute of Linguistics.
Prince, Alan S., and Paul Smolensky
    1993   Optimality theory. Constraint interaction in generative grammar. Technical Report #2, Rutgers University Center for Cognitive Science. ROA 537; published in 2004 by Blackwell Publishers.
Raffelsiefen, Renate
    2004   Absolute ill-formedness and other morphophonological effects. *Phonology* 21:91–142.
Rehg, Kenneth L.
    2001   Pohnpeian possessive paradigms: The smart solution, the dumb solution and the Pohnpeian solution. In *Issues in Austronesian Morphology. A focusschrift for Byron W. Bender*, Joel Bradshaw and Kenneth L. Rehg (eds.), 217–233. (= *Pacific Linguistics 519*.) Canberra: Research School of Pacific and Asian Studies, The Australian National University.
Rice, Curt
    2005   Optimal gaps in optimal paradigms. *Catalan Journal of Linguistics* (4)1: 155-170. Special issue on phonology in morphology edited by Maria-Rosa Lloret and Jesús Jiménez.
Rubach, Jerzy, and Geert Booij
    2001   Allomorphy in Optimality Theory: Polish iotation. *Language* 77: 26–60.

Scobbie, James M.
  1993 Constraint Violation and Conflict from the Perspective of Declarative Phonology. *Canadian Journal of Linguistics* 38: 155–168.
Stump, Gregory T.
  2001 *Inflectional Morphology. A Theory of Paradigm Structure*. Cambridge: Cambridge University Press.
Welmers, William Evert
  1976 *A Grammar of Vai* (= *University of California Publications in Linguistics 84*). Berkeley: University of California Press.
Winfield, W. W.
  1928 *A Grammar of the Kui Language*. Calcutta: Asiatic Society of Bengal.
Wilson, Colin
  2003 Experimental investigation of phonological naturalness. In *Proceedings of the 22nd West Coast Conference on Formal Linguistics*, Gina Garding and Minu Tsujimura (eds.), 101–114.
Wolf, Matthew
  2005 For an autosegmental theory of mutation. Ms., University of Massachussets, Amherst. ROA 754.
Yu, Alan
  2004 The Morphology and Phonology of Infixation. Ph.D. diss., University of California, Berkeley.
Zuraw, Kie
  2005 The role of phonetic knowledge in phonological patterning: Corpus and survey evidence form Tagalog. Ms., UCLA. ROA 791.

Chapter 5
A freer input: Yowlumne opacity and the Enriched Input Model

Orhan Orgun and Ronald Sprouse

1. Introduction

Rule-based approaches to grammar often include devices that impose limits on underlying representations (UR) and on structural changes. In early generative phonology, constraints on UR were thought to be essential in capturing language-wide restrictions on root shapes. Structural changes that rules could effect were constrained by locality and restrictions on rule types. In Optimality Theory (OT; Prince and Smolensky 1993), linguistic generalizations follow from the ranking of universal constraints and restrictions on UR and structural mappings are shunned.

We introduce a new dimension of freedom that is available to OT. We propose that the input for an Input-Output mapping is not necessarily identical to the UR. Lexical representation is instead the definition of an infinite candidate Input set; each candidate Input contains the UR plus any amount of additional structure. The constraint ranking evaluates candidate Input-Output pairs and selects the winning pair.

We present opacity effects in Yowlumne that require reference to a representation that is not present in either UR or surface form. Our model, the Enriched Input Model (EIM), handles these types of opacity while formally maintaining OT as a two-level theory.

2. Suppletion and the Enriched Input Model

We begin with a discussion of allomorphy, from which EIM derives much inspiration. A coherent analysis of phonologically-conditioned suppletion requires the evaluation of competing Input-Output pairs, with each allomorph providing a separate Input candidate. Furthermore, phonologically opaque

94 *Orhan Orgun and Ronald Sprouse*

conditioning of allomorphy requires Input wellformedness constraints. These two concepts – (1) EVAL compares multiple Input-Output pairs (section 2.1); (2) wellformedness constraints may target either Input or Output candidates (section 2.2) – form the core ideas of EIM, along with a third concept, the 'Enriched Input' (section 2.3).

2.1. Suppletive allomorphy in Turkish

Turkish provides a revealing case of phonologically-conditioned suppletion. The possessive suffix has allomorphs sensitive to the root-final segment: *-i* appears with C-final roots, *-si* with V-final roots.

(1)   Turkish *-i/-si* allomorphy
      sepet 'basket'   sepet-i 'basket 3. POSS.'
      kene 'tick'   kene-si 'tick 3. POSS.'

Following Kager (1996), we assume that the tableau for a form containing a morpheme with suppletive allomorphs includes Input candidates containing either allomorph. Implicit in this is the fact that the winning candidate is an Input-Output pair. NOCODA and *V.V (no hiatus) are sufficient to account for the allomorph distribution: *-i* attaches to C-final roots to avoid a NOCODA violation, *-si* to V-final roots to avoid a *V.V violation. In (2) the winning forms select an Input candidate allomorph: /kene-si/ → [kenesi] selects *-si*, and /sepet-i/ → [sepeti] selects *-i*.

(2)   Turkish *-i/-si* selection

/kene-{i/si}/	NOCODA	*V.V
kene-i		*!
☞ kene-si		
/sepet-{i/si}/		
☞ sepet-i		
sepet-si	t!	

Kager does not show faithfulness, as it is not relevant to his discussion. However, since both allomorphs are present in Input, DEP and MAX must be evaluated with respect to each allomorph.

Example (3) repeats the tableau in (2) in a notational variant that makes the Input-Output pairs explicit and includes faithfulness. The first column shows candidate Input forms. The second column shows Output candidates. Each Output candidate is repeated for each Input candidate, forming a complete set of Input-Output pairs.

(3) Turkish -*i*/-*si* selection with explicit Input-Output pairs

		NOCODA	*V.V	DEP, MAX
/kene-i/	kenei		*!	
	kenesi			s!
/kene-si/	kenei		*!	s
☞	kenesi			
☞ /sepet-i/	sepeti			
	sepetsi	t!		s
/sepet-si/	sepeti			s!
	sepetsi	t!		

2.2. Opaque allomorph selection in Turkish

Intervocalic velar deletion (Lewis 1967) obscures the distributional generalizations of the Turkish possessive allomorphs: -*i* attaches to a *k*-final root, but the /k/ is deleted, creating a surface *V.V violation (4).

(4) Opaque Turkish -*i*/-*si* allomorphy
    emek 'labor'   eme-i 'labor 3. POSS.'   (*emek-i, *eme-si)

While velar deletion obscures the -*i*/-*si* generalizations in surface forms, the generalizations hold true of input forms: -*i* attaches to C final input roots, and -*si* attaches to V final input roots. The solution is to make NOCODA an Input wellformedness constraint. *VkV bars surface intervocalic velars. In the following and subsequent tableaus we mark Input wellformedness constraints with the subscript 'In'; unmarked constraints are on Output. DEP outranks *V.V in tableau (5). In section 2.4 we modify *V.V to be an Input constraint, which will affect its ranking.

The high ranking of NOCODA$_{In}$ rules out Input-Output pairs that use the -*si* allomorph since Input /bebek-si/ violates it, but /bebek-i/ does not.

(5) Opaque Turkish -i/-si selection

		NOCODA$_{In}$	*VkV	DEP	*V.V	MAX
☞/bebek-i/	bebei				*	k
	bebeki		*!			
	bebesi			s!		k
	bebeksi			s!		
/bebek-si/	bebei	*!			*	ks
	bebeki	*!	*			s
	bebesi	*!				k
	bebeksi	*!				

2.3. The enriched input

EIM takes evaluation of Input-Output pairs to be the rule, not the exception to be invoked only for suppletion. The main innovation of our approach is that instead of taking UR to be the Input, UR can be considered to define the Input. This is seen in the schematized version of EIM, shown in (6).

(6) Enriched Input model

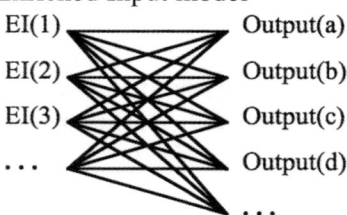

The right side of (6) is the set of candidate Outputs of the classic OT (C-OT) model. EI(1), EI(2), EI(3), etc., designate Enriched Input candidates (1), (2), (3), and so on. These are analogous to suppletive allomorphs.

Each EI candidate contains all of the information in UR. The Enriched Input set thus echoes the one-level approach of Bird and Ellison 1994; UR is a *partial description* of the Input set. Thus, UR does not constitute a separate level from Input.

The C-OT tools that evaluate Input-Output mappings also exist in EIM: 1) Correspondence constraints to evaluate faithfulness of Input-Output pairs; 2) Wellformedness constraints to evaluate candidate Outputs. EIM wellformedness constraints have the additional possibility of evaluating Input candidates.

EIM maps each EI candidate to each candidate Output: EI(1) maps to Output candidates (a–d...), EI(2) maps to Output candidates (a–d...), and so on. Each mapping from an EI candidate to the set of Output candidates is equivalent to the C-OT Input-Output mapping. In these mappings information may be lost or gained: epenthesis, deletion and feature changing are allowed in the mapping from EI to Output candidates.

We turn to another Turkish example to illustrate EIM.

2.4. Opaque alternations in Turkish

An example of the kind of opacity that escapes analysis in C-OT is found in Turkish, where epenthetic vowels break up what seem to be input consonant clusters. Turkish restricts coda clusters (Clements and Sezer 1982). Impermissible clusters are broken up by an epenthetic vowel (7).

(7) Epenthesis after C-final roots before consonantal suffix
     /temel/   [temel]   'foundation'
     /temel-m/   [temelim]   'my foundation'

     /somun/   [somun]   'loaf'
     /somun-m/   [somunum]   'my loaf'

     /kesa:fet/   [kesa:fet]   'turbidity'
     /kesa:fet-m/ [kesa:fetim] 'my turbidity'

Epenthesis is triggered by a constraint against impossible codas, $*CC]_\sigma$.

Epenthesis is more remarkable in (8). Many root-final *k*s delete intervocalically.[1] *k*-deletion obscures the environment for epenthesis. As a result, the epenthetic vowel appears between the final root vowel and a suffix consonant, not a normal epenthesis site. Epenthesis seems odd only in the surface form, however – it is readily explicable from the input, e.g. *bebek-m*, where the offending cluster is present.

The forms in (9) show that the suffix vowels in (8) are epenthetic: when the same suffix attaches to V-final roots, no epenthetic segment intervenes:

Besides the fact that epenthesis in (8) yields a universally marked structure, hiatus is particularly marked in Turkish. Hiatus created through suffixation causes an epenthetic glide to be inserted (10).[2]

Glide insertion is triggered by *V.V. The tableau in (11) demonstrates the problem that (8) presents. We present the constraints without ranking them

(8) Epenthesis with opaque /k/-deletion
/bebek/   [bebek]   'baby'
/bebek-m/   [bebeim]   'my baby'
            cf. [bebekler] 'baby-pl'

/doruk/   [doruk]   'summit'
/doruk-m/   [doruum]   'my summit'

/yenik/   [yenik]   'moth-eaten place'
/yenik-m/   [yeniim]   'my moth-eaten place'

(9) No epenthesis after V-final stems before same suffix
/araba/   [araba]   'car'
/araba-m/   [arabam]   'my car'

(10) C-epenthesis after V-final stem before V-initial suffix
/baba-Im/   [babayim]   'I am a father'
/anne-Im/   [anneyim]   'I am a mother'
(cf. /adam-Im/ adamim   'I am a man' *adamyim)

since ranking cannot fix the problem (the desired winner in (b) is harmonically bounded by the incorrect winner in (c).

(11) C-OT analysis of Turkish

	/bebek-m/	*CC]$_\sigma$	*VkV	*V.V	DEP	MAX
a.	bebekim		*!		i	
b.	bebeim			*!	i	k
☺c.	bebem					k
d.	bebekm	*!				
e.	bebeyim				yi!	k

By definition an epenthetic vowel is not in UR, and therefore is not part of Input, where the triggering environment exists. Epenthetic vowels are present in Output, but there is no consonant cluster to break up in the output form. How then are we to motivate an output form like *bebeim*?

EIM solves the problem by making *CC]$_\sigma$ an Input as well as an Output constraint, a setting indicated by the 'In' subscript.

The Enriched Input set includes candidates that contain the information in UR /bebek-m/, crucially including [be]$_\sigma$[be]$_\sigma$[kim]$_\sigma$, which has the epenthetic *i*. *CC]$_{\sigma In}$ rules out Input-Output pairs based on the Input candidate [be]$_\sigma$-[bekm]$_\sigma$. The faithfulness constraints MAX and DEP favor the Output can-

(12) Turkish epenthesis and deletion; UR /bebek-m/

	EI / Output	*VkV	*CC]$_{\sigma In}$	*CC]$_\sigma$	MAX	DEP	*V.V
	[be]$_\sigma$[bekm]$_\sigma$						
1a	[be]$_\sigma$[bekm]$_\sigma$		*!	*			
1b	[be]$_\sigma$[be]$_\sigma$[kim]$_\sigma$	*	*!			i	
1c	[be]$_\sigma$[be]$_\sigma$[im]$_\sigma$		*!		*	i	*
1d	[be]$_\sigma$[bem]$_\sigma$		*!		*		
1e	[be]$_\sigma$[be]$_\sigma$[yim]$_\sigma$		*!			yi	
	[be]$_\sigma$[be]$_\sigma$[kim]$_\sigma$						
2a	[be]$_\sigma$[bekm]$_\sigma$			*!		i	
2b	[be]$_\sigma$[be]$_\sigma$[kim]$_\sigma$	*!					
2c	☞ [be]$_\sigma$[be]$_\sigma$[im]$_\sigma$				k		*
2d	[be]$_\sigma$[bem]$_\sigma$				*ki!		
2e	[be]$_\sigma$[be]$_\sigma$[yim]$_\sigma$				k	y!	

didate [be]$_\sigma$[be]$_\sigma$[im]$_\sigma$, yielding the optimal Input-Output pair [be]$_\sigma$[be]$_\sigma$-[kim]$_\sigma$ → [be]$_\sigma$[be]$_\sigma$[im]$_\sigma$.

With one small modification this analysis extends to a second source of opacity in -i/-si allomorph selection. k-final roots take the -i allomorph even though the k deletes, yielding a surface V-final root. Normally V-final roots undergo glide insertion (10), but not with opaque -i selection (4). If *V.V is a constraint on Input, glide insertion is favored in Input candidates, where the environment is not present, as shown in (13).

We turn now to the more complex case of Yowlumne.

3. Yowlumne – the descriptive facts

The opaque alternations in Yowlumne have a long history of discussion including rule-based (e.g. Archangeli 1988; Lakoff 1993) and constraint-based analyses (e.g. Archangeli 1988; Zoll 1993; Cole and Kisseberth 1996; Archangeli and Suzuki 1997; McCarthy 1999; Zoll 2001). Most previous analyses draw data from Newman 1944 and are based on the state of the language in the early 1930s. For discussion of the state of opacity in Yowlumne in the 1990s, see Hansson and Sprouse (1999).

(13) Opaque -i/-si selection; no glide insertion; UR /bebek-{i,si}/

	EI / Output	NoCoda$_{In}$	*VkV	*CC]$_{\sigma In}$	*CC]$_\sigma$	Max	Dep	*V.V$_{In}$
	[be]$_\sigma$[be]$_\sigma$[ki]$_\sigma$							
1a	[be]$_\sigma$[be]$_\sigma$[ki]$_\sigma$		*!					
1b ☞	[be]$_\sigma$[be]$_\sigma$[i]$_\sigma$					k		
1c	[be]$_\sigma$[be]$_\sigma$[yi]$_\sigma$					k	y!	
	[be]$_\sigma$[bek]$_\sigma$[si]$_\sigma$							
2a	[be]$_\sigma$[be]$_\sigma$[ki]$_\sigma$	*!	*			s		
2b	[be]$_\sigma$[be]$_\sigma$[i]$_\sigma$	*!				ks		
2c	[be]$_\sigma$[be]$_\sigma$[yi]$_\sigma$	*!				ks	y	
2d	[be]$_\sigma$[be]$_\sigma$[si]$_\sigma$	*!				k		

The interaction of five phonological processes is of interest. These are Template association, Epenthesis, Harmony, Lowering, Shortening. We first illustrate each alternation alone, then turn to forms exhibiting more than one alternation and investigate their interactions.

3.1. Basics of template association

Yowlumne is well known for its templatic morphology. We present just enough detail to demonstrate opaque interactions between template association and phonological processes. For detailed exposition, see, e.g., Noske 1985; Archangeli 1988, 1991; Zoll 1993. The cornerstone of the system is an inventory of three template shapes (Newman 1944: 38), which can be defined in prosodic terms (14), as in Archangeli (1991).

(14) Template inventory: σ_μ, $\sigma_{\mu\mu}$, $F_{iamb} = \sigma_\mu \sigma_{\mu\mu}$

The segments of the verb root associate to these templates. Generally, a verb root contains one vowel (/i/, /u/, /a/ or /o/) and two or three consonants. Each verb selects one default template (15).

Default template selection may be overridden. Some verbal affixes select one of the templates in (14) and impose it on the root. Examples of affixes imposing their own template are shown in (16) and (17). In (16), the adjunctive

(15) Root-supplied (default) templates
    a. σ_μ: luk'l-ut   'bury PASS. AOR.'
    b. $\sigma_{\mu\mu}$:   doos-it   'report PASS. AOR.'
    c. F_{iamb}:   hudook'-ut 'straighten PASS. AOR.'

suffix imposes its iambic template, regardless of whether the root's default template is monomoraic (a), bimoraic (b), or iambic (c).

(16) Affix imposed template: F_{iamb} (-ʔeey ~ -ʔiy 'adjunctive')
    a. **t'uloo**-ʔuy   'burn ADJ.'
        (cf. root's monomoraic default template, *t'ul-*)
    b. **tanaa**-ʔeey   'go ADJ.'
        (cf. root's default bimoraic template, *taan-*)
    c. **c'uyoo**-ʔoy-nu 'urinate ADJ. IND. OBJ.'
        (cf. root's default template, also iambic: *c'uyoo-*)

Example (17) shows the desiderative suffix, which imposes the monomoraic template. We show this suffix overriding default root templates of the monomoraic (a), bimoraic (b), and iambic (c) type.

(17) Affix imposed template: σ_μ (-*hatin* 'desiderative')
    a. **linc'**-atin-mi   'speak GER.'
        (cf. default root template, also monomoraic, *linc'-*)
    b. **wuʔy**-atin-xɔɔ-nit 'go to sleep DES. DUR. FUT./present'
        (cf. root's default bimoraic template, *wooʔy-*)
    c. **liʔ**-hatin-hin   'sink AOR.'
        (cf. default iambic root template, *liʔee-*)

Examples of suffixes imposing the bimoraic template are hard to come by. This gap is a result of closed syllable vowel shortening, which causes the templatically imposed long vowel to shorten in the surface form.

Following McCarthy and Prince's (1993) Generalized Alignment approach, we analyze template association by using constraints on stem size. These constraints come from two sources. First, each root has a constraint requiring it to appear in its default templatic shape. Second, each affix that imposes a specific template has its own templatic constraint, which outranks the root constraints. Consider the forms in (18), with the roots' default templates. In these examples, the suffix -*in* does not bring its own templatic constraint and the root's default template emerges.

(18) Default root template
    a. Monomoraic /luk'l-in/   Stem=σ_μ
                ☞   luk'.l-un
                    look'.l-un   *!
                    lu.k'oo.l-un   *!

    b. Bimoraic   /dus-in/   Stem=$\sigma_{\mu\mu}$
                      du.s-un   *!
                ☞   doo.s-un
                      du.soo-n   *!

    c. Iambic   Stem=F_{iamb}
                      hud.k'-un   *!
                      hood.k'-un   *!
                ☞   hu.doo.k'-un

Technically, all of the candidates in (18) seem to violate the stem shape constraints, since each root ends in a consonant that serves as onset to the following syllable. Thus in none of the candidates shown above does the root correspond exactly to a metrical constituent. One means of dealing with this is to assume that stem shape constraints stipulate the amount of metrical structure *headed* by root material. The resyllabification of the root-final consonant in (18) does not then violate Stem=σ_μ, because the root *luk'l*, heads one mora, which heads one syllable, precisely as Stem=σ_μ specifies.

Constraint ranking handles the interaction between root and affix templates. Affix requirements are outrank root templates. For example, in (19), the adjunctive suffix -*ʔuy* imposes the iambic template.

(19) Affix imposed iambic template

/t'ul + ʔuy/	Stem=F_{iamb}	Stem=σ_μ
	(affix imposed)	(root default)
t'ul-ʔuy	*!	
t'ool-ʔuy	*!	*
☞ t'uloo-ʔuy		*

3.2. Epenthesis

The maximal syllable of Yowlumne is CVX. Unsyllabifiable clusters are broken up by epenthesis of a high vowel, which undergoes vowel harmony (discussed in section 3.3). Examples are shown below.

(20) Epenthesis
    luk'l-ut   'bury PASS. AOR.'   (no epenthesis)
    luk'ul-hanaa   'bury PASS. V. N.'   (epenthesis of [u])
    ʔilk-eeni   'sing RESULT. GER.' (no epenthesis)
    ʔilik-mix   'sing COMIT.'   (epenthesis of [i])

Epenthesis can be handled by using a syllable structure constraint, *CC]$_\sigma$, which outranks DEP.

(21) Epenthesis

		/luk'l + hanaa/	*CC]$_\sigma$	MAX	DEP
	a.	luk'l-hanaa	*!		
	b.	luk'-hanaa		*!	
☞	c.	luk'ul-hanaa			*

Epenthesis affects the metrical shape of the root. In this particular example, the suffix does not supply a template (Archangeli 1988: 206), and the root template for *luk'l* is monomoraic, yet the root surfaces as iambic in *luk'ul-hanaa*. Is this a violation of stem shape? No: stem shape constraints are evaluated on the metrical structure *headed* by roots. *luk'ul* satisfies Stem=σ_μ; only the first syllable is headed by an underlying root segment.

3.3. Vowel harmony

Yowlumne vowels undergo harmony, such that they agree in rounding and backness with the preceding vowel. Harmony applies only to vowels of the same [high] value. Thus, [i] becomes [u] after [u], but is unaffected after [o]. Likewise, [a] becomes [o] after [o], but not after [u] (22):

(22) Harmony applying to high vowels (following another high vowel)[3]
    Aorist: -hin ~ -hun   pulwiy-hin   'pop out'
                            doolul-hun   'climb'

    Passive aorist: -it ~ -ut   k'oʔ-it   'throw'
                                  luk'l-ut   'bury'

(23) Harmony applying to non-high vowels (following a non-high V)
    Dubitative: -al ~ -ol   xat-al   'eat'
                              ṣoog-al   'pull out unfastened object'
                              di'ṣ-al   'make, repair'
                              hoṭn-ol   'take the scent'

    Imperative: -k'a ~ -k'o   t'uy-k'a   'shoot'
                                  lan-k'a   'hear'
                                  t'oyix-k'a   'give medicine'
                                  woowul-k'a   'stand up'
                                  yoloow-k'o   'assemble'
                                  xoṣxoṣ-k'o   'rub repeatedly'

3.4. Lowering

Long vowels may not be high in Yowlumne. Long high vowels become mid, whether they are underlyingly long or long because of templatic requirements (in the bimoraic or iambic templates). Examples of the lowering of templatic long vowels are given in (24).

(24)   t'ul-   'burn'   (root's default monomoraic template)
        t'uloo-   (with suffix imposed bimoraic template)

        bineet-iyo-x   'ask PRIO. PREC.'

Lowering can be handled by *VV[+high], a constraint that bans long high vowels (see Archangeli & Suzuki 1997 for phonetic motivation). Lowering must outrank IDENT[high], which preserves input height specifications.

(25) Lowering

		/tul-/	Template	Lowering	IDENT[high]
	a.	tuluu-		*!	
☞	b.	tuloo-			*
	c.	toloo-			**!

3.5. Shortening

The maximal syllable is CVX and long vowels shorten in closed syllables.

(26) hortatory/prioritive *-iyoo ~ -iyo*
  t'ababwiy-iyoo-hun   'lie down on the belly PRIO. AOR.'
  bineet-iyo-x   'ask PRIO. PREC.'

Shortening results from syllable structure constraints. *CVVC enforces a prohibition on superheavy syllables by dominating the Correspondence constraint IDENT(μ), which demands that moraic affiliations not change in the mapping from Input to Output.

(27) Shortening

		/bineet + iyoo + x/	*CVVC	IDENT(μ)
	a.	bineet-iyoo-x	*!	
☞	b.	bineet-iyo-x		*

3.6. Transparent interactions

The phonological and morphological processes we have seen interact with each other in complex ways, some opaque. In this section, we examine the transparent interactions. We turn to opacity in the next section.

Template association may feed Epenthesis, Lowering, and Shortening. In triconsonantal roots that select the monomoraic template (either by default or due to suffix imposed templatic requirements), Epenthesis is observed unless a vowel-initial suffix follows:

(28) Template association feeds Epenthesis (monomoraic template)
a. /luk'l/   luk'ul-hanaa   'bury PASS. V. N.'   *C-initial suffix*
                                                 [u] epenthesis
b. /luk'l/   luk'l-ut   'bury PASS. AOR.'   *no epenthesis*

Templates that include a long vowel create the environment for Lowering, as in (29), where the stem-final vowel [oo] is a templatically induced copy of the root vowel [u], lowered to [oo] because it is long.

(29) Template association feeds Lowering (iambic template)
a. /tul/   t'uloo-ʔuy   'burn ADJ.'
b. /c'uy/   c'uyoo-ʔoy-nu   'urinate ADJ. IND. OBJ.'

Another transparent interaction is found between Epenthesis and Harmony: Epenthesis feeds Harmony. We show examples of epenthetic vowels undergoing Harmony in (30), where both verb stems are shown in the monomoraic template; the second stem vowel is epenthetic in each case.

(30) Epenthesis feeds Harmony
/luk'l/   luk'ul-hanaa   'bury PASS. V. N.'
/ʔilk/   ʔilik-mix-hin   'sing COMIT. AOR.'

3.7. Opaque interactions

The processes we have seen interact in various opaque ways. In this section, we present the data, which we analyze in later sections.

3.7.1. Lowering and Harmony

Lowering and Harmony interact opaquely in two sets of circumstances. Harmony applies only between vowels of like height, as in (31). The mid vowel /o/ does not trigger harmony on the following high vowel in (b):

(31) a. High vowel triggers harmony on following [i]:
         luk'l-ut   'bury PASS. AOR.'
     b. Underlying non-high vowel [o] does not trigger harmony on following [i] (transparent):
         doos-it   'report PASS. AOR.'
         bok'bok'-it   'find repeatedly PASS. AOR.'

Harmony can also apply opaquely, as in (32), where an underlyingly high vowel that surfaces as low triggers harmony on following high vowels:

(32) Underlying high vowel triggers harmony even when lowered
     hudook'-ut   'straighten PASS. AOR.'   second root vowel is copy of first [u], but lowered
     coom-ut   'destroy PASS. AOR.'   underlying [u] can be seen in monomoraic template, see (35)(b)

Opacity also occurs when underlyingly high vowels that undergo Lowering are followed by non-high vowels. As in (33), nonhigh vowels (here /o/) trigger harmony on following non-high vowels. However, underlyingly high vowels that lower do not trigger harmony on following vowels, even when on the surface both vowels are non-high. In (33), surface /oo/ from underlying /u/ does not trigger harmony on the following /a/.

(33) a. Harmony (root vowel underlyingly [o])
     hoṭn-ol   'may take the scent'
   b. No Harmony ([u] lowered to [oo]; does not trigger harmony)
     ṣoog-al   'might pull out'

3.7.2. Lowering and shortening

Lowering and Shortening also interact opaquely. A long vowel that shortens in a closed syllable nonetheless undergoes Lowering. This is shown in (34) by the hortatory/prioritive suffix /-iyuu/. When followed by a CV-initial suffix or by no suffix, the hortatory/prioritive surfaces as /-iyoo/, transparently lowering (34)a. With a following C suffix, as in (34b–c), the suffix vowel shortens. Even though the environment for Lowering is not met on the surface, the underlying long vowel surfaces as non-high.

(34) Shortening: hortatory/prioritive /-iyuu/
   a. tanaa-yoo-hin   'take PRIO. AOR.'   /uu/ lowers to /oo/
   b. woʔy-uyo-k'   'get PRIO. IMP.'   /uu/ lowers, shortens in closed syllable
   c. bineet-iyo-x   'ask PRIO. PREC.'   /uu/ lowers, shortens in closed syllable

One may ask why the suffix vowel is analyzed as underlyingly high; the answer is that it triggers harmony, which we know to be height-dependent, on following high vowels. This harmony is visible in (34a).

3.7.3. Templatic lengthening, lowering, harmony, shortening

Roots that are subject to the bimoraic or iambic templates show opaque interaction between Lowering and Shortening. Underlyingly high vowels in the portion of the stem required by the template to be bimoraic surface as low, even when the syllable they are in requires them to be short.

(35) Shortening counterbleeds Lowering

    a. wo?y-uyo-k'   (root's default bimoraic
        'go to sleep PRIO. IMP.'   template, woo?y-)

        cf. wu?y-atin-xoo-nit   (suffix imposed monomo-
        'go to sleep DES. DUR. FUT.' raic template)

    b. c'om-hun   (root's default bimoraic
        'devour AOR.'   template: c'oom-)

        cf. c'umo-hnool-aw   (suffix imposed iambic
        'devour PASS. CONS. ADJ. LOC.' template; second root vowel lowered in long templatic position though shortened in closed syllable)

It is not clear from the surface syllable structure of the first forms in (a) and (b) why they should be subject to Lowering. Both stems are subject to a root-based bimoraic template. In both cases the only stem syllable is CVC; the fact that long vowels in closed syllables must be short shows that CVC syllables are bimoraic. The question is why the stem vowels in these forms undergo Lowering, which we know presupposes vowel length.

Facts like these reveal a paradox involving coda consonants in Yowlumne: they do not count as moraic for Template Association (which creates long vowels and feeds Lowering), but they do for Shortening.

The fact that underlyingly short vowels which also surface as short pattern with long vowels (in undergoing Lowering) has struck past researchers as well. Archangeli (1991) deals with it derivationally, assuming that for templatic association only vowels are moraic. By contrast, for purposes of syllabification, coda consonants are moraic. Zoll (1993), in a nonderivational framework, assumes parallel representations, one (the template plane) in which only vowels are moraic and one (the suffixation plane) in which vowels and coda consonants are moraic and *CVVC holds. The crucial competition is between the following rankings:

(36) Ranking paradox:
Moraic codas: *CVVC ≫ *Cμ   *for surface syllabification*
Nonmoraic codas   *Cμ ≫ *CVVC   *for template satisfaction*

The surface ranking is *CVVC ≫ *Cμ; yet the opposite ranking must also have an effect in order to generate the opaque Lowering effects observed. Harmony and Lowering are sensitive to underlying and templatic, not surface, vowel height; Shortening obscures underlying and templatic length. Both opaque interactions are shown in the following example, in which an underlying high vowel: i) appears in a template with a long vowel position, ii) triggers harmony, iii) lowers, and iv) shortens:

(37) Opaque Template association, Lowering, Harmony, and Shortening
c'om-hun   'devour AOR.'   (underlying [u] lowers in bimoraic template, shortens in closed syllable, triggers harmony)

4. EIM analysis

We turn now to the EIM analysis of the opaque interactions.

4.1. An excursus on harmony

We begin by developing an approach to Harmony. We adopt McCarthy's (2004) theory of headed spans with a couple of amendments to deal with the high/rnd interaction. McCarthy's span approach to harmony provides four types of constraints: one type prefers autosegmental spreading, one controls the direction of spread, and two prefer lack of spreading or disharmony. Of these last two, one requires faithfulness to input feature values (lack of harmony), while the other requires certain types of segments to have a specific value for the harmonizing feature (blocking of harmony). Yowlumne requires an extension of this model in order to deal with what one might call "parasitic harmony"; further examples can be seen in Cole and Trigo 1988. In this type of case, segments that share a certain feature (here, [high]) must harmonize in another feature (here, [rnd]). We propose two additions to McCarthy's model: first, retain the use of IDENT-F constraints, which require output correspondents of input segments to have the same F specifications (McCarthy proposes to subsume these in span constraints; we show the need for both types of constraints). Second, we propose constraints that require spans for multiple features to coincide with one another (in this case, each [high] domain must also be a [rnd] domain).

Rounding spreads from left to right when the target and trigger vowels have the same [high] value. Pairs of like-height vowels are [a, o] and [i, u] ([e] occurs only as the output of the lowering of [i:]). Front/back is not contrastive and is assumed to be absent from Yowlumne (input or output) representations. Alternatively, one could assume that markedness constraints governing front/back outrank all competing faithfulness constraints. An inventory of Harmony patterns is provided in (38).

(38) Inventory of Yowlumne Harmony patterns

Input	Output
iu	ii
ui	uu
ao	aa
oa	oo
ia	ia
ua	ua
ai	ai
au	au

Our analysis consists of:

– Constraints that force like-height vowels to constitute spans

– A constraint that forces a [high] span to coincide with a [rnd] span

– A constraint that enforces the L→R directionality of harmony

(42) Span creation

	aiia	IDENT	*A-SPAN	FAITHHEAD
	[aaaa]	*!*		***
☞	[a][ii][a]		**	*
	[a][i][i][a]		***!	

First, [high] spans; this is the most complicated part of the analysis. McCarthy provides two constraints that control span assignment. The, *A-SPAN, penalizes adjacent spans. The second, FAITHHEADSPAN, requires each segment to head a span (violated by segments in nonhead span positions). With these two constraints, we could have one of two situations: the whole form is one span, or each segment is its own span. To force a word to divide into multiple spans, McCarthy provides a markedness constraint that requires certain types of segments to head a span (for example, an obstruent might be required to head a [−nas] span). In Yowlumne, however, high or non-high vowels alike can be in head or non-head positions. The restriction is that a span must start with each vowel that has a [high] value differing from its neighbor. What we need is a constraint that will force like-height vowels into a span without forcing [high] to spread. In McCarthy's approach, span-sharing and spreading are controlled by the same constraints. We need a constraint that evaluates faithfulness to input feature values without regard to span membership. The traditional IDENT fits the bill. Here are the constraints and ranking we propose.

(39) *A-SPAN(HIGH)
No adjacent [high]-spans.

(40) FAITHHEADSPAN(±HIGH): [±HIGH]
Vowels must head a [high] span (McCarthy's faithfulness constraint, here violated).

(41) IDENT(±HIGH)
Output correspondents must retain input [high] values (traditional faithfulness).

Ranking: IDENT ≫ *A-SPAN ≫ FAITHHEAD

We show a schematic example where [aiia] is assigned three [high] spans. From this point on, we consider only candidates with the proper span structure. We therefore omit the above constraints from our tableaus. Our next task is to force a [high] domain to also constitute a [rnd] domain. We do this by using a constraint that requires the features to share a span: SHPAN(High, Rnd). A candidate in which high and [rnd] spans do not coincide violates this constraint. SHPAN outranks all other constraints on [rnd] domains. Assignment of left-headedness to spans and faithfulness to span heads completes the analysis.

(43) SHPAN(HIGH, RND)
A [high] span must be coextensive with a [rnd] span, i.e. their edges must coincide.
FAITHHEADSPAN(±RND)
Vowels head [rnd] spans (Nonhead vowels violate this regardless of feature values; therefore they may harmonize at no cost with respect to this constraint).
SPAN HEADL(RND)
The head of a [rnd] span is at the left edge.

No tableau seems necessary; /ui/, for example has a single span: [uu]. In the remainder of this paper, we simplify the presentation by using "Harmony" as a cover for the constraints in this section. This concludes our discussion of Harmony; we now turn to its interaction with other alternations.

4.2. Epenthesis and Harmony

As noted above, Epenthesis and Harmony can apply simultaneously in C-OT in the absence of opacity. It suffices to apply each constraint in (45) to Output candidates. *CC]$_\sigma$ is the constraint that triggers epenthesis. Harmony stands in for the set of constraints presented in section 4.1.

The tableau in (44) demonstrates that satisfaction of the constraints in (45) results in a winner that undergoes Epenthesis and Harmony. C-OT would be sufficient if these were the only constraints needed.

(44) Simultaneous application of Epenthesis and Harmony

		/luk'l-t/	*CC]$_\sigma$	textscHarmony
☞	a.	luk'lut		
	b.	luk'lit		*!
	c.	luk'lt	*!	

Since (a) is the correct output, DEP must be ranked below *CC]$_\sigma$ and

A freer input 113

Harmony in a C-OT analysis. DEP has been left out because it will not figure in the EIM analysis below.

In EIM, each constraint in (45) may pertain to Input or Output representations. Because the interactions in (45) are transparent there is no need based on these data to tie the constraints to Input. However, the opaque interactions in section 3.7 do require the constraints to be input-sensitive, and that is how they are portrayed below.

(45)   *CC]$_{\sigma EI}$:   No complex codas.
        HARMONY$_{EI}$:   Spread [rnd] left-to-right in [high] spans.

These constraints choose the Output *luk'i ut* as optimal, based on the optimality of the Input *luk'l-ut* and of the faithful mapping between that Input and the opaque Output *luk'l-ut*.

(46) Epenthesis and Harmony

		/luk'l-t/	*CC]$_{cEI}$	HARMONY$_{EI}$	FAITH
	1a.	luk'l-t → luk'l-t	*!		
	1b.	luk'l-t → luk'l-it	*!		*
	1c.	luk'l-t → luk'l-ut	*!		*
	2a.	luk'l-it → luk'l-t			*!
	2b.	luk'l-it → luk'l-it		*!	
	2c.	luk'l-it → luk'l-ut			*!
	3a.	luk'l-ut → luk'l-t			*!
	3b.	luk'l-ut → luk'l-it			*!
☞	3c.	luk'l-ut → luk'l-ut			

In (46), Input candidate (1) *luk'lt* violates *CC]$_{\sigma EI}$, ruling out pairs (1a-c). Input candidate (2) *luk'lit* violates HARMONY$_{EI}$, ruling out (2a-c). The input candidates in (3) all pass the EI-specific constraints; however, pairs (3a) and (3b) violate FAITH-IO (specifically, DEP and IDENT[rnd]) since Input (3a) *luk'lut* possesses a vowel that Output (3a) *luk'lt* lacks, and Input (3b) *luk'lut* and Output (3b) *luk'lit* differ in the rounding of their second vowel. Pair (3c) emerges as the winner since it is based on the well-formed Input *luk'lut* and has a completely faithful Input-Output mapping.

Notice that the only candidates incurring faithfulness violations are those with differences between Input and Output. Differences between UR and Input are not regulated by faithfulness constraints; this is a defining concept in EIM.

We turn now to the question of why epenthesis and harmony must apply to input candidates, as stipulated in (45).

4.3. Templatic lengthening, lowering and shortening

Although not mentioned above, the tableau in (46) involves a root whose default template is monomoraic and a suffix that imposes no template of its own. In such cases, the application of phonological alternations is transparent. In (54), we deal with a stem that is subject to a root-supplied bimoraic template, and develop an EIM analysis of the resulting opacity. Templatic Lengthening and Lowering are enforced on Input, while Shortening is enforced on Output.

The two constraints below, copied from section 3.1, impose the bimoraic template. The *$C_{\mu-EI}$ constraint imposes the restriction that only vowels can satisfy moraic requirements of templates:

(47) Stem=$\sigma_{\mu\mu-EI}$: Bimoraic template

(48) *$C_{\mu-EI}$: Consonants do not license a mora.

Shortening is, by contrast, an Output constraint.

(49) *CVVC

For a root with bimoraic template that is followed by a C suffix, the three constraints above derive templatic length in the Input (50). The results in (50) are provisional. The full analysis of /cum-t/ is in (54).

(50) Templatic Lengthening, Lowering

	/cum-t/	Stem=$\sigma_{\mu\mu-EI}$	*$C_{\mu-EI}$	*CVVC	FAITH
1a.	cum-t → cum-t	*!			
2a.	cum$_\mu$-t → cum$_\mu$-t		*!		
3a.	cuum-t → coom-t			*	*

Where does Lowering fit in? Lowering applies to a vowel that is long either in UR or as a result of templatic lengthening (even if it surfaces as short). In EIM the conditions on Lowering find simple expression: Lowering applies to a vowel that is long in the input. We state Lowering as below, adopting the same formulation as Archangeli & Suzuki (1997: 203).[4]

(51) Lowering: *V.V$_{EI}$ → V[+high]
"Output correspondents of an input long vowel are [−high]"

The EIM tableau in (52) shows how Lowering interacts with Input imposed Templatic Lengthening and Output imposed Shortening.

(52) Templatic Lengthening, Lowering, Shortening

/cum-t/		Stem=σ$_{\mu\mu}$−EI	LOWERING	*CVVC	FAITH
1a.	cum-t → cum-t	*!			
1b.	cum-t → com-t	*!			*
2a.	cuum-t → cuum-t		*!	*	
2b.	cuum-t → coom-t			*!	*
3a.	cuum-t → cum-t		*!		*
☞ 3b.	cuum-t → com-t				**

This tableau differs from the one in (50) in displaying candidates with and without the effects of Lowering. The (b) candidates surface with lowered vowels; the (a) candidates have Outputs which are faithful in vowel quality to their Inputs. Lowering knocks out the faithful Input-Output pairings in (2a) and (3a). The winning candidate, (3b), violates IO-FAITH twice: once because a long Input vowel is short in Output, and once because a [+high] Input vowel is [−high] in Output. However, of all the candidates (3b) best satisfies the higher-ranked markedness constraints.

In stating Templatic Lengthening on Input and Lowering and Shortening on Output, EIM is faithful to the central insight of Archangeli's templatic analysis of Yowlumne, in which statements about well-formed prosodic structure are different at different levels of the grammar. In this respect EIM is also reminiscent of Goldsmith 1993's emphasis on linguistic levels as a way of organizing statements of well-formedness.

4.4. Lowering and harmony

We now turn to the interaction of Harmony with Templatic Lengthening, Lowering, and Shortening. Recall that the crucial height-agreement condition on Harmony must be satisfied by *input* vowel height, even when Lowering renders Input height obscure in Output. The simplest way to capture the Input-sensitivity of Harmony in EIM is to enforce the Harmony constraints on Input.

(53) HARMONY$_{EI}$: Spread [rnd] left-to-right in shared [high] spans.

Recall the definitional requirement of EIM that Inputs contain UR. Does enforcing harmony on Inputs conflict with this principle? No, because, unlike Lowering, Harmony is not necessarily structure-changing. If we make the common-sense assumption that harmonic suffix vowels lack their own values for the harmonizing feature [rnd], then the EI set of a suffix vowel will contain both harmonic and non-harmonic inputs.

The tableau in (55) shows the opaque interaction between Harmony and Lowering in a form whose root vowel is underlyingly high, whose stem template is bimoraic, whose high suffix vowel harmonizes with the root, and whose root vowel is lowered and shortened. This tableau is larger than the others because its Inputs vary according to whether or not they show Templatic Lengthening – (1) and (2) vs. (3) – and whether or not they conform to Harmony – (1) vs. (2) and (3). The Outputs vary according to whether or not they obey Lowering (the a-d candidates vs. the e-h ones, for (1) and (2)), whether or not they obey Shortening (the a-b and e-f candidates in (1) and (2)). Finally, each Input-Output mapping is evaluated for faithfulness, which in this tableau specifically comprises faithfulness to mora count and to values for the features [rnd] and [high].

Harmony also targets Epenthetic vowels. We provide a tableau showing the interaction of Epenthesis and Harmony. Because epenthetic vowels undergo Harmony (an EI constraint), Epenthesis must also be an EI constraint, Recall that *CC]$_\sigma$ is the constraint motivating Epenthesis. The tableau below illustrates the outcome for a stem consisting of root + consonantal suffix in which the stem must conform to a bimoraic template:

Pairs based on the Input cumut in candidate (4) fail because *cumut* fails to associate properly to the bimoraic template. Pairs based on the Input in (1), *cuumt*, satisfy the template association but have a *CC]$_\sigma$ violation, and pairs based on *cuumit* (3) satisfy both the template and *CC]$_\sigma$ but have epenthetic vowels which fail to undergo Harmony. Of the remaining pairs, (2a) with opaque Harmony is preferred over (2c) with transparent Harmony since Harmony applies to Input candidates. It is clear from (54) why Harmony

(54) Template association, epenthesis, harmony, lowering, shortening

		/sug-nIt/	Template	Harmony	Lower	Shorten	Faith
	1a.	suug.nit → suug.nit		*!	*	*	
	1b.	suug.nit → suug.nut		*!	*	*	*
	1c.	suug.nit → sug.nut		*!	*		**
	1d.	suug.nit → sug.nit		*!	*		*
	1e.	suug.nit → soog.nit		*!		*	*
	1f.	suug.nit → soog.nut		*!		*	**
	1g.	suug.nit → sog.nut		*!			***
	1h.	suug.nit → sog.nit		*!			**
	2a.	suug.nut → suug.nit			*	*!	*
	2b.	suug.nut → suug.nut			*	*!	
	2c.	suug.nut → sug.nut			*!		*
	2d.	suug.nut → sug.nit			*!		**
	2e.	suug.nut → soog.nit				*!	**
	2f.	suug.nut → soog.nut				*!	*
☞	2g.	suug.nut → sog.nut					**
	2h.	suug.nut → sog.nit					***!
	3a.	sug.nut → suug.nit	*!				*
	3b.	sug.nut → soog.nit	*!				**
	3c.	sug.nut → sug.nut	*!				
	3d.	sug.nut → sug.nit	*!				*
	3e.	sug.nut → suug.nut	*!				
	3f.	sug.nut → soog.nut	*!				*
	3g.	sug.nut → sog.nut	*!				*
	3h.	sug.nut → sog.nit	*!				**

and *CC]$_\sigma$ must be Input constraints – they cannot apply simultaneously with Lowering, as their environment may be obscured by Lowering's application.

5. Conclusion

EIM adds a new dimension of freedom to the C-OT model in order to account for opaque alternations while enriching the theory as little as possible. The

(55) Opacity of Harmony and Lowering

	UR /cum-t/	Template	*CC]σIn	Harmony	Lower	FAITH
1a.	cuumt → coomut		*!			*
1b.	cuumt → coomit		*!			*
1c.	cuumt → cuumut		*!		*	
1d.	cuumt → cuumit		*!		*	
☞ 2a.	cuumut → coomut					*
2b.	cuumut → coomit					**!
2c.	cuumut → cuumut				*!	
2d.	cuumut → cuumit				*!	*
3a.	cuumit → coomut			*!		**
3b.	cuumit → coomit			*!		*
3c.	cuumit → cuumut			*!	*	*
3d.	cuumit → cuumit			*!	*	
4a.	cumut → coomut	*!				*
4b.	cumut → coomit	*!				**
4c.	cumut → cuumut	*!				
4d.	cumut → cuumit	*!				*

simultaneous evaluation of Input-Output pairs is non-derivational, within the spirit of Optimality Theory; moreover, it is already needed and *used* in C-OT to handle suppletive allomorphy.

The innovation introduced by EIM is to treat the presence and evaluation of Input-Output pairs as the norm, rather than as an exceptional case reserved for allomorphy. The Input set introduced by EIM consists of candidates defined by UR. UR serves as a partial description of the Input set. While it is convenient and familiar to treat UR as the minimal partial description allowed by the set of Input candidates, this description of UR has exactly the same empirical consequences as treating the Input set itself as UR, a characteristic of the model that is a consequence of the fact that Correspondence constraints do not relate UR and Input representations.

Selection of the winning candidate in EIM requires the comparison of two strings only – Input and Output. EIM thus accounts for otherwise difficult opacity facts without unduly increasing the richness of OT.

Notes

1. See Zimmer and Abbott 1978; Sezer 1981; Inkelas and Orgun 1994; Inkelas 1995a, b; Inkelas and Orgun 1995; Inkelas 1996 for details of intervocalic velar deletion, including exceptions and sensitivity to derived environment s.
2. There is some disagreement on whether these suffixes are underlyingly consonantal (appearing with epenthetic vowels when necessary), or underlyingly VC (with the vowel deleting in hiatus). See Orgun 2000 for details of these approaches and their merits and shortcomings.
3. Internally, the *pulwiy-* violates Harmony since both vowels are of the same height but only the first is [+rnd]. Such forms constitute a large group of exceptions to Yowlumne harmony, discussed in detail by Newman (1944: §7, §10). Harmony does apply consistently across the stem-suffix boundary.
4. Archangeli & Suzuki dub (51) an Anti-Faithfulness constraint. This use of correspondence is anticipated in McCarthy and Prince (1995):

    One topic worthy of future investigation is the potential for stating constraints other than the faithfulness variety on correspondent pairs in input and output. Developments along this line can produce the same general effect as the 'two-level' rules ... (270)

    Researchers have found evidence for Anti-Faithfulness constraints in transderivational identity effects (Alderete 1999), quantity assignment in Yupik (Baković 1996), and repetition avoidance in reduplication (Yip 1995).

References

Alderete, John
    1999   Morphologically governed accent in Optimality Theory. Ph. D. diss., University of Massachussets, Amherst.

Archangeli, Diana
    1988   *Underspecification in Yawelmani Phonology and Morphology*. New York: Garland.
    1991   Syllabification and prosodic templates in Yawelmani. *Natural Language and Linguistic Theory* 9(2): 231–283.

Archangeli, Diana and Keiichiro Suzuki
    1997   The Yokuts challenge. *Derivations And Constraints in Phonology*, Iggy Roca (ed.), 197–226. Oxford: Clarendon Press.

Baković, Eric
    1996   Foot harmony and quantitative adjustments. Ms., University of California, San Diego.

Bird, Steven and Mark Ellison
    1994   One-Level Phonology: Autosegmental rules and representations as finite automata. *Computational Linguistics* 20(1): 55–90.

Clements, G. N and Engin Sezer
    1982   Vowel and consonant disharmony in Turkish. *The Structure of Phonological Representations, part II*, Harry van der Hulst and Norval Smith (eds.), 213–255. Dordrecht: Foris.

Cole, Jennifer S. and Charles W. Kisseberth
    1996   Restricting multi-level constraint evaluation: Opaque rule interaction in Yawelmani vowel harmony. Ms., University of Illinois Urbana-Champaign.

Cole, Jennifer and Lauren Trigo
    1988   Parasitic harmony. *Features, Segment Structure And Harmony Processes*. Harry van der Hulst and Norval Smith (eds.), 19–38. Dordrecht: Foris.

Goldsmith, John
    1993   Harmonic phonology. *The Last Phonological Rule*, John Goldsmith (ed.), 21–60. Chicago: University of Chicago Press.

Hansson, Gunnar and Ronald Sprouse
    1999   Factors of change: Yowlumne vowel harmony then and now. WSCLA IV, Vancouver, Department of Linguistics, University of British Columbia.

Inkelas, Sharon
    1995a   The consequences of optimization for underspecification. *Proceedings of the 25th Meeting of the North Eastern Linguistics Society*, Jill Beckman (ed.), 287-302. Amherst, Mass.: GSLA.
    1995b   Underspecification and Optimization. Ms., University of California, Berkeley.
    1996   The interaction of word and phrase rules in Turkish: An apparent paradox for the prosodic hierarchy. *The Linguistic Review* 13: 193-217.

Inkelas, Sharon and Cemil Orhan Orgun
    1994   Level economy, derived environment effects and the treatment of exceptions. *Theorie des Lexikons 56: Recent Developments in Lexical Phonology*, Richard Wiese (ed.) 63–90. Düsseldorf: Heinrich-Heine Universität.
    1995   Level ordering and economy in the lexical phonology of Turkish. *Language* 71(4): 763–793.

Itô, Junko, Armin Mester, and Jaye Padgett
    1995   Licensing and underspecification in Optimality Theory. *Linguistic Inquiry* 26(4): 571–613.

Kager, René
    1996   On affix allomorphy and syllable counting. *Interfaces in Phonology*. Ursula Kleinhenz (ed.). Berlin, Akademie Verlag: 155–171.

Lakoff, George
    1993   Cognitive phonology. In *The Last Phonological Rule*, John Goldsmith (ed.), 117–145. Chicago: University of Chicago Press.

Lewis, Geoffrey
    1967   *Turkish Grammar*. Oxford: Oxford University Press.

McCarthy, John J.
    1999   Sympathy and phonological opacity. *Phonology* 16(3): 331–399.
    2004   Headed spans and autosegmental spreading. Ms., University of Massachussetts, Amherst.

McCarthy, John J. and Alan S. Prince
    1993   Generalized alignment. *Yearbook of Morphology*, Gert Booij and Jaap van Marle (eds.), 79–153. Dordrecht: Kluwer.
    1995   Faithfulness and reduplicative identity. In *University of Massachusetts Occasional Papers in Linguistics* 18, Jill Beckman, Laura Walsh Dickey and Suzanne Urbanczyk (eds.), 249–384. Amherst, Mass.: GLSA Publications.

Newman, Stanley
  1944   *Yokuts Language of California*. New York: Viking Fund Publications.
Noske, Roland
  1985   Syllabification and syllable changing processes in Yawelmani. *Advances in Nonlinear Phonology*, Harry van der Hulst and Norval Smith (eds.), 335–361. Dordrecht: Foris.
Orgun, Cemil Orhan
  2000   Review of Turkish by Jaklin Kornfilt. *Studies in Language* 24(1): 204–221.
Prince, Alan S., and Paul Smolensky
  1993   Optimality theory. Constraint interaction in generative grammar. Technical Report #2, Rutgers University Center for Cognitive Science. ROA 537; published in 2004 by Blackwell Publishers.
Sezer, Engin
  1981   The k/Ø alternation in Turkish. *Harvard Studies in Phonology*. G. N. Clements (ed.), II: 354-382. Bloomington: Indiana University Linguistics Club.
Yip, Moira
  1995   Repetition and its avoidance: The case of Javanese. *Arizona Phonology Conference 4: Features in Optimality Theory*. Keiichiro Suzuki and Dirk Elzinga. Tucson: University of Arizona.
Zimmer, Karl and Barbara Abbott
  1978   The k/Ø alternation in Turkish; some experimental evidence for its productivity. *Journal of Psycholinguistic Research* 7: 35–46.
Zoll, Cheryl
  1993   Directionless syllabification and ghosts in Yawelmani. Rutgers Optimality Workshop I, Rutgers University.
  2001   Segmental phonology in Yawelmani. *Ken Hale: A Life in Language*. Michael Kenstowicz, (ed.), 427–458. Cambridge, MA: MIT Press.

Chapter 6
Derived Environment Effects and Consistency of Exponence*

Marc van Oostendorp

1. Coloured Containment

1.1. Consistency of Exponence

In this article, I defend the assumption that the generator function GEN of Optimality Theory should be restricted by a principle called *Consistency of Exponence* and I show how this assumption helps us understand so-called Derived Environment Effects .

Consistency of Exponence was introduced almost in some of the earliest work on Optimality Theory (McCarthy and Prince 1993b, 1994) as a reasonable restriction on the way the phonology works, and in particular on the way it interacts with the lexical specification of morphemes.[1] Over the course of the past 15 years, very few explicit arguments have been provided against it – those that have will be discussed in section 1.3 – and we will show in section 1.2 that several well-known families of constraints are dependent on it. Nevertheless, the principle never received the attention it deserved. Here is the original definition:

(1)   *Consistency of Exponence*
   "No changes in the exponence of a phonologically-specified morpheme are permitted." (McCarthy and Prince 1993b, 1994)

The principle was explained by McCarthy and Prince (1993b,1994) in the following way:

> [Consistency of Exponence] means that the lexical specifications of a morpheme (segments, prosody, or whatever) can never be affected by GEN. In particular, epenthetic elements posited by GEN will have no morphological affiliation, even when they lie within or between strings with morphemic

identity. Similarly, underparsing of segments – failure to endow them with syllable structure – will not change the make-up of a morpheme, though it will surely change how that morpheme is realized phonetically. Thus, any given morpheme's phonological exponents must be identical in underlying and surface form.

Underlying this is an important assumption on what GEN can do to morphology: it can only concatenate morphemes, it cannot change the morphemes themselves to something completely different. Phonologically, we are free; we can spread features from one morpheme to another, insert various types of material and decide not to pronounce other parts; but this will never affect the morphological status of the phonological material involved. If we decide not to pronounce the final *t* of *cat*, or if we insert a vowel at its end ([kætə]), this does not change the fact that the morpheme is /kæt/.

It may be instructive to consider an example. Let us consider a hypothetical input morpheme /takp/ in some language L; and let us furthermore assume that this morpheme would be pronounced as [tapi] in isolation. Consistency of Exponence gives the following output representation:

(2)
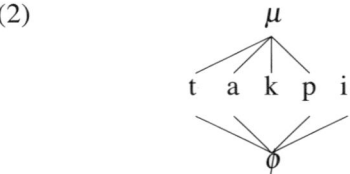

In this picture, the μ denotes the morphological structure: there is one morpheme, which 'consists' of the segments /t, a, k, p/, and will always consist of these segments. ϕ denotes the phonological structure, which does not include the deleted /k/, but it does contain a segment [i], which is phonologically present.

In van Oostendorp (2005), I propose a slightly different notation, one which is based on colours – reproduced here as subscripts.[2]

(3)
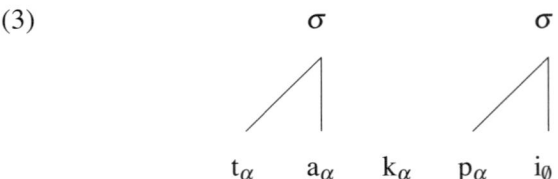

Every morpheme has its own colour which is distributed over all segments and other material – features, moras, etc. – which make it up. In this simple example, there is only one morpheme with the 'colour' α. The epenthetic segment does not have any morphological colour, denoted here by giving $\emptyset$ as its subscript. In terms of colours, Consistency of Exponence states that GEN cannot change the colour of any phonological element: it cannot give colour to epenthetic material, and it cannot alter the colours of underlying material.

A second principle restricting GEN in McCarthy and Prince (1993b, 1994) is called *Containment*. This can be seen as a special case of Consistency of Exponence in most cases:[3]

(4) *Containment*
No element may be literally removed from the input form. The input is thus contained in every candidate form.

This is a special case of Consistency of Exponence, since also the latter principle says that everything which is part of a morpheme should stay part of that morpheme. We thus do not need Containment independently of Consistency of Exponence, but it is useful to have a separate name for it, since Containment refers to one of the more controversial aspects of Consistency of Exponence.[4]

Prince and Smolensky (1993) have implemented the idea of Containment in one specific way, the so-called PARSE & FILL Model, named after the two constraints which take care of the most important aspects of faithfulness theory, deletion and insertion respectively:

(5) a. PARSE: 'Every phonological element needs to be parsed into the prosodic structure.' (I.e. deleted elements are 'not parsed' in the phonological structure.)
b. FILL: 'Syllable positions are filled with segmental material.' (I.e. inserted segments are 'empty'.)

The PARSE & FILL Model is fraught with problems, in particular with respect to the theory of epenthesis, i.e. the FILL component (van Oostendorp 2005). For instance, inserted segments have to be 'empty' in order to be recognizable as inserted at all: if we would allow non-empty epenthetic segments, the constraint FILL would not be violated, and hence we would have no theoretical device to prevent gratuitous epenthesis in all languages of the world. We thus have to prevent features from being inserted or from spreading into epenthetic vowels if we use FILL. This means for instance that we can have no phonological analysis of vowel harmony to epenthetic vowels, clearly an undesirable result.

Instead of this particular implementation of Containment, van Oostendorp (2005) therefore proposes an alternative implementation, called *Coloured Containment*, of which the most important constraints are:

(6) a. PARSE-$\phi(\alpha)$: The morphological element α must be incorporated into the phonological structure. (No deletion.)
 b. PARSE-$\mu(\alpha)$: The phonological element α must be incorporated into the morphological structure. (No insertion.)

As in the PARSE & FILL Model, we assume that underlying material which is not pronounced, is still present – it just fails to be incorporated into the prosodic structure. The phonetics will only pronounce the material that is prosodically parsed and leave the rest behind ('Stray Erasure').

PARSE-$\phi(\alpha)$ forces everything to be in the phonological structure, and thus counts as a constraint against 'deletion'. PARSE-$\mu(\alpha)$, inversely, disallows any material which is not part of a morpheme. Since something can only be part of a morpheme when it is underlying, this forbids epenthesis (cf. Golston 2007 for a proposal which integrates epenthetic segments into the input). Since faithfulness violations can always be decomposed into deletion + insertion, this gives us the machinery needed to describe the relations between lexicon and the phonetic output.

Notice that we have so far not really introduced anything new into the theory. Given Consistency of Exponence, the relevant properties of a theory of faithfulness theory follow for free, and the enrichment with Correspondence Theory seems largely superfluous.

Correspondence Theory is a more powerful theory of faithfulness than Containment-based models, involving more abstract relations (the correspondence relations between input and output), and allowing for analyses which are unavailable in Containment – such as unbounded metathesis and changing the morphological affiliation of segments. It remains to be seen whether we need this power independently, but this is not the goal of this paper. The literature so far has not given uncontested evidence to this effect (see van Oostendorp 2005 for more discussion).

The structure of the argumentation is as follows. I will first set out to show that Consistency of Exponence is implicit in much of the current literature: people routinely invoke constraints which assume that the morphological affiliation of phonological material cannot be changed (section 1.2); and furthermore, the only published attacks on Consistency of Exponence, proposing to make it a violable constraint rather than a restriction on GEN, are not succesful (1.3). Having thus established that Consistency of Exponence seems to be a principle restricting GEN, I turn to Derived Environment Effects and show how these can be captured in a model which takes Consistency of Exponence seriously. It will turn out that we can formulate the relevant constraint without problems, assuming that morphological affiliation is a visible property.

1.2. The need for colours

Consistency of Exponence is not often referred to in the literature, but there are a few exceptions. In the first place, there is a fairly large amount of literature which refers to the morphological colours implicitly, using constraints which do not make sense if we can freely change the morphological status of morphemes. In the second place, there are a few explicit rejections of Consistency of Exponence in the literature.

Among the examples of constraint families which crucially use the unchangeability of morphological affiliation are positional faithfulness constraints such as FAITH-root and FAITH-affix. McCarthy and Prince (1995) cite several examples of this:

(7) a. *Turkish vowels are distinctively [±back] in roots, but not in affixes*
IDENT$_{Root}$(back) ≫ *[back] ≫ IDENT$_{Affix}$(back)
b. *Sanskrit roots contain onset clusters, but affixes do not*
MAX$_{Root}$ ≫ *COMPLEX ≫ MAX$_{Affix}$
c. *Arabic roots contain pharyngeals, but affixes do not*
IDENT$_{Root}$(Place) ≫ *[Pharyngeal] ≫ IDENT$_{Affix}$(Place)

In Dutch (as in most Germanic languages), inflectional affixes only contain coronal consonants, whereas in roots we can distinguish three places of articulation (coronal, labial, velar). This could be described in terms of the following ranking:

(8)   IDENT_Root(Place) ≫ *[velar], *[labial] ≫ IDENT_Affix(Place) ≫ *[coronal]

Yet if GEN could freely change the morphological status of segments, it could change every root consonant into an affix consonant, and then reduce it; this would actually be the preferred winner (in the following tableau the subscript 'r' stands for 'root' and 'a' for 'affix'; I assumed the nonsensical suffix -/p/ for illustrative purposes):

(9)

/spɛm/ 'to spam' -/p/ 3SG	IDENT_R	*[labial]	IDENT_A	*[coronal]
s_r p_r ɛ_r m_r p_a		*!**		*
✘ s_r p_r ɛ_r m_r t_a		*!*	*	**
s_r t_r ɛ_r n_r t_a	*!*		*	****
☞ s_a t_a ɛ_r n_a t_a			***	****

In this tableau, ✘ marks the candidate which should win; however, it is bested in this analysis by the candidate marked with ☞, in which all segments have turned affixal.

A potential way out of this would be to have root and affix faithfulness constraints refer to the *underlying* morphological status of phonological material only. Under such assumptions, which can be implemented in Correspondence Theory, the morphological status no longer has to be visible in the output form in the form of colours. But constraints would still be sensitive to colours in the input.

This means that, even if we allow our GEN function to change the morphological status of segments, we have to restrict our theory such that only the underlying morphological status is visible for the constraints. The changes that GEN makes to this are thus vacuous, since they are never going to affect constraint violation. In other words, the constraints only see *consistent* exponence of morphemes. Consistency of Exponence is thus still satisfied: since containment follows logically from this, Correspondence Theory is thus superfluous.

Another example is provided by the FAITH-Noun constraint family of Smith (2001) and related work. Smith observes that nouns usually allow for more contrasts than other categories, and she implements this by having a special faithfulness constraint on nouns. But again, if GEN is allowed to change the label "Verb" into the label "Noun" for free, FAITH-Noun cannot do any work.

Finally, also constraints aligning morphological to phonological structure such as ALIGN-(M, Φ) (sometimes referred to as ANCHOR) have to rely on a stable morphological affiliation of phonological material during the phonological derivation. In German and (The Netherlands) Dutch, prefix-stem boundaries cannot be crossed by syllable boundaries, so that a Dutch form like *op+eet* 'eat up' is pronounced as [ɔp.et], not as *[ɔ.peet] (McCarthy and Prince 1993a).[5] A constraint aligning the lefthand side boundary of stems to the lefthand side boundary of phonological word (ALIGN(R, ω)) may be considered responsible for this. Again, if we would be allowed to freely change the status of morphological material, this would change the analysis completely:

(10)

/op/ + /et/	ALIGN(R, ω)	ONSET
✘ ɔₐpₐ.eᵣtᵣ		*!
ɔₐ.pₐeᵣtᵣ	*!	
☞ ɔᵣpᵣeᵣtᵣ		

Whether or not we want to be able to formalize all these distinctions, is an empirical matter; but we can only formalize them if we keep track of the morphological status of segments. Of course there is one alternative to restricting GEN by Consistency of Exponence, and this is by introducing a violable constraint into CON which does the same job: this constraint would be high ranked in the cases just discussed. We will turn to this alternative now.

1.3. Attacks on Consistency of Exponence

Even though Consistency of Exponence is usually ignored in the literature, the only explicit attacks against it of which I am aware are Walker and Feng (2004) and Łubowicz (2005). These authors suggest that Consistency of Exponence is not a restriction of GEN, but a set of violable constraints in CON, controlling the output of GEN. GEN will be able to change the morphological affiliation of phonological material, but in many cases these constraints will filter out candidates with those changes. The argumentation in favour of such a position should be that Consistency of Exponence is sometimes violated by a winner candidate in some natural language; this is the type of argument Walker and Feng provide.

The data are from Anxiang, a Chinese dialect spoken in the Hunan Province in central China. In this dialect, a diminutive is formed of a noun by adding Cər, where C is a copy of the stem consonant, and ə an epenthetic vowel.

(11)

Stem	Diminutive	Gloss
pʰa	pʰapər	'claw'
ke	kekər	'square'
to	totər	'pile'
pʰwu	pʰwupʰwər	'shop'
pʰau	pʰaupʰər	'bulb'

The diminutive form thus consists of the stem, a copy of the consonant of the stem, a schwa and an /r/. Since the schwa may be considered an epenthetic vowel, Walker and Feng assume that the underlying structure of the diminutive suffix is /r/.

Walker and Feng (2004) argue that we need two constraints for our analysis of these facts. First we have the following constraint on the morphology-phonology interface:

(12) ALIGN[σ]: 'Each morpheme should occupy exactly one syllable and *vice versa*'

This constraint is argued to be a very general one on the phonology-morphology interface in this dialect of Chinese in which every morpheme has the size of exactly one syllable – and every syllable therefore corresponds to exactly one morpheme.

Next to this well-formedness constraint, Walker and Feng (2004) propose the following faithfulness constraint, which is essentially a violable version of Consistency of Exponence:

(13) IDENT-MM: 'Let α be a morpheme in the input, and β be its correspondent morpheme in the output. If α has phonological content ϕ, then β has phonological content ϕ and *vice versa*.'

In order to show that IDENT-MM is not a restriction on GEN, we need to show that it is sometimes violated in the winning candidate. This is exactly what happens in Anxiang, according to Walker and Feng (2004), as illustrated by the following tableau:

(14)

ke₁, r₂	ALIGN[σ]	IDENT-MM
a. [ke]₁[r]₂	*!	
b. [ke]₁kə[r]₂	*!	
☞ c. [ke]₁[kər]₂		*

The winning candidate here is the one in which the 'copied' consonant and the epenthetic vowel have become part of the morpheme on the surface. This would prove that Consistency of Exponence is indeed violable.

Yet very much depends on our interpretation of the constraint ALIGN[σ]. Under one interpretation, we could argue that this constraint is violated in (14a) both by the morpheme *ke-* and by the morpheme *-r* – because neither corresponds exactly to one syllable –, so this form has two violations of that constraint. On the other hand, (14b) has only one (for *r*, but not for *ke*). This means that even if we do not take (14c) into consideration (because this is not generated under Consistency of Exponence) the correct surface string *kekər* would still win.

(15)

ke₁, r₂	ALIGN[σ]	IDENT-MM
a. [ke]₁[r]₂	**!	
☞ b. [ke]₁kə[r]₂	*	

Although it is a little less explicit, another proposal for a violable interpretation of Consistency of Exponence can be found in Łubowicz (2005), who analyzes phenomena in Palauan and Akkadian, and argues that these should be understood as the result of 'morpheme absorption': infixed elements become part of the morphological stem. I will discuss the Palauan facts here, but I believe a similar reanalysis can be made for Akkadian.

In Palauan, then, there is a morpheme /m(ə)/ which behaves sometimes as a prefix and sometimes as an infix; the status of the schwa is irrelevant. Łubowicz (2005) argues that the choice between these two options is non-phonological and made on morphological grounds only.

(16)

Prefixation	dakt	'fear'		mə-dakt	'be/get fearful'
	rur	'shame'		mə-rur	'be/get ashamed'
Infixation	láŋəl	'crying'		l-m-áŋəl	'cry'
	rurt	'running'		rə-m-urt	'run'

The prefix and the infix behave differently with respect to one phonological phenomenon: (long distance) dissimilation. If the verb already contains a labial consonant, the infix nasal turns into a rounded vowel [u], whereas the prefix nasal is not affected:

(17)
Prefixation	dub	'poison'		mə-dub	'be/get poisoned/ bombed'
	kimud	'cut hair'		mə-rur	'been cut (hair)'
Infixation	rébət	'action of falling'		r-u-ébət	'fall (from)'
	ʔárm	'suffering'		ʔ-u-árəm	'suffer'

Łubowicz (2005) claims that the relevant constraint is a version of the OCP indexed for morphological category:

(18) OCP_{root}(C-lab): Avoid more than one labial consonant in the root domain.

The idea is that this constraint is violated in the infixed cases, but not in the prefixed cases. But this idea only makes sense if the infix is part of the root (it has been 'absorbed' by it), whereas the prefix stays outside.

In order to get this effect, Łubowicz (2005) invokes two constraints: one is a violable version of Consistency of Exponence, which she dubs MORPHEME-DEPENDENCE (M-DEP), and another constraint MORPHEME-LOCALITY (M-LOC) which disallows discontinuous morphemes:

(19) a. M-DEP: Let M_i be a morpheme and S_j be a phonological element in two related morpho-phonological representations, M_1 and S_1 ∈ Input, M_2 and S_2 ∈ Output, $M_1 \mathscr{R} M_2$, and $S_1 \mathscr{R} S_2$, If $S_2 \in M_2$, then $S_1 \in M_1$.
b. M-LOC: Let M be a morpheme, and xyz be segments, where xyz ∈ Output: If xyz are adjacent, and $x \in M \wedge z \in M$, then $y \in M$

A ranking M-LOC≫M-DEP gives the right morphological parsing (given that the status of the morpheme as an infix is predetermined by the morphology):

(20) a.

/l-m-atk/	M-LOC	M-DEP
☞ [lmatk]		*
[l[m]atk]	*!	

b.

/m-dakt/	M-Loc	M-Dep
☞ [mə][dakt]		*!
[mədakt]		

In (20a), the morphology has decided that /m/ is an infix; however, M-Loc does not like to see infixes at the surface, and it therefore turns the segment into a part of the stem, creating a violation of M-Dep. On the other hand, there is no potential problem with M-Loc in (20b), so that in this case M-Dep (=Consistency of Exponence) decides.

This analysis has to determine the placement of affixes as infix or prefix *before* any phonology can take place. The reason for this is that in the output form [lmatk], the morphology would no longer be able to check that /m/ has indeed turned into an infix: as a matter of fact the relevant adjectivising suffix has become completely invisible, since it is 'absorbed' by the stem. This means that morphological constraints can no longer be operative at this level. This implies a type of serialism however – doing morphology before phonology – which runs counter to one central tenet of classical OT, where the placement of affixes can be determined by the interaction of phonological and morphological constraints (Prince and Smolensky (1993); see also Golston (1995)).

Given this architecture of the grammar, it is furthermore unclear why we need to have morphological structure in the output of the phonological module at all. The morphological constraints are no longer operative at this level, so why would we need to see the difference between stems and affixes at all? The answer to this is: because phonological constraints like OCP_{root}(C-lab) need to see them. But this actually turns the root in these cases into a purely prosodic category, which is only there to establish the domain of phonological phenomena.

If that is the case, however, we might just as well abandon the problematic assumption that morphological grammar precedes phonological grammar, and reformulate the OCP constraint directly into prosodic terms:[6]

(21) OCP_{PW}(C-lab): Avoid more than one labial consonant in the phonological word.

In this case, we will have to make sure that infixes become part of the phonological word, whereas prefixes stay outside. We do not need to relativize Consistency of Exponence for this, however. Under the assumption that embedded phonological word structures such as (22a) are universally impossible, we only need a constraint for Alignment of phonological and morphological categories. And even if we would allow GEN to produce structures such as this, we could still have a high-ranking constraint against such center-embedding phonological structures, parallelling Łubowicz (2005)'s M-LOC.

(22) a.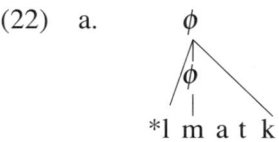
   b. Φ-LOC: Phonological words must be contiguous (=M-LOC, applied to phonological words).
   c. ALIGN: The edges of a morpheme should correspond to the edges of a phonological word.

We can now build exact parallels to the structures in (20).

(23) a.

/latk/+/m/	Φ-LOC	ALIGN
☞ (lmatk)		**
(l(m)atk)	*!	

b.

/dakt/+/m/	Φ-LOC	ALIGN
☞ (mə)(dakt)		
(mədakt)		*!

The first candidate in (23a) violates ALIGN since there is a morpheme boundary which does not correspond to a phonological word boundary. As a matter of fact there are two such 'illicit' boundaries (both before and after the morpheme). Yet there is no way to not violate ALIGN in this case, without violating higher-ranking Φ-LOC. In the case of (23b), on the other hand, we can satisfy both constraints by keeping the prefix and the stem separate, following a strong cross-linguistic trend for boundaries between prefixes and stems to have strong phonological correlates (Booij and Rubach 1984, 1990).[7]

I believe that this analysis is not just a notational variant of the one which turns Consistency of Exponence into a violable constraint. It is conceptually superior to because it interleaves morphological and phonological constraints in a way that is well-established and does not use morphological categories as phonological diacritics. Instead, it uses the category of the phonological word, which is independently needed. We thus see that neither Walker and Feng (2004)'s nor Łubowicz (2005)'s attempt to turn Consistency of Exponence into a violable constraint is very succesful. From this we conclude that its status as a restriction on GEN is uncontested.

2. Derived Environment Effects and colouring

2.1. Some examples of derived environment effects

One important aspect of the phonology-morphology interface which has been discovered in the second half of the twentieth century, is that some phonological processes only apply in derived environments, that is to say, they do not apply to underlying monomorphemic forms (Kiparsky 1973, 1993; Kenstowicz and Kisseberth 1977, Anttila 2005). Traditionally, two types of derived environment are recognized: phonologically and morphologically derived environments. Morphologically derived environments consist of material from more than one morpheme. Phonologically derived environments can be monomorphemic, but at least one of the elements has to be created by an earlier phonological rule or process. In so far as these effects are real, phonological theory needs to account for them, and I propose that Coloured Containment is optimally suitable for that.

In order to illustrate this point, I will consider five rather well-known instances of Derived Environment Effects (DEE), from Korean, Turkish, Finnish, and Polish.

Korean has a rule of *palatalisation*, affecting coronal stops before front high vowels, roughly formulated as in (24a) and illustrated in (24b). This rule only applies across morpheme boundaries however; it does not apply in the form in (24c), where the /t/ and /i/ are already adjacent at the underlying level (Iverson 1993; Polgárdi 1998; Rhee 2002, to mention just a few recent sources).

(24) a. t, t^h → tʃ, tʃ^h / __ i
　　 b. hæ tot+i → hæ doʥi 'sunrise-NOM'
　　 c. mati → madi 'knot'

The second example comes from Vowel Harmony in Turkish. As is well known, Turkish has both backness and roundness harmony (subject to different phonological constraints) (25a). Roots can be disharmonic; although the forms in (25b) are of foreign etymology, they have been integrated into the Turkish phonology in other respects. (25c) shows that epenthetic vowels are sensitive to vowel harmony.

(25) a.

	nom.sg.	gen.sg.	nom.pl.	gen.pl.
'rope'	ip	ipin	ipler	iplerin
'girl'	kız	kızın	kızlar	kızların
'face'	yüz	yüzün	yüzler	yüzlerin

b. *vali* 'governor', *ķitap* 'book', *hareket* 'movement', *hesap* 'bank account', *bobin* 'spool'

c.

	careful form	colloquial form
'fetters'	pranga	pıranga
'cruiser'	kruvazör	kuruvazör

We can see this blocking of productive harmony to roots as a DEE. The fact that a vowel within a root can be subject to harmony only if it is epenthetic lends further credence to such a view.

A third example of a DEE comes from Colloquial Helsinki Finnish Vowel Coalescence, as has been demonstrated by Anttila (2005). This particular dialect of Finnish has a rule of Vowel Coalescence, which turns /makea/ 'sweet' for instance into [má.keː]; the rule is optional, so that [má.ke.a] is also possible. I assume that in vowel coalescence, all the features of one vowel spread onto the other vowel position.

Anttila (2005) notes that Vowel Coalescence is subject to a quantitative DEE effect:

- Vowel Coalescence is categorically blocked in **non-derived environments** if the structural change is highly marked. If the structural change is unmarked, it may apply.

- Vowel Coalescence is quantitatively dispreferred in **derived environments** if the structural change is highly marked. If the structural change is unmarked, it is quantitatively preferred.

All in all, we will thus find more vowel coalescence in derived environments. There is vowel coalescence in underived environments as well, but it is much less frequent. It is quite interesting that there is quantitative variation of this type, and Anttila (2005) offers an analysis of the statistic effect, which falls beyond the scope of our present concerns. But the fact that there is variation of this quantitative type at all, shows that the DEE is real within the synchronic grammar of Finnish. There is a way in which coalescence is perfectly acceptable in derived environments, while it is less acceptable in underived environments.

A fourth example of a DEE is Polish Spirantisation (Rubach 1984); as a matter of fact this is at present probably the most widely discussed instance of this phenomenon within Optimality Theory because of the work of Łubowicz (2002, 2005). The process is slightly more complicated: an underlying /g/ turns into a [ʒ] before an [e]. This can be seen as palatalisation of /g/ to [j], and subsequent spirantisation to [ʒ] (26a). It is this spirantisation which is subject to a DEE, since underlying /j/ does not undergo it (26b).

(26) a. /rog+ek/ → [roʒek], *[rojek]
     b. /brij+ek/ → [brijek]

2.2. Colours show Derived Environments

Now that we have set up a catalogue of (hopefully representative) examples, we will build an analysis of DEE in constraint-based theory. In order to do this, we need to be able to evaluate both input and outputs. We thus need aspects of both faithfulness and markedness. I argue that the advantage of Coloured Containment is that it offers both in one representation, while in Correspondence, on the other hand, the separation between F and M is too large, causing problems of locality.

From the rule-based work on DEE, we know that there are several correlates to DEE-sensitivity (lexical rules, structure-building, etc) but also that there are problems with these diagnostics. I propose a different diagnostic here: DEE will always involve spreading. This seems to be tenable at least for the examples studied here.

The application of Coloured Containment to DEE can be easily illustrated on the basis of Turkish. Consider the form in (27), the genitive of the word *kruvazör* 'cruiser', with an epenthetic vowel inserted within the first cluster, and a suffix -*ın* added at the end (we use the subscripts 'r' for 'root' and 'a' for 'affix' for mnemotechnic convenience)

Now let us compare those structures which are allowed, to those which are not (28).

138   Marc van Oostendorp

(27) k_r 1 r_r u_r v_r a_r z_r $ö_r$ r_r l_a n_a

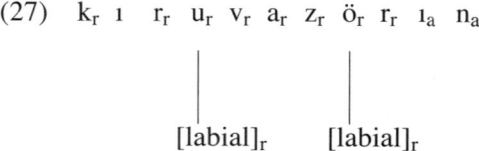

(28)

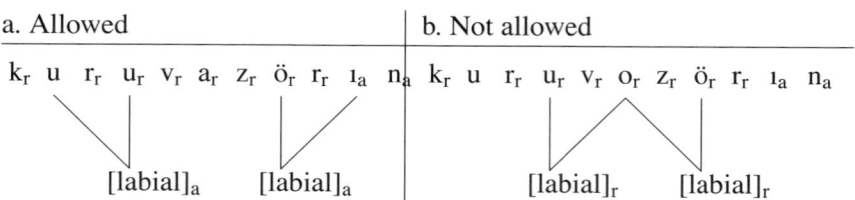

A comparison of these forms teaches us that it is possible to associate a feature and a segment of different colour (either because the segment is epenthetic or because the feature is in a different morpheme than the segment), but it is not possible to associate a feature and a segment of the same colour. On the other hand, we obviously do not want our constraint to disallow underlying associations between segments and features, such as that between the two /u/ segments and their feature [labial].

One way of implementing this would be to assume that association lines, like other elements of a phonological representation have a morphological colour. If an association line is underlying, it has the colour of the morpheme to which it belongs; if it is not underlying, it does not have a colour. Revithiadou (2007) provides a better formalisation of this, but for our purposes the following constraint will suffice:

(29)   ALTERNATION: If an association line links two elements of colour α, the line should also have colour α.

The structure in (28b) violates this constraint since it links the feature [labial] to a segmental node which is in the same morpheme, hence has the same colour. The structure in (28a) on the other hand is fine, since the features and the segments to which they are linked have the same colour. The underlying association lines in both structures have the same colour as the elements they link (by definition) and hence they are fine as well.

This analysis can be easily extended to the other languages we have discussed. Compare for instance the licit form of palatalisation in Korean on the lefthand side and the illicit form on the righthand side.

(30)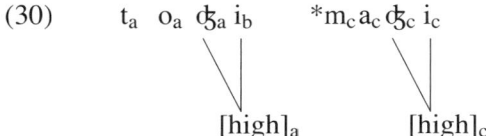

The form on the righthand side is characterised by a new (colourless) association line linking two elements of the same colour, which is not allowed by ALTERNATION. In the form on the lefthand side, on the other hand, the two elements which are linked have different colours, hence the association line is allowed.

Similarly, it becomes quite clear what happens in Finnish once we draw the right association lines. Remember that we are dealing in this case with vowel coalescence, and we are assuming that this means that all features of one vowel spread onto the other vocalic position.

(31)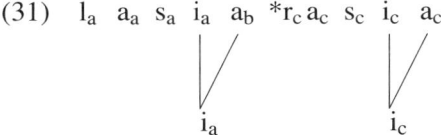

Again, the preferred structure is characterized by new association lines linking elements of different colours, whereas the dispreferred structure has a new link between material which is already underlyingly present in the same morpheme.

The situation is a bit complicated in this case by the fact that we are dealing with statistical preferences rather than an absolute categorical distinction. Anttila (2005) proposes to deal with these preferences by way of variable constraint ranking. Suppose we have three constraints $\mathscr{C}_1$, $\mathscr{C}_2$ and $\mathscr{C}_3$. These constraints can be ranked in six different ways. Suppose furthermore, that given an input α, four of these rankings give an output β, whereas the remaining two rankings give an output γ. We predict that this will correspond to twice as many β than γ in the input.

In this case, it could be the constraint ALTERNATION which is ranked in a variable way. If it is ranked very low, vowel coalescence will be allowed both in derived environments and in non-derived environments. If it is ranked very high, it will block coalescence in non-derived environments but not in derived environments. This is how we get a difference in preference.[8]

In this approach, there thus is no qualitative difference between phonologically and morphologically derived environments. In both cases there is a difference in colour; in phonologically derived environments since one of the elements is epenthetic, i.e. colourless, and in morphologically derived environments since different morphemes each contribute their own colour.

The situation is a little more complicated for the case of Polish spirantisation. In the examples just discussed, a whole segment was 'new', either because it was phonologically derived or because it belonged to a different morpheme. In Polish, this is not the case: the difference between [roʒek], *[rojek] and [brijek] is not that the former contains a new segment in any sense in which the latter does not. The difference is that the former contains a segment which has been *changed*.

In order to describe this properly, then, we need to resort to Feature Geometry and assume that ALTERNATE works at a subsegmental level in this language.

An independent advantage of introducing Feature Geometry, may be that it allows us to express the intimate connection between [continuant] and Place. Within other approaches to the Polish facts (such as Łubowicz 2002, 2005) it is essentially a coincidence that the derived environment for spirantisation – a change in [continuant] – is created by palatalisation – a change in Place feature specification. However, it is well known that there is an intimate connection between these features, which has been expressed in various ways; here we will choose the analysis of Padgett (1991), according which [continuant] depends on the Place features (so it can be a daughter of Coronal, Velar or Labial).

A few more representational assumptions are in order. In line with a very long-standing tradition, we assume that palatalisation is 'assimilation' with the vowel on the righthand side. With Rubach (1984) we also assume that the relevant context for spirantization is the lefthand side, since it happens after vowels and sonorants, but not after obstruents.

(32) a. róg 'horn' → ro[ʒ]ek (DIM), potęga 'power' → potę[ʒ]ny (ADJ),
 b. skarga 'complaint' → skar[ʒ]yć 'complain'

I will assume that this is progressive assimilation of continuancy (cf. Mascaró 1983; Harris 1984).

To fully understand what happens in Polish, it is useful to first study the structure of these two words when only palatalisation has applied:

(33)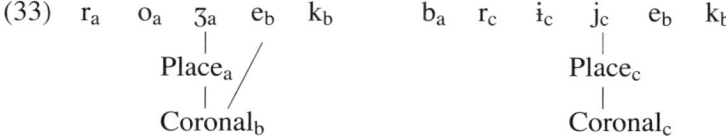

In the case of /rog+ek/, the Coronal feature will spread from the /e/ to the /g/, perhaps because of a constraint which disallows a configuration of a non-palatalized velar consonant followed by a front vowel. This spreading conforms to the constraint ALTERNATION. For /brıjek/, no change is necessary, since the structure already conforms to all well-formedness constraints. Now we extend the structure and look at the interaction of this with spirantisation.

(34)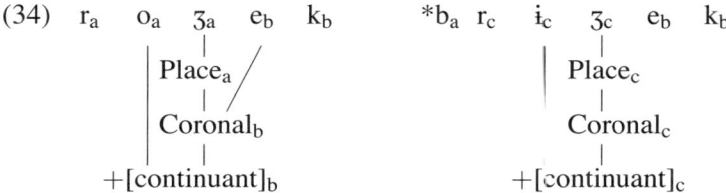

Spirantisation is allowed in [roʒek], since the feature [continuant] links to a feature [Coronal] which has a different colour. Spirantisation is not allowed in [brıjek], on the other hand, since the place feature and [continuant] have the same colour in this case.

We have thus seen that all cases of DEE from the previous section are the result of implementing a feature spreading analysis in a Coloured Containment frame. It remains to be seen whether this is true for all DEE, and if not, how other cases are to be analysed. This also requires a theory of faithfulness to association lines, possibly one which is based on Turbidity Theory (Goldrick 2000; see Revithiadou 2007).

2.3. Comparison to other models

Hitherto, various analyses have been proposed to deal with DEE within Optimality Theory, usually based on Correspondence models of faithfulness. We will briefly discuss these alternatives, in order to compare them with the analysis just proposed. By necessity, all these models share some mixing of faithfulness and markedness: we are talking about derived environments, hence phonological environments which are derived (faithfulness) and require some phonological process to apply (markedness).

The most well-known analysis of DEE within OT is couched in terms of Constraint Conjunction (Łubowicz 2000). Under this approach, DEE are seen as the result of conjunction of Faithfulness and Markedness constraints. For the Polish case we have discussed, this is [*ʤ&IDENT-[CORONAL]]$_{segment}$, i.e. a markedness constraint requiring spirantisation which is coupled with a faithfulness constraint on palatalisation: if this constraint is high-ranked, only those instances of [ʤ] which are the result of palatalisation (hence, which invoke a violation of IDENT-[coronal]) will be subjected to this constraint.

Several objections can be raised against this account. We have already pointed out that the linking of spirantisation and palatalisation is purely accidental for this account, since any two constraints could be linked. In as far as these processes are indeed intimately linked, the explanation should come from outside the theory of constraint conjunction – possibly from some form of phonetic grounding, although it is not clear how grounding could interact with a purely formal operation such as constraint conjunction. In the Coloured Containment model, only features which are linked in the Feature Geometry can establish a relation of this type.

Further, Constraint Conjunction did not have a theory of locality its original formulation. There is no principled reason why it refers to a violation of *ʤ and of IDENT-[coronal] within the same segment. This unrestrictiveness predicted unattested long-distance effects. For instance, if we assume that [*ʤ&IDENT-[CORONAL]]$_{word}$ would be conjoined within the domain of the word in some language, we would get the effect that palatalisation of a consonant at the end of the word could cause spirantisation of a consonant at the beginning of the word. We thus could get derivations of the following type:

(35)   ʤem+ik+ek → ʒemičhek

These derivations seem unattested, however, and we therefore want to rule them out. A proposal to this effect is provided by Łubowicz (2005) using McCarthy's (2003) idea of a so-called *locus function*. The details of this are not important here, but essentially this minimizes the domain of all constraints to the segment: only segments can violate constraints. This restriction seems too general: it is certainly incompatible with the assumption of autosegmental representations. On the other hand, within Coloured Containment, the locality comes for free: palatalisation of one segment in a word will have no representational effect on another palatal in the same word, so a derivation as in (35) can never be derived.

A second approach to DEE in the existing literature, is *Comparative Markedness* (CM, McCarthy 2003). Like Coloured Containment, CM refers to differences between 'old' and 'new' material, but it is couched in a Correspondence framework. The central idea of CM is that markedness constraints can refer to 'old' violations (those already underlyingly present) vs. 'new' violations (those created by GEN). To be precise, for every traditional markedness constraint, CM posits two versions: one referring only to old violations, and one only to new violations. In the case of Polish, this would involve for instance a high ranking constraint *$ʤ_{New}$: old /ʤ/ is unaffected by this constraint, but those instances of [ʤ], for instance created by palatalisation, are ruled out by it.

CM is in a certain sense a Correspondence sister (or historically and genetically, a mother) of Coloured Containment theory. Like Constraint Conjunction, CM is however crucially based on the Locus function, which, as we have seen, is incompatible with autosegmental representations. Opinions may of course differ as to whether this is a positive or a negative aspect of the theory, but in the presence of an overwhelming amount of evidence in favour of autosegmental representations, we consider it wise to be conservative.

Furthermore, in order to describe cases of morphologically DEE, CM has to refer to a very special version of 'newness', viz. Output-Output$_{New}$, satisfied if the violation was not yet there in the underived word. However, introduction of such a constraint type implies simultaneous introduction of a constraint referring to Output-Output$_{Old}$, i.e. violations which only count if there is a base form in which they are already present. This has the undesirable result of deriving anticyclicity. For instance, we predict a language like Turkish*, which is like Turkish, except that we find spreading of [−back] only in embedded domains.

(36) a. Underived form for /kitap/ 'book': *kitap*
b. Derived form: *kitep-lar* (SPREAD$_{Old}$ applies to stem element, which has a base, but not to suffix, which is new).
c. Derived form: *kitep-ler-an* (SPREAD$_{Old}$ applies to *kitepler*, which has a base, but not to the whole word)

Patterns like this have not been attested, and this seems an undesirable result of CM.

A third approach, *Root Faithfulness* is proposed as a device to describe Derived Environment Effects in Anttila (2005). This gives very similar effects as Coloured Containment; for instance, both suffix vowels and epenthetic vowels in Turkish are not part of the root. If we assume FAITH-Root ≫ SPREAD, this is why they can both assimilate, whereas vowels in the root are blocked from doing so.

It comes as no surprise that the two approaches yield similar results. We have seen in section 1.2 that Root Faithfulness constraints need an idea of morphological colour for their implementation. Inversely, Coloured Containment can be seen as an implementation of Root Faithfulness.

It is not clear, however, how we could derive the phonological derived environment effects of Polish in a Root Faithfulness approach, without taking recourse to more sophisticated phonological representations, since [±continuant] and [Coronal] represent different dimensions from the point of view of autosegmental phonology.

3. Conclusions

In this article, I have defended the classical assumption that Consistency of Exponence restricts the Generator function. I have shown that this assumption is needed in the interpretation of various constraints which are available in the literature, and that objections which have recently been raised to it are not strong enough to abandon this assumption.

Consistency of Exponence expresses a generalisation about the interaction between phonology on the one hand and morphology and syntax on the other which seems quite strong: phonology cannot influence morphology or syntax. Phonology can decide to interpret morphemes in some way, but it cannot decide that the vowel at the end of one syntactic word will be at the beginning of the next syntactic word instead.

It should be noted that it follows from Consistency of Exponence that Correspondence is probably superfluous. The output representations are already very rich under Consistency of Exponence, so that we do not need to refer to overly abstract correspondence relations with an independent input representation. Certain types of opacity also follow from containment. Consistency of Exponence thus leads us to adapt a purely monostratal model, one in which all constraints refer to one representation only.

An important goal of this article was to argue that Derived Environment Effects are basically expected under Coloured Containment, at least in as far as they can be seen as involving the spreading of features.

A final important note is that none of these claims can be evaluated without some basic assumptions about phonological representations. Since we are dealing with a monostratal model, we will have to read off the faithfulness status of a given segment from its representation. Whereas a Correspondence-based model of faithfulness is basically independent from the internal structure of the input and output representations. The only requirement is that the representations consist of discrete elements which can be related to each other. This is not true for Containment models, where there is an intimate link between markedness and faithfulness. It is this link which allows us to express Derived Environment Effects, but it is also this link which makes a very precise reconsideration of representations necessary. We consider this to be a positive aspect, since it makes the theory into a tighter unit, where subtle changes in one assumption will have implications for many other aspects of the analysis. Phonological analysis becomes more difficult because of this, but that is not necessarily a bad thing.

Notes

* Thanks are due to Ben Hermans, Anthi Revithiadou, Christian Uffmann, the audiences at my talks in Tromsø, August 2005 and London, December 2005 and the reviewers and editors. All errors are mine.
1. The idea of Containment predates Consistency of Exponence, as it is found already in Prince and Smolensky (1993). The term Containment is from McCarthy and Prince (1993b,1994).
2. See Blaho and Bye (2005) for a partially similar approach, rooted in Correspondence Theory.
3. A third principle governing GEN is *Freedom of Analysis*: "posit any amount of structure". Freedom of Analysis can hardly be seen as a restriction on GEN.
4. Logically speaking, there are a few cases where the two principles work differently. Consider for instance the case of an underlying segment without morphological affiliation, in other words an 'underlying epenthetic segment' (this point has been brought to my attention by Curt Rice, p.c.). Containment would disallow deletion of such a segment, whereas Consistency of Exponence would not. It is unclear, at present, whether such devices as underlying epenthetic segments are ever really needed in phonological analysis, and thus, whether an independent status for Containment is warranted.
5. See Noske (2005) for an argument that in Flemish syllables may cross morpheme boundaries.
6. I am not claiming that the OCP could not refer to roots in some cases, but only that it

does not need to refer to the morphological category of a root in cases like this, where it could also refer to the prosodic word.
7. Notice that it has to be assumed here, as in Łubowicz (2005) that independent, higher-ranking and purely morphological constraints decide that the morpheme is an infix in (23a) and a prefix in (23b).
8. This sketches only a rough approximation of the relevant facts. See Anttila (2005) for a more precise approach, which can easily be made compatible with the present proposal.

References

Anttila, Arto
2005 Derived environment effects in colloquial Helsinki Finnish. To appear in *Festschrift for Kiparsky*.

Blaho, Sylvia, and Patrik Bye
2005 Cryptosonorants and the misapplication of voicing assimilation in Biaspectual Phonology. To appear in *Proceedings of the 31st Annual Meeting of the Berkeley Linguistics Society*, Yuni Kim (ed.). ROA 759.

Booij, Geert, and Jerzy Rubach
1984 Morphological and prosodic domains in lexical phonology. In *Phonology Yearbook* 1:1–27.

Goldrick, Matthew
2000 Turbid output representations and the unity of opacity. *Proceedings of the 30th Meeting of the North East Linguistic Society*, Masako Hirotani, Andries Coetzee, Nancy Hall, and Ji-yung Kim (eds.), 231–245. Amherst, Mass.: GLSA. ROA 368.

Golston, Chris
1995 Syntax outranks phonology: Evidence from Ancient Greek. *Phonology* 12:343–368.
2007 Variables in Optimality Theory. This volume.

Harris, James
1984 La espirantización en castellano y su representación fonológica autosegmental. In *Estudis grammaticals*, Bartra et al. (eds.), 149–167. Universitat Autònoma de Barcelona.

Iverson, Gregory
1993 (Post)lexical rule application. In *Studies in lexical phonology* 4, Sharon Hargus and Ellen Kaisse (eds.), 255–275. San Diego: Academic Press.

Kenstowicz, Michael, and Charles Kisseberth
1977 *Topics in Phonological Theory*. New York: Academic Press.

Kiparsky, Paul
1973. Abstractness, opacity, and global rules. In *Three Dimensions of Linguistic Theory*, Osamu Fujimura (ed.), 5–56. Tokyo: TEC.
1993 Blocking in non-derived environments. In *Studies in Lexical Phonology*, ed. Sharon Hargus and Ellen Kaisse. San Diego, Cal.: Academic Press.

Łubowicz, Anna
2000. Derived environment effects in Optimality Theory. *Lingua* 112:243–280.

2002	Contrast preservation in phonological mappings. Ph.D. diss., University of Massachusetts at Amherst.
2005a	Infixation as morpheme absorption. ROA 773.
2005b	Locality of conjunction. In *Proceedings of the 24th West Coast Conference on Formal Linguistics*, John Alderete, Chung-hye Han, and Alexei Kochetov (eds.), 254–262. Somerville, Mass.: Cascadilla Press.

Mascaró, Joan
1983   Three Spanish variations and a Majorcan theme. Ms., Universitat Autònoma de Barcelona.

McCarthy, John J.
2003   Comparative markedness. *Theoretical Linguistics* 29:1–51.

McCarthy, John J., and Alan S. Prince
1993a   Generalized Alignment. In *Yearbook of Morphology*, Geert Booij and Jaap van Marle (eds.), 79–153. Dordrecht: Kluwer.
1993b   Prosodic Morphology: constraint interaction and satisfaction. ROA 485.
1994   The emergence of the unmarked: Optimality in prosodic morphology. *Proceedings of the 24th Annual Meeting of the North East Linguistic Society*, Mercè Gonzalez (ed.), 333–379.
1995a   Faithfulness and reduplicative identity. *University of Massachusetts Occasional Papers* 18:249–384.

Noske, Roland
2005   A prosodic contrast between northern and southern Dutch: A result of a Flemish-French *Sprachbund*. In *Organizing Grammar. Linguistic Studies in Honor of Henk van Riemsdijk*, Hans Broekhuis, Norbert Corver, Riny Huybregts, Ursula Kleinhenz, and Jan Koster (eds.), 474–482. Berlin/New York: Mouton De Gruyter.

van Oostendorp, Marc
2005   The theory of faithfulness. Ms., KNAWL, Amsterdam.

Padgett, Jaye
1991   Stricture in feature geometry. Ph.D. diss., University of Massachusetts at Amherst, Amherst, Mass..

Polgárdi, Krisztina
1998   Vowel harmony. an account in terms of government and optimalityu theory. Ph.D. diss., Leiden University.

Prince, Alan S., and Paul Smolensky
1993   Optimality theory. Constraint interaction in generative grammar. Technical Report #2, Rutgers University Center for Cognitive Science. ROA 537; published in 2004 by Blackwell Publishers.

Rhee, Sang Jik
2002   Empty nuclei in Korean. Ph. D. diss., University of Leiden.

Revithiadou, Anthi
2007   Colored turbid accents and containment: A case study from lexical stress. This volume.

Rubach, Jerzy
1984   *Cyclic And Lexical Phonology. The Structure of Polish*. Dordrecht: Foris.

Rubach, Jerzy, and Geert Booij
    1990   Syllable structure assignment in Polish. *Phonology* 7:121–158.
Smith, Jennifer L.
    2001   Lexical category and phonological contrast. In *Papers in Experimental And Theoretical Linguistics 6: Workshop on the Lexicon in Phonetics and Phonology*, ed. Robert Kirchner, Joe Pater, and Wolf Wikely, 61–72. Edmonton: University of Alberta.
Walker, Rachel, and Bella Feng
    2004   A ternary model of morphology-phonology correspondence. In *Proceedings of the 23rd West Coast Conference on Formal Linguistics*, Vineeta Chand, Ann Kelleher, Angelo J. Rodríguez, Benjamin Schmeiser (eds.) 787–800. Somerville, Mass.: Cascadilla Press.

Chapter 7
Colored turbid accents and containment: A case study from lexical stress*

Anthi Revithiadou

1. Introduction

In contemporary Optimality-theoretic research (OT; Prince and Smolensky 1993), the focus has been primarily on constraint typology and the role of constraints in assessing the relative 'harmony' of candidate outputs. Representational issues and, especially, questions pertaining to possible restrictions imposed by representational assumptions on the phonological make-up of linguistic forms have received little attention. This paper aims at exploring, among other things, such restrictions on *Freedom of Analysis*. The empirical investigation focuses on lexical accent systems and, in particular, Greek and Russian. In such systems, stress can occur on any syllable of the word regardless of syllable structure, weight or edge-orientation. Accentuation can be straightforwardly accounted for only if direct reference to morphological constituent structure and the inherent accentual properties of morphemes is assumed. Although the literature is replete with examples of morpho-accentual processes[1] and discussions of the formal problems they pose for phonological theory, some issues still need to be further explored. In this paper, the focus is on the representation of lexical accents and the interface constraints that control accentuation.

There is little consensus in the literature regarding the way lexically-encoded information is represented. Most representational approaches attribute unpredictable or irregular stress to differences in the lexical specification of certain morphemes. For instance, in a language like Greek, the contrast between *monáxos* 'alone' and *monaxós* 'monk' derives from the different accentual status of the root. In the former word, the root bears an accent itself, whereas in the latter word, the root is post-accenting; that is, it places its inherent accent on the following element, i.e. the suffix *-os*. Likewise, an affix may require its inherent accent to land on the immediately preceding morpheme as in the case of the pre-accenting genitive singular ending -*u*, e.g. *anθróp-u* 'man GEN. SG.'. However, as we will show in the following sections, analyses that adopt a representational approach to lexical stress face various drawbacks at the theoretical and/or empirical level. The most important one is that they cannot provide a uniform representation and analysis for post-accentuation and pre-accentuation. Both accentual patterns share two basic properties: first, the accent always surfaces on a vowel of different morphological affiliation (migration) and, second, it never lands further than the immediately neighboring syllable (locality). Crucially, morphological affiliation and locality also characterize accent migration phenomena triggered by violations of window restrictions or deletion of vocalic material. Greek once again serves as an illustrative example. In pairs such as *fúrnaris* 'baker NOM. SG.', *furnárides* 'baker NOM. PL.', the root is lexically accented but its accent shifts one syllable to the right in the plural form in order to comply to the three-syllable window restriction. Here, accent migration is also minimal but, nevertheless, strictly limited within the morpheme it belongs to. We argue that the two types of migration, i.e. migration within the sponsoring morpheme and migration outside the sponsoring morpheme, are two different sides of the same coin and the locality effects they both exhibit are intimately related to their common origin. No previous account has managed to bring all these different aspects of lexical accentuation under the same roof and provide a uniform explanation for them. This task is undertaken in the present paper. More specifically, we propose a theory of enriched representations that builds upon Goldrick's (1998, 2000) *Turbidity Theory* (TT). A lexical accent is treated as an autosegmental feature that is associated with its sponsoring vowel by means of two relations: (a) a *projection* relation, that is, an abstract, structural relationship, part of a morpheme's lexical representation, and (b) a *pronunciation* relation which represents the output realization of structure and is subject to phonetic interpretation. We show that this dichotomy between input and output representations offers promising insights for the understanding of migration phenomena and locality effects in the distribution of accents and, more importantly, it makes accurate typological predictions about the inventory of accentual patterns crosslinguistically.

The morphology-oriented nature of lexical stress extends beyond the affiliation of lexical accents to specific morphological domains. Certain morphemes are accentually dominant in the sense that they claim stress from other morphemes within the word. For this reason, lexical accent systems provide a promising field for research on the morphology-phonology interface as well as on the typology of interface constraints. One way of explaining how morphological (and lexical) information is encoded in phonology is by means of *indexed* constraints. Anttila (2002) states that these are mainly faithfulness constraints, which are indexed to refer to various aspects of morphological structure.[2] Critics of the indexed-constraint approach, however, call attention to the fact that in practice constraints can be indexed for almost anything (Anttila 2002). Moreover, indexing is not limited to faithfulness constraints alone since nothing precludes markedness constraints from also being indexed (Inkelas and Zoll 2003). The latter constraints, however, do not regulate the relation between morphological structure and prosodic form, therefore, it is only natural to assume that they should never be allowed to refer to aspects of the interface and, accordingly, be labeled for this. We propose instead that van Oostendorp's (2004, 2007) *Colored Containment* (CC) model provides a principled basis for the formulation of interface constraints. The most important aspect of this model is that it allows phonology to 'see' the morphological affiliation, i.e. the morphological color, of phonological elements. Ideally, phonology 'mirrors' morphology in the sense that it provides enough cues to 'recover' morphological structure from prosodic form. This visibility proves valuable both for representational issues as well as for the formulation of interface constraints. We show that when such a theory is combined with a representational device such as TT, which offers the possibility to encode and track the morphological color of lexical accents by drawing a distinction between underlying structure and pronounced structure, it acquires the necessary explanatory power to successfully analyze complex morpho-accentual phenomena like the ones encountered in the languages under investigation.

To sum up, we show that the TT/CC model advanced in this paper unifies the representation of pre/post-accenting morphemes, it accounts for accent migration and locality phenomena and makes accurate typological predictions about the cross-linguistic distribution of accentual patterns. Moreover, we argue that it offers a restrictive theory of the morphology-phonology interface and, especially, the formulation of constraints that control the mapping between morphological structure and prosodic form.

The remainder of the paper is organized as follows: In section 2, we present some representative examples of Greek and Russian stress and discuss a few interesting cases of accent migration. In section 3, we review various representational accounts of lexical stress and propose an enriched representational device along the lines of TT. In section 4, we investigate a range of accent migration phenomena and provide an analysis based on the premises of CC. We also provide a more principled formulation of interface constraints than indexed-constraint accounts and offer a TT/CC analysis of lexical stress that relies on the notion of morphosyntactic headedness. An alternative analysis of the same morpho-accentual phenomena is discussed in section 5. In section 6, we conclude this paper.

2. Lexical accent systems: The facts

Greek is a bounded trochaic system; the scope of primary stress is limited to the last three syllables of the word. Syllable structure lacks distinctions of phonological weight. The same applies to Russian although the language lacks the window restriction. Words in both languages minimally consist of a root and an inflectional ending, e.g. Greek *anθrop-os* 'man', Russian *zérkal-o* 'mirror'. Representative examples from the Greek and Russian nominal system of are given in (1) and (2), respectively:

(1) a. ánθropos anθrópu   'man-NOM./GEN. SG.'
    b. θálasa   θalasón   'sea NOM. SG./GEN. PL.'
    c. fantáros fantáru   'soldier-NOM./GEN. SG.'
       stafíða   stafíðon 'raisin NOM. SG./GEN. PL.'
    d. uranós   uranú   'sky-NOM./GEN. SG.'
       aɣorá   aɣorón   'market NOM. SG./GEN. PL.'

(2) a. skovorodá skóvorody 'frying pan NOM. SG./PL.'
    b. rabóta   rabóty   'work NOM. SG./PL.'
    c. gospožá   gospoží   'lady NOM. SG./PL.'

Let us begin with the examination of the Greek stress facts. In (1), stress is located on any of the three positions allowed by the window. The examples *ánθropos*, *fantáros*, *uranós* are morphologically equivalent but differ in the location of stress. Furthermore, in examples like (1a) and (1b) stress moves from the antepenultimate syllable in nominative singular to the penultimate syllable in genitive singular (*-os* class) and the ultimate syllable in genitive plural (*-a* class), respectively. Such stress shifts reveal the internal prosodic structure of suffixes.

Greek stress can be straightforwardly accounted for by reference to the inherent metrical structure of morphemes. More specifically, three accentual classes of roots are distinguished: (a) accentless roots, e.g. /anθrop-/, which lack a pre-assigned accent; (b) accented roots, which bear an accent on some syllable e.g. /fantár-/, and (c) post-accenting roots, which carry an accent themselves but push it onto a following morpheme, e.g. /uran^-/, /aɣor^-/.[3] The same accentual typology applies to suffixes. An accentless root will be stressed by the language-specific *default* (i.e. antepenultimate stress for Greek) when combined with an equally accentless suffix. It will, however, lose stress to an inherently accented suffix. For instance, given that the roots /anθrop-/ and /θalas-/ are both accentless, the antepenultimate stress in the nominative results from the default. The stress mobility in the genitive, then, is attributed to the pre-accenting status of the suffix /-^u/ and the accented status of the suffix /-ón/, respectively. In Russian, accentuation works in a similar fashion with the difference that the default stress is initial (Halle 1973; Melvold 1990).

A few remarks with respect to post- and pre-accenting morphemes are in order at this point. In the languages under examination, such morphemes place their accent on an immediately following or preceding syllable. For instance, in the Russian word *gospož-ámi* 'lady-INSTR. PL.' the accent sponsored by the root lands on the first syllable of the suffix which is the closest one to the root. Similarly, in pre-accentuation, the accent of the suffix never docks further than the last syllable of the root, e.g. *anθróp-u* 'man GEN. SG.'. In conclusion, in both cases the accent does not migrate too far from its morpheme of origin.

As mentioned in section 1, there are more instances of accent migration besides post-/pre-accentuation that are relevant for the analysis to be developed in the ensuing sections. In Greek, window restrictions often cause an accent to move away from its original position. For instance, the word *fúrnaris* (< /fúrnar-i(ð)-s/ [root - thematic constituent - inflection]) 'baker NOM. SG.' is accented on the initial syllable but when an extra syllable is added in the plural, *furnaríðon* 'baker GEN. PL.', the distance between the accent and the right edge of the word is inevitably increased. Given the inviolability of the window, the accent must either reclaim the lost space or remain unpronounced. The surface form *furnáriðon* suggests that the latter option is chosen. It should be noted that the antepenultimate stress in this case can never originate from the default because the suffix *-on* is pre-accenting. The ungrammaticality, therefore, of a hypothetical form such as **furnaríðon* clearly shows that what keeps stress on the root is its inherent accent.

Accents may also migrate when the vowel that sponsors them deletes or loses its vocalic status. The following example from Greek is telling in this respect. The high front vowel /i/ turns into a palatal fricative before another vowel. For instance, in the genitive singular of neuter nouns, /i/ loses its vocalic status, as shown in (3b).[4] In this case, the accent moves to another vocalic peak of the same morpheme.

(3) a. /peð-í/ [peðí] 'child NOM. SG.'
    b. /peð-íu/ [peðjú] 'child GEN. SG.'

We now turn to the issue of accent resolution. Elaborate prosodic structures arise when many morphemes with inherent accentual properties meet in the same word. Due to culminativity (Alderete 1999 and references cited therein) only one accent must prevail in the word. In *aɣorón* (post-accenting root + accented suffix), both root and suffix accent yield final stress. In *uranú* (post-accenting root + pre-accenting suffix), however, there is an accentual conflict, which is resolved in favor of the root accent.

In (4) and (5), we provide some representative examples from derivational morphology. The situation here is slightly different. In Greek, the diminutive/pejorative suffix *-ak* combines with nominal roots of various accentual patterns. Similarly in Russian, the derivational suffix *-ást*, which derives adjectives from nominals, attaches to roots of different accentual categories. Stress is on the (accented) derivational suffix regardless of the underlying accentual properties of the other morphemes.[5]

(4) a. ageláku   /agel-ák-ˆu/   'little angel GEN. SG.'
    b. papaɣaláku   /papaɣál-ák-ˆu/   'little parrot GEN. SG.'
    c. misθáku   /misθˆ-ák-ˆu/   'small salary GEN. SG.'

(5) a. borodásta   /borod-ást-á/   'heavily bearded NOM. SG.'
    b. gorlásta   /górl-ást-á/   'loud-mouthed NOM. SG.'
    c. jazykásta   /jazykˆ-ást-á/   'sharp-tongued NOM. SG.'

To conclude, in this section we presented the basic patterns of nominal stress in Greek and Russian. The discussion made clear that any account of stress in these systems must refer to morphological structure. The formal details of the analysis are presented in section 4. The next section addresses the issue of representation of lexical accents.

3. The representation of lexical accents

3.1. Previous approaches

Most representational accounts concur that lexical stress should be prespecified in the lexicon.[6] They differ, however, on how this information should be represented. Due to space limitations, we focus only on the prespecified foot and the autosegmental/grid-mark approach. We begin with a critical review of both accounts and continue with introducing an enriched autosegmental device along the lines of TT.

Inkelas (1994), on the basis of exceptional stress in Turkish, proposes that some morphemes are affiliated with a trochaic foot structure. To explain, both accented and pre-accenting suffixes are underlyingly specified with a trochaic foot. In pre-accenting suffixes, this foot has a segmentally empty prosodic head. However, representing lexical stress as an underlying foot is unmotivated in systems such as Turkish that show no other metrical evidence for footing. Building on Inkelas' idea, McCarthy (1995: 45–47, 2000: 158–159) formulates prosodic faithfulness as a requirement on corresponding segments occupying particular prosodic roles, e.g. head or tail of a foot. Thus, given the appropriate ranking, morphemes with foot-initial segmental anchors, e.g. /(íyor)/ 'PROGRESSIVE', will retain their inherent metrical structure. But this idea is not devoid of problems either. Although in such a model locality comes for free due to the boundedness of prosodic feet, post- and pre-accenting morphemes do not receive a uniform representation. Post-accenting morphemes are specified with iambic heads, V1($_w$V2, whereas pre-accenting morphemes are specified with trochaic tails, V1)$_w$V2. More importantly, however, this approach makes the wrong empirical predictions. Recall the *fúrnaris – furnáriðon* example from Greek. Let us assume that the initial syllable of the root is pre-specified as a foot-head, /(fúrnar-/, and the ending *-on* is pre-specified as a foot-tail, /-on)/. Strikingly, a form like *furnaríðon /($_s$furna) (ríðon)$_w$/ is incorrectly predicted to be grammatical; it respects the window and satisfies the faithfulness requirements of both the suffix and the root (provided that faithfulness is satisfied when the foot-head anchor is not primary stressed). In contrast, the grammatical form *furnáriðon* massively violates faithfulness to foot-internal positions. We conclude, therefore, that constructing the correct analysis on the basis of the proposed representational assumptions is a quite demanding task.

Alternatively, a lexical accent can be represented as an autosegmental unit, a grid mark which is projected onto the stress plane as an idiosyncratic property of a vocalic peak. However, this approach also faces a few drawbacks on the technical side. First, formulating faithfulness as a requirement on the prosodic structure itself makes it impossible to capture faithfulness in the segmentally-empty portion of prosodic structure in post-/pre-accenting morphemes (6a). A possible way out is to invoke empty vocalic positions, as shown in (6b), but this solution leads to further technical complications that, unfortunately, cannot be addressed here.

(6) a.
$\quad\quad\quad\quad\quad\quad *\quad\quad\quad *$
$\quad\quad V_1\quad V_2\quad -\quad\quad -\quad V_1\quad V_2$

b.
$\quad\quad\quad\quad\quad\quad *\quad\quad\quad\quad *$
$\quad\quad V_1\quad V_2\quad \square -\quad\quad -\quad \square\quad V_1 V_2$

Second, stress shifts of the *fúrnaris – furnárides* type raise another thorny technical problem for the autosegmental approach. Alderete (1999), based on morpho-accentual processes in Cupeño, argues that an accent is an autosegmental unit, namely a grid mark, which is encoded as an intrinsic feature of a vowel. Furthermore, he accounts for accent migration by means of the constraint NO-FLOP-PROM, stated in (7). Alternatively, one could also appeal to faithfulness constraints pertaining to the preservation (MAX-link) or insertion (DEP-link) of association lines.

(7) NO-FLOP-PROM (Alderete 1999: 18): For x a prominence, y a sponsor, and z an autosegmental link, $\forall x \forall y \forall z$ [x and y are associated via z in $S_1 \rightarrow \exists x' \exists y' \exists z'$ such that (x, y, z) $\Re$ (x', y', z') and x' and y' are associated via z' in S_2]. 'Corresponding prominences must have corresponding sponsors and links.'

NO-FLOP-PROM is violated in the output form in (8) because the prominence has shifted to another vocalic peak yielding a correspondence violation to IO prominences, their vocalic sponsors and their links. In this paper, we claim that constraints such as the one in (7) should be banned from Universal Grammar. Association lines are not linguistic entities like moras, segments or features; they rather indicate a relation holding between an autosegmental unit and its sponsor and, as such, they cannot be subject to faithfulness.[7] We, therefore, need a representational device that will be able to capture accent migration from one vocalic peak to the other without resorting to movement of the association line that links the respective autosegmental elements.

(8) $\begin{matrix} * \\ | \\ V_1V_2\text{-}V_3V_4 \end{matrix}$ input $\rightarrow$ $\begin{matrix} * \\ | \\ V_1V_2\text{-}V_3V_4 \end{matrix}$ output

Despite the technical problems, in this paper, we adopt the autosegmental approach because it allows us to develop a uniform representation for post- and pre-accentuation. These accentual patterns seem to be the mirror-image of each other. Intuitively, a post-/pre-accenting morpheme desires to push the lexical accent outside its domain (migration) but not too far away (locality). A successful representational theory, among other things, must also be able to articulate the inverse relation that seems to hold between different accentual patterns and migration (i.e. migration is always within the sponsor in accented morphemes but outside the sponsor in post-/pre-accenting ones), and tie it to locality. We, therefore, conclude that a better model for the representation of lexical accents is needed. In the next section, we explore the possibilities offered by TT towards this direction.

3.2. The Turbidity Theory of accents

Goldrick (1998, 2000) in an attempt to handle opacity effects (Kiparsky 1971 *et seq.*) in OT develops a richer representational device which allows for *turbid* (covert) structures. This means that "the output of the grammar will contain unpronounced material which 'can' influence the surface – the portion of the output which is pronounced" (Goldrick 2000: 2). According to *Turbidity Theory*, two relations hold between a vowel and, in general, any autosegmental feature sponsored by it:

- projection (up-arrow ↗): an abstract, structural relationship holding between the vowel and the autosegmental unit.

- pronunciation (down-arrow ↘): an output relation that holds between the autosegmental unit and the vowel and describes the output realization of structure.

The unmarked case is for projection and pronunciation to match.[8] The result then is a transparent, non-turbid relation. Structural harmony constraints, however, can override this pressure and give rise to opaque relations. To illustrate with an example, in Luganda, vowel length is contrastive but vowel deletion in hiatus triggers lengthening of the surviving vowel (Goldrick 2000). For instance, the input form /ka-oto/ surfaces as *ko:to* 'fireplace-DIM.' (cf. /ka-tiko/→ *katiko* 'mushroom'). In traditional autosegmental terms, hiatus resolution triggers re-association of the mora of the deleted vowel to the second vowel, as shown in (9a). In TT, however, the story is as follows: the first vowel projects its mora which is then pronounced on the second vowel, as depicted in (9b). As a consequence, the first vowel is silenced.

(9) a. μ_1 μ_2 b. μ_1 μ_2
         V_1 V_2 V_1 V_2

An implementation of TT for accentuation translates as follows: In accented morphemes, there is a transparent relation between the vocalic peak and the accent. As shown by the abstract example in (10), the accent is projected and pronounced by V1.

(10)   *
         $V_1 C\ V_2 - V_3$

Although the default case for the accent is to be pronounced on the vowel that projects it, other forces may cause it to be pronounced elsewhere. Remarkably, this split between projection and pronunciation paves the way for handling accent shifts triggered by structural constraints (e.g. *fúrnaris – furnári-ðon, peðí – peðjú*). In this case, the accent will still be projected by V_1 but it will be pronounced on V_2. In its current version, however, TT leaves unaccounted for the fact that the accent cannot be pronounced on a neighboring syllable of a different morpheme (e.g. outputs such as **furnaríðon* and **péðju* are ungrammatical). In contrast, a turbid relation is assumed to hold between accents and their vocalic peaks in post-/pre-accented morphemes. In particular, we claim that the accent is floating, hence not bound by projection to a specific vowel of its sponsor in this case. In (11a) the accent is sponsored by the root but is pronounced on the suffix, whereas in (11b) the opposite holds. Note, however, that we still cannot explain why the accent migrates instead of being pronounced on its sponsor.

(11) a.   *   b.   *

    V₁ C V₂ - V₃   V₁ C V₂ - V₃

To summarize, TT constitutes an advantageous representational apparatus because it represents all lexical accents as autosegmental units. Furthermore, the split between projection and pronunciation lines allows us to capture accent migration phenomena without having to resort to movement of association lines. This offers a possible solution to the faithfulness problem of previous autosegmental approaches. However, in its current version, the model does not really preclude movement of projection lines. Ideally, the representational device should also be able to encode morphological information, which seems to be important for explaining the inverse relation that holds between type of accent (i.e. linked vs. floating), on the one hand, and domain of migration, on the other.

The explanatory force of TT can easily be enhanced, if we add some 'morphological color'. Van Oostendorp's (2004, 2007) *Colored Containment* model offers the appropriate theoretical framework for such an endeavor. In the classical version of OT, GEN is restricted by *Consistency of Exponence* (CoE) (McCarthy and Prince 1993a, b):

(12) No changes in the exponence of a phonologically-specified morpheme are permitted.

This means that "the phonological specifications of a morpheme (segments, moras, or whatever) cannot be affected by GEN" (McCarthy and Prince 1993a: 22). CoE implies that morphological affiliation is visible to phonology and, therefore, can distinguish between elements of different morphological affiliation or no morphological affiliation at all (e.g. epenthetic material). Classic OT also endorses *Containment* (Prince and Smolensky 1993):

(13) No element may be literally removed from the input form. The input is contained in every candidate form.

Thus, for a given input /takp/, the output [tak] is assumed to contain the unpronounced segment /p/ as well. Van Oostendorp (2004, 2007) proposes that CoE and containment should be integrated again into OT. In this model, the different morphological affiliation of phonological elements is visualized in terms of colors. For instance, in the abstract word CV_1C-V_2, V_1 is affiliated to the root (blue color) whereas V_2 is affiliated to the suffix (red color). The most important aspect of CC is that it allows the morphological affiliation of phonological elements to be 'visible' in the surface structure. It is precisely this visibility that will help us solve the migration puzzle.

Lexical accents are born with a specific morphological color because they are part of the input. Here, we extend this claim to projection lines as well. To explain, we take projection lines to represent the lexical state of affairs, that is, to be part of the lexical representation of a morpheme and hence to have the same color as their sponsor. In conformity with CoE, therefore, they cannot be altered by GEN. Such a move would be tantamount to changing the structure of a morpheme but, in CC, CoE is a principle of grammar and not a violable constraint (*contra* Walker and Feng 2004). In the same spirit, a floating accent cannot be assigned a projection line simply because it lexically lacks one. This means that a representation such as (15) can never be a legitimate member of the candidate set for either input in (14a, b). Given input (14a), the projection line of output (15) moves one syllable to the right thus changing the phonological exponent of the morpheme. Given input (14b), output (15) also defies CoE because a projection line has been added that was not present in the input. In this case, the projection line is inevitably of a different color than the sponsoring morpheme and, given the inviolability of CoE, it is not legitimate to assume that it will be morphologically absorbed by the color of the sponsoring morpheme. Consequently, only pronunciation lines, which are not part of the input, can be subject to the function GEN.

(14)   a.   *   b.   *
              ↑
              V_1 V_2 V_3-V_4 V_1 V_2 V_3-V_4

(15)   *
              ↑
              V_1 V_2 $V_3$$V_4$

The combined effects of TT and CC, therefore, yield the following restriction on Freedom of Analysis.

(16) projection lines are not alterable by GEN.

The proposed model provides the analytical tools to account for accent migration without resorting to faithfulness to association line constraints. According to (16), projection lines cannot move. Thus, migration of linked accents can only result from the manipulation of pronunciation lines. In light of CC, the constraints on the pronunciation and projection of lexical accents are formulated as follows:[9]

(17) a. V↗LA: A vowel V of morpheme/color M which carries a lexical accent LA must project it at the phonological level.
b. LA↘: Lexical accents must be pronounced.
c. RECIPROCITY$^{LA}{}_V$: If a vowel V of morpheme/color M projects a lexical accent LA, then the lexical accent LA must be pronounced on the vowel V of morpheme/color M.

As shown in (18), these constraints favor as optimal an output in which the lexical accent is pronounced on the vowel that projects it. Candidate (18b) pronounces the accent on another vowel whereas candidate (18c) leaves the accent unpronounced. Consequently, both are doomed to fail. Note that RECIPROCITY is violated when a projection line is not matched by pronunciation or is not pronounced at all.

(18)

$\acute{V}_1\ V_2\text{-},\ \text{-}V_3$	V↗LA	RECIPROCITY$^{LA}{}_V$	LA↘
☞ a. ⁎ ↑↓ $V_1\ V_2\text{-}V_3$			
b. ⁎ ↑ ↘ $V_1\ V_2\text{-}V_3$		*!	
c. ⁎ ↑ $V_1\ V_2\text{-}V_3$		*!	*

To conclude, TT makes sense only within the CC model because the latter guarantees that lexical accents and underlying projection lines will not be literally removed or changed. The split between projection and pronunciation is superfluous, if underlying material is freely allowed to delete. Deleted material cannot enforce any pronunciation relation thus rendering this dimension redundant. Furthermore, CC enables the encoding of morphological information on phonological representations. This piece of information is crucial for understanding the different behavior of linked and unlinked accents in migration. Inversely, TT becomes handy for a theory like CC. More specifically, the split between underlying and surface structure at the representational level allows CC to: (a) handle certain migration phenomena without having to resort to movement of association lines and, consequently, faithfulness constraints that refer to non-linguistic entities (e.g. MAX/DEP/PARSE-link), and (b) account for deletion without actually appealing to the physical removal of features, a significant benefit for any theory that endorses containment.

4. A TT/CC analysis of lexical accentuation

4.1. Accent migration and locality

In this section, we examine accent migration as exhibited by post-/pre-accentuation and various accent shift phenomena. Locality is closely related to both types of migration and needs to be accounted for as well. We will begin with the first type of migration. Why are floating accents not pronounced within their sponsoring morpheme? RECIPROCITY$^{LA}_V$ guarantees locality in the realization of linked accents. Ideally, an accent is pronounced on the vowel it is lexically associated with. In the case, however, that such a lexical association is not provided, migration is not bound by the color of the accent. But what drives the accent away? Recall the restriction in (16): projection lines cannot be added, if they are not lexically present, or changed, if they are present. In some abstract sense, therefore, the migration of floating accents has a *derived environment* flavor. A floating accent cannot be associated with 'old' material, and all vowels of the same color constitute 'old' material. Therefore, the accent has to migrate to another domain. In other words, in the absence of projection lines, the scope of the lexical accent is inevitably broadened and automatically all vowels of the same color are cancelled out as potential docking (pronunciation) sites. As a consequence, the accent either has to migrate or, alternatively, be left unpronounced. We claim that the principle responsible for floating accent migration is *Invariance*:[10]

(19) INVARIANCE: A lexical accent *LA* is pronounced within morpheme/color *M* iff it is projected by a vowel *V* of morpheme/color *M*.

The effects of (19) are illustrated in (20). The optimal output is the one in which the accent of the root is pronounced on the suffix. Outputs that choose to locally pronounce their accent (20b) or leave it unpronounced (20c) (the acute here is due to the default) fare worse than (20a) and, consequently, they are rejected.

(20)

$V_1\ V_2\hat{\ }\text{-},\ \text{-}V_3$	V⁄LA	INVARIANCE	DEFAULT[11]
☞ a. $\ \ \ \ \ \ \ \ \ \ \ \ \ *$ $V_1\ V_2\text{-}\ \ \ V_3$			*
b. $\ \ \ \ \ \ \ \ \ \ *$ $\ \ \ \ \ \ \ \ \ \ \downarrow$ $V_1\ V_2\text{-}V_3$		*!	*
c. $\ \ \ \ \ \ \ \ \ \ *$ $\acute{V}_1\ V_2\text{-}V_3$	*!		

Invariance is also responsible for accent migration triggered by window restrictions or vowel deletion. In the by now familiar example *fúrnaris – furnárides* 'baker NOM. SG./PL.', the accent does not really move to the right because in TT/CC projection lines cannot 'move'. It is simply pronounced on a vowel that satisfies the window requirement, as shown in (21a). Furthermore, due to invariance, the accent sticks to the same color and never migrates to a different morpheme, e.g. the thematic constituent *-ið*. The same applies to the case of hiatus resolution in (21b).[12]

(21) $\ \ \ \ \ \ \ \ \ \ \ \ *\ \ \ \ \ \ \ \ \ \ \ \ \ \ \ *$
$\ \ \ \ \ \ \ \ \ \ \ \ \ \ \uparrow\downarrow\ \ \ \ \ \ \ \ \ \ \ \ \ \ \uparrow$
   a.   furnar-is   furnar-ið-es
   b.   peð-i   peð-ju

Turning now to the issue of locality, by migrating to another morpheme, a floating accent expands its scope, that is, the domain of possible associators, by *1, 2,...n* number of syllables, depending on how far from its source it drifts away. What pulls the accent back to its birthplace is SCOPE, stated in (22). This is a gradient constraint which is violated every time the 'old' territory of an accent is expanded by the addition of 'new' material. The tableau in (23) illustrates how this constraint works. [A subscript letter indicates the affiliation of the accent; *r* stands for root, *s* stands for suffix.]

(22)   SCOPE(LA) ≡ M
       The scope in which a lexical accent *LA* of morpheme/color *M* is pronounced equals the total number of segments the morpheme/color *M* consists of and no other.

(23)

	$V_{1r}\ V_{2r}\hat{\ }\text{-},\ \text{-}V_{3s}V_{4s}$	SCOPE(LA) ≡ M
☞ a.	$*_r$ ↓ $\{V_{1r}\ V_{2r}\}\text{-}V_{3s}V_{4s}$	
b.	$*_r$ ↘ $\{V_{1r}\ V_{2r}\text{-}V_{3s}\}V_{4s}$	$*V_{3s}$
c.	$*_r$ ↘ $\{V_{1r}\ V_{2r}\text{-}V_{3s}V_{4s}\}$	$*V_{3s}*V_{4s}$

Interestingly, the interaction of SCOPE with the other constraints of the system results in the typology in (24). Ranking (24a) yields local migration of floating accents in languages like Greek and Russian.[13] This is illustrated by the tableau in (25) where only candidates with pronounced accents are taken into consideration. Ranking (24b), in which SCOPE crucially outranks INVARIANCE, leads to pronunciation of all accents (linked and floating) within their morphological color and, consequently, to neutralization of the accented vs. post-/pre-accenting distinction. This ranking characterizes languages which lack post-/pre-accenting morphemes, e.g. Cappadocian. Finally, ranking (24c) causes floating accents to be left unpronounced. The effects of unpronounced floating accents can be witnessed in various downstep phenomena.

(24) a. LA↘ ≫ INVARIANCE ≫ SCOPE(LA) ≡ M
      b. LA↘ ≫ SCOPE(LA) ≡ M ≫ INVARIANCE
      c. INVARIANCE, SCOPE(LA) ≡ M ≫ LA↘

We conclude from the above that the TT/CC approach to lexical accentuation enjoys certain advantages. First, it offers a uniform representation and analysis for post-/pre-accenting morphemes. Second, it predicts a restricted and attested typology for floating accents. Third, it provides the means to

(25)

V_{1r} $V_{2r}\hat{}$-, -$V_{3s}V_{4s}$	INVARIANCE	SCOPE(LA) ≡ M
a. $*_r$ ↓ {V_{1r} V_{2r}}-$V_{3s}V_{4s}$	*!	
☞ b. $*_r$ ↘ {V_{1r} V_{2r}-V_{3s}}V_{4s}		*V_{3s}
c. $*_r$ ↘ {V_{1r} V_{2r}-$V_{3s}V_{4s}$}		*V_{3s}*V_{4s}!

express and analyze accent deletion/non-realization phenomena, without invoking additional machinery. Fourth, it brings migration of lexical accents and locality under the same roof: INVARIANCE restrains migration of linked accents but triggers migration of floating ones. Locality in both cases is a side-effect of the requirement that the accent must stick to its morphological color.

Alternatively, a Correspondence Theoretic analysis (McCarthy and Prince 1995) of floating accent migration and related locality effects must employ a faithfulness constraint like NO-FLOP in (7) and a markedness constraint such as *DOMAIN (Revithiadou 1999, after Myers and Carleton 1996), given in (26).[14]

(26) *DOMAIN: *LA$_\alpha$
                |
           [...V...]$_\alpha$

In languages like Greek this constraint must be modified to refer to association lines that link floating accents to their sponsors. This is because linked accents migrate within their domain, *contra* to the dictates of (26). Migration, therefore, is articulated rather crudely as a prohibition against the association of a floating accent to the morphological domain α of its sponsor. The actual docking site of the floating accent is decided by some alignment constraint which, preferably, will also derive the locality effect. It is obvious that such a solution falls short in explanatory power since, first, it fails to establish a connection between migration and locality and, second, it employs markedness constraints that are indexed to refer to an underlyingly distinct class of morphemes, i.e. those that lack inherent association lines.

4.2. Accent resolution at the interface

In this section, emphasis is on accent resolution. In Greek and Russian, derivational suffixes that carry an accent are dominant when competing with other elements in the word, whereas root accents prevail in inflected constructions. In Revithiadou (1999), it is proposed that the morpho-syntactic head of the word is the element that determines which accent will eventually surface with stress prominence.[15] Following Hoeksema and Janda (1988: 220), the notion 'head' is defined in terms of the more basic notions 'functor' and 'argument':[16]

(27) $\text{Head}(f(\alpha)) = \alpha$ if $\text{Cat}(\alpha) = \text{Cat}(f(\alpha))$
$\qquad\qquad\quad\ \ = f$ otherwise

The definition in (27) basically states that the output category of a functor + argument combination $f(\alpha)$ is specified by the functor category. If, however, the functor is a modifier, it can be viewed as an operator performing the identity operation on the category of its argument. In this case, the argument determines the category of the combination.

Head dominance is an instantiation of the 'mirroring' relation that holds between morphology and phonology. Van Oostendorp (2004, 2007), proposes that the principle behind mirroring is *morphological recoverability* (Kaye 1974) which, roughly, states that ideally morphological structure should be reconstructed from the prosodic form. This principle gives rise to a range of interface constraints, called here *mirroring constraints*, that require the two dimensions to be parallel. From this perspective, RECIPROCITY$^{LA}{}_V$ can be viewed as a mirroring constraint that requires a projection line, which is a morphological entity, to match with the pronunciation line, which is its phonological realization.

In order to delve into the nature of interface constraints, however, we first need to determine which aspects of morphology are *visible* to phonology. CC offers some interesting insights into this issue. Phonology can 'see' morphological colors and domains. We take this statement one step further and extend visibility to hierarchical relations holding between nodes, i.e. headedness. This idea is captured by the following constraint:

(28) MIRROR-HEAD (MH): The lexical accent of the morphological head is the head of the prosodic word.

MH guarantees that in accentual conflicts the score is settled by the head element of a particular construction. This is because the head of the prosodic word must mirror the head of the morphological word. In inflected words, this element is the root. The abstract example in (29) helps us visualize this point. The winning candidate, (29a), is the one that pronounces the accent of the head.

(29)

		$V_{1r}\ \acute{V}_{2Head}\text{-},\ \text{-}V_3$	MH	LA↘
		* *		
☞	a.	↑↓ ↑ $V_1\ V_2\text{-}V_3$		$*_{infl}$
		* *		
	b.	↑ ↑↓ $V_1\ V_2\text{-}V_3$	*!	$*_{root}$

An approach that endorses TT/CC has some significant implications for phonological theory and, especially, for common assumptions about the nature of interface constraints. Under TT/CC, 'not anything goes'. Interface constraints are simply faithfulness constraints that control the mapping between morphology and phonology. Markedness constraints do not regulate the relation between morphological structure and prosodic form; therefore, they can never refer to (aspects of) the interface. Moreover, because visibility derives from mirroring, interface constraints can only refer to strictly morphological information such as morphemes, domains, and hierarchical relations between nodes, but never to lexical information (e.g. affix classes, lexical strata, individual lexemes, and so on).

5. An alternative: Transderivational Anti-Faithfulness

Alderete (1999, 2001a, b) proposes the theory of *Transderivational Anti-Faithfulness* (TAF) in order to account for morpho-accentual processes like the ones discussed in this paper. He draws a distinction between root-controlled and affix-controlled accent (ACA). The latter refers to dominance effects triggered by suffixes and is morpheme-specific. Alderete argues that the two types of morphologically-governed accentual phenomena must receive separate treatment. McCarthy and Prince's (1995) Root-Affix metaconstraint can easily treat root-controlled accent whereas TAF is introduced to exclusively handle ACA. TAF operates between morphologically-related words and encourages dissimilation between them. Strict base-mutation is one of its most important properties. An example will clarify how this model works.

In Russian inflected words, root-accent prevails, as shown by the examples in (30) (Alderete 1999: 163–170). Alderete assumes the default stress to be on the post-stem syllable. In short, there are no lexically specified post-accenting roots in Russian. This assumption is crucial, as will be shown below.

(30)   a.   /rák-u/   ráku   'crayfish-DAT. SG.'
       b.   /stol-u/   stolú   'table-DAT. SG.'

TAF accounts for ACA exhibited by the words in (31). The suffix -úx, which attaches to adjectival and verbal roots to form nouns, is accented. Moreover, it is dominant and base-mutating, i.e. it changes the accentual status of the root it attaches to. For instance, the bases s'ív- and skak- are accented and accentless, respectively. However, the accent of the base in s'ív' 'gray', does not survive in the derived form because of the base-mutating character of the suffix -úx.[17] This implies that the morpheme-specific (and hence indexed) anti-faithfulness constraint $\neg OO_{Dom}(ACC)$ outranks the other constraints of the system and, especially, the one that encourages similarity between morphologically related forms, i.e. OO(ACC). The latter constraint requires, for instance, a stressless root to remain stressless in all of its derivatives.

(31)   a.   /s'ív-úx-a/   siv'úxa   'raw alcohol'
       b.   /skak-úx-a/   skakúxa   'frog'

In contrast, recessive suffixes such as -ic (see endnote 15), for instance, belong to another affixal class which is associated with the anti-faithfulness constraint $\neg OO_{Rec}(ACC)$. The effects of $\neg OO_{Rec}$, however, are masked by a ranking in which this constraint is placed at the bottom of the hierarchy: $\neg OO_{Dom}(ACC) \gg OO(ACC) \gg \neg OO_{Rec}(ACC)$.

The TAF approach enjoys several merits, the most important one being that it can handle a wide range of morpho-accentual processes. However, it faces some serious drawbacks. Due to space limitations, we focus on the most significant ones here (see also Apoussidou 2003 for detailed discussion). First, it misses the generalization that, in Russian, recessive suffixes are always non-heads, regardless of whether they are inflectional or derivational. There is a principled reason behind the dominant vs. recessive distinction, but TAF accounts for it by means of suffix class-specific constraints. This, in turn, suggests that suffixes have a more elaborate specification than roots since they encode information on inherent accents as well as class membership (dominant vs. recessive). Second, an empirical problem is raised by the assumption that base-mutation is a property of dominance. Imagine a situation where a post-accenting root, e.g. Greek /uran^-/, combines with a dominant post-accenting suffix, e.g. /-ik^/. The result is a word with stress on the inflectional ending, *uranikós* 'of heaven'. But no base-mutation is exhibited in this case: the root remains stressless. Thus, the very architecture of the TAF model leads Alderete (1999: 214) to preclude the existence of post-accenting roots (hence the post-stressing default in Russian), which is of course empirically false. Finally, the locality restrictions exhibited by post-/pre-accenting morphemes are derived with the help of an extra mechanism, namely constraint conjunction (see Alderete 1999 *et seq.* for details).

To summarize, we end up with a rather heavy theoretical apparatus that employs lexical specification, metaconstraints, morpheme-specific constraints, paradigmatic identity relations and constraint conjunction. In contrast, the proposal advanced in this paper can capture both root- and affix-controlled dominance and, at the same time, provide a uniform interpretation for various instances of accent migration and locality that are in effect in lexical accent systems by means of a model of enriched representations and an interface theory that incorporates CoE and the principle of mirroring in its theoretical apparatus.

6. Conclusions

In this paper, we took a fresh look at morpho-accentual processes that carry heavy lexical baggage and crucially call upon the assistance of interface constraints. More specifically, we developed an analysis that makes use of enriched representations and builds on an interface theory that endorses two basic principles of classic OT, namely containment and CoE. Enriched representations allow us to capture the difference between linked and unlinked accents and also describe a wide range of accent migration phenomena. CC provides an explanation for the locality conditions that accompany accent migration. In addition, the proposed account offers a more principled and restrictive typology for interface constraints than alternative analyses (e.g. TAF). Finally, because TT and CC both rely on the notion of 'visibility' in phonology, an interface theory that brings them together attains the explanatory force required to resolve the intricacies of lexical stress. It also offers exciting possibilities for current challenges to OT that hinge on hidden structure such as, for instance, opacity.

Notes

* I am grateful to Marc van Oostendorp and the two anonymous reviewers for providing useful feedback. I also wish to thank the attendees of the Workshop on Freedom of Analysis (1–2 September 2005, CASTL, University of Tromsø) and OCP3 (17–19 January 2006) for discussion and valuable comments. All errors are my own.
1. E.g. Sanskrit (Kiparsky 1982), Russian (Halle 1973; Melvold 1990; Alderete 1999; Revithiadou 1999), Cupeño (Alderete 1999 *et seq.*), among others.
2. I.e., individual morphemes or lexemes (Hammond 1995), lexical strata (Fukazawa *et al.* 1998; Itô and Mester 1999), roots vs. affixes (McCarthy and Prince 1995; Alderete 1999), affix classes (Benua 1995, 1998), and so on.
3. The superscript circumflex '^' indicates that the accent is placed on a syllable outside the sponsoring morpheme.
4. The underlying form of the suffix, namely /-íu/, surfaces in archaic nouns and place names that tolerate hiatus in this environment, e.g. *monastiríu* 'monastery GEN. SG.', *vrisakíu* 'Vrysaki GEN. SG..
5. Revithiadou (1999) explains why an analysis based on lexical strata is not preferable for the Greek and Russian stress facts.
6. Non-representational accounts and their drawbacks are discussed in Revithiadou (1999). Representational approaches to lexical stress have been proposed by: Halle and Vergnaud (1987); Idsardi (1992); Halle and Idsardi (1995); McCarthy and Prince (1995); Alderete (1999 *et seq.*), among others.
7. I wish to thank Marc van Oostendorp for pointing out this problem to me and also for the stimulating discussion that followed his comment.
8. This is achieved by high ranking the constraint RECIPROCITY (If Y projects to X, then X must pronounce Y, Goldrick 2000: 3).
9. Drawing a parallelism between the constraints in (17) and traditional OT constraints is not an easy task. Constraints linking pronunciation to projection and *vice versa* resemble markedness constraints because they strive towards wellformedness of phonological structure. At the same time, however, they act as traditional faithfulness constraints (e.g. PARSE, IDENT) because they keep track of whether, for instance, the underlying form (projection) is pronounced by the phonetics (pronunciation), i.e. the relevant feature is associated in the output to the element it is associated to underlyingly.
10. This constraint is inspired by Wheeler's (1981, 1988) Principle of Invariance which states that once an interpretation has been established for a constituent, that interpretation cannot be changed.
11. DEFAULT is a cover term for constraints that derive antepenultimate stress.
12. The analysis developed here correctly predicts that an accented /i/ that belongs to a root will shift its accent to the left, e.g. /oksí-/ 'acid', *óks(j)-os* 'vinegar'.
13. The choice of domains comes for free in constructions that consist of two morphemes.

The system described here, however, remains agnostic with respect to the pronunciation site of a floating accent sponsored by a derivational suffix in constructions such as [root-der.suffix-infl.suffix]. In this case, the decision is left on the markedness system. For instance, in Russian and Greek, the accent is pronounced in outermost domains, whereas in Turkish, it is pronounced in innermost domains. This analysis predicts that there cannot be post- and pre-accenting patterns within the same morphological category of suffixes, e.g. derivational suffixes or inflectional suffixes. Greek confirms this prediction.

14. The same effect can also be achieved with an indexed DEP constraint which prohibits insertion of a lexical accent to specific morphemes.
15. An interesting prediction of head theory is that elements that are not heads will not exhibit accentual dominance effects, even if they carry an accent. This prediction is empirically confirmed. For instance, in Russian, the diminutive suffix -íc(-a) is accented, e.g. /čast'/ (fem) 'part' částíca (fem). However, because it is morphologically transparent and hence not a head, it loses stress to an accented root, e.g. /lúž-a/ (fem) 'puddle' lúžica (fem).
16. A *functor* is an element that carries information about its combination with other constituents. It is an incomplete expression that receives as an *argument* an element that is chosen on the basis of its subcategorization information.
17. Alderete (1999) does not discuss examples such as (31b) where the root is accentless and the suffix fails to show any base-mutating effects.

References

Anttila, Arto
2002   Morphologically conditioned phonological alternations. *Natural Language and Linguistic Theory* 20: 1–42.

Alderete, John
1999   Morphologically governed accent in Optimality Theory. Ph. D. diss., University of Massachusetts, Amherst, Mass..
2001a   Dominance effects as Transderivational Anti-faithfulness. *Phonology* 18: 201–253.
2001b   *Morphologically Governed Accent in Optimality Theory.* New York: Routledge.

Apoussidou, Diana
2003   The deformity of Anti-Faithfulness. In *Proceedings of the Stockholm Workshop on 'Variation within Optimality Theory'*, Jennifer Spenader, Anders Eriksson & Östen Dahl (eds.), 15–24. Department of Linguistics, Stockholm University.

Fukazawa, Haruka, Mafuyu Kitahara, and Mitsuhiko Ota
1998   Lexical stratification and ranking invariance in constraint-based grammars. In *Proceedings of the 34th Meeting of the Chicago Linguistic Society. 2 The Panels*, M. Catherine Gruber, Derrick Higgins, Kenneth S. Olson, and Tamra Wysocki (eds.), 47–62. Chicago: Chicago Linguistic Society.

Goldrick, Matthew
1998   Optimal opacity: Covert structure in phonology. Ms., John Hopkins University, NJ.

2000 Turbid output representations and the unity of opacity. In *Proceedings of the 30th Meeting of the North East Linguistic Society*, Masako Hirotani, Andries Coetzee, Nancy Hall, and Ji-yung Kim (eds.), 231–245. University of Massachusetts, Amherst, Mass.: GLSA.

Halle, Morris
1973 The accentuation of Russian words. *Language* 49: 312–348.

Halle, Morris and Jean-Roger Vergnaud
1987 *An Essay on Stress*. Cambridge, Mass.: MIT Press.

Halle, Morris and William Idsardi
1995 General properties of stress and metrical structure. In *The Handbook of Phonological Theory*, John A. Goldsmith (ed.), 403–443. Oxford and Cambridge, Mass.: Blackwell.

Hammond, Michael
1995 There is no lexicon!. Ms., University of Arizona, Tuscon.

Hoeksema, Jack and Richard D. Janda
1988 Implications of process-morphology for Categorial Grammar. In *Categorial Grammars and Natural Language Structures*, Richard T. Oehrle, Emmon Bach, and Deirdre Wheeler (eds.), 199–247. Dordrecht: Reidel.

Idsardi, William
1992 The computation of prosody. Ph. D. diss., MIT, Cambridge, Mass..

Inkelas, Sharon
1994 Exceptional stress-attracting suffixes in Turkish: Representations versus the Grammar. Published in 1999, in *The Prosody-Morphology Interface*, René Kager, Harry van der Hulst, and Wim Zonneveld (eds.), 134–87. Cambridge: Cambridge University Press.

Inkelas, Sharon and Cheryl Zoll
2003 Is Grammar dependence real?. Ms., UC Berkeley and MIT, Cambridge, Mass..

Itô, Junko and Armin Mester
1999 The structure of the phonological lexicon. In *A Handbook of Japanese Linguistics*, Natsuko Tsujimura (ed.), 62–100. Malden/Oxford: Blackwell.

Kaye, Jonathan
1974 Opacity and recoverability in phonology. *Canadian Journal of Linguistics* 19: 13–149.

Kiparsky, Paul
1971 Historical linguistics. In *A Survey of Linguistic Science*, W.O. Dingwal, (ed.), 577–649. College Park, Maryland: University of Maryland.
1982 The lexical phonology of Vedic accent. Ms., Stanford University, California.

McCarthy, John J.
1995 Extensions of faithfulness: Rotuman revisited. Ms., University of Massachusetts, Amherst.
2000 The prosody of phase in Rotuman. *Natural Language and Linguistic Theory* 18: 147–197.

McCarthy, John J. and Alan S. Prince
1993a Generalized alignment. In *Yearbook of Morphology* 1993, Geert Booij and Jaap van Marle (eds.), 79–153. Dordrecht: Kluwer.

1993b	Prosodic morphology I: Constraint interaction and satisfaction. Report no. RuCCS-TR-3, Rutgers University Center for Cognitive Science, New Brunswick, NJ.
1995	Faithfulness and reduplicative identity. In *Papers in Optimality Theory*, Jill N. Beckman, Laura Walsh Dickey, and Suzanne Urbanczyk (eds.), 249–384. University of Massachusetts, Amherst, Mass.: GLSA.

Melvold, Janis Leanne
   1990   Structure and stress in the phonology of Russian. Ph. D. diss., MIT, Cambridge, Mass.

Myers, Scott and Troi Carleton
   1996   Tonal transfer in Chichewa. *Phonology* 13: 39–72.

van Oostendorp, Marc
   2004   The theory of faithfulness. Ms., Meertens Instituut/ KNAW, Amsterdam.
   2007   Derived Environment Effects and Consistency of Exponence. This volume.

Prince, Alan S., and Paul Smolensky
   1993   Optimality theory. Constraint interaction in generative grammar. Technical Report #2, Rutgers University Center for Cognitive Science. ROA 537; published in 2004 by Blackwell Publishers.

Revithiadou, Anthi
   1999   *Headmost Accent Wins: Head Dominance And Ideal Prosodic Form in Lexical Accent Systems*. Ph. D. diss., HIL. The Hague: HAG.

Walker, Rachel and Bella Feng
   2004   A ternary model of morphology-phonology correspondence. In *Proceedings of the 23rd West Coast Conference on Formal Linguistics*, Vineete Chand, Ann Kelleher, Angelo J. Rodriguez, and Benjamin Schmeiser (eds.), 787–800. Somerville, Mass.: Cascadilla Press.

Wheeler, Deirdre
   1981   Aspects of a Categorial Theory of phonology. Ph. D. diss., University of Massachusetts, Amherst, MA.
   1988   Consequences of some categorially-motivated phonological assumptions. In *Categorial Grammars and Natural Language Structures* Richard T. Oehrle, Emmon Bach, and Deirdre Wheeler (eds.), 467–488. Dordrecht :Reidel.

Chapter 8
Freedom, Interpretability, and the Loop*

Paul de Lacy

1. Introduction

The aim of this chapter is to propose the 'Interpretive Loop'. The Loop is a limited feedback mechanism: if the winning phonological candidate is phonetically uninterpretable, the Loop eliminates it from the candidate set and EVAL finds a new winner; this process of elimination and re-EVALuation continues until an interpretable form wins. The Loop is needed to maintain the broadest conception of Freedom of Analysis. The alternative is to prevent GEN from creating uninterpretable forms; I will argue that such prevention is neither empirically nor conceptually desirable.

In its broadest conception, Freedom of Analysis allows GEN to create all possible candidates, limited only by restrictions on the formal properties of the available objects and relations (Prince & Smolensky 2004, McCarthy & Prince 1993). Therefore, GEN can create phonetically uninterpretable phonological candidates as well as interpretable ones. An interpretable candidate is one that can be converted by the post-phonological interpretive components (i.e. the phonetic module(s)) into motor commands; an uninterpretable candidate cannot be so converted.

Current theories of phonological representation allow a myriad of uninterpretable forms to be created. For example, a segment with the features [+high, +low] is phonologically well formed. However, it cannot be interpreted (i.e. converted into motor commands) as it requires the tongue to be in two different positions at once (from an articulatory point of view – Chomsky & Halle 1968:305; the same sort of contradiction arises in an auditorist phonetic implementation). Such cases of phonologically well-defined but phonetically contradictory forms have been and continue to be present in all generative theories (see e.g. Hale *et al.* 1977). Freedom of Analysis also allows GEN to create interpretively incomplete forms: candidates that lack crucial specifications such as features, prosodic structure, precedence relations, and so on.

The standard view is that an uninterpretable output dooms the derivation (i.e. causes 'crash'). For example, if a winning candidate has a [+high, +low] vowel it cannot be converted into motor commands by the phonetic component. So, there will be no speech output for the particular input involved (often called 'absolute ungrammaticality' or 'ineffability').

Absolute illformedness through uninterpretability is far from innocuous because some uninterpretable candidates are harmonic bounds for many interpretable attested ones: in some (perhaps all) situations uninterpretable candidates always win. Section 2 discusses the pervasiveness of the problem, showing that phenomena such as types of harmony, assimilation, and metathesis always favour uninterpretable candidates, and so should not occur under standard conceptions of grammar. In short, uninterpretable candidates must be eliminated otherwise the grammar will not function.

Uninterpretable candidates can be eliminated through the 'Interpretive Loop'. The Loop prevents the derivation from failing if the phonological output is uninterpretable. If the winner is uninterpretable, it is deleted from the candidate set. Eval is then applied again and a new winner is picked. The Loop is described fully in section 3.

(1)   *The Interpretive Loop*

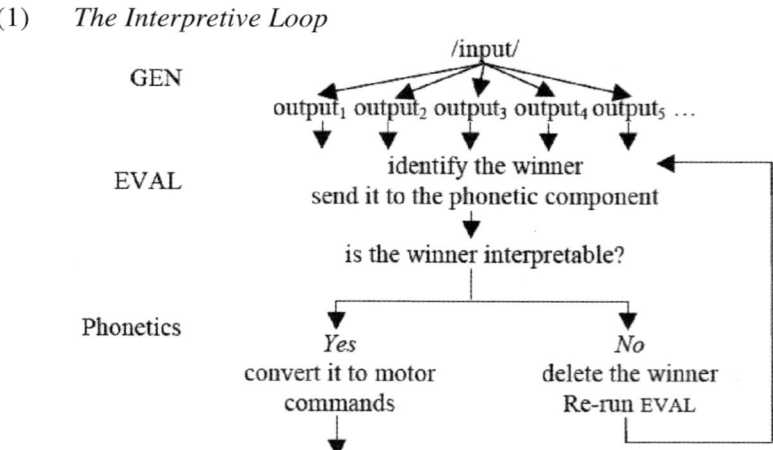

Section 4 discusses alternatives. One is to restrict Freedom of Analysis and ban GEN from producing uninterpretable candidates. Another is to allow the phonetic component to repair uninterpretable forms. I will argue that Freedom of Analysis should not be restricted and the phonetic component cannot repair uninterpretable forms. The Loop's implications are discussed in section 5: it allows many putative phonological constraints to be eliminated. Section 6 presents conclusions.

To avoid unnecessary entanglement later on, it's necessary to mention a few assumptions up front. The Loop is proposed for a unidirectional two-level OT theory of phonology based on innatist (i.e. not functionalist) principles. For comments on bidirectionalism see footnote 7 and on the Loop's compatibility with functionalism and number of levels see section 4.1. I also assume full featural specification, as argued in Steriade (1995), de Lacy (2006:sec.8.4) and references cited therein.

2. The Uninterpretability Problem

This section identifies the problem with allowing GEN to create uninterpretable forms. The main point is that uninterpretable forms are harmonic bounds for attested interpretable ones. They should therefore block those interpretable forms from ever appearing, contrary to observation. Section 2.1 provides some background to interpretability. Section 2.2 identifies ways in which uninterpretable forms affect the derivation.

2.1. What is interpretability?

Interpretability is an issue in all models of phonology in which phonological representation does not directly specify motor commands (i.e. every generative theory of phonology). In such theories, the phonological component generates abstract representations. These representations are converted into motor commands by the 'phonetic component' (Keating 1988, 1990);[1] the conversion process is 'phonetic interpretation'. A phonological form is uninterpretable when the phonetic component cannot convert it into motor commands. Every generative theory proposed so far has the capability of producing uninterpretable forms.

It will be useful to distinguish two types of uninterpretability. One is 'contradiction': where a phonological structure is phonetically interpreted as requiring opposing motor commands. For example, a [+high, +low] vowel requires the tongue to be in two different positions (or in an acoustic approach for different levels of F_1 to be produced simultaneously). Therefore [+high,

+low] cannot be converted into coherent motor commands.

Structures can be contradictory too. The representation in (2) poses an unresolvable problem for interpretation (Sagey 1988, Hammond 1988, Bird & Klein 1990, cf. Boersma 2003). ||H|| must temporally precede ||L|| (||H|| refers to the interpretation of the phonological symbol 'H' – it is read as "the phonetic realization of H"), and ||a|| must temporally precede ||o||. However, the association lines require ||H|| and ||o|| to occur at the same time, and the same for ||L|| and ||a||. There is therefore a contradiction: for ||H|| and ||o|| to be simultaneous and for ||a|| to precede ||o||, ||H|| must follow ||L||.

(2) *Structural contradiction: crossed association lines*

There are many interpretively contradictory structures. Many segmental feature combinations require incompatible realizations (e.g. [−sonorant, +approximant], [−voice, implosive], [strident, glottal]). All of these combinations are phonologically well-formed: they are simply combinations of representational primitives, and so are not formally distinct from interpretable combinations like [+voice,−continuant], [+ATR,+high] and so on.

The other major type of uninterpretability relates to having too little structure. For example, a phonological form that lacks prosodic structure is uninterpretable because it does not provide enough information to create a complete set of motor commands relating to pitch, loudness, and duration. Such forms are 'interpretively incomplete'. (Recall that full specification is assumed here – see section 5 for further discussion).

There may seem to be an obvious and easy way to avoid uninterpretable phonological outputs: simply prevent GEN from creating them. The problems with this approach are discussed in section 4.1.

2.2. Uninterpretability in Optimality Theory

In all models of phonology (and syntax) I am aware of, if an uninterpretable form wins, the derivation ends: if an uninterpretable form is sent to the phonetic component it cannot be converted into motor commands, so no speech will result. If GEN is allowed to create uninterpretable forms, significant problems arise because in many cases – perhaps all – uninterpretable forms will win. In many cases, uninterpretable forms are harmonic bounds for interpretable ones. Examples involving interpretive contradictions are easy to identify: schematically they involve cases where an underlying segment is [αF,αG], a phonological process forces the segment to become [βG], and [αF, βG] is interpretively contradictory. For example, [high] harmony should produce uninterpretable [+high, +low] vowels given the right conditions. Pasiego Montañes Spanish provides a relevant example (McCarthy 2002). McCarthy states that "... all nonlow vowels in a word must agree with the stressed [nonlow] vowel in the value of the feature [high]." The examples in (3) provide alternations. (There is an independent requirement that all vowels agree in tenseness, and a vowel reduction process affects word-final vowels (or perhaps more accurately vowels in the weak position of a foot), requiring them to be one of [a e u ʊ] (e.g. [sentémus], *[sentémos])). The underlying value of the root vowel can be seen when the stressed vowel is [a].

(3) Pasiego Montañes [high] harmony
    a. harmony with [+high]
        /beb/ 'drink'
        [bib-íːs] 2. PL. PR. IND.   [beb-ér] INF.
        [bib-íu] PAST PPL. MASC. SG. COUNT. [beb-ámus]1. PL. PR. SUB.
        /kox/ 'take'
        [kux-í] 1SG. PERF.   [kox-ér] INF.
        [kux-irían] 3. PL. COND.   [kox-áis] 2. PL. PR. SUB.
    b. harmony with [−high]
        /sint/ 'feel'
        [sent-émus]1. PL. PR. IND.   [sint-ír] INF.
                                            [sint-áis] 2. PL. PR. SUB.

The restriction in Pasiego relates to [high] and not to another vowel feature. It is clearly not [ATR] harmony as there is a separate requirement that all vowels in a word agree in tenseness: e.g. [bindiθír] cf. [pɪθígʊ]; [abidúl] 'birch tree' cf. [trænkílʊ] 'quiet (count)'. The requirement that all vowels agree in [high] applies both to tense mid vowels and lax ones: the lax mid vowel [ɔ] is permitted, but it never appears in the same word with a [+high] vowel (e.g. [ækɔlɔdræʊ] 'long, thin').

Tableau (4) presents a straightforward analysis of [high] harmony: a constraint AGREE[high] outranks IDENT[high]. The winner is [bibís]; it contains no interpretive contradictions (or incompleteness), so can be successfully converted to motor commands. σ-IDENT[high] is responsible for the stressed syllable retaining its underlying [high] specification (i.e. for eliminating *[bebéːs]); its ranking cannot be determined in this competition.

(4) *Pasiego Montañes [high] harmony ranking*

/beb-íːs/	AGREE[high]	IDENT[high]
☞ a. bibíːs		*
b. bebíːs	*!	

The low vowel [a] now presents a problem. Low vowels do not undergo height harmony: e.g. /sal/ 'leave', [sal-ír] {INF.}, [sal-íːs] {2. PL. PR. IND..}, [sal-émus] {1pl. PR. IND.}. However, the ranking requires that with input /sal-iːs/, the output should be the uninterpretable [sᵆlíːs], where [ᵆ] is used here to symbolize a [+high, +low] vowel. Tableau (5) illustrates; the uninterpretable winner is marked with ☠.

The winner (a) is the least marked and most faithful. It does not violate AGREE[high] because all its vowels are [+high] – i.e. [i] and [ᵆ]. The attested form (b) [salíːs] fatally violates AGREE[high] by having a [+high] [i] and a [−high] [a]. Candidate (c) is an important competitor: it is the most faithful interpretable candidate that has [high] harmony by changing the /a/s [+low] feature to [−low], producing [e]. However, candidate (a) is a harmonic bound for (c): candidate (c) violates IDENT[high] and IDENT[low], while (a) violates only IDENT[high]. In other words, the uninterpretable [ᵆ] is the most faithful way of satisfying the markedness constraint AGREE[high].

(5)

/sal-iːs/	IDENT[low]	AGREE[high]	IDENT[high]
☠ a. sᵆlíːs			*
b. salíːs		*!	
c. selíːs *!	*		*

So, if there is [high] harmony and an input has a low vowel, the most faithful and least marked form will always be one with a [+high, +low] vowel [ᵆ]. If an uninterpretable winner means the end of the derivation, the practical effect is that if a language has [high] harmony, all inputs with a [+low] vowel and a [+high] vowel should be unpronounceable. Forms like [bibía] show this prediction to be false.

There may seem to be a couple of easy solutions to this problem. For example, why not invoke a constraint *{+high,+low} that outranks IDENT

[low]? Unhappily, there are two problems with this approach. One is that it would require CON to contain constraints that ban uninterpretable structures; this again raises the issue of how CON came to contain such constraints (see section 4.1). It also makes the wrong typological predictions. If there is a constraint *{+high,+low}, it is possible that in some language with [high] harmony it *will* be ranked below IDENT[low], so that every input with a low and high vowel will produce a winner with a [ɐ̈]; therefore, for every input with a low and high vowel, no speech should result. No such language has been reported: in every case of harmony, potential uninterpretability is always avoided through failure to undergo harmony or alteration to an interpretable vowel. Having a constraint *{+high,+low} is therefore an inadequate solution.

Does this whole line of argumentation rely on the existence of the features [high] and [low]? Not at all: [high] and [low] are merely used here to illustrate a general property of all extant feature systems: the possibility for interpretive contradiction. It's possible to appeal to 'local' solutions for this particular case, like adopting features like [1height], [2height], [3height]. However, weeding out interpretive contradiction from the entire feature system is much harder, probably impossible (Hale *et al.* 1977); the Loop makes doing so unnecessary.

In short, under current conceptions of OT and phonology-phonetics interaction, /sal-iːs/ should have the output [sɐ̈líːs] and be phonetically uninterpretable; therefore, /sal-iːs/ should have no pronounceable output. The general problem this case illustrates – where an uninterpretable candidate is the most faithful least marked candidate – cannot be avoided by introducing constraints to CON or by redefining features so that uninterpretable combinations are impossible.

The Pasiego Montañes Spanish situation arises in all cases where an underlying segment S is specified as [αF, αG], S must become [βG] through an assimilation/harmony/neutralization process, and [αF, βG] segments are interpretively contradictory.

Lokaa ([lòkɔ́ɔ́]) provides an analogous example, but instead with autosegmental relations. Akinlabi (to appear) describes a process of tonal metathesis whereby /H+LH/ → [HHL] (for arguments against alternative accounts, see Akinlabi's work). Examples are given in (6).

(6) *Lokaa tone metathesis*
   a. /H+LH/ → [HHL]
   [lèdʒí] 'palmseed'   cf. [έplá jɔ́ lédʒì] 'palmseed market'
   [lètú] 'head'   cf. [úkpò wɔ́ léːtù] 'head towel'
   b. Other sequences remain faithful
   [kétə̀m] 'lizard'   cf. [έplá jɔ́ kéːtə̀m] 'lizard's market'
   [éfém] 'crocodile'   cf. [úkwá wɔ̀ éːfém] 'crocodile's canoe'

The attested response to input /HLH/ is to metathesize to [HHL]. Metathesis involves two changes: (a) reversing the order of tones, and (b) reassociating the tones to new segmental sponsors. However, such a candidate is harmonically bounded by an uninterpretable candidate with crossed association lines, as illustrated in (7). Candidate (a) satisfies the constraint that motivates metathesis (called *HLH here – see Akinlabi to appear for a complete analysis) by being minimally unfaithful – it only violates LINEARITY-tone (the constraint that preserves underlying precedence relations between tones – after McCarthy & Prince 1995). In contrast, the attested interpretable candidate (c) satisfies *HLH, but in doing so violates both LINEARITY-tone and MAX-Association (Myers 1987). In short, candidate (a) is a harmonic bound for candidate (b).

(7) *Tone metathesis should doom the derivation*
   Input /H L H/
           | | |
           jə le tu

   a. Most faithful candidate that avoids [HLH]
      [H L H]
       | ✕
       jə le tu

      – avoids HLH, preserves input associations
   b. Best interpretable candidate that avoids [HLH]
      [H H L]
       | | |
       jə le tu

      – avoids HLH, *unfaithful* to input associations

As with Pasiego Montañes Spanish, the most faithful way of satisfying a constraint results in an uninterpretable winner: one that places contradictory ordering demands on the tonal and segmental tiers.

One way to avoid this result would be to claim that there is a ban on crossed association lines, either in GEN or as a constraint in CON. The problem with appealing to a restriction in GEN is that it is then necessary to explain how GEN came to have a restriction whose sole purpose is to avoid uninterpretability (more on this in section 4.1). An additional problem with proposing that there is a constraint against crossed lines is that it predicts that there could be some language in which an input failed to have any pronounceable output every time it presented the environment for metathesis. No such language has been reported, to my knowledge.[2]

To generalize, in all cases of metathesis the most faithful response is to reverse the order of the offending tones/features only. However, such a local reverse results in an uninterpretable form. The consequence is that metathesis should not occur in natural language as every time metathesis is motivated the winning candidate is uninterpretable.

The same issue arises with interpretively incomplete forms, but in a more striking way. The constraint ONSET is violated when the leftmost node in a syllable is part of the nucleus (or moraic, depending on the theory). The most minimal way to satisfy ONSET through epenthesis is to insert a root node with no features: i.e. /i/ → [•i], where • is a featureless root node. [•i] is a harmonic bound for all other [Ci] candidates (where C is a more fully specified segment) as it does not violate any featural markedness constraints. For example, a prime competitor is [ti], but it violates constraints against coronals and AGREE[Place] (which favours [tʃi] over [ti]).[3] Therefore, the most harmonic candidate with epenthesis will always contain [•]. However, [•] is interpretively incomplete (cf. proposals in underspecification theories – see de Lacy 2006: §8.4 for discussion and references). Therefore, epenthesis should not occur: every input which is forced to undergo epenthesis will have an uninterpretable winner, which of course cannot be pronounced.

The same point can be made for many – perhaps all – phonological processes. For deletion, the most faithful candidate would delete just the offending feature, not the entire segment (deleting the segment results in violations of MAX and CONTIGUITY, deleting the feature alone violates nothing in faithfulness theories with IDENT[F] and not MAX[F]).

An even more surprising point is that uninterpretable candidates should always win regardless of the input. Prosodic structure is non-contrastive (apart from length and main stress), so either prosodic structure is not present in input forms or there are no faithfulness constraints that preserve prosody. Either way, the implication is the same: the most harmonic form will have no prosodic structure. For an input like /tata/, the interpretable output [{(.tá.ta.)}] – i.e. syllabified, footed, and enclosed in a PrWd – inevitably violates several markedness constraints, including constraints on the relation between sonority and syllable constituents, syllable structure, foot form, and PrWd shape. In contrast, the output [tata], with no prosodic structure at all, is equally as faithful as [{(.tá.ta.)}], but violates a proper subset of markedness constraints.[4] Therefore, the most harmonic candidate for any input is one without any prosodic structure; such a candidate is interpretively incomplete, so all words and sentences should be unpronounceable, given current assumptions about OT and the fate of uninterpretable forms.

3. The Interpretive Loop

The preceding section has argued that uninterpretable forms cause a serious problem in OT. At worst, they win in every derivation, meaning that nothing should be pronounceable. At best, they should always win in processes such as epenthesis, metathesis, harmony/assimilation, deletion, and so on; such processes should therefore not be visible. In short, uninterpretable forms are a problem.

There are several potential places to eliminate uninterpretable candidates: GEN, CON, and in a post-phonological component. They could be eliminated in GEN by restricting Freedom of Analysis or in CON by devising constraints against uninterpretable feature combinations and structures. Section 4 will examine the GEN and CON approaches in detail, and will reject them. Instead, a post-phonological mechanism will be proposed here called the 'Interpretive Loop'. Section 3.1 outlines the form of the Loop and shows how it deals with uninterpretable forms. Section 3.2 discusses the implications of an infinite candidate set for the Loop.

3.1. The Interpretive Loop

The source of the uninterpretability problem is the assumption that uninterpretable winners spell doom for the derivation. I propose that when a phonological winner is uninterpretable, the derivation does not end. Instead, the winner and its associates are deleted from the candidate set, and EVAL runs again with the new candidate set.[5] This process of deletion and candidate set re-evaluation continues until an interpretable winner is found.

The Loop can be illustrated with Pasiego Montañes Spanish [high] harmony. The problem identified in section 2 was that the form [sᵊ•líːs] (with an uninterpretable [+high, +low] vowel [ᵊ•]) will always beat every other interpretable candidate that has undergone [high] harmony, such as [selíːs]. It will also beat the candidate in which [high] harmony has been blocked: i.e. [salíːs]. However, the Loop allows [sᵊ•líːs] to be eliminated, summarized in (8).

(8) *The Loop in Pasiego Montañes Spanish [high] harmony*
    a.   GEN(/sal-iːs/) → candidates {..., [salíːs], [sᵊ•líːs], [selíːs], ...}
            GEN produces a candidate set.
    b.   EVAL({..., [salíːs], [sᵊ•líːs], [selíːs], ...}) → [sᵊ•líːs]
            EVAL identifies the winner.
    c.   INTERP([sᵊ•líːs]) → failure
            The interpretive component cannot produce an output.
    d.   WINNOW → delete [sᵊ•líːs] from the candidate set.
            The uninterpretable winner is deleted from the candidate set.
    e.   EVAL({..., [salíːs], [selíːs], ...}) → [salíːs]
            EVAL is run again without [sᵊ•líːs]. [salíːs] wins.
    f.   INTERP([salíːs]) → success
            The interpretive component produces an output.
            The derivation ends.

GEN creates a candidate set related to the input /sal-iːs/ (8a). The candidate set contains [salíːs] (the attested form in which [high] harmony has been blocked), [selíːs] (an interpretable form in which [high] harmony has taken place), and the uninterpretable [sᵊ•líːs], among many other candidates (e.g. [slíːs], [saléːs], etc.). EVAL identifies the winning candidate (8b). As shown in tableau (5), the ranking AGREE[high] ≫ IDENT[high] means that [sᵊ•líːs] will win as all its vowels are [+high] and they are minimally unfaithful. EVAL does not rank-order the entire candidate set (Prince & Smolensky 2004; cf. Coetzee 2004). Therefore, at this point [salíːs] and [selíːs] are both losers and are not ordered with respect to each other. The winner [sᵊ•líːs] is sent to the interpretive component (8c). As it cannot be interpreted, a function winnows down the candidate set (i.e. WINNOW) (8d). The winnowing involves deleting the uninterpretable winner [sʔ◆líːs]. After the candidate set has been cut down, EVAL runs again (8e). In this pass, the primary competition is between [salíːs] and [selíːs]. Both are interpretable. It just so happens in Pasiego Montañes Spanish that blocking of [high] harmony is preferred to altering a low vowel by means of the ranking IDENT[low] ≫ AGREE[high], so [salíːs] beats [selíːs].

(9)   EVAL, *pass II*

/sal-iːs/	IDENT[low]	AGREE[high]	IDENT[high]
☞ a. salíːs		*	
b. selíːs	*!		*

As tableau (9) shows, [salíːs] wins. As it is also interpretable (8f), it can be successfully converted into motor commands and the derivation ends.

In summary, post-phonology candidate deletion allows interpretable losers to ultimately win. Of course, the result generalizes to all situations where the 'first' winner is uninterpretable. For Lokaa, the candidate with crossed tone association lines wins, but is eliminated by the Loop, and eventually the interpretable metathesized candidate wins.

3.2.   The size of the candidate set

The Loop continues to apply as long as EVAL picks uninterpretable winners. Alan Prince (p.c.) has raised a significant issue: what guarantee do we have that, for some input, an interpretable winner will ever be found? Could there be a situation where all interpretable forms are harmonically bounded by an *infinite* number of uninterpretable forms? In such a case, the derivation would loop back forever. This will be called the 'Infinity Problem' here.

The Infinity Problem is different from the oft-discussed issue of whether there are an infinite number of candidates. It is not the number of candidates that is at issue here, it is whether it is ever possible to find an interpretable winner under certain rankings.

The Infinity Problem is easy to construct. For Pasiego Montañes Spanish, it is evident in the candidate [ʔisʔ◆líːs], which has an initial epenthetic [ʔi]. If DEP ranks below AGREE[high] and IDENT[low], [ʔisʔ◆líːs] will be the next most harmonic form after [sʔ◆líːs]. The next most harmonic form after [ʔisʕlíːs] will be [ʔiʔisʕlíːs], and so on with an infinite number of uninterpretable forms with epenthesis [ʔi… ʔisʕlíːs].

In short, the Infinity Problem means that in some cases no interpretable form will ever win; the derivation will continue looping indefinitely.

For Pasiego Montañes, the easy solution is to have DEP outrank AGREE [high], then [salíːs] will beat all candidates with epenthesis [… ʔisʕlíːs]. However, in some languages DEP is necessarily ranked below featural faithfulness constraints to generate other phenomena. In these languages, the Infinity Problem is unavoidable.

The Infinity Problem arises in segmental epenthesis, splitting, and perhaps in prosodification. It does not affect segmental deletion or featural change. The problem does not arise with deletion or feature change because for any length string the number of candidates without epenthesis is finite (these are candidates in which every segment corresponds to a segment in the input form). The finitude follows from the fact that (a) deletion has an upper bound of the length of the input string and a lower bound of 0 and (b) there are a finite number of features.

Consequently, if DEP outranks MAX in a language an interpretable candidate will ultimately be reached. There is always one deletion candidate that can win – one without any phonological content at all ('∅'). The ∅ candidate is interpretable as 'no motor commands', and exists in every candidate set.

The Infinity Problem may apply to prosodification. If there are a finite number of prosodic nodes and prosodic recursion is banned in GEN, then the number of different ways a form can be prosodified is also finite. However, if GEN allows recursion of prosodic nodes, then such structures also pose an Infinity Problem. For example, if the string [ta] can have a candidate with one syllable node, a candidate with two syllable nodes (one on top of the other [[ta]$_\sigma$]$_\sigma$), one with three ([[[ta]$_\sigma$]$_\sigma$]$_\sigma$]), and so on, there is the potential for an infinite number of uninterpretable forms to beat all interpretable forms.

The simplest way to avoid the Infinity Problem is to place an arbitrary upper bound on segmental epenthesis and splitting, and restrict prosodification. For example, if GEN contains a finite number of prosodic nodes and prosodic recursion is banned (or limited to some arbitrary high finite number), for a string of any length there will be a finite number of possible prosodifications. The idea that there are a finite number of prosodic categories is implicitly accepted in most work. Recursion has been extremely limited as well – it has fallen out of favour for prosodic categories such as the σ and Ft nodes (e.g. Hayes 1981 cf. Hayes 1995), but is still accepted in a limited way for PrWds

(Selkirk 1995, Peperkamp 1997) and perhaps higher units.

Segmental epenthesis can be similarly restricted. Łubowicz (2003:§1.2.1.2) proposes that "there can be only as many segments added to the underlying form as there are segments in it plus 1." So, for an input of length n candidates can contain $2n+1$ segments or fewer.

I suggest that the restriction be raised somewhat, to at least $4n$. The size of the restriction does not matter, as long as it is finite. The motivation for raising the $2n+1$ restriction is that Łubowicz bases it on the idea that "there is only one spot adjacent to each segment in a string of segments available for an epenthetic filler." However, adjacent epenthetic elements do occur: e.g. Slave /t͡saɣ/ 'he was crying' is augmented to [het͡saɣ] for minimal word reasons (Rice 1989:133), and the same for Axininca Campa /na/ → [nata] 'carry' (Payne 1981). While the Slave and Axininca Campa outputs do end up with fewer epenthetic segments than the number of input segments and so – strictly speaking – fit within Łubowicz's proposal, the restriction predicts that an input like /n/ in Axininca would not be able to augment to [nata] as this contains three epenthetic segments while the input has only one. One can imagine a case where there is a single input consonant /p/ and word minimality and head augmentation pressures result in [(patá?)], where there are four epenthetic segments. Consequently, $4n$ seems a reasonable minimal restriction.

The same sort of restriction can be placed on prosodic recursion. A generous restriction is that a node n can be recursed only for as many segments as there are in the candidate. So, for [pat] there can be a candidate with three recursed PrWd nodes, but no more.

Arbitrary limits on the number of epenthetic segments per input and prosodic recursions may provoke a sense of unease. However, they provide the most effective way of avoiding the Infinity Problem. An alternative is to delete not only the uninterpretable winner but all candidates that share its uninterpretable property. The challenge in such an approach is in determining which part of a candidate is uninterpretable, translating this uninterpretability into phonological representation, and then deleting all candidates that contain this information. The Interpretive Loop mechanism is much simpler if segmental epenthesis and prosodification are restricted.

Restricting segmental epenthesis and prosodification is clearly a limitation on GEN, and therefore on Freedom of Analysis. However, it is a fundamentally different kind of restriction than preventing GEN from creating uninterpretable forms. 'Epenthesis' and 'prosodic structure' are defined solely in terms of phonological representation. Restricting epenthesis and prosodic structure in GEN therefore has a straightforward and well defined expression and formulation in phonological terms. In contrast, 'uninterpretability' is not a phonological concept – it is a phonetic one. Restrictions on phonological forms that are uninterpretable in another component therefore do not admit of a straightforward expression in phonological terms. Section 4 discusses this issue in more detail.

To summarize, restrictions on epenthesis and prosodic recursion mean that there are a finite number of candidates for any input. There is at least one candidate which is interpretable for any input: the contentless candidate ∅. Therefore, if the Loop re-applies enough times an interpretable form will be reached.

4. Alternatives examined

Section 3 presented a solution to the uninterpretable candidate problem that relied on a post-phonology mechanism. There are alternative methods of avoiding uninterpretable candidates. For example, restrictions could be placed on GEN (i.e. on Freedom of Analysis), preventing uninterpretable candidates from being generated. Alternatively, constraints against uninterpretable structures could be introduced in CON. Finally, the phonetic component could be allowed to repair uninterpretable forms. These options will be examined in turn and argued to be inadequate.[6]

4.1. GEN cannot ban uninterpretable structures

There are empirical and conceptual problems with claiming that GEN cannot produce uninterpretable candidates.

The empirical problem relates to underlying forms. GEN has two roles. It creates output candidates, and it creates underlying forms of lexical items. The process of learning an underlying form requires generation of potential underlying forms for a particular winner (e.g. Tesar & Smolensky 1998). As the only candidate-creation mechanism in the grammar, GEN must therefore create these underlying forms. So, if a lexical entry has an uninterpretable underlying form GEN must have created it, and so GEN must be capable of creating uninterpretable forms.

Lexical items certainly can have uninterpretable underlying phonological forms: the underlying form of lexical items can be interpretively incomplete. For example, underlying forms can contain only part of a segment (Akinlabi 1996 and references cited therein). Such 'featural morphemes' are interpretively incomplete on their own, as are morphemes that contain a single tone. If such lexical items were sent to the interpretive component alone, they would not be pronounced. As GEN can create such uninterpretable underlying forms, it therefore follows that there is no restriction on creating uninterpretable candidates.

Underlying forms also lack prosodic structure, accounting for why there are no languages that have contrastive syllabification, footing, and other prosodic constituents (of course, length and primary stress are exceptions). Forms without prosodic structure are uninterpretable, therefore GEN can create uninterpretable forms. An alternative is to say that all underlying forms have prosodic structure and are therefore interpretively complete in that respect, but that faithfulness constraints do not preserve such structure. The problem with this view is that McCarthy (2000) has argued that there are faithfulness constraints that preserve prosodic structure – they apply on the output-output dimension, and also between opaque candidates and outputs (McCarthy 1999, 2003). Clearly, faithfulness constraints that preserve prosodic structure do exist, but they are effective on every dimension except Input → Output. The most consistent way of accounting for this gap is to assume that underlying forms do not have prosodic structure.

Lexical items can also be interpretively incomplete by lacking segmental features. For example, Inkelas, Orgun, and Zoll (1997) argue that Turkish has three types of lexical items when it comes to the feature [voice]: those that are [−voice], those that are [+voice], and those that lack a [voice] feature. If an obstruent is underlyingly [+voice] or [−voice] it surfaces faithfully in all environments (e.g. /etyd/: [e.tyd] 'study', [e.tyd.-ler] 'study-plural'; /devlet/: [dev.let] 'state', [dev.le.t-i] 'state-accusative'). However, if an obstruent has no [voice] feature underlyingly, it alternates: [ka.nat] 'wing' cf. [ka.na.d-ɯ] 'wing-accusative'). Assuming that a segment is interpretively complete only if it contains all features, the underlying form for [ka.nat] is interpretively incomplete because its final obstruent lacks a [voice] feature.

It is also possible that GEN allows interpretive contradiction in underlying forms. This possibility is far less well documented, and finding evidence for it is difficult in any case. If, for example, an input segment is [+high] and [+low], it may act chameleonic, surfacing as a high vowel in some environments and low in others. The possibility of interpretive contradiction in lexical entries requires further exploration.

In short, if GEN creates underlying forms and (at least) some underlying forms are uninterpretable, GEN must be able to create uninterpretable forms. If GEN is capable of creating uninterpretable underlying forms, the least complex assumption is that it can create uninterpretable output candidates.

There are also conceptual reasons for thinking that GEN can create uninterpretable candidates. Suppose there are restrictions in GEN that prevent uninterpretable structures. These restrictions would include bans on [+high, +low] vowels, crossed association lines, lack of prosodic structure, lack of features, and a myriad of other restrictions. The restrictions are clearly not phonologically unified: there is no single phonological property that they all share. The only factor they have in common is that the structures they ban are not interpretable by the phonetic component. So, how did such restrictions come about?

A functionalist perspective provides a straightforward response: there must be a mechanism that allows construction of phonological restrictions based on performance factors, such as interpretability and other phonetic considerations. The mechanism would detect failures in interpretability, identify the source of the interpretability, and create a restriction in GEN to avoid such situations. Adopting such an approach effectively swings the door open to proposing that all phonological constraints and GEN restrictions are functionally motivated and not innate.

From a formalist/innatist perspective, the existence of a myriad of restrictions in GEN whose sole purpose is to avoid uninterpretable structures would be startling and a remarkably suspicious coincidence. The only justification for such restrictions would be that they are necessary to make the system work – i.e. 'minimally conceptually necessary' in Minimalist terminology (Chomsky 2001). In other words, the restrictions exist because without them there would be no way for the grammar to produce any output. This approach works for some phonological restrictions. Every output candidate needs prosodic structure to be interpretable. If forms without prosodic structure are harmonic bounds for all of those with prosodic structure, a GEN restriction that requires prosodic structure on candidates would have to evolve for there to be any output at all (if, of course, the Loop does not exist). So, it would be no surprise that such a GEN restriction exists: without it, there would be no speech.

However, many interpretability restrictions are not essential for the grammar to work. For example, if there was no GEN restriction on [+high, +low] vowels very few derivations would be doomed – only those inputs with underlying [+high, +low] vowels or those with a low and a high vowel that underwent [high] or [low] harmony would have no output. The same goes for a ban on crossed association lines: crossed lines only arise in specific situations, not in every derivation. To summarize, an innatist approach that appeals to GEN restrictions on uninterpretable structures has the problem of explaining why those restrictions exist. They are not all 'minimally conceptually necessary', so one would have to appeal to a massive amount of coincidental random mutation/exaptation to account for their existence.

If one wishes to avoid functionalism, the Loop avoids a solution to the problems identified above. With the Loop, GEN is free to create uninterpretable forms. Consequently, lexical items can have uninterpretable underlying forms. There are no restrictions on uninterpretable structures in GEN, so there is no need for a mechanism that 'looks ahead' to the phonetic component and constructs restrictions based on what can and cannot be interpreted.

4.2. CON cannot ban uninterpretable structures

Instead of putting restrictions on GEN, one could appeal to constraints in CON: i.e. there are constraints for every uninterpretable structure. For example, there would be a constraint *[+high, +low], a constraint against crossed lines, and constraints requiring full prosodification.

Constraints against uninterpretable forms make a range of incorrect predictions. If a constraint against an uninterpretable structure exists, it can be ranked so that for some input an uninterpretable output will always win. For example, if there is a constraint *[+high, +low] and it ranks below IDENT[low] and AGREE[high] in a language with [high] harmony, every input with both a [+high] and a [+low] vowel will have an uninterpretable winner with a [+high, +low] vowel. I am not aware of such pervasive effects in harmony systems where an underlying combination of low and high vowels spells doom for the derivation.

In short, having constraints against uninterpretable structures predicts pervasive types of ineffability that are not observed.

4.3. The Interpretive component cannot repair uninterpretable forms

An alternative is to restricting GEN or CON is to allow the phonetic component to repair uninterpretable forms. For example, if the phonetic component encounters a [+high, +low] vowel, it could interpret it as a low vowel. However, there are several problems in allowing the phonetic component such power.

A central problem is that the same uninterpretable form would have to be interpreted differently in different grammars. For example, in Pasiego Montañes Spanish [high] harmony, the winner is the uninterpretable [sælíːs]. The phonetic approach would be to invoke an interpretative principle whereby [æ] is interpreted as a low vowel – i.e. phonetically [salíːs]. However, in another language low vowels may participate in [high] harmony, becoming [silíːs] (cf. Jingulu – Pensalfini 2002); the phonetic approach would have to allow another interpretive procedure whereby [æ] is interpreted as a high vowel. The learner would have to choose which interpretive rule to use. At this point the phonetic component effectively has the power to alter contrastive phonological specifications, and therefore to 'do' phonology.

Giving the phonetic component such power also means that it does not have to respect phonological restrictions. For example, [æ] could be interpreted phonetically as [a] even if the language's phonology bans this segment.

The ultimate result of permitting the phonetic component to repair uninterpretable structures is that it is thereby given power to alter, add, and delete phonological structures on a language-specific basis. In effect, it takes over the role of the phonological component.

With the Loop, the phonetic component can be restricted in terms of what it can and cannot do. While the phonetic component may introduce elements that have no phonological correlate (e.g. interpolation between tone specifications, intrusive segments through gestural overlap), it cannot eliminate features or segments or ignore phonological precedence relations. In short, the Loop allows the roles of the phonology as providing sound specifications and of the phonetics as an interpretive component to be maintained.

5. Implications of the Loop

The Loop allows Freedom of Analysis to have a great deal of freedom in positing different types of structure. It also allows GEN and CON to be simplified significantly: GEN and CON do not need to contain restrictions and constraints whose sole purpose is to ensure interpretability. Identifying all such constraints would require a complete theory of phonetic interpretation (i.e. what the phonetic component can and cannot interpret and what it requires in order to produce a complete set of motor commands), so I offer only a few suggestions and examples here.

Prosodic structure is converted to information about duration, loudness, intensity, pitch targets, and so on. Without such information, a candidate is uninterpretable. Since the Loop will eliminate unprosodified candidates, there is therefore no need for constraints or GEN restrictions to require prosodic structure. So, there is no need for GEN to require every segment to be syllabified, or for every candidate's prosodic structure to contain each member of the prosodic hierarchy. This contrasts with constraints like PARSE-σ "Every syllable must be part of a foot" – violation of PARSE-σ does not mean uninterpretability, and languages differ on the degree of syllable parsing. Therefore, the Loop does not affect the existence of PARSE-σ.

It is possible that the hierarchical order of prosodic nodes is also determined by interpretability. If a structure in which a σ node dominates a Ft node is uninterpretable, there is no need to have a restriction in GEN that imposes the correct dominance relations on the prosodic hierarchy.

The requirement that every prosodic constituent has a head is also essentially an interpretive requirement (Selkirk 1984, 1995; cf. Crowhurst 1996 cf. de Lacy 1999). A head is interpreted as the locus of duration enhancement, raised pitch, and so on. If a constituent's head is not marked in a candidate, it is therefore interpretively incomplete. The effects of the constraint HEADEDNESS (Selkirk 1995) are therefore an epiphenomenon of the Loop.

There is no need for constraints against interpretively incompatible features. For example, a constraint *[+high, +low] is unnecessary as all winners with [+high, +low] vowels are uninterpretable and will be eliminated as contenders for pronunciation. Similarly, there is no need for a ban on crossed association lines, either as a restriction on GEN or as a constraint. Crossed association lines are uninterpretable as they impose contradictory precedence requirements; consequently, any winner with crossed association lines will be eliminated, so there is no need for a ban on them in CON or GEN.

Assuming that the phonetic component cannot fill in missing feature values, only candidates with fully featurally specified segments will ever survive phonetic interpretation. Consequently, there is no need for constraints that require 'full specification' – i.e. that all segmental features be present for every segment in every candidate.

The Loop allows restrictions on the formal properties of phonological relations like precedence to be removed. For example, precedence (the ordering relation between nodes on a tier) is transitive, asymmetric, and irreflexive: i.e. [tak] is (informally abbreviated[7]) {t<a, t<k, a<k}. There is no need for GEN to require that precedence is irreflexive. GEN can generate precedence relations between any members; it could generate a candidate {t<a, a<a}. However, {t<a, a<a} is uninterpretable: it requires that $\|a\|$ temporally precede its realization. The same goes for the symmetry property: the precedence relations {t<a, a<t} require that $\|t\|$ precedes $\|a\|$ and $\|a\|$ precedes $\|t\|$ – again an interpretive contradiction. Therefore, there is no need to specify that precedence is asymmetric – any candidates with a symmetric relation that is to be interpreted as temporal order are interpretively incompatible.

Of course, the Loop cannot eliminate every GEN restriction or CON constraint. It can only eliminate 'inviolable' properties or constraints; if a property differs from language to language it must be controlled by a constraint.

The Loop can also apply to syntax. Some proposals have already been made to eliminate syntactic restrictions and consider them as following from interpretive restrictions. For example, Heim & Kratzer (1998) propose that syntactic trees that are not binary branching are semantically uninterpretable. They define the interpretive mechanism of functional application so that it requires two daughters of every node (effectively one to provide the function and the other as its argument). Functional application therefore cannot apply to ternary- or unary- branching trees, so all such trees will be eliminated. With the Loop, there is therefore no need for a syntactic principle that demands binarity. Hale & Keyser (1993) and Heim & Kratzer (1998:51ff) make a similar argument for theta theory.

Apart from constraints, the Loop has implications for levels and 'intermediate forms'. Interpretability is only relevant for the winner. All other forms (underlying and intermediate forms) do not have to be interpretable. For underlying forms, this has no surprising implication – extant theories assume that underlying forms are uninterpretable in that they lack a great deal of structure (e.g. prosodic constituency).

However, problems arise for 'intermediate' forms – candidates that are not the winner but influence it, as in Sympathy or Cumulativity Theory (McCarthy 1999, 2003 resp.). The sympathetic candidate does not have to be interpretable because it does not pass through the interpretive component. For example, McCarthy (1999) discusses a case of opacity in Tiberian Hebrew where /deʃʔ/ is realized as [de.ʃe] – the winner's epenthetic vowel only appears in the winner because it aims to be faithful to the sympathetic (and unrealized) form [de.ʃeʔ]. The proposal works because [de.ʃeʔ] is the most harmonic of a designated set of losing candidates (all those that preserve input consonants). However, if having prosodic structure is not demanded by GEN, there is a more harmonic form: [deʃʔ] with no prosodic structure at all. This form is superior to [de.ʃeʔ] in faithfulness (it does not violate DEP) and in markedness because it has no syllable structure and so does not violate constraints like NOCODA. There is no way to eliminate unprosodified [deʃʔ] as the sympathetic winner because lack of prosody is only 'banned' by passing through the interpretive component, and the sympathetic candidate form never passes through it. The same applies to other theories such as Bye's (2001) 'virtual phonology'.

In a nutshell, the problem is that the intermediate form in analyses of opacity must be interpretable. However, if interpretability is an 'epiphenomenon' of the Loop and intermediate forms never pass through the interpretive component, there is no way to require that they be interpretable. The same goes for multi-level theories (e.g. Kiparsky 2006, McCarthy 2007): the output of every non-final level will be uninterpretable.

The Loop therefore implies that the grammar is strictly two-level with no reference to intermediate forms and losing candidates. I note this as a consequence of the Loop, and not self-evidently a good or bad thing. The majority of theories of opacity so far have used reference to a losing form (or at least uninterpreted form – e.g. McCarthy 1999, 2003, Jun 1999, Bye 2001), though some have not (McCarthy 1994, Goldrick 1999).

A final comment is that the Loop guarantees that for every input there will be an interpretable output. This raises the issue of what to do when an input has no (obvious) output (see Fanselow & Féry 2002 for discussion). An example is the English input *beautiful+er{comparative}*, which has no obvious output realization (*beautifuller, *beauter). In syntactic theories (e.g. Minimalism) it is common to ascribe ineffability to uninterpretability, but the Loop eliminates doing so as an option. In contrast, recent proposals about ineffability have not appealed to uninterpretability as a means of accounting for ineffability; instead, Prince & Smolensky (2004) argue that a 'null parse' candidate can account for some cases, and a variety of other proposals have also been made (see McCarthy 2002: 198 ff. for an overview).

The Loop also has implications for pruning the candidate set. Samek-Lodovici & Prince (1999) observe that there are 'perpetual losers' in the candidate set – those that are singly or collectively harmonically bounded by interpretable candidates. If all perpetual losers could be eliminated, the candidate set would be finite. Riggle (2004) proposes an algorithm along these lines. However, uninterpretable candidates are harmonic bounds for interpretable ones. For example, from input /tak/ the candidate [tak] with no prosodic structure incurs a proper subset of markedness violations of those of any prosodified form. So, if all candidates that are harmonically bounded were eliminated from contention, there would be no interpretable competitors left. A straightforward solution to incorporate Riggle's proposal is to regenerate candidate sets for each loop: the Loop can ban a member of the candidate set from being generated, so GEN will be run again and again and eventually all uninterpretable candidates will be banned: then interpretable candidates will no longer be harmonically bounded.

6. Conclusions

The first aim of this article was to show that uninterpretable candidates pose significant problems in Optimality Theory. In many cases – perhaps all – uninterpretable candidates are harmonic bounds for interpretable ones. The standard belief that uninterpretable winners cause the derivation to stop ('crash') means that many inputs should have no pronounceable output, contrary to fact.

The second aim was to show that Freedom of Analysis can remain free: GEN can generate uninterpretable candidates as long as there is an Interpretive Loop. If the winning output is uninterpretable, it is eliminated from the candidate set and evaluation is run again, and so on until an interpretable winner emerges. This proposal requires limiting the candidate set to a finite number of candidates by restricting segmental epenthesis and prosodic recursion.

The Loop has implications for the constraint component CON. It eliminates all constraints whose sole purpose is to impose interpretability, such as the ban on crossed association lines, bans on interpretively incompatible feature combinations, and prosodic requirements such as exhaustive parsing and HEADEDNESS.

The Loop also has implications for the alphabet of phonological features and relations. The Loop means that not every phonological feature must be phonetically interpretable; the Loop will eliminate every winner that contains inherently uninterpretable features. Of course, for the phonological component to do its job (i.e. produce some interpretable form), it must contain enough features and relations to make some interpretable segment(s). However, the Loop makes it possible for the phonological component to function even if it contains uninterpretable features and relations and – of course – if GEN can create uninterpretable forms.

The next step is to determine how much the Loop is responsible for. The Loop provides the *potential* for Freedom of Analysis to be extremely free. However, the Loop has limitations: a putative GEN-restricting principle can only be ascribed to the Loop if it bans an uninterpretable structure; the Loop has nothing to say about violable restrictions.

Notes

* My thanks to two anonymous reviewers, and to John McCarthy, Alan Prince, John Kingston, Lisa Selkirk, and Steve Parker for commenting on earlier versions of this work. The proposals in this chapter were presented in several different venues over the past several years. My thanks to the phonology group at the University of Massachusetts, Amherst in 1999, the MIT Phonology Circle in 2000, the audience at Concordia University in 2000 (in particular Charles Reiss), and the audience at Rutgers University in 2004.

1. I use 'motor commands' to refer to the output of the phonetic component. The output may be articulatory commands or acoustic targets – see Kingston (2006) for an overview. The relevant issue here is that the phonetic component converts the phonological output into a different representation, whatever that representation might be like.
2. Another approach is to deny that there is ordering on the tonal tier. However, the existence of floating tones in output forms shows that there must be precedence relations between tones (Pulleyblank 1986).
3. There is no consonant that perfectly satisfies all featural markedness constraints – see de Lacy (2006: §1.3.4).
4. Of course, this argument assumes that candidates should be fully prosodified (or only minimally unprosodified (e.g. only at edges)). This assumption sits comfortably with recent views that the effects of putative extraprosodicity are due to constraint interaction (e.g. Hung 1994). The only constraint an unprosodified form might violate is one that requires segments to belong to syllables ('PARSE-seg'). In more general terms, to get a prosodically complete form to beat a prosodically incomplete form, there would have to be constraints that required the presence of every prosodic level. The problem this approach raises is that it predicts languages that cannot pronounce words that violate some prosodic constraint. For example, the ranking ‖ MAX, DEP, NO-CODA ≫ PARSE-SEG ‖ means that the winning candidate for /pat/ is [pat] with no prosodic structure (prosodified [.pa.ti.], [.pa.], and [.pat.] are all ruled out). Therefore, /pat/ should not be pronounceable. In any case, the Loop allows constraints like PARSE-SEG to be eliminated from CON: note that PARSE-SEG's sole role is to ensure interpretability.
5. Coetzee (2004) proposes that all candidates are rank-ordered – winners as well as losers. This full rank-ordering is achieved by removing the winner from a candidate set and

running EVAL with the smaller candidate set (p.3) Despite its superficial similarity to the Loop, Coetzee's proposal is fundamentally different. The mechanism Coetzee describes does not literally eliminate candidates from the candidate set – it rank-orders losers. In contrast, the Loop really eliminates candidates, and losers are not rank-ordered. The Loop is compatible with Prince & Smolensky's (2004) proposal that EVAL picks the winner in a candidate set but does not distinguish between the winners. In short, Coetzee's proposal rank-orders losers and does not eliminate candidates, while the Loop does not rank-order losers and does eliminate candidates.
6. All of the discussion in this chapter assumes a uni-directional production model of OT. Some versions of bi-directional OT require every syntactic form to have a semantic interpretation, and this could in principle be applied to phonology phonetics: every phonological form could be required to have a phonetic interpretation, so ruling out uninterpretable candidates (see Beaver & Lee 2003 for discussion of various bi-directional models). The possibility that some version of a bi-directional model might be used to ban uninterpretable candidates is in itself uninteresting for the purposes of this article as the focus here is on uni-directional theories. It would be interesting if uni-directional models could not deal with the uninterpretability problem; however, as this chapter argues, they can if the Loop exists. This chapter eliminates the uninterpretability problem as a challenge for uni-directional OT; it provides no insight as to which of bi- and uni-directionalism is correct.
7. To be accurate, a tier is a string, and a string can be defined as a function from a finite set of elements S (drawn from a denumerably infinite set of elements (like natural numbers)) to phonological primes (features, nodes); precedence relations hold between the members of S, not between the phonological primes.

References

Akinlabi, Akinbiyi
    1996   Featural affixation. *Journal of Linguistics* 32(2): 239–289.
    to appear   The prosodic organization of Lokaa tones. In *Proceedings of the 24th West African Languages Congress*.
Beaver, David I. and Hanjung Lee
    2003   Input-output mismatches in OT. In *Optimality Theory and pragmatics*, Reinhard Blutner and Hank Zeevat (eds.), 112–153. Palgrave: MacMillan.
Bird, Steven and Ewan Klein
    2000   Phonological events. *Journal of Linguistics* 26: 33–56.
Boersma, Paul
    2003   Nasal harmony in functional phonology. In *The phonological spectrum, Vol. 1: Segmental Structure*, Jeroen van de Weijer, Vincent J. van Heuven and Harry van der Hulst (eds.), pp. 3–35. Amsterdam: John Benjamins.
Bye, Patrik
    2001   Virtual Phonology: Rule sandwiching and multiple opacity in North Saami. Ph. D. diss, University of Tromsø. ROA 498.
Chomsky, Noam
    1993   A minimalist program for linguistic theory. In *The view from Building 20:*

Essays in honor of Sylvain Bromberger, Kenneth Hale and Samuel J. Keyser (eds.), pp. 1–52. Cambridge, Mass.: MIT Press.

Chomsky, Noam
2001 Derivation by Phase. In *Ken Hale: A life in language*, Michael Kenstowicz (ed.), pp. 1–52. Cambridge, Mass..: MIT Press.

Chomsky, Noam and Morris Halle
1968 *The sound pattern of English*. New York: Harper & Row.

Coetzee, Andries
2004 What it means to be a loser: Non-optimal candidates in Optimality Theory. Ph. D. diss., University of Massachusetts, Amherst. ROA 687.

Crowhurst, Megan
1996 An optimal alternative to conflation. *Phonology* 13:409–424.

Fanselow, Gisbert and Caroline Féry
2002 Ineffability in grammar. In *Resolving Conflicts in Grammars*, Gisbert Fanselow & Caroline Féry (eds.), 265–307. (Sonderheft der Linguistischen Berichte) Hamburg: Buske.

Goldrick, Matthew
1999 Turbid output representations and the unity of opacity. In *Proceedings of the 30th Annual Meeting of the North East Linguistic Society*, Ji-Yung Kim and Mako Hirotani (eds.), 231–245. Amherst, Mass.: GLSA Publications.

Goldsmith, John
1976 Autosegmental phonology. Ph. D. diss., MIT.

Gordon, Matthew
2006 Functionalism in phonology. In *The Cambridge Handbook of Phonology*, Paul de Lacy (ed.), ch.2. Cambridge: Cambridge University Press.

Hale, Kenneth, LaVerne Masayesva Jeanne, and Paul Platero
1977 Three cases of overgeneration. In *Formal Syntax*, Peter W. Culicover, Thomas Wasow, and Adrian Akmajian (eds.), 379–425. New York; London; San Francisco: Academic Press.

Hale, Kenneth and Samuel J. Keyser
1994 On argument structure and the lexical expression of syntactic relations. In *The View from Building 20: Essays in Linguistics in Honor of Sylvain Bromberger*, Kenneth Hale & Samuel Jay Keyser (eds.), 53–109. Cambridge, Mass.: MIT Press.

Hammond, Michael
1988 On deriving the Well-formedness Condition. *Linguistic Inquiry* 19: 319–325.

Hayes, Bruce
1981 A metrical theory of stress rules. Ph. D. diss., MIT.
1995 *Metrical Stress Theory: Principles And Case Studies*. Chicago: University of Chicago Press.

Heim, Irene and Angelika Kratzer
1998 *Semantics in Generative Grammar*. Malden, Mass.: Blackwell.

Inkelas, Sharon, Cemil Orhan Orgun, and Cheryl Zoll
1997 The implications of lexical exceptions for the nature of grammar. In *Derivation and Constraints in Phonology*, Iggy Roca (ed.), 393–418. Oxford: Oxford University Press.

Jun, Jongho
  1999 Generalized sympathy. In *Proceedings of NELS 29*, Pius Tamanji, Masako Hirotani, and Nancy Hall (eds.), 121–135. Amherst, Mass.: GLSA.
Keating, Patricia
  1988 The Phonology-Phonetics Interface. In *Linguistics: The Cambridge Survey, Volume I: Grammatical Theory*, Frederick Newmeyer (ed.), 281–302. Cambridge, UK: Cambridge University Press.
  1990 Phonetic representations in a generative grammar, *Journal of Phonetics* 18: 321–334.
Kingston, John
  2006 The phonetics-phonology interface. In *The Cambridge Handbook of Phonology*, Paul de Lacy (ed.), ch. 17. Cambridge: Cambridge University Press.
Kiparsky, Paul
  2006 *Paradigmatic effects and opacity*. Chicago, Ill.: University of Chicago Press.
Łubowicz, Anna
  2003 Contrast preservation in phonological mappings. Ph. D. diss., University of Massachusetts, Amherst. ROA 554.
de Lacy, Paul
  1999 Sympathetic stress. ROA 294.
  2006 *Markedness: Reduction and preservation in phonology*. Cambridge: Cambridge University Press.
McCarthy, John J.
  1984 Theoretical consequences of Montañes vowel harmony. *Linguistic Inquiry* 15(2): 291–328.
  1994 Remarks on phonological opacity in Optimality Theory. ROA 79.
  1999 Sympathy and Phonological Opacity. *Phonology* 16: 331–399.
  2000 The Prosody of Phase in Rotuman. *Natural Language and Linguistic Theory* 18: 147–197.
  2002 *Optimality Theory: A thematic guide*. Cambridge: Cambridge University Press.
  2003 Sympathy, Cumulativity, and the Duke-of-York Gambit. In *The Optimal Syllable*, Caroline Féry and Ruben van de Vijver (eds.), 23–76. Cambridge: Cambridge University Press.
  2007 Restraint of Analysis. This volume.
McCarthy, John J. and Alan S. Prince
  1993 Prosodic morphology I: Constraint interaction and satisfaction. Rutgers Technical Report TR-3. New Brunswick, Rutgers University Center for Cognitive Science. ROA 482.
  1995 Faithfulness and reduplicative identity. ROA 60.
Myers, Scott
  1997 OCP effects in Optimality Theory. *Natural Language and Linguistic Theory* 15(4): 847–892.
Payne, David L.
  1981 *The phonology and morphology of Axininca Campa*. Summer Institute of Linguistics Publications in Linguistics 66. Dallas, Texas.: SIL.
Pensalfini, Rob
  2002 Vowel harmony in Jingulu. *Lingua* 112: 561–586.

Peperkamp, Sharon
1997   Prosodic words. HIL Dissertations 34. The Hague: Holland Academic Graphics.
Prince, Alan S., and Paul Smolensky
1993   Optimality theory. Constraint interaction in generative grammar. Technical Report #2, Rutgers University Center for Cognitive Science. ROA 537; published in 2004 by Blackwell Publishers.
Rice, Keren D.
1989   *A Grammar of Slave*. Berlin/New York: Mouton de Gruyter.
Riggle, Jason
2004   Contenders and Learning. In *Proceedings of the 23rd Annual Meeting of the North East Linguistic Society*, Benjamin Schmeiser, Vineeta Chand, Ann Kelleher and Angelo Rodriguez (eds.), 101-114. Somerville, Mass.: Cascadilla Press.
Sagey, Elisabeth
1988   On the ill-formedness of crossing association lines. *Linguistic Inquiry* 19: 109–118.
Samek-Lodovici, Vieri and Alan Prince
1999   Optima. Ms., Rutgers University. ROA 363.
Selkirk, Elizabeth
1984   *Phonology and Syntax: The relation between sound and structure*. Cambridge, MA.: MIT Press.
1995   The prosodic structure of function words. In *Papers in Optimality Theory*, Jill Beckman, Laura Walsh Dickey and Suzanne Urbanczyk (eds.), 439–470. (University of Massachusetts Occasional Papers 18.) Amherst, Mass., GLSA.
Steriade, Donca
1995   Underspecification and markedness. In *The Handbook of Phonological Theory*, John Goldsmith (ed.), 114–174. Cambridge, Mass.: Blackwell.
Tesar, Bruce and Paul Smolensky
1998   Learnability in Optimality Theory. *Linguistic Inquiry* 29: 229–268.

Chapter 9
Restraint of Analysis

John J. McCarthy

1. Introduction

In Optimality Theory (Prince and Smolensky 1993), GEN is the grammatical component that performs linguistic operations. *Freedom of analysis* is the phrase introduced by McCarthy and Prince (1993a) to describe GEN's ability to transform any input form into a wide range of output candidates. Under Correspondence Theory (McCarthy and Prince 1995; McCarthy and Prince 1999), GEN even supplies [dɔg] as one of the candidates for input /kæt/. The mapping /kæt/ → [dɔg] is unattested, of course, but that is not GEN's concern. Instead, the limits on possible mappings follow from the assumptions that there is a universal constraint component CON and that grammars are permutations of CON. The /kæt/ →[dɔg] mapping never occurs in any language because [dɔg] is not the most harmonic member of /kæt/'s candidate set under any ranking of CON.

This much is OT orthodoxy. But there are inklings of a heterodox view of freedom of analysis in Prince and Smolensky's analysis of Berber syllabification and a few other works (Black 1993; McCarthy 2000; McCarthy 2002:159–63; McCarthy 2007; Norton 2003). The *locus classicus* is this quotation:

> Universal grammar must provide a function Gen that admits the candidates to be evaluated. In the discussion in chapter 2 we have entertained two different conceptions of Gen. The first, closer to standard generative theory, is based on serial or derivational processing: some general procedure (Do-α) is allowed to make a certain single modification to the input, producing the candidate set of all possible outcomes of such modification. This is then evaluated; and the process continues with the output so determined. In this serial version of grammar, the theory of rules is narrowly circumscribed, but it is inaccurate to think of it as trivial. There are constraints inherent in the limitation to a single operation and in the requirement that each individual operation in the

sequence improve Harmony. (An example that springs to mind is the Move-x theory of rhythmic adjustments in Prince (1983); it is argued for precisely on the basis of entailments that follow from these two conditions, pp. 31–43.) (Prince and Smolensky 2004:94–95)

In this statement, Prince and Smolensky are sketching an alternative architecture for OT based on *restraint* rather than freedom of analysis. In classic OT, maximal harmony is reached in one fell swoop because GEN supplies candidates that may show the simultaneous effects of many phonological operations. The quotation describes a different version of OT, one in which maximal harmony is achieved in small steps of gradual harmonic improvement, because a more restrained GEN is limited to making modest changes in the input one at a time. What restrained GEN lacks in freedom, however, it makes up for in persistence: the most harmonic candidate selected by EVAL is fed back into restrained GEN as an input, whence it yields a new candidate set that is subject to a new round of evaluation. The GEN → EVAL → GEN → ... loop continues until there is nothing left to do. I will, accordingly, refer to this alternative architecture as persistent OT. (The earlier literature calls it harmonic serialism.)

In this chapter, I explore some of the differences between classic OT with free GEN on the one hand and persistent OT with restrained GEN on the other. We will see, as Prince and Smolensky suggest, that the single-operation and harmonic-improvement requirements do indeed have consequences that are different from those of the familiar OT model. This chapter's goal is not to decide squarely for one version of OT over the other, though elsewhere (McCarthy 2007) I argue in favor of a derivative of persistent OT called OT-CC (for OT with candidate chains).

This chapter is organized as follows. In §2, I summarize the relevant aspects of Prince (1983), which Prince and Smolensky mention parenthetically at the end of the quotation. I then apply similar ideas to OT. In §3 and §4, some basic properties of this modified theory are discussed, while §5 identifies some situations where this theory makes novel predictions.

2. A single harmony-improving operation

In the quotation, Prince and Smolensky cite the work of Prince (1983:31–43), and so we will begin there. Prince analyzes the rhythmic stress shift observed in English and other languages; the standard example is *thir̩teen* 'men → ˌthirteen 'men. In Prince's system, stress prominence is represented by a metrical grid with the following properties:

- Every syllable projects a grid position, marked by an x.
- Syllables that are more prominent project taller stacks of xs.
- Grid positions are subject to a Continuous Column Constraint: except for the bottom level of the grid, every x is supported by another x on the level immediately below it.

In a typical rhythmic shift situation, such as (1), an x moves leftward from a position of stress clash, thereby improving the rhythmic alternation.

(1) Rhythmic stress shift

```
            x                   x
     x      x         x         x
  x  x      x         x  x      x
  thirteen men    →   thirteen men
```

Prince analyzes stress shift with an elementary operation on metrical grids and conditions on the application of that operation. The operation is called Move-x, and it does exactly what its name implies: it moves any x to a different syllable while remaining in the same row and not skipping over any xs in that row. Speaking a bit anachronistically, Move-x only applies when it improves harmony by eliminating stress clashes, such as the clash between *teen* and *men* highlighted in (1). But Move-x cannot apply when it would introduce violations of the Continuous Column Constraint. That is why the stress clash in *an'tique ˌstore* remains unresolved (see (2)).

(2) Unresolved clash in *an'tique ˌstore*

```
       x              x              x
    x  x        x     x           x  x
  x x  x      x x     x         x x  x
  antique store  →  *antique store   *antique store
```

By assumption, only one x can be moved at a time, and each movement must effect a harmonic improvement by resolving clash without violating the Continuous Column Constraint. Example (2) shows that these assumptions do real work in the analysis. The problem in (2) is that all leftward movements of a single x violate the Continuous Column Constraint. (Rightward movement never occurs in English, so ˌantique ˈstore is not a possible resolution.) If two *x*s could be moved leftward at the same time, then it would be possible to resolve the clash and satisfy the Continuous Column Constraint at the same time, yielding *ˈantique ˌstore. But two *x*s cannot be moved at once, *ex hypothesi*. The clash therefore remains unresolved, and a general prediction is obtained: clash is never resolved by shifting the location of the stronger of two clashing stresses. The Continuous Column Constraint is the basis for this prediction, but only if Move-*x* is limited to one-at-a-time application.

This example shows, as Prince and Smolensky promised, that significant results can be derived from the assumption that derivations are limited to one harmony-improving operation at a time. We will now study how a similar limitation can affect OT.

3. Restraint of analysis and finiteness

The classic OT candidate set is infinite because, under freedom of analysis, GEN includes unrestricted structure-building operations, of which epenthesis is the most obvious example. With an epenthesis operation in GEN and with no limit on the number of epenthesis operations that a candidate can undergo, there is no upper bound on the length of a candidate. Classic OT's GEN has unrestricted epenthesis for reasons of theoretical parsimony: all observed limits on epenthesis are adequately explained by factorial typology. Excessive epenthesis brings additional faithfulness violations with no concomitant improvement in markedness performance, so there is no need for a GEN-internal restriction on iterated epenthesis.

In persistent OT, the candidate set after each pass through GEN is finite. This conclusion follows from the assumptions that restrained GEN allows only one phonological operation at a time and that the number of distinct phonological operations in GEN is finite. The restriction to one operation at a time is, of course, the hypothesis we are exploring here. That the number of distinct operations in GEN is finite is a universal but usually tacit assumption in classic OT as well. There is a short list of licit phonological operations, each of which is associated with some faithfulness constraint: epenthesis, deletion, alterations of feature values, and various transformations on autosegmental and metrical structures. The number of different ways in which a finite input string can be altered by one application of one of these operations is therefore finite. In short, there is an upper bound on the number of ways that GEN can apply a single operation to an input.

The derivations in persistent OT are also finite. That is, there is an upper bound on the number of passes that must be made through the GEN → EVAL → GEN → ... loop. The existence of this bound follows from the results in Moreton (2003). Moreton shows that, under certain assumptions, OT grammars have a property he dubs *eventual idempotency*. A function f is idempotent if and only if $f(a) = f \circ f(a)$ for any a – that is, if the result of applying f to a is the same as the result of applying f to the result of applying f to a, so reapplications of the function to its own output have no effect. Any generative grammar, including an OT grammar, is a function G(/in/) → [out]. This function G is *eventually* idempotent if and only if, for any input, there comes a point when repeated application of G to its own output yields no further changes. That is, $\forall$/in/ $\exists n$ s.t. G^n(/in/) = G^{n+1}(/in/). Eventual idempotency is provably true of OT grammars if CON is finite and is limited to markedness and faithfulness constraints, and if GEN supplies the faithful candidate [in] as a member of the candidate set for any input /in/.

To say that every classic OT grammar is eventually idempotent is therefore to say that there is always an upper bound on any input's potential for harmonic improvement; if the grammar is repeatedly given its own output as input, there will always come a point when the output is identical to the input because no further harmonic improvement is possible. These results apply with equal force to persistent OT, which is not different in any relevant respect. This means that there is always a limit on how many passes will be possible through the GEN → EVAL → GEN → ... loop before there is convergence, when the most recent output of the grammar is the same as the most recent input. This limit exists for any input and any permutation of CON.

Consider again the problem of iterated epenthesis. The classic OT candidate set for input /pa/ is infinite because there is no limit on how many epenthesis operations GEN can perform: [paʔ], [paʔə], [paʔəʔ], [paʔəʔə], ... In persistent OT, it is possible to derive iterated epenthesis by repeated passes through the GEN → EVAL → GEN → ... loop: /pa/ → [paʔ] → [paʔə] → ... But because OT grammars are eventually idempotent, there is always an upper bound on how many iterations are possible before they cease to be harmonically improving.[1]

Intuitively, the result about eventual idempotency follows from the basic character of OT constraints. Faithfulness constraints alone cannot compel unfaithful mappings, so no faithfulness constraint by itself could cause epenthesis. We must therefore focus on markedness constraints. In principle, a markedness constraint could favor [paʔə] over [paʔ] or even [paʔəʔə] over [paʔəʔ], relative to the input /pa/. But there are only finitely many markedness constraints, so growth by iterated epenthesis must eventually cease to be harmonically improving. Alternative assumptions about CON, such as constraints favoring antifaithfulness (Alderete 2001a, b) or morpheme realization Kurisu (2001), could undermine these results, but that is perhaps sufficient reason to approach these alternatives with skepticism.

To complete the picture, we ought to consider other potential sources of unbounded candidate growth besides iterated epenthesis. Two come to mind: nonbranching recursion ([... [[*dog*]$_{PWd}$]$_{PWd}$ ...]$_{PWd}$) and iterated construction of empty constituents ([*pa*]$_\sigma$ [ ]$_\sigma$ [ ]$_\sigma$ ...). In classic OT, candidates like these lose because of markedness constraints that have structural economy effects (Gouskova 2003, 2004; Grimshaw 2002). If we assume that insertion of a prosodic constituent node is among the operations that restrained GEN is limited to doing one at a time, then those same structural economy constraints will account in persistent OT for why no derivation ever heads off in the direction of [... [[*dog*]$_{PWd}$]$_{PWd}$ ...]$_{PWd}$ or [*pa*]$_\sigma$ [ ]$_\sigma$ [ ]$_\sigma$ ...

The finiteness of the candidate sets and derivations in persistent OT is not an uninteresting result, but neither is it very significant from a computational point of view. It is the responsibility of linguistic theory to define the function G that maps inputs to outputs. The responsibility to offer a well-defined G is entirely separate from the question of whether G is efficiently computable, a point that has often been emphasized by Chomsky (e.g. 1965:9; 1968:117). The study of computation must be conducted using the theories and methods of that field. The "challenge" of the infinite candidate set comes from assuming that the computational model looks just like the competence model, struggling with the Sisyphean task of sorting an infinite set into harmonic order. Serious work in computation does not proceed in this way (see, e.g., Tesar 1995a, b).

4. Ranking arguments in persistent OT

Persistent OT can require certain constraints to be ranked even when they are nonconflicting and therefore unrankable in classic OT. This situation can occur when at least two operations are required to map the underlying form to the surface form. This difference in constraint rankability is by itself neither an advantage nor a disadvantage of persistent OT; it is merely a difference from classic OT. But in §5 we will see that this difference leads to novel predictions about what kinds of linguistic systems can be analyzed in persistent OT.

The reason for the rankability difference is that persistent OT approaches the ultimate output gradually, through a succession of intermediate forms. Each intermediate form must improve harmonically over its predecessor if it is to win on its pass through EVAL. Constraints can and do conflict over the choice of an intermediate form, sometimes even if they do not conflict over the choice of an ultimate output form in classic OT.

Prince and Smolensky's (2004:141) analysis of augmentation in Lardil illustrates this point nicely. As shown in (3), unaffixed monomoraic roots are augmented by epenthesizing [Ca], where C is a stop that is homorganic with the preceding consonant. Augmentation is a response to the requirement that feet be bimoraic, FT-BIN, which dominates DEP. But FTBIN would be satisfied just as well even if only [a] were epenthesized, yielding *[ṭila], so another constraint is required to force epenthesis of the [C] part of the [Ca] augment. In Prince and Smolensky's analysis, that constraint is ALIGN-R(MWord, σ), which is satisfied only if the rightmost segment in the (underlying) morphological word (MWord) is also syllable final. Since it compels consonant epenthesis, ALIGN-R(MWord, σ) must also dominate DEP. These classic OT ranking arguments are summarized in tableau (4).[2] (Where relevant, word-internal syllable boundaries are indicated by a period/full stop.)

(3) Lardil augmentation (Hale 1973; Klokeid 1976; Wilkinson 1988)
    Root   Nominative   Locative
    /ṭil/   ṭil.ta   ṭil.e   'neck'
    /tal/   tal.ta   ta.le   'vulva'
    /maṛ/   maṛ.ta   ma.ṛe   'hand'
    /kaŋ/   kaŋ.ka   ka.ŋe   'speech'

(4) FT-BIN, ALIGN-R(MWord, σ) ≫ DEP in Lardil

/ṭil/	FT-BIN	ALIGN-R(MWord, σ)	DEP
☞ ṭil.ta			2
a. ṭi.la		W_1	L_1
b. ṭil	W_1		L

In classic OT, the /ṭil/ → [ṭil.ta] mapping does not supply evidence about how FT-BIN and ALIGN-R(MWord, σ) are ranked with respect to one another; since [ɽil.ta] obeys both of these constraints, they are not in conflict. In persistent OT, though, there is another basis for ranking these constraints: conflict over the selection of an intermediate form in the derivation. Under the assumption that restrained GEN can epenthesize only one segment at a time, the direct mapping /ɽil/ → [ɽil.ta] is not possible. Persistent OT instead requires a derivation with an intermediate stage where only one epenthesis operation has occurred, either /ɽil/ → [ɽi.la] → [ɽil.ta] or /ɽil/ → [ɽilt] → [ɽil.ta].[3] The latter derivation begins with a mapping, /ɽil/ → [ɽilt], that is not harmonically improving: [ɽilt] violates DEP without purchasing better performance on FT-BIN. (Codas are never moraic in Lardil.) So the intermediate form must instead be [ɽi.la].

The derivation /ɽil/ → [ɽi.la] → [ɽil.ta] is possible only if the mapping /ɽil/ → [ɽi.la] is possible. And the mapping /ɽil/ → [ɽi.la] is possible only if FT-BIN dominates ALIGN-R(MWord, σ), as tableau (5) shows. This tableau presents a kind of ranking argument that is possible in persistent OT but not classic OT. Intermediate [ɽi.la] must improve harmonically over faithful [ɽil] if it is to be favored by EVAL on the first pass through the GEN → EVAL → GEN → ... loop. The constraints FT-BIN and ALIGN-R(MWord, σ) conflict over [ɽi.la] and [ɽil], and that is why they must be ranked.

(5) Intermediate-form ranking argument: FT-BIN ≫ ALIGN-R

/ɽil/	FT-BIN	ALIGN-R(MWord, σ)	DEP
☞ ɽil.la		1	1
ɽil	W_1	L	L

The /ɽil/ → [ɽi.la] derivation in (5) is not complete. The form [ɽi.la] is submitted to another pass through GEN, and among the candidates emitted are [ɽi.la] and [ɽil.ta]. ALIGN-R(MWord, σ) favors the latter, as shown in (6). After this, no further harmonic improvement is possible.[4]

(6) Final stage of /ɽil/ → [ɽila] → [ɽilta]

/ɽil/	FT-BIN	ALIGN-R(MWord, σ)	DEP
☞ ɽil.ta			2
ɽi.la		W_1	L_2

The ranking result obtained from an intermediate form in (5) is independently supported by a conventional ranking argument – that is, a ranking argument where the winner is the final output form and not one of the intermediate forms. The [C] part of the [Ca] augment is omitted when the result would be an illicit cluster: /jak/ → [ja.ka], *[jak.ka] 'fish' because geminates are prohibited; /teɾ/ → [te.ɾa], *[teɾ.ta] 'thigh' because [ɾt] clusters are prohibited. These examples show that vocalic augmentation occurs even when it results in bad alignment in the ultimate output form, so FT-BIN must dominate ALIGN-R(MWord, σ). The ranking argument appears in (7).

(7) Ultimate output ranking argument: FT-BIN ≫ ALIGN-R(MWord, σ)

/teɾ/	*ɾt	FT-BIN	ALIGN-R(MWord, σ)	DEP
☞ te.ɾa			1	1
teɾ		W$_1$	L	L

Tableau (7) shows the persistent (and classic) OT derivation /teɾ/ → [te.ɾa]. This derivation is complete because no further phonological operations will produce a harmonically improving result. The operation of interest is consonant epenthesis, and in (8) it fails to win because of an undominated markedness constraint against [ɾt] clusters. This is *convergence*: the output of a pass through GEN and EVAL is identical to the input, so further attempts at harmonic improvement are pointless.

(8) Convergence after (7)

/teɾa/	*ɾt	FT-BIN	ALIGN-R(MWord, σ)	DEP
☞ te.ɾa			1	1
~ teɾ.ta	W$_1$		L	W$_2$

In Lardil, the ranking argument based on an intermediate form in (5) is confirmed by a ranking argument based on a final form in (7). But it can also happen that persistent OT will require a ranking that, while not contradicted by final-form ranking arguments, is not necessarily supported by them either. Augmentation in Axininca Campa (Arawakan, Peru) is an example (McCarthy and Prince 1993a; McCarthy and Prince 1993b; Payne 1981; Spring 1990).[5] Under certain conditions, stems must be minimally bimoraic to satisfy FT-BIN. Monomoraic roots like /tʰo/ augment to bimoraicity by epenthesizing the syllable [ta]: [tʰota]. Since the [t] and the [a] cannot be epenthesized in a single operation, the derivation requires an intermediate step, presumably /tʰo/ → [tʰo.a] → [tʰota].[6] For [tʰo.a] to be the intermediate form, it must be more harmonic and therefore less marked than faithful [tʰo].

As shown in (9), this is only true if FT-BIN dominates ONSET, trading [tʰo]'s monomoraicity for [tho.a]'s onsetless syllable.

(9) Intermediate-form ranking argument: FT-BIN ≫ ONSET

/tʰo/	FT-BIN	ONSET	DEP
☞ tʰo.a		1	1
tʰo	W₁	L	L

In the McCarthy and Prince (1993a) analysis of Axininca Campa, FTBIN and ONSET are unrankable because they do not conflict over any output forms. The ranking required in the persistent OT analysis is therefore compatible with but not independently supported by the ranking obtained from conventional argumentation.[7]

The general point is this. In classic OT, if a language with the constraint hierarchy $\mathcal{H}$ maps /A/ unfaithfully to [B], then [B] must be less marked than [A] according to the markedness constraints in CON as they are ranked in $\mathcal{H}$. If /A/ and [B] differ by the effect of two or more phonological operations, however, persistent OT imposes a stricter requirement: there must be a harmonically improving path of forms linking /A/ to [B] by single operations. That is, there must be a sequence of forms $[I_1], [I_2], \ldots, [I_n]$ meeting the following two conditions:

- The mappings /A/ → $[I_1]$, $/I_n/$ → [B], and $/I_j/$ → $[I_{j+1}]$, $1 \leq j < n$, each require exactly one phonological operation (however "operation" is defined).

- $\mathcal{H}$ imposes the harmonic order [B] ≻ $[I_n]$ ≻ ... ≻ $[I_1]$ ≻ [A].

These properties of persistent OT may require constraint rankings that are unjustifiable in (though not inconsistent with) classic OT, as we have already seen. They may also make some phonological mappings impossible, as I will show in the next section.

5. Persistent OT and language typology

If /A/ and [B] differ by the effect of two or more phonological operations, then persistent OT requires a derivation with one or more intermediate forms $[I_j]$. Each intermediate form must be chosen by EVAL from the limited candidate set provided by restrained GEN. In consequence, the intermediate form must be more harmonic than its predecessor and less harmonic than its successor. The various dimensions of phonological difference between /A/ and [B] must be decomposable into a derivation that has these properties. Sometimes, this is not possible, either universally or given other ranking requirements of the system in which the /A/ → [B] mapping is embedded. When that happens, classic OT and persistent OT can make different predictions, even when they incorporate identical assumptions about CON. I will illustrate this phenomenon first with an example based on Lardil. This example has the virtue of familiarity, but it yields a rather uninteresting prediction. I will then present some more substantial examples.

Recall the constraint ranking in Lardil: ALIGN-R(MWord, σ) dominates DEP to account for the consonantal part of the augment in [ʈilta]; and FT-BIN dominates ALIGN-R(MWord, σ) to account for the intermediate stage [ʈila] and for augmentation without the consonant in [teɹa]. Now suppose we change this ranking from ⟦FT-BIN ≫ ALIGN-R(MWord, σ) ≫ DEP⟧ to ⟦ALIGN-R(MWord, σ) ≫ FT-BIN ≫ DEP⟧. In classic OT, this permuted ranking predicts that vocalic augmentation will be blocked just in those cases where consonantal augmentation is blocked, as shown in (10) (cf. (7)). Augmentation of /teɹ/ fails entirely because there is no way of augmenting while maintaining good alignment and satisfying the prohibition on [ɹt] clusters. Augmentation still goes through in those forms like [ʈilta] where there is no problem with augmenting while still satisfying ALIGN-R(MWord, σ).

(10) Effect of ⟦ALIGN-R(MWord, σ) ≫ FT-BIN ≫ DEP⟧ in classic OT

		*ɹt	ALIGN-R(MWord, σ)	FT-BIN	DEP
/ʈil/					
☞	ʈil.ta				2
a.	ʈi.la		W_1		L_1
b.	ʈil			W_1	L
☞	teɹ				
c.	teɹ.ta	W_1		L	W_2
d.	te.ɹa		W_1	L	W_1

In persistent OT, however, the same ranking blocks augmentation across the board, for all inputs: /ʈil/ → [ʈil] and /teɹ/ → [teɹ], as shown in (11). With ALIGN-R(MWord, σ) ranked above FT-BIN, there is no way to get from

/ɾil/ to [ɾil.ta], since intermediate [ɾi.la], which violates ALIGNR(MWord, σ), does not improve harmonically over faithful [ɾil], which violates FT-BIN.[8]

(11) Effect of ⟦ALIGN-R(MWord, σ) ≫ FT-BIN ≫ DEP⟧ in persistent OT

		*rt	ALIGN-R(MWord, σ)	FT-BIN	DEP
/ɾil/					
☞	ɾil			1	
a.	ɾi.la		W$_1$	L	W$_1$
☞	teɾ			1	
b.	te.ɾa		W$_1$	L	W$_1$

The upshot is that classic OT and persistent OT describe different languages under the ranking ⟦ALIGN-R(MWord, σ) ≫ FT-BIN ≫ DEP⟧. In classic OT, the [a] part of [Ca] augmentation is blocked whenever the [C] part is blocked, but otherwise [Ca] augmentation occurs. In persistent OT, there is no augmentation anywhere, the same as if the ranking were ⟦DEP ≫ FT-BIN⟧. In short, classic OT predicts the existence of a language Lardil' with /ɾil/ → [ɾilta] and /teɾ/ → [teɾ], while persistent OT denies that there could be such a language – keeping all the *cetera* exactly *paria*, of course.

In classic OT, where fully realized output forms compete with one another, [ɾilta]'s advantage in satisfying both ALIGN-R(MWord, σ) and FTBIN wins the day. In persistent OT, though, [ɾilta]'s advantage is not apparent at the earlier stage of the derivation, when only [a] has been epenthesized. The ranking ⟦ALIGN-R(MWord, σ) ≫ FT-BIN ≫ DEP⟧ never allows [ɾilta] to see the light of day because it blocks the derivation at the [ɾila] intermediate step. Abstractly, this example is the same as *an'tique ˌstore* in (2): if both *x*s could be moved at once, then *'antique ˌstore* would be the result, but there is no way to get to that result by moving one *x* at a time while satisfying the Continuous Column Constraint along the way.

In these situations, [ɾil] and *an'tique ˌstore* are *local minima* in potential for harmonic improvement. The picture in (12) is intended to illustrate this concept. The ball has rolled part of the way down the hill, but it is stuck in a local minimum of the terrain. The global minimum – the next valley – is more attractive but unreachable. Winning candidates in classic OT are guaranteed to be at the global minimum for further harmonic improvement: there is no more harmonic candidate from the same input. Winning candidates in persistent OT are at some local minimum that may or may not be the same as the global minimum. Like the ball in (12), they can get stuck when the global minimum is reachable only by way of one or more operations that fail to improve harmony. (These are the equivalent of the ball rolling uphill to crest the next rise.)

(12)   Stuck in a local minimum

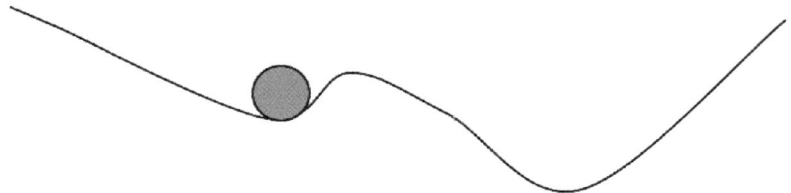

The difference between local and global minima is the basis for all of the predictions that distinguish between persistent OT and classic OT. A hypothetical apocope phenomenon supplies another example. The constraint FINAL-C requires that every phonological word end in a consonant (Gafos 1998; McCarthy 1993; McCarthy and Prince 1994; Wiese 2001). When combined with a constraint CODA-COND that prohibits syllable-final obstruents (Itô 1989; Zec 1995), FINAL-C will favor words that end in sonorant consonants. If both FINAL-C and CODA-COND are ranked above MAX, then all words will be truncated after the rightmost sonorant consonant, as shown in the classic OT tableau (13).

(13)   Effect of FINAL-C, CODA-COND ≫ MAX in classic OT

/palasanataka/		FINAL-C	CODA-COND	MAX
☞	palasan			5
a.	palasanataka	W_1		L
b.	palasanatak		W_1	L_1
c.	palasanata	W_1		L_2
d.	palasanat		W_1	L_3
e.	palasana	W_1		L_4

In tableau (13), the winning candidate [palasan] is the global minimum in potential for further harmonic improvement. In persistent OT, however, this global minimum is unattainable using these constraints. The persistent OT derivation gets stuck in a local minimum: the local minimum is faithful [palasanataka] if CODA-COND dominates FINAL-C (see (14)) and it is [palasanatak] if FINAL-C dominates CODA-COND (see (15)). With CODA-COND top-ranked, there can be no truncation, since truncating the final vowel of /palasanataka/ produces a forbidden coda. With FINAL-C at the top, we get [palasanatak] with vowel truncation, but further truncation is impossible because [palasanata] violates FINAL-C.

(14) Effect of CODA-COND ≫ FINAL-C ≫ MAX in persistent OT

/palasanataka/	CODA-COND	FINAL-C	MAX
☞ palasanataka		1	
palasanatak	W_1	L	W_1

(15) Effect of CODA-COND ≫ FINAL-C ≫ MAX in persistent OT

a. First pass through GEN and EVAL

/palasanataka/	FINAL-C	CODA-COND	MAX
☞ palasanatak		1	1
palasanataka	W_1	L	L

b. Second pass through GEN and EVAL

palasanatak	FINAL-C	CODA-COND	MAX
☞ palasanatak		1	
palasanataka	W_1	L	W_1

Classic OT and persistent OT make different predictions in this situation, and these predictions are at least in principle testable. In classic OT, the grammar (13) describes a language where words are truncated after the rightmost sonorant consonant, or not at all if there is no sonorant consonant in the word. In persistent OT, the same grammar describes a language that truncates the final vowel in /...CV/ words (if FINAL-C is topranked), or a language that limits this truncation to words where C is a sonorant (if CODA-COND is top-ranked). Readers may judge for themselves which predictions are more plausible; certainly, no known language works like (13).

It may go without saying, but it should nonetheless be said, that all such results depend on substantive assumptions about the contents of CON. For example, suppose CON were to include the dubious gradient alignment constraint ALIGN-R(Word, [+son, +cons]). which measures the distance in segments between the rightmost sonorant consonant and the right edge of phonological word. Since every deletion of a segment in the trailing string /ataka/ purchases better performance on this constraint, the mapping /palasanataka/

→ [palasan] would be possible in persistent OT. This is one of many dubious results that follow from adopting gradient alignment constraints (McCarthy 2003).

It is important to note that truncation, even truncation of long sequences of segments, is not impossible in principle in persistent OT. For example, like classic OT, persistent OT can describe a pattern of truncation that reduces all words to a single foot. Among the constraints responsible for this pattern is PARSE-SYLL "every syllable belongs to some foot" (McCarthy and Prince 1994). If PARSE-SYLL dominates MAX, then there can be a harmonically improving derivation like (16). (The foot is delimited by parentheses.) This derivation eliminates syllables outside the word's sole foot by deleting their nuclei and cleaning up the excess consonants, one segment at a time. It is harmonically improving if PARSESYLL dominates *COMPLEX-CODA, which itself also dominates MAX.

(16) Persistent OT derivation
Assumed ranking: PARSE-SYLL ≫ *COMPLEX-CODA ≫ MAX

Underlying	/kamasapata/	Improvement
	('kama)sa.pa.ta	✓ PARSE-SYLL
	('kama)sa.pat	✓ PARSE-SYLL
	('kama)sapt	✓ PARSE-SYLL
	('kamaspt)	✓ PARSE-SYLL
	('kamasp)	✓ *COMPLEX-CODA
	('kamas)	✓ *COMPLEX-CODA
Surface	[('kamas)]	

We have seen two different patterns of truncation. In one of them, words are truncated from the right until a satisfactory word-final segment is found. In the other, words are truncated from the right until only a single disyllabic foot is left. Persistent OT cannot accommodate the first pattern, but it can accommodate the second. What is the reason for this difference?

The mapping /palasanataka/ → [palasan] in (13) requires multiple phonological operations in pursuit of a distant goal: satisfaction of FINAL-C and CODA-COND. Taken individually, the operations offer no harmonic improvement; the harmonic improvement is realized only when all of the operations have applied. This behavior is well within the analytic scope of classic OT, since the candidates that are evaluated may show the simultaneous effects of many processes. But persistent OT cannot elide the intermediate steps between /palasanataka/ and [palasan]. Persistent OT requires local harmonic improvement at each step in the derivation. Under the grammar in (13), the /palasanataka/ → [palasan] mapping offers only global harmonic improvement: if all of the segments in /ataka/ are deleted, then and only then will FINAL-C and CODA-COND be satisfied.

In (16), on the other hand, there is local harmonic improvement because each vowel that is eliminated also eliminates a violation of PARSESYLL and each consonant that is omitted improves performance on *COMPLEX-CODA. It is significant that the system with only global harmonic improvement in (13) is not only unattested but almost surely impossible. It is equally significant that systems with local harmonic improvement like (16) are attested in prosodic morphology and language acquisition (McCarthy and Prince 1994; Pater 1997). This match between prediction and reality suggests that local harmonic improvement may be an authentic property of human language and that persistent OT is on the right track.

metathesis processes present further opportunities for studying this difference between classic and persistent OT. If ONSET or NO-CODA is ranked above the antimetathesis constraint LINEARITY, classic OT can force /apekto/ to map to [paketo] by double metathesis (/ap/ → [pa] and /ek/ → [ke]). Tableau (17) shows how this happens.

(17) Double metathesis in classic OT

/apekto/		ONSET or NO-CODA	LINEARITY
☞	paketo		2
a.	apekto	W_1	L
b.	pa.ekto	W_1	L_1
c.	apketo	W_1	L_1

In persistent OT, however, this mapping is not possible. I will make the natural assumption that GEN includes a phonological operation that transposes a pair of adjacent segments: /ab/ → [ba]. The /apekto/ → [paketo] mapping involves two applications of this operation, so there must be an intermediate derivational step, either [pa.ekto] or [apketo]. Neither intermediate step is harmonically improving, however. The mapping /apekto/ → [pa.ekto] swaps one ONSET violation for another, and the mapping /apekto/ → [apketo] swaps one NO-CODA violation for another. Persistent OT, then, cannot obtain the /apekto/ → [paketo] mapping from the constraints in (17). Since double metathesis of this type has never been reported and seems improbable, persistent OT's more limited descriptive power is supported by this example.

Long-distance metathesis shows very clearly the difference between local and global harmonic improvement. Synchronic long-distance metathesis is attested in only a couple of morphologized processes (Carpenter 2002; Hume 2001: 7; Poser 1982),[9] but it is relatively easy to construct rankings that allow it. For example, to obtain the long-distance metathesis of /art/ → [tar] in classic OT requires only that a CODA-COND prohibiting obstruent codas dominate LINEARITY. This ranking result is shown in (18).

(18) Long-distance metathesis in classic OT

/art/		CODA-COND	LINEARITY
☞	tar		2
a.	art	W$_1$	L
b.	atr	W$_1$	L$_1$
c.	rat	W$_1$	L$_1$

The situation in persistent OT is different, however. The path from /art/ to [tar] must go by way of [atr], so the /art/ → [atr] mapping must be harmonically improving. It is not. The pattern of long-distance metathesis illustrated in (18), though consistent with classic OT, is predicted to be impossible in persistent OT. This pattern is also unattested.

In general, although persistent OT does not prohibit long-distance metathesis categorically, it establishes relatively stringent conditions under which it can be possible. In classic OT, the unfaithful mapping /abc/ → [cab] requires that distantly metathetic [cab] be less marked than faithful [abc] and locally metathetic [acb] or [bac]. Succinctly, [cab] ≻ [abc], [acb], [bac]. Persistent OT imposes an additional requirement: locally metathetic [acb] must be less marked than faithful [abc] ([acb] ≻ [abc]). As metathesis gets more distant, the markedness requirements become even stricter, since every intermediate step must improve over its predecessors. Long distance metathesis must be analyzable as a succession of harmonically improving local metatheses under the persistent OT regime, and in most situations that will be impossible.[10]

The difference between local and global harmonic improvement also becomes apparent when we examine processes that manipulate autosegmental association lines. We will look first at flop and then at long-distance spreading.

In autosegmental flop processes, a feature or tone is delinked from one host and relinked to another. Flop rules were introduced in the earliest work on autosegmental phonology (Goldsmith 1976) and flop mappings can be found in various classic OT analyses. Esimbi (Niger-Congo, Cameroon) supplies a nice example (Clements 1991; Hyman 1988; Stallcup 1980; Walker 1997; Walker 2001). In this language, the height of a prefix vowel is determined by the underlying height of the root vowel, and the root vowel neutralizes to [+high]. For example, as shown in (19), the infinitival prefix is a back rounded vowel that alternates among [u], [o], and [ɔ], depending on the underlying vowel of the following root. Hyman and Walker analyze this as a flop process: the height features of the root vowel are transferred to the prefix syllable, and the root vowel becomes high by default.

(19) Esimbi vowel alternations

Underlying root	Infinitive	
/ri/	u-ri	'to eat'
/zu/	u-zu	'to kill'
/se/	o-si	'to laugh'
/to/	o-tu	'to insult'
/dzə/	o-dzɨ	'to steal'
/rɛ/	ɔ-ri	'to daub'
/hɔ/	ɔ-hu	'to knead'
/ba/	ɔ-bɨ	'to come'

It is reasonable to assume that flop is not a primitive operation in GEN and that all instances of flop involve two operations, deletion and insertion of association lines. Flop phenomena, then, require persistent OT derivations that go through an intermediate stage. Two logical possibilities for this intermediate step are illustrated in (20) and (21). The derivation in (20) involves a temporary floating feature, and it is not obvious how this intermediate step constitutes a harmonic improvement. The derivation in (21), on the other, turns out to be fully compatible with Walker's (2001) analysis. I therefore pursue the idea that (21) is the right persistent OT analysis of this phenomenon.

(20) Flop as delinking and reassociation

$$\begin{array}{ccccc} \text{U-sA} & \to & \text{U-sA} & \to & \text{U-sA} \\ | & & & & \backslash \\ [-\text{hi}, +\text{lo}] & & [-\text{hi}, +\text{lo}] & & [-\text{hi}, +\text{lo}] \end{array}$$

i.e., /usa/ → [usɨ] → [ɔsɨ]

(21) Flop as spreading and delinking

   U-sA → U-sA → U-sA
    | \ | \
  [-hi, +lo]   [-hi, +lo]   [-hi, +lo]
 i.e., /usa/ → [ɔsa] → [ɔsɨ]

Walker argues that flop in Esimbi is a response to two markedness constraints. LIC([−high], $_{Wd}$[σ]) requires any token of a [−high] feature value to be linked to a word-initial syllable (cf. Zoll 2004), and CRISP(σ, [high]) prohibits any token of the feature [high] from being linked to more than one syllable at a time (cf. Itô and Mester 1999). These constraints are ranked above IDENT(high), as shown in (22).

(22) Esimbi in Walker (2001)

/u-sa/ | [−hi, +lo]	LIC([−high], $_{Wd}$[σ])	CRISP(σ, [high])	ID(high)
☞ /ɔ-sɨ/ \\ [−hi, +lo]			2
a. /u-sa/ | [−hi, +lo]	W$_1$		L
b. /ɔ-sa/ \\ | [−hi, +lo]		W$_1$	L$_1$

In Walker's classic OT analysis (22), LIC([−high], $_{Wd}$[σ]) and CRISP(σ, [high]) cannot be ranked relative to one another because both are obeyed by every winning candidate. In persistent OT, however, they are rankable based on the first step in the derivation /usa/ → [ɔsa] → [ɔsɨ] (see (23)). For [ɔsa] to improve harmonically over faithful [usa], a temporary violation of CRISP(σ, height) must be tolerated in exchange for immediate satisfaction of LIC([−high], Wd[σ]). This is another case where harmonic improvement in a derivation requires ranking two constraints that are unrankable in classic OT, since they do not conflict in surface forms of the language.

 This reanalysis of Esimbi implies the claim that all instances of the flop phenomenon are reducible to combinations of spreading and delinking. If

(23) Esimbi in persistent OT
a. First pass through GEN and EVAL

/u-sa/ | [−hi, +lo]	LIC([−high], $_{Wd}$[σ])	CRISP(σ, [high])	ID(high)
☞ /ɔ-sa/ \ | [−hi, +lo]		1	1
/u-sa/ | [−hi, +lo]	W_1	L	L

b. Second pass through GEN and EVAL

/ɔ-sa/ \ | [−hi, +lo]	LIC([−high], $_{Wd}$[σ])	CRISP(σ, [high])	ID(high)
☞ /ɔ-sɨ/ \ [−hi, +lo]			2
/ɔ-sa/ \ | [−hi, +lo]		W_1	L_1

this surmise is correct, then flop should have properties that are similar to assimilatory spreading processes in other languages. This flop/assimilation connection seems right. For example, dialects of Emakhuwa (Bantu, Mozambique) differ in whether a particular process involves tone spreading or tone flop (Cassimjee and Kisseberth 1999). More generally, this approach to flop makes strong predictions: all proposed restrictions on assimilation, such as locality, should also be possible restrictions on flop, since flop is assimilation with an additional derivational step.

Long-distance autosegmental spreading has obvious relevance to persistent OT. A natural assumption is that GEN is limited to adding one association line at a time, so long-distance spreading involves a succession of local spreading operations (see (24)).

For derivations like (24) to show steady harmonic improvement, there must be some markedness constraint that imposes the harmonic ordering ... ≻ [tátátá...] ≻ [tátáta...] ≻ [tátata...]. Such a constraint is equally

(24) Long-distance spreading in persistent OT

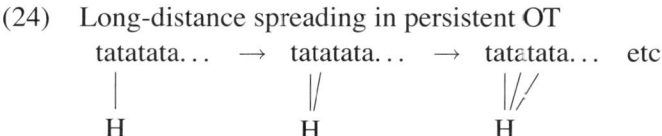

necessary in classic OT analyses to account for those cases where an autosegment spreads as far as it can until it encounters a blocking segment (McCarthy 2003; Wilson 2003, 2004): /tátatatàta/ → [tátátátàta]. This is why gradient alignment constraints have been favored as the impetus for autosegmental spreading (Archangeli and Pulleyblank 1994; Cole and Kisseberth 1995; Kirchner 1993; Pulleyblank 1996; Smolensky 1993 etc.). There are alternatives to gradient alignment, some of which have the necessary properties and some of which do not. For discussion, see McCarthy (2004).

In persistent OT, long-distance autosegmental spreading or flop cannot be compelled by markedness constraints that do not impose harmonic orderings like ... ≻ [tátátá...] ≻ [tátáta...] ≻ [tátata...]. This is a point of difference from classic OT, which allows a much wider range of markedness constraints to produce spreading or flop. The following example is based on José and Auger's (2004) analysis of Vimeu Picard (Romance, France).

In Vimeu Picard, voiced stop codas become nasals after nasalized vowels: /repɔ̃d/ → [repɔ̃n] 'to answer' (cf. [repɔ̃dy] 'answered'). José and Auger propose that nasalization of coda /d/ has essentially the same explanation as devoicing of coda obstruents in German. According to Lombardi (1999; 2001), coda devoicing satisfies the context-free markedness constraint *VCDOBST, which is violated by any voiced obstruent. The positional faithfulness constraint IDENTONS protects onset consonants from alteration. As tableau (25) shows, the only real difference between German and Vimeu Picard is that the crucially dominated faithfulness constraint is IDENT(nasal) rather than IDENT(voice).

Coda nasalization is subject to an important limitation: it can only happen by spreading from an adjacent segment (preceding or following). For example, the failure of coda nasalization in /berlœd/ → [berlœd], *[berlœn] 'old ewe' shows that the feature value [+nasal] cannot be epenthesized, only spread. (This form also shows that coda devoicing does not occur as an alternative.) The constraint DEP(nasal), ranked above *VCDOBST, accounts for this observation (see (26)). In forms like [repɔ̃n], [+nasal] is present in the underlying representation, so DEP(nasal) is satisfied (see (27)).

In classic OT, *VCDOBST could in principle compel spreading of [+nasal]

(25) Coda nasalization in Vimeu Picard

		IDENT (voice)	IDENT ONS (nasal)	*VCD OBST	IDENT (nasal)
	/repɔ̃d/				
☞	re.pɔ̃n				1
a.	re.pɔ̃d			W₁	L
b.	re.pɔ̃t	W₁			L
	/repɔ̃dy/				
☞	re.pɔ̃.dy			1	
c.	re.pɔ̃.ty	W₁		L	
d.	re.pɔ̃.ny		W₁	L	W₁

(26) DEP(nasal) ≫ *VCDOBST in Vimeu Picard

		IDENT (voice)	DEP (nasal)	*VCD OBST	IDENT (nasal)
	/berlœd/				
☞	berlœd			1	
a.	berlœn | [+nas]		W₁	L	W₁
b.	berlœt	W₁		L	

from a more distant host. For example, *VCDOBST would favor mapping hypothetical /mad/ to [mãn] or /nead/ to [nẽãn].[11] In these forms, [+nasal] is spreading from a nonadjacent segment to satisfy *VCDOBST, and only low-ranking IDENT(nasal) is violated. Distant spreading does not seem to happen in Vimeu Picard, and additional constraints ranked above *VCDOBST could be invoked to block it. But a language-particular solution to this problem misses the point: it is likely that *no* language could do what Vimeu Picard does not do. That is, the local advantage of avoiding a violation of *VCDOBST cannot be achieved by long-distance spreading in any language.

This typological claim is problematic in classic OT. Classic OT's unrestrained GEN offers up output candidates like [nẽãn] for /nead/, and *VCD OBST favors [nẽãn] over faithful [nead] and other alternatives. In persistent OT, however, restrained GEN can only get from /nead/ to [nẽãn] by a succession of local spreading operations: /nead/ → [nẽad] → [nẽãd] → [nẽãn]. On

(27) Spreading does not violate DEP(nasal)

		IDENT (voice)	DEP (nasal)	*VCD OBST	IDENT (nasal)
	/repɔ̃d/ | [+nas]				
☞	repɔ̃n // [+nas]				1
a.	repɔ̃d / [+nas]			W₁	L
b.	repɔ̃t / [+nas]	W₁			L
c.	repɔ̃n // [+nas][+nas]		W₁		1

the first pass through the GEN → EVAL → GEN → ... loop, the candidate set includes [nẽad] and faithful [nead]. But *VCDOBST does not favor [nẽad], so the derivation terminates. Faithful [nead] is a local minimum, so [nẽãn] is unreachable from /nead/ with a grammar like the one in Vimeu Picard.

Nonlocal autosegmental spreading of [+nasal] is possible in persistent OT if the grammar has IDENT(nasal) ranked below a constraint that imposes the harmonic ordering [nẽãn] ≻ [nẽãd] ≻ [nẽad] ≻ [nead]. But *VCDOBST is not such a constraint – all it says is [nẽãn] ≻ [nẽãd], [nẽad], [nead]. In general, markedness constraints that offer a harmonic advantage only after several segments have been traversed can never compel nonlocal spreading in persistent OT, even though they are free to do so in classic OT. Persistent OT, then, offers a restrictive typology of harmony and tone-spreading processes.

6. Conclusion

This chapter began with a quotation from Prince and Smolensky. They describe an alternative implementation of OT in which progress toward maximal harmony is gradual. GEN is subject to restraint rather than freedom of analysis, but GEN and EVAL apply repeatedly as long as greater harmony can be achieved. We looked at an important early precedent for this approach, the analysis of rhythmic stress shift in Prince (1983). We have seen various ways in which persistent OT differs from classic OT.

Persistent OT can impose stricter ranking requirements than classic OT because of the need to ensure harmonic improvement in the intermediate forms as well as the ultimate output. For the same reason, persistent OT predicts a more restrictive language typology. As we have seen, this more restrictive typology conforms rather well to observation.

What else can be gained from this alternative way of looking at OT? In McCarthy (2007) I argue that persistent OT's derivations are the candidates that the grammar evaluates. This means that EVAL can optimize the properties of the derivations themselves as well as the forms that those derivations produce. This leads to a new perspective on the problem of phonological opacity in Optimality Theory.

Notes

1. This result harks back to Tesar's (1995b) syllabic parsing model, which proceeds directionally rather than derivationally but with the same basic idea.
2. Throughout, I follow Prince (2002) in using comparative tableaux. The winning candidate appears to the right of the arrow, and losers are in the rows below it. Subscripted integers stand for the number of violation marks incurred by a candidate, replacing the familiar strings of asterisks. In loser rows, the effects of the constraints are indicated by W and L, W if the constraint favors the winner and L if it favors the loser.
3. Persistent OT derivations like /ɾil/ → [ɾi.la] → [ɾil.ta] show that the resyllabification that accompanies epenthesis cannot count for the one-operation-at-a-time restriction on GEN. An "operation", in the relevant sense, is an unfaithful mapping, and resyllabification is not in itself unfaithful. See McCarthy (2007) for discussion.
4. Tableau (6) reckons faithfulness violations relative to the local input rather than the underlying representation. This is a point on which implementations of persistent OT might differ. See McCarthy (2007) for a different approach.
5. I am indebted to Nicole Nelson for pointing this out.
6. The derivation cannot be /tʰo/ → [tʰot] → [tʰota]. Since codas are not moraic in this language, [thot] does not improve performance on FT-BIN.
7. In the analysis of Axininca Campa sketched by Downing (1998:18–22), ranking (the equivalent of) FT-BIN over ONSET can be independently justified using conventional

argumentation. This ranking accounts for the difference in reduplicative behavior between short and long vowel-initial roots: initial onsetless syllables are forced into the reduplicative base when the root is short ([asi-asi] 'cover more and more') but not when the rest of the root is long enough ([osampisampi] 'ask more and more').

8. What about [ṭil.a] as the intermediate step from /ṭil/ to [ṭil.ta]? In Lardil, ONSET must dominate ALIGN-R(MWord, σ) to account for the syllabification [te.ra] rather than *[ter.a]. Therefore, the mapping /ṭil/ → [ṭil.a] is not harmonically improving.
9. Hume (2001): "all regular cases of synchronic metathesis involve adjacent segments".
10. These observations about metathesis in persistent OT are relevant to Horwood's (2004) proposal that infixation is reducible to metathesis. In his view, infixation in Tagalog /umsulat/ → [sumulat] 'to write (actor focus)' is the result of a LINEARITY-violating transposition. If each transposition of a pair of adjacent segments requires a separate operation, as I have assumed, then this mapping would have to be obtained with a derivation like /umsulat/ → [usmulat] → [sumulat]. To my knowledge, nothing in Tagalog phonology explains how the initial step /umsulat/ → [usmulat] could be harmonically improving. Horwood's proposal would be a better fit to persistent OT if the entire morpheme /-um-/ could be shifted in a single operation. Something like this may be necessary anyway to explain why infixal morphemes normally remain contiguous even when the roots that they are infixed into do not.
11. These examples presuppose that spreading of [+nasal] never skips over segments. When feature or tone spreading is allowed to skip over segments or syllables, the differences between classic and persistent OT become less obvious, but they do not disappear entirely. For arguments that spreading never skips, see Gafos (1999), Ní Chiosáin and Padgett (2001), Rose and Walker (2004), and Walker (1998), among others.

References

Alderete, John
    2001a   Dominance effects as transderivational anti-faithfulness. *Phonology* 18: 201–253.
    2001b   *Morphologically Governed Accent in Optimality Theory*. New York/London: Routledge.
Archangeli, Diana, and Douglas Pulleyblank
    1994   Kinande vowel harmony: Domains, grounded conditions, and one-sided alignment. Ms., University of Arizona and University of British Columbia.
Black, H. Andrew
    1993   Constraint-Ranked Derivation: A Serial Approach to Optimization. Ph.D. diss., Department of Linguistics, University of California, Santa Cruz.
Carpenter, Angela
    2002   Noncontiguous metathesis and adjacency. In *University of Massachusetts Occasional Papers in Linguistics 26*, Angela Carpenter, Andries Coetzee and Paul de Lacy (eds.), 1–26. (Papers in Optimality Theory II.) Amherst, Mass.: GLSA.
Cassimjee, Farida, and Charles Kisseberth
    1999   A conspiracy argument for Optimality Theory: Emakhuwa dialectology. In

UPenn Working Papers in Linguistics 6(1), Jim Alexander, Na-Rae Han and Michelle Minnick Fox (eds.), 81–96. Philadelphia: Department of Linguistics, University of Pennsylvania.

Chomsky, Noam
1965 Aspects of the Theory of Syntax. Cambridge, Mass.: MIT Press.
1968 Language and Mind. New York: Harcourt Brace Jovanovich.

Clements, G. N.
1991 Vowel height assimilation in Bantu languages. In *BLS 17S: Proceedings of the Special Session on African Language Structures*, Kathleen Hubbard (ed.), 25–64. Berkeley: Berkeley Linguistic Society.

Cole, Jennifer S., and Charles Kisseberth
1995 An Optimal Domains theory of harmony. Urbana: University of Illinois.

Downing, Laura J.
1998 On the prosodic misalignment of onsetless syllables. *Natural Language and Linguistic Theory* 16: 1–52.

Gafos, Adamantios
1998 Eliminating long-distance consonantal spreading. *Natural Language and Linguistic Theory* 16: 223–278.
1999 *The Articulatory Basis of Locality in Phonology*. New York: Garland.

Goldsmith, John
1976 An overview of autosegmental phonology. *Linguistic Analysis* 2: 23–68.

Gouskova, Maria
2003 Deriving economy: Syncope in Optimality Theory. Ph.D. diss., Department of Linguistics, University of Massachusetts Amherst.

2004 Minimal reduplication as a paradigm uniformity effect. In *The Proceedings of the 22nd West Coast Conference on Formal Linguistics*, Vineeta Chand, Ann Kelleher, Angelo J. Rodriguez and Benjamin Schmeiser (eds.), 265–278. Somerville, Mass.: Cascadilla Press.

Grimshaw, Jane
2002 Economy of structure in OT. In *University of Massachusetts Occasional Papers in Linguistics 26*, Angela Carpenter, Andries Coetzee and Paul de Lacy (eds.), 81–120. (Papers in Optimality Theory II.) Amherst, Mass: GLSA.

Hale, Kenneth
1973 Deep-surface canonical disparities in relation to analysis and change: An Australian example. In *Current Trends in Linguistics*, Thomas Sebeok (ed.), 401–458. The Hague: Mouton.

Horwood, Graham
2004 Order without Chaos: Relational Faithfulness and Position of Exponence in Optimality Theory. Ph.D. diss., Department of Linguistics, Rutgers University.

Hume, Elizabeth
2001 Metathesis: Formal and functional considerations. In *Surface Syllable Structure and Segment Sequencing*, Elizabeth Hume, Norval Smith and Jeroen van de Weijer (eds.), 1–25. Leiden: Holland Institute of Linguistics (HIL).

Hyman, Larry
 1988 Underspecification and vowel height transfer in Esimbi. *Phonology* 5: 255–273.
Itô, Junko
 1989 A prosodic theory of epenthesis. *Natural Language and Linguistic Theory* 7: 217–259.
Itô, Junko, and Armin Mester
 1999 Realignment. In *The Prosody-Morphology Interface*, René Kager, Harry van der Hulst and Wim Zonneveld (eds.), 188–217. Cambridge: Cambridge University Press.
José, Brian, and Julie Auger
 2004 *(Final) nasalization as an alternative to (final) devoicing: The case of Vimeu Picard.* In Indiana University Linguistics Club Working Papers Online, Brian José and Ken De Jong (eds.). Bloomington, In.: Indiana University Linguistics Club.
Kirchner, Robert
 1993 Turkish vowel harmony and disharmony: An Optimality Theoretic account. Los Angeles: UCLA.
Klokeid, Terry
 1976 Topics in Lardil Grammar. Ph.D. diss., Department of Linguistics, MIT.
Kurisu, Kazutaka
 2001 The Phonology of Morpheme Realization. Ph.D. diss., Department of Linguistics, University of California, Santa Cruz.
Lombardi, Linda
 1999 Positional faithfulness and voicing assimilation in Optimality Theory. *Natural Language and Linguistic Theory* 17: 267–302.
 2001 Why Place and Voice are different: Constraint-specific alternations in Optimality Theory. In *Segmental Phonology in Optimality Theory: Constraints and Representations*, Linda Lombardi (ed.), 13-45. Cambridge: Cambridge University Press.
McCarthy, John J.
 1993 A case of surface constraint violation. *Canadian Journal of Linguistics* 38: 169–195.
 2000 Harmonic serialism and parallelism. In *Proceedings of the North East Linguistics Society* 30, Masako Hirotani (ed.), 501–524. Amherst, Mass.: GLSA Publications.
 2002 *A Thematic Guide to Optimality Theory.* Cambridge: Cambridge University Press.
 2003 OT constraints are categorical. *Phonology* 20: 75–138.
 2004 Headed spans and autosegmental spreading. Ms., University of Massachusetts, Amherst.
 2007 *Hidden Generalizations: Phonological Opacity in Optimality Theory.* London: Equinox Publishing.
McCarthy, John J., and Alan S. Prince
 1993a *Prosodic Morphology: Constraint Interaction and Satisfaction.* New Brunswick, NJ: Rutgers University Center for Cognitive Science

1993b Generalized Alignment. In *Yearbook of Morphology*, Geert Booij and Jaap van Marle (eds.), 79–153. Dordrecht: Kluwer.

1994 The emergence of the unmarked: Optimality in prosodic morphology. In *Proceedings of NELS 24*, Mercè Gonzàlez (ed.), 333–379. Amherst, Mass.: GLSA Publications.

1995 Faithfulness and reduplicative identity. In *University of Massachusetts Occasional Papers in Linguistics* 18, Jill Beckman, Laura Walsh Dickey and Suzanne Urbanczyk (eds.), 249–384. Amherst, Mass.: GLSA Publications.

1999 Faithfulness and identity in Prosodic Morphology. In *The Prosody-Morphology Interface*, René Kager, Harry van der Hulst, and Wim Zonneveld (eds.), 218–309. Cambridge: Cambridge University Press.

Moreton, Elliott
2003 Non-computable functions in Optimality Theory. In *Optimality Theory in Phonology: A Reader*, John J. McCarthy (ed.), 141–163. Malden, MA, and Oxford, UK: Blackwell.

Ní Chiosáin, Máire, and Jaye Padgett
2001 Markedness, segment realization, and locality in spreading. In *Segmental Phonology in Optimality Theory: Constraints and Representations*, Linda Lombardi (ed.). New York: Cambridge University Press.

Norton, Russell J.
2003 Derivational Phonology and Optimality Phonology: Formal comparison and synthesis. Ph.D. diss., Department of Linguistics, University of Essex.

Pater, Joe
1997 Minimal violation and phonological development. *Language Acquisition* 6: 201–253.

Payne, David L.
1981 *The Phonology and Morphology of Axininca Campa*. The Summer Institute of Linguistics and University of Texas at Arlington.

Poser, William
1982 Phonological representations and action-at-a-distance. In *The Structure of Phonological Representations*, Harry van der Hulst and Norval Smith (eds.), 121–158. Dordrecht: Foris.

Prince, Alan S.
1983 Relating to the grid. *Linguistic Inquiry* 14: 19–100.
2002 Arguing optimality. In *Papers in Optimality Theory II*, Angela Carpenter, Andries Coetzee and Paul de Lacy (eds.), 269–304. (University of Massachusetts Occasional Papers 26) Amherst, Mass.: GLSA.

Prince, Alan S., and Paul Smolensky
1993 Optimality theory. Constraint interaction in generative grammar. Technical Report #2, Rutgers University Center for Cognitive Science. ROA 537; published in 2004 by Blackwell Publishers.

Pulleyblank, Douglas
1996 Neutral vowels in Optimality Theory: A comparison of Yoruba and Wolof. *Canadian Journal of Linguistics* 41: 295–347.

Rose, Sharon, and Rachel Walker
2004 A typology of consonant agreement as correspondence. *Language* 80: 475–531.
Smolensky, Paul
1993 Harmony, markedness, and phonological activity. Rutgers Optimality Workshop I, New Brunswick, NJ.
Spring, Cari
1990 Implications of Axininca Campa for Prosodic Morphology and reduplication. Ph.D. diss., Department of Linguistics, University of Arizona.
Stallcup, Kenneth L.
1980 Noun classes in Esimbi. In *Noun Classes in the Grassfields Bantu Borderland*, 139–153. Los Angeles: Dept. of Linguistics, University of Southern California.
Tesar, Bruce
1995a Computational Optimality Theory. Ph.D. diss., Department of Linguistics, University of Colorado.
1995b *Computing Optimal Forms in Optimality Theory: Basic Syllabification.* Boulder, CO: Department of Computer Science, University of Colorado
Walker, Rachel
1997 Faith and markedness in Esimbi feature transfer. In *Phonology at Santa Cruz*, Rachel Walker, Motoko Katayama and Dan Karvonen (eds.), 103–115. Santa Cruz, CA: Linguistics Research Center, UC Santa Cruz.
1998 Nasalization, neutral segments, and opacity effects. Ph.D. diss., Department of Linguistics, University of California, Santa Cruz.
2001 Positional markedness in vowel harmony. In *Proceedings of the 5th HIL Phonology Conference*, Caroline Féry, Antony Dubach Green and Ruben van de Vijver (eds.), 212–232. Potsdam, Germany: University of Potsdam.
Wiese, Richard
2001 The structure of the German vocabulary: Edge marking of categories and functional considerations. *Linguistics* 39: 95–115.
Wilkinson, Karina
1988 Prosodic structure and Lardil phonology. *Linguistic Inquiry* 19: 325–334.
Wilson, Colin
2003 Unbounded spreading in OT (or, Unbounded spreading is local spreading iterated unboundedly). Paper presented at the 8th South Western Optimality Theory Workshop, Tucson, Ariz.
2004 Analyzing unbounded spreading with constraints: Marks, targets, and derivations. Los Angeles: UCLA
Zec, Draga
1995 Sonority constraints on syllable structure. *Phonology* 12: 85–129.
Zoll, Cheryl
2004 Positional asymmetries and licensing. In *Optimality Theory in Phonology: A Reader*, John J. McCarthy (ed.), 365–378. Malden, Mass./Oxford, UK: Blackwell.

Chapter 10
The roles of GEN and CON in modeling ternary rhythm*

Curt Rice

1. Introduction

Structures absent from the set of well-formed representations in natural language can be avoided by restricting the alphabet or the operations which are inherently available in Universal Grammar. Alternatively, they can be suppressed by restrictions articulated in every individual grammar. In Optimality Theory, the first of these strategies would be modeled through restrictions on GEN, and the second via the interaction of constraints in CON (Prince and Smolensky 1993).[1] The present article aims to elucidate these options by considering competing strategies for approaching metrical analyses of ternary rhythm in OT.

I begin by setting the theoretical stage for further exploration of a division of labor between GEN and CON, including a selective review of the guidance offered in the literature on this matter. This is followed by a reminder of the analytical challenges which ternary rhythm presents as we review the two dominant strategies found in metrical theory for modeling such patterns. The remainder of the paper is devoted to schematic discussion of OT strategies and their implications for GEN and CON as potential subdivisions in which restrictions on structure might reside.

The contributions of the paper are twofold. Specific problems are identified where a solution could either be in GEN or CON, and the relative merits of those possible solutions are discussed. In this way, I aspire to stimulate more explicit engagement with the properties of GEN including specific restrictions on freedom of analysis. Secondarily, the paper makes clear that we currently lack an OT strategy for modeling ternary rhythm which achieves its results exclusively as an emergent effect from constraint interaction. Instead, I demonstrate that even the best effort has explicit ternary-specific stipulations lurking in the shadows. While my intention here is not to provide an analysis of ternary rhythm – which is introduced for the present purposes to occasion a discussion of the division of labor between GEN and CON – a set of issues are nonetheless identified which future work on ternary rhythm must consider.

2. Phonological structure in OT

The advent of Optimality Theory correlates chronologically with the near cessation of work on the structure of phonological entities. The severed lines of research include many of those most prominent in the 1980s, such as feature geometry, the internal structure of the syllable and the metrical theory of stress, to name just a few.

Part of the responsibility for this state of affairs surely resides in the fact that OT is itself not a theory of structure. Indeed, no theory of the structure of any grammatical entity is inherently in conflict with an OT approach to modeling grammar; arguments advancing one theory of structure against another therefore have no bearing on the validity of OT. With OT, the focus of research shifts to the properties of constraints and their interaction and to other aspects of the theory, in part with the goal of determining the potential of a parallel model *vis-à-vis* derivational approaches.

There is a second culprit bearing responsibility for the reduction in work on phonological structure, namely the GEN-defining principle of *freedom of analysis* which simply states that 'any amount of structure may be posited' McCarthy and Prince (1993b: 21).[2] GEN receives an input, and freedom of analysis operates to posit structure, spouting candidates which may be identical to the input, but which may also have either less or more structure than the input.

> [Gen] generates for any given input a large space of candidate analyses by freely exercising the basic structural resources of the representational theory. The idea is that the desired output lies somewhere in this space, and the constraint system of the grammar is strong enough to single it out.
> (Prince and Smolensky 1993: 6)

One nearly reads the reference to 'basic structural resources' as an invitation to pursue research on the nature of said resources, but acceptance is hindered by frequent assertion of the proliferation of unrestricted structure.

> The GEN function for syllable structure should admit every conceivable structure, with every conceivable array of affiliations and empty and filled nodes.
> (Prince and Smolensky 1993: 26)

We see with these quotes that GEN with its principle of freedom of analysis is presented in classical OT as producing any structure, thereby undermining the need for research to identify which particular structures should be available for manipulation. The division of labor between GEN and CON in the foundational OT literature is clear: GEN can do anything, we needn't say more; for results, look to CON.

And although the door to research on basic structural resources is at times cracked open to rule out definitionally ill-formed structures – syllables dominating feet, crossing association lines, perhaps nonextant distinctive features – the opening just isn't quite wide enough to step through with a serious scientific agenda in hand.

> Since GEN is the same in every language, it initially seems like a good place to deposit a wide variety of "hard" universals [...] There is a flaw here, though. Hardwiring universals into GEN is inevitably a matter of brute-force stipulation, with no hope of explanation or connection to other matters – it is the end of discussion rather than the beginning.
>
> (McCarthy 2002: 8–9)

Hardwiring may indeed be the end of a discussion. But that need not make the discussion itself any less interesting or important, nor does it make the conclusion incorrect. Furthermore, it is not *a priori* inconceivable that hardwired universals can be connected 'to other matters'. Finally, in the context of this quote, the student of OT might be forgiven for thinking that at least in practice, solutions derived from CON – e.g. through the positing of new constraints – aren't immune from the charge of being 'brute-force' either.

Solutions in CON are successful when typological effects emerge from the interaction of independently motivated constraints. Effects which do not emerge in this way might legitimately find their explanation in the structure of GEN. To pursue a discussion of the roles of these two potential solution loci, we turn now to the matter of ternary rhythm.

3. Ternary rhythm in metrical theory

Iterative ternary rhythm in natural language is well-documented, as is the lack of consensus about the implications of these patterns for foot typology.[3] Of particular relevance for us is the disagreement about whether the existence of iterative ternary rhythm compels positing ternary metrical feet. If it does, what are the properties of these feet, e.g. can the head be anywhere in the foot, do the feet have internal structure? Should those properties follow from GEN or CON? If ternary rhythm does not compel ternary feet, should they be ruled out in UG by a restriction on freedom of analysis? Should they be banned in CON by a single constraint or does their absence follow from the interaction of several constraints? In short, what are the contributions of GEN to the analysis of ternary rhythm? What are the contributions of CON and Eval?

Consider first some patterns and the initial reactions to these patterns in the metrical phonology literature. The Bolivian language Cayuvava shows a ternary alternation which can be schematized as in (1), where stress is on every third syllable counting from the right edge of the word Key (1961, 1967). Each number represents a syllable; 0 represents no stress; 1 represents primary stress; 2 represents secondary stress. The words are right-justified because the pattern is claimed to emanate from the right edge of the word. Words of such length are provided in the source materials.

In her analysis of Cayuvava, Levin (1988) relaxes metrical theory to allow for amphibrachs, i.e. ternary feet with prominence on the middle syllable. To give Cayuvava an amphibrachic parse correctly locating stress, Levin uses final extrametricality, which can be overridden when necessary to build at least one foot on the (minimal) disyllabic words. In longer words, initial lone syllables are left unfooted. In (1), parentheses indicate feet and angled brackets mark extrametricality.

(1)   *Ternary alternations parsed into amphibrachs*
        a.   (10)
        b.   (10)⟨0⟩
        c.   (010)⟨0⟩
        d.   0(010)⟨0⟩
        e.   (20)(010)⟨0⟩
        f.   (020)(010)⟨0⟩
        g.   0(020)(010)⟨0⟩
        h.   (20)(020)(010)⟨0⟩
        i   (020)(020)(010)⟨0⟩

Halle and Vergnaud (1987) pursue Levin's strategy and limit UG to this one type of ternary foot, arguing that there is no compelling case of iterative dactyls or anapests. Their strategy is to parameterize a *head terminal* requirement, with amphibrachs having the negative value. A [−head terminal] constituent is one which allows the head to be separated from the edge of the constituent by maximally one syllable (or mora), generating the possibility of iterative amphibrachs, cf. Rice (1988) for related discussion. The ternary foot approach receives further elaboration and restriction in the metrical theory literature, including an approach with internal structure, advocated in works such as Dresher and Lahiri (1991) and Rice (1992); see also related discussion in van der Hulst (1999).

The alternative to an analysis with ternary feet begins with the assumption that UG is limited to the foot inventory in (2) (Hayes 1995).

(2) *The Hayesian foot typology*
    a.   Syllabic trochee (x .)
                                  σ σ

    b.   Moraic trochee   (x .)   (x)
                                  L L or H

    c.   Iamb   (. x)   (x)
                                  L σ or H

Ternary rhythm, of course, cannot be modeled with the exhaustive parsing of a string using any of these feet. But it can be modeled with non-exhaustive parsing, and that is the strategy which Hayes advocates. Instead of being endowed with a particular type of ternary foot, UG is endowed with a parameter which requires with its so-called *weak local parsing* setting that feet be constructed iteratively but non-exhaustively, with an unparsed syllable between each foot. By limiting the intervening material to maximally one (light) syllable, there can be maximally two unstressed syllables between stressed ones, giving a ternary pattern – but not more – using only binary feet.

For a ternary pattern such as that seen in Cayuvava, trochees are constructed from right to left, with final extrametricality and with weak local parsing. In (3c), the final syllable is unfooted by extrametricality and the initial syllable is unfooted because it is too little to be a foot. In (d) the powerful effects of weak local parsing are seen; here there is in fact sufficient material to form a foot, but doing so would result in adjacent feet, which is not allowed by the parsing strategy. Not until we have six syllables, as in (e),

(3) *Ternary alternations parsed into nonexhaustive binary feet*
    a.   (10)
    b.   (10)⟨0⟩
    c.   0(10)⟨0⟩
    d.   00(10)⟨0⟩
    e.   (20)0(10)⟨0⟩
    f.   0(20)0(10)⟨0⟩
    g.   00(20)0(10)⟨0⟩
    h.   (20)0(20)0(10)⟨0⟩
    i   0(20)0(20)0(10)⟨0⟩

is there sufficient space to build two non-adjacent – i.e. weakly local parsed – feet.

4. Amphibrachs in OT

I begin an investigation of the roles of GEN and CON in modeling ternary rhythm by exploring an OT analysis using amphibrachs. To accomplish this, freedom of analysis must obviously be allowed to construct candidates with ternary feet. The discussion here will contribute to our larger goal of examining the trade-off between GEN and CON through a consideration of the status of degenerate feet in a ternary system. Because I am not presenting a thorough analysis of ternary stress, but am rather using ternary stress as an occasion to discuss the architecture of OT, I will make some assumptions which must ultimately be justified in a theory of ternary rhythm. For example, I will follow Halle and Vergnaud (1987) in assuming the absence of dactyls and anapests, and will say nothing more about this here. I will also leave aside any discussion of feet larger than ternary ones.

4.1. Optimizing amphibrachs

To optimize a parse with amphibrachs, CON must be augmented with a constraint which can dominate the well established FOOTBINARITY constraint that requires a foot to be parsable as binary at the level of either the syllable or the mora (Prince and Smolensky 1993). One strategy for optimizing amphibrachs would be a constraint which explicitly rewards parses with this foot type. Prince and Smolensky achieve footing with the constraint RHTYPE=I/T which they describe as 'a constraint which sets the rhythmic type at either iambic or trochaic' with clear reference to the Hayesian typology (Prince and Smolensky 1993: 56). Amphibrachs could be optimized if this constraint were provided with a third setting, RHTYPE=I/T/A, allowing the specification of an amphibrach, which would be violated by any foot not having a series of three syllables with stress on the middle one. Such an approach would correspond to expanding Hayes' typology in (2) to include the amphibrach, a foot which has a flat ternary structure dominating three light syllables or three morae, the middle of which bears stress.

The effect of final extrametricality can be achieved with high ranking NONFINALITY, which prohibits the head foot of the prosodic word from being word-final (Prince and Smolensky 1993: 45), along with ALIGNR(WD, H_{PrWd}), which requires the same foot to be aligned with the right edge of the word (McCarthy and Prince 1993: 34). When NONFINALITY is highest, these two constraints will place the first amphibrach as in the parses in (1). In the tableaux below, these two constraints are assumed in the suggested ranking and we therefore consider only candidates which satisfy NONFINALITY and which violate ALIGNR(WD, H_{PrWd}) exactly once, i.e. candidates which have one 'extrametrical' syllable.

4.2. Degenerate ternary feet

The challenging patterns in (1) are those with imperfect parses, such as (1d) and (1e), with five and six syllables, respectively. With the six syllable string, the optimal candidate should include an initial degenerate foot. This suggests the prioritization of parsing, such that the relevant grammar will rank PARSE above RHTYPE=A.

(4)   *A disyllabic degenerate foot is (correctly) optimal*

σσσσσσ	PARSE	RHTYPE=A
a. σσ(σόσ)σ	**!*	
☞ b. (όσ)(σόσ)σ	*	*

Recall however that (1d) shows the pattern 0(010)⟨0⟩; the final syllable is extrametrical, the initial syllable is left unparsed, and the middle three form an amphibrach. Of course, the optimization of a form lacking a degenerate foot will fail with the grammar developed in (4), as seen in (5).

(5) *A monosyllabic degenerate foot is (incorrectly) optimal*

σσσσσ	PARSE	RHTYPE=A
a. σ(σσ́σ)σ	**!	
☞ b. (σ́)(σσ́σ)σ	*	*

Tableaux (4) and (5) bring out one of the central challenges for characterizing ternary rhythm, namely that there are two conceivable flavors of degenerate foot: binary and unary. In the Cayuvava patterns, and in analyses of other cases of ternary rhythm, degenerate feet are minimally binary; if the language is syllable counting, a degenerate foot is minimally disyllabic, if it is mora counting, the minimum is two morae.

Typological studies of stress patterns make it clear that there is variation regarding the footing of material smaller than a foot. For example, a language with a left-to-right trochaic stress pattern may or may not show stress on the final syllable of an odd-parity string. In OT, this can be modeled by changing the relative ranking of FOOTBINARITY and PARSE. When FOOTBINARITY is relatively high, a final lone syllable will be left unfooted. When PARSE is high, a final lone syllable will be footed.

We continue to assume for this discussion that the footing in (1) is the goal of an analysis, given foot boundary sensitive processes identified in other ternary rhythm languages, cf. Leer (1985); Rice (1992) *inter alia*. Under this assumption, the challenge of degenerate footing leaves us with a paradox. When a single syllable is left at the end of a parse, it remains unfooted, suggesting that PARSE does not compel ill-formed feet because it is lower ranked than the constraint compelling the correct foot type. When two syllables are left at the end of a parse, they are footed, suggesting that PARSE does compel ill-formed feet and should therefore be ranked above the foot type constraint. It's clear, then, that the relative ranking of PARSE and the 'don't parse' constraint (usually FOOTBINARITY, but in the present discussion RHTYPE=A) is not going to be enough to solve this problem. Candidates with monosyllabic feet will have to fail in another way, yet the generation of unary feet cannot be banned outright, since many languages with binary patterns show stress on stray monosyllables.

The problem with unary feet in ternary systems is not just that they are degenerate, but that they are too degenerate. Degenerate feet must be allowed, but only those which are minimally smaller than a full foot. By appealing to this generalization – that a degenerate foot is the size of a full foot minus one terminal – freedom of analysis could be restricted such that parses including ternary feet are prohibited from including unary ones. Alternatively, the generalization could be encoded in a constraint, preserving freedom of analysis and leaving the job of eliminating unary feet to CON, albeit not as an effect of PARSE.

To the extent that all ternary systems prohibit unary ternary feet, a solution in CON would require a universal high ranking since the factorial typology of constraints would otherwise lead us incorrectly to expect variation on this point. Having to resort to a stipulated universal high ranking might itself be taken as a reason to read the restriction into GEN.

When (5b) is eliminated as a candidate by restricting GEN such that a parse with ternary feet cannot include unary feet, (5a) can be optimized. Of course, there are other candidates which must be considered in a more thorough discussion of the analysis of ternary stress, but our primary concern here has been to highlight the trade-offs between GEN and CON.

4.3. GEN and CON for amphibrachs

Although a complete analysis using amphibrachs has not been offered above, we have seen enough to abandon the effort. This approach simply cannot be claimed to model any deep insights into the nature of the patterns. Feet with three syllables can be optimal, but this requires enhancing CON with a constraint RHTYPE=A which does nothing more than explicitly favor feet which are amphibrachs. And – as with the non-OT amphibrach analyses – the generalization about the size of degenerate feet is only available through stipulation, either in GEN or with a stipulatively highly ranked constraint in CON. Results achieved with ad hoc constraints rather than from constraint interaction are not particularly enlightening. So, although a descriptively correct analysis can be imagined by bringing the amphibrach into OT, the analysis is unsatisfying at several levels.[4]

As a final comment in this section, one might question how a constraint RHTYPE=I/T could be better formulated. Markedness constraints are usually formulated to punish ill-formed structures, yet this constraint is phrased positively. More fundamental, though, is that the constraint encodes at least two properties of feet, namely their size and their headedness. And, indeed, it probably encodes more, since RHTYPE=T, for example, is probably intended to punish not only iambs but also left-headed feet not present in the

Hayesian typology, (2), e.g. (HL) trochees. It would be preferably to derive the constellation of properties present in well-formed feet through the interaction of various constraints, such as FOOTBINARITY and perhaps alignment constraints positioning the head of a foot at either the right or left edge of the constituent; for related discussion see Eisner (1998). An enhancement of the constraint (family) to include the amphibrach, however, renders the alignment strategy is unavailable, since the correct position for the head of an amphibrach is exactly where misalignment is achieved; this is yet another reason to delay adoption of an analysis employing iterative amphibrachs.

5. Weak local parsing in OT

Questions about the division of labor between GEN and CON also arise when attempting to model ternary rhythm with binary feet, in the spirit of Hayes' (1995) weak local parsing. For example, if feet are universally maximally disyllabic, should GEN emit trisyllabic feet which are then ruled out by CON, or should GEN build maximally disyllabic feet, leaving to CON the responsibility for optimizing ternary rhythm without having to eliminate ternary feet? The present section presents a strategy for achieving ternary rhythm with binary feet in OT, drawing heavily on the analysis in Elenbaas and Kager (1999), and showing that this approach also makes crucial assumptions which may limit freedom of analysis.

5.1. ALL-FOOT-L/R ≫ PARSE

The footings seen in (3) will incur several violations of PARSE, e.g. four for the pattern in (i), 0(20)0(20)0(10)0. To make these parses optimal, they must be rewarded for their satisfaction of some constraint which dominates PARSE. The relevant constraint will be one which makes footing with fewer feet more harmonic than footing with more. The constraint invoked in the literature is ALL-FT-L/R, as proposed in McCarthy and Prince (1993a). This constraint examines each foot in a parse and awards violations for its distance from the left or right edge, using minimal violation to achieve the effect of directionality. When PARSE dominates ALL-FT-L/R, the effect will be a parse with iterative binary feet. But when ALL-FT-L/R dominates PARSE, fewer feet are favored.

(6) *Minimize the number of feet*

σσσσ	ALLFTR	PARSE
a. (όσ)(όσ)	*!*	
☞ b. σσ(όσ)		**

The two violations of ALL-FT-R in (6a) are associated with the leftmost foot in the string, which is two syllables away from the right edge of the word. When these syllables instead remain unfooted, as in (b), the alignment constraint is satisfied, but each of the unfooted syllables incurs a violation of PARSE.

The ranking in (6), however, goes too far in the pursuit of minimal parsing since it will always favor a parse with just one foot, even in longer strings. The weakly local parsed (7b) must defer to the severely underparsed (7c).

(7) *Optimize unipedal parses*

σσσσσσ	ALLFTR	PARSE
a. (όσ)(όσ)(όσ)	*!*****	
b. σ(όσ)σ(όσ)	*!**	**
☞ c. σσσσ(όσ)		****

So while the illustrated ranking of these two constraints does indeed contribute to favoring the nonexhaustive parses in (3) over exhaustive parsing, it is clear from (7) that the ranking ALL-FT-R over PARSE is not sufficient to generate ternary rhythm. Hence, the analysis must be enhanced by a constraint which stops short of PARSE, but which nonetheless limits a grammar's tolerance of unfooted material.

5.2. Limiting unparsed syllables with *LAPSE

Strings of unfooted syllables can be characterized as ill-formed because they represent unacceptably long spans lacking stress, creating a diserythmic lapse in the string (Selkirk 1984). Various *LAPSE constraints are to be found in the OT literature, e.g. Kager (1994), Green (1995), Gordon (2002), where the leading idea is that a string of more than two unstressed syllables is unacceptable.

Following Ishii (1996), an OT analysis of ternary rhythm can be based on the interaction of *LAPSE and ALL-FT-L/R. The latter compels relatively fewer feet and the former prevents long strings of unstressed syllables. Elenbaas and Kager's formulation of *LAPSE essentially says that an unstressed syllable must be adjacent to a stressed syllable or a word boundary. As we see in the following tableau, this formulation says nothing about footing, such that an unstressed syllable is licensed by a stressed one, independent of the position of foot boundaries, as with the medial unfooted syllables in (8b) and (8c).

(8) *Ternary rhythm with* *LAPSE

	σσσσσσ	*LAPSE	ALL-FT-R	PARSE
a.	(σσ́)(σσ́)(σσ́)		******!	
b.	(σσ́)σ(σσ́)σ		****!*	**
☞ c.	σ(σσ́)σ(σσ́)		***	**
d.	σσ(σσ́)(σσ́)	*!	**	**

Candidate (a) respects PARSE and thereby incurs the most violations of the higher ranked ALL-FT-R, four for the leftmost foot and two for the middle one. Among the candidates which violate PARSE twice, (c) is preferred to (b) under the pressure of ALL-FT-R. In both (b) and (c), *LAPSE is satisfied. The first syllable of candidate (c) does not violate *LAPSE even though it is not adjacent to a stressed syllable, because a word boundary also licenses an unstressed syllable. A *LAPSE violation, however, is awarded to candidate (d), where the second syllable is adjacent neither to a word boundary nor to a stressed syllable; with this fatal violation of *LAPSE, candidate (d)'s superior performance on ALL-FT-R is irrelevant.

5.3. Elenbaas and Kager (1999)

To apply this approach to the patterns in (3), we can consider the strategy advocated by Elenbaas and Kager (1999). I focus on their paper in part because of its explicitness regarding the division of labor. Specifially, Elenbaas and Kager set for themselves the goal of achieving a ternary parse through CON alone, modeling the patterns as an emergent effect of the interaction of independently motivated constraints.

We argue that these analyses [of ternary rhythm – CR] require *no ternarity-*

inducing [emphasis theirs] mechanisms, such as ternary feet or special parsing modes. Instead, ternarity emerges by LICENSING, involving interactions of the anti-lapse constraint *LAPSE [...] with standard foot-alignment constraints [...]

(Elenbaas and Kager 1999: 274)

As we will see below, even the insightful analysis which Elenbaas and Kager present does require a crucial anti-ternarity limitation on freedom of analysis. But before making this point, the core properties of the analysis are presented. Their key insight for predicting the patterns in (3) is that both ALL-FT-R and ALL-FT-L play a crucial role in the analysis. These constraints are crucially ranked, with ALL-FT-L dominating ALL-FT-R for the Cayuvava patterns. ALL-FT-L is crucial for selecting the optimal candidate when a string has the length $3x$ while ALL-FT-R is crucial for strings with the length $3x + 2$ – the so-called double upbeat data. The optimal parse in the $3x + 1$ cases is selected by both ALL-FT-L and ALL-FT-R. Three tableaux are now presented, showing strings of four, five and six syllables, where the optimal candidates show the patterns from (3c-e).

(9)   *Cayuvava 3x string* à la *Elenbaas & Kager (1999)*

σσσσσσ	*LAPSE	ALLFTL	ALLFTR	PARSE
☞ a. (σ́σ)σ(σ́σ)σ		***	*****	**
b. σ(σ́σ)(σ́σ)σ		****!	****	**

All unstressed syllables in the candidates in (9) are adjacent either to stressed syllables or word boundaries, and *LAPSE is therefore unviolated. The first foot of candidate (a) is responsible for no violations of ALL-FT-L but for four of ALL-FT-R. The second foot of candidate (a) incurs three violations of ALL-FT-L and adds one more under ALL-FT-R. When the leftmost foot is not word initial, as in candidate (b), additional violations of ALL-FT-L are incurred but fewer of ALL-FT-R. Candidate (a) is therefore optimal. Because this correctly optimal candidate is inferior on ALL-FT-R, the tableau in (9) constitutes an argument for ranking ALL-FT-L above ALL-FT-R.

Tableau (10) differs from (9) insofar as the optimal candidate for strings having $3x + 1$ syllables will be best not only on ALL-FT-L but also on ALL-FT-R.

(10) *Cayuvava* 3x + 1 *string* à la *Elenbaas & Kager (1999)*

σσσσ	*Lapse	AllFtL	AllFtR	Parse
☞ a. σ(όσ)σ		*	*	**
b. (όσ)(όσ)		**!	**	

The challenge in analyzing stress patterns from Cayuvava always arises with the $3x + 2$ strings. This is where Elenbaas and Kager's insight about the role of both All-Ft-L/R constraints becomes clear. For these strings, All-Ft-L cannot be decisive because this constraint does not distinguish two initial syllables which are unfooted from two initial syllables which are footed, as seen in candidates (a) and (b) in (11). These candidates will be distinguished, however, by their performance on All-Ft-R, which will favor the candidate in which those initial syllables are left unfooted. The lone foot in (a) is separated from the right edge by one syllable and therefore is awarded one asterisk under All-Ft-R. The same violation is found in (b), but the initial foot there adds three more violations under this constraint, with the result that candidate (a) with the double upbeat is optimal.

(11) *Cayuvava* 3x+2 *string* à la *Elenbaas & Kager (1999)*

σσσσσ	*Lapse	AllFtL	AllFtR	Parse
☞ a. σσ(όσ)σ		**	*	***
b. (όσ)(όσ)σ		**	**!**	*
c. (όσ)σ(όσ)		***!	***	*

On the basis of (9), (10) and (11), it is clear that Elenbaas and Kager's approach successfully uses binary feet to get ternary rhythm. But because we are interested in the roles of Gen and Con, and because of freedom of analysis, we should also consider candidates with ternary feet. After all, an analysis which aspires to get ternary rhythm with binary feet as an emergent effect in Con must consider any output of Gen. In the next three tableaux, the optimal candidates from (9), (10) and (11) are shown to compare unfavorably with candidates making use of amphibrachs.

In each of these tableaux, the two candidates have stress on the correct syllables. The difference between them is that in each of the (a) candidates, the rightmost foot is a trochee preceded by an unfooted syllable, while in the (b) candidates, the rightmost foot is an amphibrach. The effect of this in each case is to move the leftmost boundary of the rightmost foot one syllable further to the left, such that the candidate with the amphibrach will

The roles of GEN *and* CON *in modeling ternary rhythm* 247

be better by one when the performance of the two candidates on ALL-FT-L is evaluated. Since all the candidates satisfy *LAPSE, ALL-FT-L is decisive, and in each case, it favors the parse with an amphibrach.

(12) *Cayuvava 3x string allowing amphibrachs*

σσσσσσ	*LAPSE	ALLFTL	ALLFTR	PARSE
a. (όσ)σ(όσ)σ		***!	*****	**
☞ b. (όσ)(σόσ)σ		**	*****	*

(13) *Cayuvava 3x+1 string allowing amphibrachs*

σσσσ	*LAPSE	ALLFTL	ALLFTR	PARSE
a. σ(όσ)σ		*!	*	**
☞ b. (σόσ)σ			*	*

(14) *Cayuvava 3x+2 string allowing amphibrachs*

σσσσσ	*LAPSE	ALLFTL	ALLFTR	PARSE
a. σσ(όσ)σ		**!	*	***
☞ b. σ(σόσ)σ		*	*	**

In these tableaux, we see that the parses with amphibrachs harmonically bound the ones with trochees, such that no reranking can save the parses with binary feet. To save Elenbaas and Kager's analysis, the candidates with the amphibrachs must be eliminated in some other way. This, of course, can be accomplished either in GEN – by limiting freedom of analysis such that ternary feet are not produced – or in CON, perhaps with FOOTBINARITY. With the stated goal of deriving ternarity as an emergent effect, we should think that Elenbaas and Kager would propose eliminating these candidates with a constraint. And, clearly, when FOOTBINARITY is included in the grammar in a position dominating ALL-FT-L, the (b) candidates in (12), (13) and (14) will be eliminated. But as we see in the following section, an appeal to FOOTBINARITY masks other assumptions in this analysis.

5.4. Binary vs. ternary systems

The use of FOOTBINARITY to eliminate candidates with ternary feet is also important for Elenbaas and Kager's analysis of binary systems, and by looking at this analysis we will uncover important assumptions which impact their approach to ternarity. The basic difference between binary and ternary patterns for Elenbaas and Kager is in the relative rankings of ALL-FT-L/R and PARSE, as illustrated in §5.1 above. In binary systems, PARSE dominates ALL-FT-L/R, while in ternary systems, the ranking is reversed. FOOTBINARITY is explicitly stated as relevant for both systems, and it dominates the other two constraints. Highly ranked *LAPSE can be assumed for binary systems, although for our purposes it is irrelevant. The rankings are summarized in (15) and (16).

(15) *Constraint ranking for binary rhythm*
 *LAPSE ≫ FOOTBINARITY ≫ PARSE ≫ ALL-FT-L/R

(16) *Constraint ranking for ternary rhythm*
 *LAPSE ≫ FOOTBINARITY ≫ ALL-FT-L/R ≫ PARSE

The characterization of binary systems in (15) runs into trouble with systems which foot stray syllables, i.e. systems which have degenerate feet. In that situation, the ranking of FOOTBINARITY and PARSE must be reversed to make a candidate with a degenerate foot more harmonic than one with an unfooted syllable.

(17) *Degenerate feet as* PARSE ≫ FOOTBINARITY

	σσσ	PARSE	FOOTBINARITY
a.	(σ́σ)σ	*!	
☞ b.	(σ́σ)(σ́)		*

In identifying the candidates to be considered in (17), we assume only binary feet, which can either be *proper* or *degenerate*, in Hayes' terminology. But we must also consider a candidate with a ternary foot, lest we run afoul of the hypothesis of the Richness of the Base (cf. note 2). As shown in (18), such a candidate will perform just as well as the candidate with the degenerate foot, satisfying PARSE, and violating FOOTBINARITY once.

And, indeed, the situation is even worse, because ALL-FT-L and ALL-FT-R are present in the grammar of binary systems, too; they're just relatively low ranked, as in (15). Add one of these to the tableau, and the parse with the amphibrach alone becomes optimal.

(18) *Equally optimal degenerate or ternary foot*

σσσ		PARSE	FOOTBINARITY
a.	(σ́σ)σ	*!	
☞ b.	(σ́σ)(σ́)		*
☞ c.	(σ́σσ)		*

(19) *An optimal ternary foot*

σσσ		PARSE	FOOTBINARITY	ALLFTL
a.	(σ́σ)σ	*!		
b.	(σ́σ)(σ́)		*	*!*
☞ c.	(σ́σσ)		*	

Again we face an analytical challenge which can be solved either in GEN or CON. If we solve this problem in GEN, we must restrict freedom of analysis to prohibit ternary feet. If we solve it in CON, we need two different constraints to punish deviation from the binary ideal, e.g. *[σ]$_{Foot}$ and *[σσσ]$_{Foot}$. In languages with no degenerate feet, *[σ]$_{Foot}$ asserts itself as highly ranked. But when PARSE is ranked between these two constraints, with *[σσσ]$_{Foot}$ highest, ternary feet will be ruled out while unary feet will be allowed.

(20) *Eliminating the ternary foot with* *[σσσ]$_{Ft}$

σσσ		*[σσσ]$_{Ft}$	PARSE	*[σ]$_{Ft}$	ALLFTL
a.	(σ́σ)σ		*!		
☞ b.	(σ́σ)(σ́)			*	**
c.	(σ́σσ)	*!		*	

Freedom of analysis opens for any amount of structure, such that an analysis of binary rhythm must consider candidates with ternary feet. The ranking necessary to analyze a language with unary feet at the end of a string turns out to be a ranking under which a string-final ternary foot is more harmonic than a string-final sequence of a binary foot followed by a unary one. Because FOOTBINARITY – or at least *[σ]$_{Ft}$ – must be relatively low ranked when unary feet are allowed, an optimal string final ternary foot has to be ruled out either by prohibiting ternary feet in GEN through a restriction on freedom of analysis, or with a highly ranked constraint specifically devoted to ruling out ternary feet.

5.5. GEN and CON in a model of ternary rhythm with binary feet

The solution used for analyzing binary systems will of course also be on the scene for the analysis of ternary rhythm. We noted above that highly ranked FOOTBINARITY might do the job necessary in (12), (13) and (14) by punishing the candidates with an amphibrach in their parse. But, in fact, Elenbaas and Kager have no need to refer to FOOTBINARITY in this context. The reason for this is that their analysis of binary systems – in particular those which allow degenerate feet – requires either a restriction on freedom of analysis blocking trisyllabic feet or a universally highly ranked constraint such as $*[\sigma\sigma\sigma]_{Ft}$. Either way, FOOTBINARITY is supplemented by restrictions on GEN or else replaced by more specific constraints in CON. For this reason, I suggest that the elimination of the ternary feet in those tableaux is not really accomplished by FOOTBINARITY, and the appeal to that constraint has the effect of masking a more complicated situation that includes ternary-specific mechanisms.

Given the arguments made here, one might ask whether Elenbaas and Kager achieve their stated goal of modeling ternary stress without any '*ternary-inducing* mechanisms'. Since nothing in their analysis induces ternary feet, we can concede that they have achieved their stated goal.

But analyses in OT don't need to *induce* structure; structure appears without motivation according to the hypotheses of the Richness of the Base and freedom of analysis. Because of these methodological assumptions in classical OT, the task of an analysis is not to avoid inducing a particular structure, but rather to provide a principled strategy for eliminating an unwanted structure, even one which is proposed to be universally absent.

If the correct analysis of ternary rhythm involves non-exhaustive parsing with binary feet, then the goal of an analysis must be to achieve such a parsing with no *ternary-specific* mechanisms in a way which nonetheless prefers binary feet to ternary ones; in short, parses with binary feet must harmonically bound parses with ternary ones. Ternary rhythm with binary feet must be achieved through the interaction of violable constraints, not through a ternary-specific stipulation in GEN or with a ternary-specific constraint stipulated as universally highly ranked. This is the currently unmet challenge for future attempts to develop emergent analyses of ternary rhythm.

6. Conclusion

The presentation in this paper aims to identify situations in which we are forced to look at GEN and to entertain restrictions on freedom of analysis as a strategy worthy of consideration alongside a possible solution in CON. The specific case under review involves the modeling of ternary rhythm, and the issues which arise there may be somewhat more subtle than definitional restrictions on GEN such as prohibiting crossing association lines. To say that GEN produces maximally disyllabic feet is no less stipulative than the claim that GEN produces maximally trisyllabic feet; both of these restrictions, stated in this straightforward way, are stipulations without any principled foundation.

The universal absence of ternary feet may be a hypothesis worth pursuing and it may be a consequence of a more insightful restriction on GEN – for example, specific properties of constituent structure. To move in the direction of a deeper understanding of freedom of analysis and its implications for modeling grammar and typology, we have to study GEN. We have to look at cases in which different assumptions about GEN have an impact on the details of the analysis being pursued, and then consider the relative merits of these various assumptions. Assumed restrictions on GEN can surely be found in most OT analyses; one never finds, for example, a candidate set for an analysis of stress including candidates which represent prominence with the grid alone (Prince 1983) alongside candidates which use footing, leaving it to CON to distinguish these approaches. Neither does one find analyses of syllable-based phenomena in which structures with 'every conceivable array of affiliations and empty and filled nodes' are actually considered (op.cit.). Freedom of analysis is rarely assumed to be truly free. The assumptions hidden in typical analyses must be made explicit.

By questioning GEN and asserting that research on this aspect of the theory is wanting, I take a different view than the one advocated by McCarthy (2002: 8), where we read that '[i]n phonology, there is a rough consensus about the properties of GEN.' It's difficult to imagine the basis for this claim. Certainly, one cannot reach that conclusion by reviewing the practice seen in most OT analyses, where the assumptions or properties of GEN are rarely mentioned.

But beyond practical matters, if GEN is the repository of truly universal formal structures, then McCarthy's claim boils down to an assertion that there is a consensus about such structures. Yet in fundamental areas such as the inventory of features, feature geometry, the structure of the syllable, or the inventory of metrical feet, the contemporary literature offers little basis for inferring consensus. OT doesn't require the abandonment of research on structure but it does require reconceptualization of how results related to phonological structure should be modeled. Consensus on these matters is a respectable objective, but it does not currently exist.

The quest for results emerging from the interaction of independently motivated constraints should be pursued in explicit awareness that the tools and alphabet available to UG might be limited, and that these limitations are relevant for analyses and loaded with the potential for actual insights, not least of all about the properties of linguistic structures and thereby the properties of the candidates submitted to Eval. The nature of such limitations is a legitimate focus of research, and it is one which we can hope will now assume its rightful place alongside the study of constraints and their interaction.

Notes

* This paper has emerged from presentations at the *Workshop on Freedom of Analysis* in Tromsø, a University College London colloquium, the *Variation and Stability in Grammar* workshop in Nijmegen and the *Fourth North American Phonology Conference* in Montreal; I thank the members of those audiences for their valuable input. I'm also grateful to my fellow phonologists at the Center for Advanced Study in Theoretical Linguistics (CASTL) in Tromsø – particularly Sylvia Blaho, Patrik Bye, Martin Krämer, Ove Lorentz, Bruce Morén, and Christian Uffmann – for discussion of the ideas presented here, and for the input of two anonymous reviewers.
1. A third strategy whereby such structures are simply left unconsidered by the grammar is precluded by Prince and Smolensky's (1993) hypothesis of *the Richness of the Base*. This hypothesis, or methodology, requires that we achieve surface results through formalized generalizations about surface structures, rather than by restricting potential inputs.
2. In the discussion that follows, I consider only an OT model using *harmonic parallelism* and not one using *harmonic serialism*. These two different strategies for implementing OT differ rather fundamentally in their conception of freedom of analysis. As I noted in Rice (2005: 6), 'the pursuit of a restricted theory of GEN might be facilitated by a closer examination of the serial approach to OT and a fitting version of freedom of analysis'. For related discussion, see McCarthy (2007).
3. Relevant references include Leer (1985); Levin (1985); Halle and Vergnaud (1987); Everett (1988); Levin (1988); Rice (1988); Halle (1990); Hammond (1990); Dresher and Lahiri (1991); Hewitt (1992); Rice (1992, 1993); Kager (1994); Kenstowicz (1994); Green (1995); Green and Kenstowicz (1995); Hammond (1995); Hayes (1995); Ishii (1996); Berry (1998); van de Vijver (1998); Blevins and Harrison (1999); Elenbaas (1999); Elenbaas and Kager (1999); van der Hulst (1999); Hyde (2001); Gordon (2002); Hyde (2002); Rifkin (2003); Houghton (2006).
4. Another option for eliminating a unary foot as a candidate degenerate ternary foot is to

build on Rice's (1992) proposal that ternary feet have internal structure, and that two of the three syllables in the foot form a head. The restriction which one would then propose for GEN is that a constituent consists minimally of a head, cf. relevant discussion in Dresher and van der Hulst (1998). In the case of a trisyllabic foot with a disyllabic head, this has the effect of ruling out monosyllabic feet, correctly capturing the generalization about the degenerate feet in the Cayuvava patterns. This is not available in the amphibrachic approach, where the matter requires explicit stipulation. Space restrictions preclude further discussion of this approach here.

References

Berry, Lynn
1998 Alignment and adjacency in optimality theory: Evidence from Warlpiri and Arrernte. Ph. D. diss., University of Sydney. ROA 271.

Blevins, Juliette, and Sheldon P. Harrison
1999 Trimoraic feet in Gilbertese. *Oceanic Linguistics* 38:203–230.

Dresher, B. Elan, and Harry van der Hulst
1998 Head-dependent asymmetries in phonology: Complexity and visibility. *Phonology* 15:317–352.

Dresher, B. Elan, and Aditi Lahiri
1991 The Germanic foot: Metrical coherence in Old English. *Linguistic Inquiry* 22:251–286.

Eisner, Jason
1998 FOOTFORM decomposed: Using primitive constraints in OT. In *MIT working papers in linguistics*, Benjamin Bruening (ed.), volume 31, 115–143. MIT.

Elenbaas, Nine
1999 A unified account of binary and ternary stress: Considerations from Sentani and Finnish. Ph. D. diss., Utrecht University.

Elenbaas, Nine, and René Kager
1999 Ternary rhythm and the *LAPSE constraint. *Phonology* 16:273–313.

Everett, Daniel L
1988 On metrical constituent structure in Piraha phonology. *Natural Language and Linguistic Theory* 6:207–246.

Gordon, Matthew
2002 A factorial typology of quantity-insensitive stress. *Natural Language and Linguistic Theory* 20:491–552.

Green, Thomas
1995 The stress window in Piraha: A reanalysis of rhythm in optimality theory. ROA 45.

Green, Thomas, and Michael Kenstowicz
1995 The lapse constraint. Ms., MIT. ROA 101.

Halle, Morris
1990 Respecting metrical structure. *Natural Language and Linguistic Theory* 8:149–176.

Halle, Morris, and Jean-Roger Vergnaud
    1987   *An Essay On Stress*. Cambridge, Mass.: MIT Press.

Hammond, Michael
    1990   Deriving ternarity. Ms., University of Arizona, Tucson.
    1995   Metrical phonology. *Annual review of anthropology* 24:313–42.

Hayes, Bruce
    1995   *Metrical Stress Theory: Principles And Case Studies*. Chicago: Chicago University Press.

Hewitt, Mark
    1992   Vertical maximization and metrical theory. Ph. D. diss., Brandeis University.

Houghton, Paula
    2006   Ternary stress. ROA 836.

van der Hulst, Harry
    1999   Word accent. In *Word Prosodic Systems in the Languages of Europe*, Harry van der Hulst (ed.), 3–96. Berlin: Mouton de Gruyter.

Hyde, Brett
    2001   Metrical and prosodic structure in optimality theory. Ph. D. diss., Rutgers, The State University of New Jersey. ROA 476.
    2002   A restrictive theory of metrical stress. *Phonology* 19:313–359.

Ishii, Toru
    1996   An optimality theoretic approach to ternary stress systems. In *Proceedings of the South Western Optimality Theory Workshop (SWOT II). UCI Working papers in linguistics*, volume 2, 95–111. Irvine, CA: University of California, Irvine.

Kager, René
    1994   Ternary rhythm in alignment theory. Ms., Utrecht University, ROA 35.

Kenstowicz, Michael
    1994   *Phonology in Generative Grammar*. Oxford: Blackwell.

Key, Harold H.
    1961   Phonotactics of Cayuvava. *International Journal of American Linguistics* 27:143–150.
    1967   *Morphology of Cayuvava*. Janua Linguarum, Series Practica 50. The Hague: Mouton.

Leer, Jeff
    1985   Prosody in Alutiiq. In *Yupik Eskimo Prosody Systems: Descriptive And Comparative Studies*, Michael Krauss (ed.), 77–133. Fairbanks: University of Alaska.

Levin, Juliette
    1985   Evidence for ternary feet and implications for a metrical theory of stress rules. Ms., University of Texas at Austin.
    1988   Generating ternary feet. *Texas Linguistic Forum* 29:97–113.

McCarthy, John J.
    2002   *A Thematic Guide to Optimality Theory*. Cambridge: Cambridge University Press.
    2007   Restraint of analysis. This volume.

McCarthy, John J., and Alan S. Prince
1993a   Generalized alignment. In *Yearbook of Morphology*, Geert Booij and Jaap van Marle (eds.), 79–153. Dordrecht: Kluwer.
1993b   Prosodic morphology I. Constraint interaction and satisfaction. Ms., University of Massachusetts, Amherst and Brandeis University; ROA 482.

Prince, Alan S.
1983   Relating to the grid. *Linguistic Inquiry* 14:19–100.

Prince, Alan S., and Paul Smolensky
1993   Optimality theory. Constraint interaction in generative grammar. Technical Report #2, Rutgers University Center for Cognitive Science. ROA 537; published in 2004 by Blackwell Publishers.

Rice, Curt
1988   Stress assignment in the Chugach dialect of Alutiiq. In *CLS 24: Papers from the 24th Annual Regional Meeting of the Chicago Linguistic Society*, Lynn MacLeod, Gary Larson, and Diane Brentari (eds.), 304–315. Chicago, IL: Chicago Linguistic Society.
1992   Binarity and ternarity in metrical theory: Parametric extensions. Ph. D. diss., University of Texas at Austin. Available at http://www.hum.uit.no/a/rice.
1993   A note on ternary stress in Sentani. In *University of Trondheim Working Papers in Linguistics*, 67–71. Trondheim: Department of Linguistics, University of Trondheim.
2005   Freedom ≢ anarchy. Presented at *Workshop on Freedom of Analysis*, September 1-2, 2005, Tromsø.

Rifkin, Jay I.
2003   Ternarity is prosodic word binarity. In *The Phonological Spectrum, Volume II: Suprasegmental Structure*, Jeroen van de Weijer, Vincent J. van Heuven, and Harry van der Hulst (eds.), 127–150. Amsterdam: John Benjamins.

Selkirk, Elisabeth
1984   *Phonology and Syntax: The Relation Between Sound And Structure*. Cambridge, Mass.: MIT Press.

van de Vijver, Ruben
1998   *The iambic issue: Iambs as a result of constraint interaction*. HIL Dissertations 37. Holland Institute of Generative Linguistics.

Chapter 11
Representational complexity in syllable structure and its consequences for GEN and CON*

Jennifer L. Smith

1. Introduction

The papers in this collection all address some aspect of the following question: In a phonological model developed within the framework of Optimality Theory (Prince and Smolensky 1993), what restrictions, if any, should be placed on GEN, the function that generates a candidate set from a given input form? This paper makes the case that restrictions on GEN must not be considered in isolation; their effects on CON, the constraint set, must be taken into account as well. In particular, allowing GEN a greater degree of freedom in generating subsyllabic structure actually allows for a more restrictive, functionally grounded constraint set.

After some background discussion on the relationship between representational complexity and freedom of analysis (§1.1–2), and on what it means for a constraint to be functionally grounded (§1.3), a set of explicit representational assumptions about subsyllabic structure is presented (§2). Representational complexity is then shown to have implications for CON as well as for GEN, in the context of a sonority-based analysis of liquid-specific onset restrictions (§3). Additional syllabification-related predictions of the version of GEN presented here are also considered (§4).

1.1. On freedom of analysis: Ways of restricting GEN

In principle, there are two distinct types of restrictions that can be placed on GEN. First, it is possible to delimit the space of interpretable linguistic representations by establishing an inventory of primitive representational elements and defining the configurations in which these elements can be placed. If GEN is required to produce only output candidates that conform to these specifications, then we can say that GEN is subject to general *representational restrictions*. For example, a particular phonological model might define a set of primitive elements that includes certain distinctive features and certain prosodic categories, and then specify that prosodic categories may dominate categories lower in the prosodic hierarchy (e.g., syllables may dominate moras) but not vice versa.

The second type, which can be called *content-based restrictions* on GEN, are those that exclude from the candidate set particular structures that are otherwise well formed according to whatever representational restrictions are in place. Examples might include a prohibition on the syllabification [CVC.V], or a prohibition on any candidate with more than two epenthetic segments; these restrictions go beyond general representational restrictions if CVC and V have been included in the set of licit syllable types and GEN is permitted to include epenthetic material in output candidates. The standard objection to content-based restrictions on GEN (e.g., Kager 1999: 20; McCarthy 2002: §1.1.3) is that constraint interaction is a better place to search for explanations for universally unattested structures like these, in order to uncover "connections between the universal properties of language and between-language variation" (McCarthy 2002: §1.1.3). Still, it may be that certain types of content-based restrictions on GEN will produce insightful solutions to open questions.

The focus of this paper, however, is on the first type of restriction. The argument made here is that in order to decide whether placing a particular representational restriction on GEN really simplifies a phonological model, it is essential to consider the effect of that restriction, not only on GEN, but also on the set of constraints CON. In some cases, it is worth giving GEN more freedom of analysis if doing so makes for a better-motivated constraint set.

1.2. Representational restrictions and a link between GEN and CON

Restrictions on GEN of the basic representational type are employed, implicitly or explicitly, by essentially all phonologists working in OT (for a recent, explicit example, see McCarthy 2004). The task of determining what the set of primitive linguistic elements should be, and how they should be combined, is a fundamental component of research in linguistics, and has been for many years under many theoretical frameworks. It is generally considered good practice in phonology to add more-complex representations to a phonological model only when the increased complexity is necessary for explaining phonological patterns. From the perspective of OT, keeping representational complexity to a minimum is a way of restricting the parameter space for GEN – the fewer the representational choices that are available to GEN, the smaller the number of distinct candidates that GEN will produce for a given input.

Furthermore, it has been found that working in OT may allow for the simplification of traditional phonological representations. Phenomena that would be used to motivate a complex structural representation in other frameworks can sometimes be recast in OT as the result of simpler representations, interacting with violable constraints whose incomplete satisfaction produces what looks like a complex pattern. Examples of this kind of representational simplification include McCarthy and Prince's (1993b) approach to Tagalog infixation, in which the infix appears to the right of an entire onset cluster, as in /um + gradwet/ –> [gr-um-adwet] 'graduated'. McCarthy and Prince argue that there is no need to posit a representationally defined "Onset" *constituent* under the syllable node, because the apparently constituent-like behavior of the onset cluster [gr] is an epiphenomenon of best satisfying the constraint NOCODA. Another example is the re-examination of feature geometry by Padgett (2002), who proposes that constraints that call for the spreading of a feature class (i.e., a node) are not all-or-nothing, but can be only partially satisfied in cases where the demands of a higher-ranked conflicting constraint are at stake. This approach allows for a reduction in the number of feature classes (nodes) that must be included in the model, since not every subset of features that is observed to spread together must be structurally modeled as a constituent.

Despite cases like these, however, the use of the simplest conceivable set of phonological representations is not always the best choice, even in the OT framework. This is because there is a mutual relationship between the representational space that GEN can exploit – the structures and configurations that can be present in output candidates – and the types of constraints that make up CON, the constraint set. If a particular model of CON motivates the existence of some constraint C that distinguishes between two structural representations R_1 and R_2, then for C to be phonologically active, there must be candidates that differ on the basis of R_1 versus R_2; that is, GEN must be allowed the freedom to produce both of these structures, or it would be meaningless for CON to include a constraint that distinguishes them.

The representational question considered here is the syllabification of a glide-vowel (GV) string – how many options does GEN have for assigning syllable structure to GV? A structural distinction between pre-peak glides that are syllabified as true onset segments and those that are syllabified in the rime, as part of a rising diphthong, has been motivated in non-OT models for languages such as French, English, Slovak, and Spanish (Kaye and Lowenstamm 1984; Davis and Hammond 1995; Rubach 1998; Harris and Kaisse 1999).

(1)   Structural options for glides
      a. True onset glide   b. Rimal onglide

In the following discussion, {brackets} indicate the syllable rime, so a true onset glide is represented as G{V}, while a rimal onglide is {GV}.

When the question of how glides should be represented in syllable structure is reconsidered under OT, one possibility would be to look to constraint interaction to explain why pre-peak glides seem to behave differently in different languages or different contexts, abandoning the representational distinction between true onset glides and rimal onglides shown in (1). If this approach were successful, it would be another representational simplification like those described above for onset clusters and feature geometry, restricting the freedom GEN has to produce different syllabifications for the same segmental string. However, maintaining a structural distinction between true onset glides and rimal onglides under OT has a beneficial theoretical consequence: It allows for an analysis of onset-related sonority patterns based on phonetically motivated constraints, a result that is not possible if all "onset" glides are taken to have the same structural representation.

1.3.   Functionally grounded phonological constraints

This paper follows Hayes (1999) in designating a constraint as functionally or phonetically grounded if the set of potential output forms that satisfy the constraint is preferable overall, on the basis of some particular functional consideration, to the set of potential output forms that violate the constraint. As emphasized by Hayes (1999), this means that a constraint may be stated solely in terms of abstract phonological symbols and categories, but still be functionally grounded. The *ONSET/X constraint family introduced in §3 below is one such example: it is phonologically defined, such that it only evaluates segments in a particular subsyllabic position, but it is functionally motivated, because it reflects the cross-linguistic preference for low-sonority onsets. See also Gordon (2004) and Smith (2005, to appear) for additional discussion of phonologically defined, functionally grounded constraints.

2. A model of GEN for syllable structure

The claim developed in §3 below, that recognizing two structural positions for glides allows for a more phonetically motivated constraint set, does not depend on the particular formalism by which the rime is represented. Rime segments could be identified on the basis of association to moras, or there could be a structural Rime constituent to which all rime segments belong. What is essential is that there be *some* structural distinction between the two types of glides, to which onset-related constraints can refer. So, for example, this claim is incompatible with the strong version of Blevins' (2003) proposal that phonotactic constraints should generally be stated in terms of segmental strings rather than prosodic structure.

Although various representational models would be compatible with a structural distinction between onsets and rimal onglides, the implications of representational complexity and freedom of analysis cannot be examined without choosing some explicit representational proposal. For concreteness, this discussion assumes a version of moraic theory close to that in McCarthy and Prince (1988) and Hayes (1989), with additional assumptions about the prosodic hierarchy as in Selkirk (1978, 1995). Other sets of representational assumptions concerning syllable structure can and should be explored as well. (For recent proposals that recognize an onset/rime distinction without moraic theory, see Zhang 2002; Gordon 2004).

2.1. GEN and allowable syllable shapes

In the model of GEN to be developed here, syllables dominate moras and segments, and moras dominate segments. (Prosodic structure above the level of the syllable is not considered in this paper.) These structural relationships can be enforced if GEN is subject to the restrictions in (2).

(2) Structural restrictions on GEN for syllabification (after McCarthy and Prince 1988; Hayes 1989; Selkirk 1978, 1995)
   a. A syllable node (σ) can dominate one or more segments (X) and one or more moras (μ).
   b. μ can dominate one or more segments (for phonetically motivated arguments in support of "mora-sharing," see Broselow, Chen, and Huffman 1997; Frazier 2006).
   c. Like all prosodic constituents, σ and μ have unique heads at the next lower prosodic level (heads are underlined in diagrams).

These are representational restrictions, the type of restrictions that define the space of linguistically statable representations. They prevent GEN from including candidates with structures of the following types.

(3) Candidates with the following characteristics are not generated
   a. μ dominating σ, or X dominating μ or σ
   b. multiple heads at any prosodic level
   c. moraless syllables

The representational restrictions in (2) generally seem to be typologically supported; the structures in (3a) are uncontroversially held to be ill-formed, and (3b) is also widely considered to be impossible. There may be some question about (3c), however, since reduced vowels are sometimes treated as moraless (e.g., Hammond 1997, Crosswhite 2004). If it is necessary to relax (3c) somewhat, perhaps GEN can allow for the absence of intermediate prosodic heads as long as there is a terminal head (=segment) for each prosodic constituent.

The basic structural restrictions on GEN outlined in (2) allow for the generation of the types of representations in (4), which are attested syllable structures. (For discussion of structures generated under (2) that may not be as well attested, see the Appendix.) Crucially, these representational restrictions also allow for structures of the types in (5), where the rime includes a non-head segment that precedes, rather than follows, the head. This type of structure can represent a rising diphthong, such as those found in French and Spanish (§1.2).

(4) Structures like the following can be generated

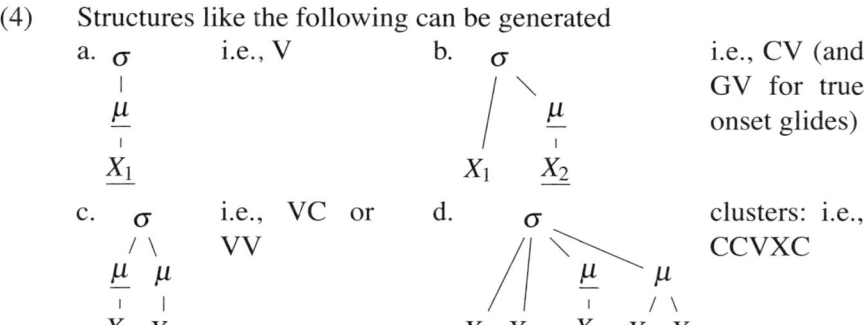

a. σ — i.e., V
b. σ — i.e., CV (and GV for true onset glides)
c. σ — i.e., VC or VV
d. σ — clusters: i.e., CCVXC

(5) Rimal onglide structures: rime segments that precede the peak

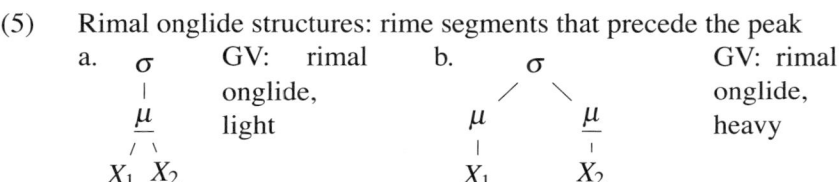

a. σ — GV: rimal onglide, light
b. σ — GV: rimal onglide, heavy

The structural distinction that GEN can make between the X_1 position in (5ab) and the X_1 position in (4b) under this model of syllable structure is what can be exploited to distinguish between true onset glides and rimal onglides. In order for this difference to be phonologically meaningful, however, the constraint set must also be sensitive to this structural distinction.

2.2. GEN, CON, and subsyllabic structure

The next step in this exploration of freedom of analysis for syllable structure is to determine, given the syllable-structure criteria for GEN specified in (2), the set of subsyllabic structures that can be representationally defined, and therefore referred to by constraints and invoked in phonological analyses.

(6) Representationally definable subsyllabic structures
   a. **Peak**: The head segment of the head μ of σ is the peak of σ.
   b. **Rime**: Any segment dominated by μ is in the rime.
      – This includes segments that have additional, non-moraic associations (not pursued here), as well as segments that are linked to μ but are not its head.
   c. **Onset**: Any pre-rime (i.e., non-moraic) segment is an onset[1].

d. **Coda**: Various possibilities, subject to empirical verification.
   i. Any ([+cons]?) segment aligned at the right edge of the syllable (McCarthy and Prince 1993a).
   ii. Any ([+cons]?) segment to the right of the peak.
   – Not all codas are necessarily [+cons]: Syllable-final glides in Diola Fogny are subject to the Coda Condition (Itô 1988); see Levi (2004) on glides that trigger vowel epenthesis when unsyllabifiable.

The following schematic diagram of a syllable illustrates how segments in various structural positions would be classified according to (6).

(7)   Example syllable

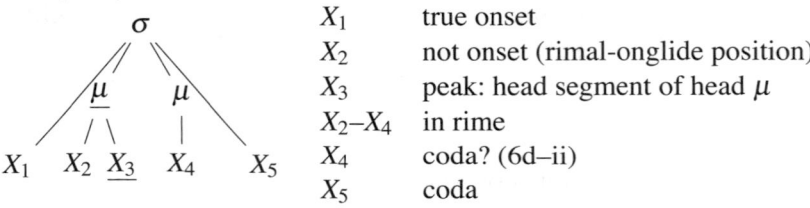

X_1 true onset
X_2 not onset (rimal-onglide position)
X_3 peak: head segment of head μ
X_2–X_4 in rime
X_4 coda? (6d–ii)
X_5 coda

For present purposes, the most crucial structural distinction to make is that between true onsets, which are dominated directly by the syllable node itself, and other pre-peak segments (e.g., rimal onglides), which are directly dominated by a mora. The constraint definition that needs to be sensitive to this distinction is that for *ONSET/X, a family of constraints that regulate the sonority of "onset" consonants. As demonstrated in §3 below, the segments that are relevant for this constraint family are specifically those that are syllabified in true onset position.

3. Freedom of analysis and onset sonority restrictions

The argument for maintaining the distinction between true onset glides and rimal onglides even within the OT framework comes from languages in which high-sonority onsets are generally avoided, but glide "onsets" are permitted. If the glides in question are analyzed as rimal onglides, they are correctly predicted not to be relevant for *ONSET/X constraints, which penalize high-sonority segments syllabified *as true onsets*. Distinguishing between true onset glides and rimal onglides thus allows for a sonority-based treatment of onset restrictions even in cases where glides, the highest-sonority consonant category, are (apparent) exceptions to the restriction.

The advantage of explaining liquid-specific onset prohibitions by means of onset-sonority constraints is that these constraints are functionally motivated. Cross-linguistically, low-sonority onsets are preferred, as shown by evidence from reduplication (Steriade 1982, 1988; McCarthy and Prince 1986) and child language (Gnanadesikan 2004; Barlow 1997). The functional motivation for this preference (see also Gordon 2003) is essentially that a low-sonority onset is more distinct from the syllable nucleus than a high-sonority onset would be (Delgutte 1997; Wright 2004), and the auditory system is particularly sensitive to rapid spectral changes such as an alternation between high- and low-sonority segments (Stevens 1989; Ohala 1992; Delgutte 1997; Warner 1998; Wright 2004).

This cross-linguistic, functionally motivated preference for low-sonority onsets can be modeled in OT by means of the *ONSET/X constraint family, which is based on the *MARGIN/X family (Prince and Smolensky 1993) but applies only to onsets, not to codas.

(8) *ONSET/X   'Onsets do not have sonority level X'

In order to exploit the distinction between true onsets and rimal onglides in the analysis of liquid-specific onset restrictions developed below, the term "onset" in (8) must specifically refer to true structural onsets, excluding rimal onglides. Therefore, *ONSET/X constraints are functionally grounded, but phonologically defined (see §1.3 above).

The *ONSET/X family consists of one constraint for each level X of the sonority hierarchy. These constraints are in a universally fixed ranking determined by the sonority scale; the constraint against the most sonorous onset is highest ranked.[2]

(9) The *ONSET/X constraint family assumed here
     *ONS/GLIDE ≫ *ONS/RHOTIC ≫ *ONS/LATERAL ≫
     *ONS/NASAL ≫ *ONS/OBSTRUENT

The sonority scale arguably includes further distinctions, including vowel height and voicing and continuancy in obstruents (e.g., Dell and Elmedlaoui 1985, 1988), but these distinctions are set aside here because they are not relevant for the languages discussed below.[3]

Because the constraints in the *ONSET/X family are in a fixed ranking, this means that if one *ONSET/X constraint is ranked high enough to be active in some language, so is any higher-ranked *ONSET/X constraint. As a consequence, a ban on onsets of a certain sonority level implies a ban on all onsets with higher sonority. A language that conforms to this prediction is the Sestu dialect of Campidanian Sardinian (Bolognesi 1998), in which both rhotic onsets and the higher-sonority glide onsets are banned in initial syllables.

(10)   Prohibition against word-initial rhotic and glide onsets
    a.   Expected [r]-initial words (Bolognesi 1998: 42)
        [arːɔza] 'rose' < L. *rosa*   [arːiu] 'river' < L. *rivus*
        [arːana] 'frog' < L. *rana*   [arːikːu] 'rich' < It. *ricco*
        [arːuβiu] 'red' < L. *rubeum*   [arːaðiu] 'radio' < It. *radio*
        [arːɔða] 'wheel' < L. *rota*
    b.   Expected [j]-initial words (Bolognesi 1998: 44)
        Sestu Campidanian   Iglesias Campidanian (see below)
        [ajaju] 'grandfather'   [jaju]
        [ajaja] 'grandmother'   [jaja]

However, there are a number of languages that ban rhotic onsets, or liquid onsets in general, with no corresponding ban on glide onsets. One example, which will be the focus of the following discussion, is the Iglesias dialect of Campidanian Sardinian (Bolognesi 1998). The Iglesias dialect is a close relative of the Sestu dialect, but differs from Sestu in that only rhotic onsets are banned in initial syllables (see 10b). Another case like Iglesias Campidanian Sardinian is Mbabaram (Australian; Dixon 1991). A related pattern, in which all liquid onsets – rhotics and laterals – are banned in initial syllables, is found in languages such as Mongolian (Poppe 1970; Ramsey 1987), Kuman (Papuan; Trefry 1969; Lynch 1983; Blevins 1994), and the Australian languages Pitta-Pitta and Guugu Yimidhirr (Blake and Breen 1971; Blake 1979; Haviland 1979; Dixon 1980; Smith to appear). Strikingly, many of these onset prohibitions apply only to initial syllables. This is part of a more general phenomenon; initial syllables are often subject to fortition or more stringent sonority requirements than other syllables. A possible case of a liquid-specific onset ban in *all* syllables is Seoul Korean (Kim-Renaud 1986; Sohn 1994: 440), recent loanwords excepted – but whether this is a case of restricted onsets in all syllables or only in initial syllables depends on whether certain medial liquids are analyzed as ambisyllabic. In any case, at least some of these onset restrictions are restricted to initial syllables (σ_1), so we need to invoke a version of *ONSET/X that is positionally relativized: [*ONSET/X]/σ_1.[4]

In Iglesias Campidanian Sardinian, rhotic onsets are avoided by means of epenthesis; this motivates the following ranking between DEP 'No epenthesis' (McCarthy and Prince 1995) and the [*ONSET/X]/σ_1 constraints.[5] That is, a candidate with epenthesis, violating DEP, is preferred to a candidate with an initial rhotic, violating [*ONS/RHOTIC]/σ_1, but all lower-sonority onsets are preferred to a candidate with epenthesis.

(11) [*ONS/GLI]/σ_1 ≫ [*ONS/RHO]/σ_1 ≫ DEP ≫ [*ONS/LAT]/σ_1 ≫ [*ONS/NAS]/σ_1 ≫ ...

However, the universal ranking of *ONSET/GLIDE above *ONSET/RHOTIC, determined by the sonority scale, means that the ranking in (11) seems to make the wrong prediction for glide-initial words in Iglesias.

(12) Liquids vs. glides in Iglesias Campidanian
    a. [aːana] 'frog' *[r(ː)ana]
    b. [jaju] 'grandfather' *[ajaju]

The problem is that ranking [*ONSET/RHOTIC]/σ_1 above DEP requires [*ONSET/GLIDE]/σ_1 to be ranked above DEP as well, so glide onsets should be avoided through epenthesis just as rhotic onsets are – the pattern that is observed in Sestu, as seen in (10) above, though not in Iglesias.

(13) Banning [r] onsets should make [j] onsets impossible

/rana/	[*ONS/GLI]/σ_1	[*ONS/RHO]/σ_1	DEP	[*ONS/LAT]/σ_1
i. rana		*!		
☞ ii. aːana			*	

/jaju/	[*ONS/GLI]/σ_1	[*ONS/RHO]/σ_1	DEP	[*ONS/LAT]/σ_1
(☞) i. jaju	*!			
☺ ii. ajaju			*	

Changing the ranking of DEP so that it dominates [*ONSET/GLIDE]/σ_1 does not solve the problem, as the fixed ranking [*ONSET/GLIDE]/σ_1 ≫

[*ONSET/RHOTIC]/σ_1 now results in avoidance of epenthesis for rhotic onsets as well as for glides.

(14)   Allowing [j] onsets should make [r] onsets possible

/jaju/		DEP	[*ONS/ GLI]/σ_1	[*ONS/ RHO]/σ_1	[*ONS/ LAT]/σ_1
	i. jaju		*		
☞	ii. ajaju	*!			

/rana/		DEP	[*ONS/ GLI]/σ_1	[*ONS/ RHO]/σ_1	[*ONS/ LAT]/σ_1
☺	i. rana			*	
(☞)	ii. arːana	*!			

In other words, the universally ranked *ONSET/X scale seems to be at odds with languages like Iglesias in which liquid onsets, but not the more highly sonorous glide onsets, are avoided.

Recognizing a representational distinction between true onset glides and rimal onglides provides a solution to this problem. The proposal to be pursued here is that glides that "escape" sonority-based initial-onset restrictions are rimal onglides, while glides that are subject to these restrictions are syllabified as true onsets. Formally, this requires that we allow GEN to create output candidates that differ with respect to the structural position of pre-peak glides, and that we define *ONSET/X constraints so that they evaluate only non-rimal segments. While this solution requires that GEN be given more freedom in generating syllable structures for output candidates, it has the advantage that the constraints that are responsible for the liquid-specific onset prohibitions, namely, *ONSET/X constraints, remain functionally grounded in the sonority hierarchy. There is moreover additional evidence that sonority is the relevant functional characteristic behind liquid-specific onset bans. Flack (2006) presents experimental evidence ruling out a "perceptibility"-based account of similar initial-liquid prohibitions in Australian languages, arguing for a sonority-based account instead. Moreover, the languages with liquid-specific onset prohibitions listed above demonstrate an implicational relationship that is compatible with the sonority scale: Lateral bans imply rhotic bans.

There are no alternative analyses of liquid-specific onset prohibitions that are as successful as the onset-sonority approach with respect to the phonetic motivation of the constraints that would be responsible for the pattern.

For example, if the model is modified to allow *ONSET/X constraints to be freely ranked in any order, then Iglesias could have the ranking [*ONSET/RHOTIC]/σ_1 ≫ DEP ≫ [*ONSET/GLIDE]/σ_1, which would select the desired candidates. However, this approach is less than appealing because it abandons the relationship between *ONSET/X and the perceptual preference for low-sonority onsets.

Another approach might be to propose a new constraint that simply bans liquid onsets. But such a constraint has no obvious functional motivation. A constraint penalizing liquids that are not post-vocalic might be phonetically motivated for some types of liquids, as there is a cross-linguistic preference for taps, flaps, and trills to occur with a preceding vowel. Crucially, however, some of the liquid-specific onset bans in the languages described above extend to approximant liquids as well, such as [l]. Mbabaram bans even [ɾ] from σ_1 onsets – this liquid is realized as "a tap, a trill, or *a rhotic continuant*" (Dixon 1991: 356, emphasis added).

A third alternative might be to assume that glides are subject to onset-sonority constraints just as much as liquids in these languages, as predicted by the *ONSET/X family, but some glide-specific faithfulness constraint intervenes to protect glides from being altered, while liquids remain unprotected (Flack 2006). This approach will not work for Iglesias Campidanian, however, since the initial-rhotic repair is vowel epenthesis. This repair simply violates DEP, not a feature-related faithfulness constraint that might be able to distinguish between rhotics and glides.

Thus, the analysis of liquid-specific onset prohibitions based on the inapplicability of *ONSET/X constraints to rimal onglides is the empirically successful approach that is most consistent with the use of functionally motivated constraints.

The representational distinction between true onset glides and rimal onglides can be applied to the difference between the Sestu and Iglesias dialects of Campidanian Sardinian as follows. Glides in Sestu pattern with rhotics, so pre-peak glides in this dialect are true onsets (15). On the other hand, glides in Iglesias are not subject to sonority restrictions, which indicates that they are syllabified as rimal onglides (16). Iglesias (and similar cases listed above) can be analyzed as in (17)–(18). In particular, the presence of syllable-initial glides in this dialect does not entail that *ONSET/GLIDE is violated, because the glides are rimal onglides. Thus, Iglesias is now compatible with the typological prediction that satisfaction of *ONSET/RHOTIC implies satisfaction of *ONSET/GLIDE.

(15) Sestu: Rhotics and glides both prohibited
a. Rhotics   b. Glides

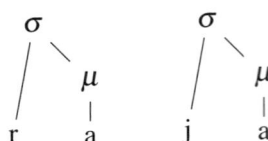

(16) Iglesias: Rhotics are prohibited, but glides appear
a. Rhotics   b. Glides

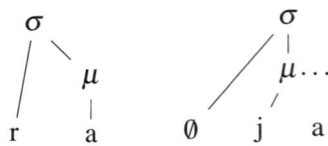

(17) The ban on [r] onsets motivates [*ONS/RHOTIC]/σ_1 ≫ DEP

/rana/	[*ONS/GLI]/σ_1	[*ONS/RHO]/σ_1	DEP	[*ONS/LAT]/σ_1
i. rana		*!		
☞ ii. a<u>r</u>ːna			*	

(18) Syllabifying [j] as rimal onglide satisfies [*ONS/GLIDE]/σ_1

/jaju/	[*ONS/GLI]/σ_1	[*ONS/RHO]/σ_1	DEP	[*ONS/LAT]/σ_1
☞ i. {ja}ju	✓		✓	
ii. j{a}ju	*!			
iii. <u>a</u>jaju			*!	

There is additional evidence in support of the claim that Sestu and Iglesias syllabify "onset" glides differently, as these two dialects treat glides differently in another context as well: Iglesias allows rising diphthongs with an onset consonant (CGV), but Sestu does not. As Bolognesi (1998: 24) states, "Rising diphthongs ... are normally prohibited in Sestu ... [T]he 'Standard' Campidanian word ˈkwa dːu ('horse') is realized as kuˈa dːu in the Sestu dialect: /u/ is short and unstressed, but distinctly longer than the corresponding glide."

Given the structural distinction between true onset glides and rimal onglides, two structures are possible for a CGV syllable (19). The fact that Sestu disallows CGV syllables means that its phonological system must rule out both (19a) and (19b). Iglesias, which allows CGV syllables, must allow either (19a) or (19b). These conclusions are compatible with the current proposal based on onset-sonority restrictions: only Iglesias allows rimal onglides. (An additional explanation is needed for why Sestu also disallows the structure in (19a), but this question is separate from the claim made here, which is that *if* the rimal onglide structure {GV} is allowed, *then* the structure [C{GV}] should also be allowed.)

(19) CGV syllables – Possible structures

a. Glide as true onset   b. Glide as rimal onglide

In summary, the account developed here invokes the functionally motivated *ONSET/X constraints to account for liquid-specific onset restrictions. For this approach to work, *ONSET/X must evaluate the sonority of true onsets but not of rimal onglides, thereby allowing a language the option of obeying *ONSET/GLIDE by syllabifying pre-peak glides as rimal onglides. Because CON is sensitive to the structural distinction between onset glides and rimal onglides, GEN must have the freedom to produce candidates with both types of structures.

4. Further implications of this model of GEN for syllabification

The diagram in (7) above, repeated here as (20), exemplifies the kinds of subsyllabic structures that can be defined, given a model of GEN operating under the representational restrictions stated in (2).

(20) Example syllable

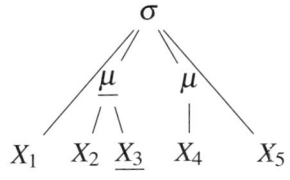

X_1 true onset
X_2 not onset (rimal-onglide position)
X_3 peak: head segment of head μ
X_2–X_4 in rime
X_4 coda? (6d–ii)
X_5 coda

Based on cross-linguistic facts about syllabification, we know that there are no universal restrictions on what segment classes can be parsed as syllable peaks (Dell and Elmedlaoui 1985, 1988; Prince and Smolensky 1993); as weight-bearing codas (Hayes 1989; Zec 1994); or as onsets (with the possible exception of low vowels; see Rosenthall 1994 for discussion). Because there exist languages that allow all segment classes to be syllabified in these positions, there can be no restrictions on what segments GEN is allowed to prosodify into these syllable positions. Of course, there are well-known *language-particular* restrictions on the segment classes that can fill these positions, but these can (must) be modeled in terms of constraint interaction, not restrictions on GEN.

These facts about segment classes and freedom of analysis, coupled with the formal implementation of syllable structure adopted here, have certain consequences for the rimal-onglide structure. The general representational conclusion to be drawn from the discussion in §3 above is that GEN allows a segment X to be syllabified in the rimal-onglide position. So far, the discussion has considered only glides ([−cons] segments) in this position. But can segments in this position ever be [+cons]? As noted above, rime subconstituents (such as weight-bearing codas) and even syllable peaks can be [+cons] segments in many languages. Thus, there is no general restriction on [+cons] segments in the rime. This predicts that there should be languages in which the segments syllabified into the 'rimal onglide' position include consonants.

What might evidence for [+cons] segments in the rimal-onglide position look like? One scenario in which consonants might be syllabified as rimal onglides would be under compulsion from *COMPLEXONSET, the constraint against onset clusters. Strong evidence for the ability of *COMPLEXONSET to force consonants into the rime would be a language in which all CV syllables are light, but all CCV syllables are heavy, parallel to light G{V} versus heavy C{GV} in Spanish (Harris and Kaisse 1999). This weight pattern would show that the second C in CCV is weight-bearing, and therefore must be rimal. However, as decades of research into interactions between onsets and stress have shown, there are very few languages in which onsets, or onset clusters, have any effect on stress assignment at all.

Another type of evidence for consonants in the rimal-onglide position due to *COMPLEXONSET would be a language that also has restrictions on rimal segments (including those in the rimal-onglide position), requiring them to be high in sonority . The combined effect of these two markedness constraints would be a language with C_1C_2 "onset clusters" where C_2 must be some high-sonority element, but does not have a fixed sonority distance from C_1 (as we would expect to see in a true onset cluster). This would be analogous to another fact about Spanish: C_1C_2 onset "clusters" have no sonority -distance restrictions if and only if C_2 is a glide (Baertsch 1998) – as predicted, since a glide in the C__V context is a rimal onglide in Spanish.

Evidence for the rimal status of pre-peak consonants might also be found in a language that takes the Iglesias Campidanian pattern one step farther, such that high-sonority segments other than glides are also driven into the rimal-onglide position by *ONSET/X constraints. stress-related evidence for a pattern of this type may exist: Davis, Manganaro, and Napoli (1987) argue that Italian second-conjugation infinitive verbs treat the antepenultimate syllable as heavy *if its onset is a sonorant*. This example appears to be morphologically restricted, but even so, it may be a case of *ONSET/X constraints for $X \geq$ NASAL forcing pre-peak sonorants into the rime.

Also suggestive in this context is the claim that speech-error patterns in Japanese (Kubozono 1989) support a model of prosodification in which all "onset" (pre-peak) segments are dominated by a mora (essentially, the version of moraic structure in Hyman 1985). If this interpretation of the speech-error data is phonologically relevant, then Japanese may be a language in which all *ONSET/X constraints are satisfied by consistently syllabifying pre-peak segments into the rime. Syllable weight is extremely significant in many aspects of Japanese phonology and prosodic morphology, so it is well established that pre-peak consonants do not contribute to syllable weight. However, this fact alone does not prove that said consonants are not rimal; monomoraic {GV} is attested (light rising diphthongs), so monomoraic {CV} is predicted to occur as well if [+cons] segments can appear in the rimal onglide position.

These potential examples from Italian and Japanese aside, if it turns out that [+cons] segments cannot be syllabified in the rimal onglide position, then the reason for this systematic gap remains an open question; perhaps it calls for content-based restrictions on freedom of analysis in addition to the basic representational restrictions in (2), or perhaps it is an effect of the interface between grammar and diachronic change (Myers 2003).

274 *Jennifer L. Smith*

5. Conclusion

Empirical and OT-internal evidence support a model in which GEN and CON distinguish true onset glides from rimal onglides. Complicating output representations with subsyllabic hierarchical structure in this way, so as to recognize two structural positions for pre-peak glides, is motivated because it allows for an account of onset restrictions that relies on cross-linguistically attested, phonetically grounded constraints. Additionally, under freedom of analysis – based on the cross-linguistic space of possibilities for assigning segments to rimal positions in the syllable – we seem to predict that consonantal segments should be able to appear in the rimal-onglide position as well; some evidence in support of this claim is available, but more investigation is needed. In any case, at least for glides, a model that takes into account the implications of representational complexity for both GEN and CON must allow GEN the freedom to syllabify pre-peak glides as either onset or rimal segments, since the best model of CON with respect to onset sonority restrictions distinguishes these two representational options.

Appendix: Slightly too much freedom of analysis?

The basic representational restrictions on syllabification proposed in (2) above generate the well-formed structures in (4) and (5), while correctly ruling out the universally problematic structures in (3). However, this model of GEN produces the following structures as well, which may not be attested.

(21)   Additional structures produced by GEN according to (2)

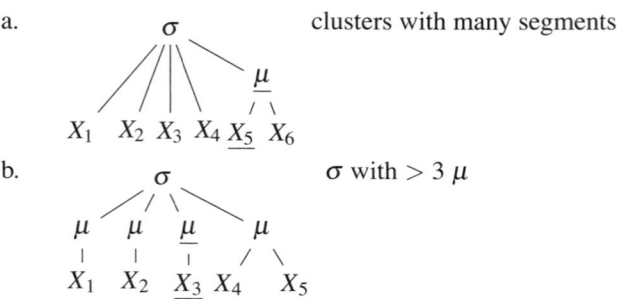

a.   σ   clusters with many segments

b.   σ with > 3 μ

c. 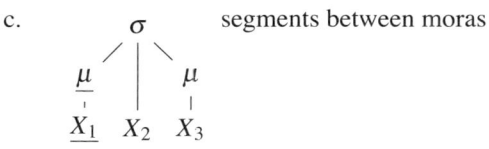 segments between moras

If these structures are allowed by GEN, and yet universally unattested, then what is responsible for ruling them out? Super-complex clusters as in (21a) can be ruled out in individual languages on the basis of constraints involving sonority -distance requirements or perceptibility considerations. But what accounts for the complete absence of such structures – is this a further example of a gap in factorial typology with a diachronic explanation (Myers 2003)? The case in (21b) is a familiar puzzle in moraic theory; there cannot be a universal bimoraic limit, as superheavy (trimoraic) syllables are attested, though comparatively rare. So why stop at *three* moras?

The structure in (21c) is not something that has received much attention in the literature, but it is quite clearly generated under the representational restrictions stated in (2), which have nothing to say about the relative ordering of segments and moras under a syllable node. Even if we add additional complexity to the current model of syllable structure and recognize a Rime node in addition to moraic structure, it is unclear what would prevent a segment from intervening *between* moras. One possible approach might be a requirement that GEN keep moras contiguous within a syllable – but this would be a content-based restriction on GEN, not a basic representational restriction as defined in §1.1, and so perhaps other solutions should be considered first (although the questionable status of the intermoraic segment in (21c) is suspiciously reminiscent of the edge-orientation of extrametrical elements). Conversely, the structure in (21c) may not be impossible at all, if this is an appropriate representation for intrusive (*svarabhakti*) vowels (see Hall 2004 for a recent review and discussion under a different representational framework).

Notes

* Discussion of the Sestu and Iglesias epenthesis patterns, and the advantages of distinguishing true onsets from rimal onglides, also appears in Smith (2003, 2005). I am grateful to Patrik Bye for encouraging me to revisit this topic from the perspective of freedom of analysis. Also, many thanks to Ian Clayton, Melissa Frazier, Elliott Moreton, and participants in the "Freedom of Analysis?" workshop for helpful comments and suggestions.

1. A consequence of this definition of "onset" is that the constraint ONSET does not actually require the presence of a *true* onset; it is satisfied as long as the syllable peak is preceded by any tautosyllabic segment (Smith 2005, to appear).
2. See also Prince (2001) and de Lacy (2002) for another approach to linguistic scales based on stringency constraints. The points made here can be recast in the stringency model; see Smith (to appear) for discussion.
3. For recent discussion and experimentation related to the sonority scale, see Parker (2002)

and Wright (2004).
4. See Smith (2005) for a general theory of markedness constraints relativized to phonologically prominent positions.
5. ONSET 'Syllables have onsets' must also rank below [*ONSET/RHOTIC]/σ_1, or the epenthetic #V in the winning candidate would be avoided.

References

Baertsch, Karen
1998 Onset sonority distance constraints through local conjunction. *Chicago Linguistic Society* 34, vol. 2: 1–15.
Barlow, Jessica
1997 A constraint-based account of syllable onsets: Evidence from developing systems. Ph.D. diss., Indiana University.
Blake, Barry J.
1979 Pitta-Pitta. In *Handbook of Australian Languages, vol. I*, Robert M. W. Dixon and Barry J. Blake (eds.), 183–242. Amsterdam: John Benjamins.
Blake, Barry J., and J. Gavan Breen
1971 *The Pitta-Pitta Dialects*. Melbourne: Monash University.
Blevins, Juliette
1994 A place for lateral in the feature geometry. *Journal of Linguistics* 30: 301–348.
2003 The independent nature of phonotactic constraints: An alternative to syllable-based approaches. In *The Syllable in Optimality Theory*, Caroline Féry and Ruben van de Vijver (eds.), 375–403. Cambridge: Cambridge University Press.
Bolognesi, Roberto
1998 *The Phonology of Campidanian Sardinian: A Unitary Account of a Self-Organizing Structure*. Amsterdam: HIL.
Broselow, Ellen, Su-I Chen, and Marie Huffman
1997 Syllable weight: Convergence of phonology and phonetics. *Phonology* 14: 47–82.
Crosswhite, Katherine
2004 Vowel reduction. In *Phonetically Based Phonology*, Bruce Hayes, Robert Kirchner, and Donca Steriade (eds.), 191–231. Cambridge: Cambridge University Press.
Davis, Stuart, and Michael Hammond
1995 On the status of onglides in American English. *Phonology* 12: 159–182.
Davis, Stuart, Linda Manganaro, and Donna Jo Napoli
1987 Stress on second conjugation infinitives in Italian. *Italica* 64: 477–498.
Delgutte, Bertrand
1997 Auditory neural processing of speech. In *The Handbook of Phonetic Sciences*, William J. Hardcastle and John Laver (eds.), 507–538. Oxford: Blackwell.
Dell, François, and Mohamed Elmedlaoui
1985 Syllabic consonants and syllabification in Imdlawn Tashlhiyt Berber. *Journal of African Languages and Linguistics* 7: 105–130.

1988	Syllabic consonants in Berber: Some new evidence. *Journal of African Languages and Linguistics* 10: 1–17.

Dixon, Robert M. W
1980	*The Languages of Australia*. Cambridge: Cambridge University Press.
1991	Mbabaram. In *Handbook of Australian Languages*, vol. IV, Robert M. W. Dixon and Barry J. Blake (eds.), 348–402. Melbourne: Oxford University Press.

Flack, Kathryn
2006	Lateral phonotactics in Australian languages. *Proceedings of the 35th Annual Meeting of the North East Linguistic Society*, Leah Bateman and Cherlon Ussery (eds.), 187–199. Amherst, Mass.: GLSA.

Frazier, Melissa
2006	Output-output faithfulness to moraic structure: Evidence from American English. *Proceedings of the 36th Annual Meeting of the North East Linguistic Society*, Christopher Davis, Amy Rose Deal and Youri Zabbal, (eds.), 1–14. Amherst, Mass.: GLSA.

Gnanadesikan, Amalia
2004	Markedness and faithfulness constraints in child phonology. In *Fixing Priorities: Constraints in Phonological Acquisition*, René Kager, Joe Pater, and Wim Zonneveld (eds.), 73–108. Cambridge: Cambridge University Press.

Gordon, Matthew
2003	The puzzle of onset-sensitive stress: A perceptually-driven approach. *West Coast Conference on Formal Linguistics* 22: 217–230.
2004	Syllable weight. In *Phonetically Based Phonology*, Bruce Hayes, Robert Kirchner, and Donca Steriade (eds.), 277–312. Cambridge: Cambridge University Press.

Hall, Nancy
2004	Gestures and segments: Vowel intrusion as overlap. Ph.D. diss., University of Massachusetts, Amherst.

Hammond, Michael
1997	Vowel quantity and syllabification in English. *Language* 73: 1–17.

Harris, James, and Ellen M. Kaisse
1999	Palatal vowels, glides and obstruents in Argentinean Spanish. *Phonology* 16: 117–190.

Haviland, John
1979	Guugu Yimidhirr. In *Handbook of Australian Languages*, vol. I, Robert M. W. Dixon and Barry J. Blake (eds.), 27–180. Amsterdam: John Benjamins.

Hayes, Bruce
1989	Compensatory lengthening in moraic phonology. *Linguistic Inquiry* 20: 253–306.
1999	Phonetically driven phonology: The role of Optimality Theory and inductive grounding. In *Formalism and Functionalism in Linguistics*, vol. I, Michael Darnell, Edith A. Moravcsik, Frederick Newmeyer, Michael Noonan, and Kathleen M. Wheatley (eds.), 243–285. Amsterdam: Benjamins.

Hyman, Larry
1985	*A Theory of Phonological Weight*. Dordrecht: Foris.

Itô, Junko
    1988   *Syllable Theory in Prosodic Phonology*. New York: Garland.
Kager, René
    1999   *Optimality Theory*. Cambridge: Cambridge University Press.
Kaye, Jonathan, and Jean Lowenstamm
    1984   De la syllabicité. In *Forme sonore du langage*, François Dell, Daniel Hirst, and Jean-Roger Vergnaud (eds.), 123–159. Paris: Hermann.
Kim-Renaud, Young-Key
    1986   *Studies in Korean Linguistics*. Seoul: Hanshin.
Kubozono, Haruo
    1989   The mora and syllable structure in Japanese: Evidence from speech errors. *Language and Speech* 32: 249–278.
de Lacy, Paul
    2002   The formal expression of markedness. Ph.D. diss., University of Massachusetts, Amherst.
Levi, Susannah
    2004   The representation of underlying glides: A cross-linguistic study. Ph.D. diss., University of Washington.
Lynch, John
    1983   On the Kuman 'liquids'. *Languages and Linguistics in Melanesia* 14: 98–112.
McCarthy, John J.
    2002   *A Thematic Guide to Optimality Theory*. New York: Cambridge University Press.
    2004   Headed spans and autosegmental spreading. Ms., University of Massachusetts, Amherst. ROA 685.
McCarthy, John J., and Alan S. Prince
    1986   Prosodic Morphology. Ms., University of Massachusetts, Amherst, and Brandeis University.
    1988   Quantitative transfer in reduplicative and templatic morphology. In *Linguistics in the Morning Calm 2*, Linguistic Society of Korea (ed.), 3–35. Seoul: Hanshin.
    1993a   Generalized alignment. *Yearbook of Morphology* 1993: 79–153.
    1993b   Prosodic Morphology I: Constraint interaction and satisfaction. Rutgers University Center for Cognitive Science Technical Report RUCCS TR-3.
    1995   Faithfulness and reduplicative identity. In *Papers in Optimality Theory*, Jill Beckman, Laura Walsh Dickey, and Suzanne Urbanczyk (eds.), 250–384. (University of Massachusetts Occasional Papers 18.) Amherst, Mass.: GLSA.
Myers, Scott
    2003   Gaps in factorial typology: The case of voicing in consonant clusters. Ms., University of Texas, Austin.
Ohala, John J.
    1992   The segment: Primitive or derived? In *Papers in Laboratory Phonology II: Gesture, Segment, Prosody*, Gerard J. Docherty and D. Robert Ladd (eds.), 166–183. Cambridge: Cambridge University Press.
Padgett, Jaye
    2002   Feature classes in phonology. *Language* 78: 81–110.

Parker, Steve
    2002   Quantifying the sonority hierarchy. Ph.D. diss., University of Massachusetts, Amherst.

Poppe, Nikolaus
    1970   *Mongolian Language Handbook*. Washington, D.C.: Center for Applied Linguistics.

Prince, Alan S.
    2001   Invariance under reranking. Paper presented at the 20th West Coast Conference on Formal Linguistics, University of Southern California.

Prince, Alan S., and Paul Smolensky
    1993   Optimality theory. Constraint interaction in generative grammar. Technical Report #2, Rutgers University Center for Cognitive Science. ROA 537; published in 2004 by Blackwell Publishers.

Ramsey, S. Robert
    1987   *The Languages of China*. Princeton: Princeton University Press.

Rosenthall, Sam
    1994   Vowel/glide alternation in a theory of constraint interaction. Ph.D. diss., University of Massachusetts, Amherst.

Rubach, Jerzy
    1998   A Slovak argument for the onset/rime distinction. *Linguistic Inquiry* 29: 168–179.

Selkirk, Elisabeth
    1978   On prosodic structure and its relation to syntactic structure. In *Nordic Prosody II*, Thorstein Fretheim (ed.), 111–140. Trondheim: Tapir.
    1995   The prosodic structure of function words. In *Papers in Optimality Theory*, Jill Beckman, Laura Walsh Dickey, and Suzanne Urbanczyk (eds.), 439–469. (University of Massachusetts Occasional Papers 18.) Amherst, Mass.: GLSA.

Smith, Jennifer L.
    2003   Onset sonority constraints and subsyllabic structure. Ms., University of North Carolina, Chapel Hill. [Submitted to: Phonologica 2002, John R. Rennison, Friedrich Neubarth, and Markus A. Pöchtrager (eds.).]
    2005   *Phonological Augmentation in Prominent Positions*. New York: Routledge.
    To appear Phonological constraints are not directly phonetic. *Chicago Linguistic Society* 41, vol. 1.

Sohn, Ho-Min
    1994   *Korean*. New York: Routledge.

Steriade, Donca
    1982   Greek prosodies and the nature of syllabification. Ph.D. diss., Massachusetts Institute of Technology.
    1988   Reduplication and syllable transfer in Sanskrit and elsewhere. *Phonology* 5: 73–155.

Stevens, Kenneth N.
    1989   On the quantal nature of speech. *Journal of Phonetics* 17: 3–46.

Trefry, David
    1969   *A Comparative Study of Kuman and Pawaian. (Pacific Linguistics B-13.)* Canberra: Australian National University.

Warner, Natasha L.
- 1998 The role of dynamic cues in speech perception, spoken word recognition, and phonological universals. Ph.D. diss., University of California, Berkeley.

Wright, Richard
- 2004 A review of perceptual cues and cue robustness. In *Phonetically Based Phonology*, Bruce Hayes, Robert Kirchner, and Donca Steriade (eds.), 34–57. Cambridge: Cambridge University Press.

Zec, Draga
- 1994 *Sonority Constraints on Prosodic Structure*. New York: Garland.

Zhang, Jie
- 2002 *The Effects of Duration and Sonority on Contour Tone Distribution – A Typological Survey and Formal Analysis*. New York: Routledge.

Chapter 12
Restricting GEN*

Christian Uffmann

1. Introduction

Explorations into the candidate generator function GEN are conspicuously absent from the literature on Optimality Theory (Prince and Smolensky 1993, McCarthy and Prince 1993). Even today, GEN is usually seen as a black box which emits a potentially infinite number of candidates. Instead, the research focus has been on the universal constraint set CON and the evaluator function EVAL which contains a language-specific ranking of these constraints. This is hardly surprising, since in OT the primary locus of explanation and variation lies within the constraint set and possible rankings thereof. Phonological generalizations and factorial typologies are understood as constraint interaction. The function of GEN then is simply to provide the candidates, of which the more sensible ones are then picked by the phonologist for comparison in tableaux.

This concentration on constraint interaction as the sole source of phonological generalizations has led to an ever-increasing constraint set, many additional constraint classes having been proposed over the years. The result is somewhat paradoxical: While a model of OT which incorporates all proposed additions to CON would be fairly unconstrained, overgenerating and predicting all kinds of unattested phonological behavior, there are still many unresolved issues (e.g. opacity, locality issues and many aspects of segment interaction). This paper will therefore pursue the question to which extent GEN can play a role in explaining grammatical and typological variation, arguing that GEN is by definition not unconstrained. By defining and delimiting the shape of the candidate space we might be able to relieve CON and EVAL of some of the burden they are carrying at present. Such a constrained version of GEN is not against the spirit of Freedom of Analysis as one of the fundamental principles of OT. Rather, this freedom is fully present within the bounds of a properly defined theory of representations. Our main aim will therefore be to suggest a research program which probes into the questions how the choice of a theory of representations impacts on the shape of CON and what the space of variation is within which a theory of constraint interaction operates. The simple fact is often neglected that representational assumptions also impact on OT analyses. Any discussion about the adequacy and the explanatory value of a phonological analysis should thus not only take into account the set of constraints proposed in this analysis; the structure of representations is equally important, hence up for discussion. A desideratum of present-day OT is that representational assumptions are often not made explicit. We will not propose a theory of representations for OT in detail here. Rather, we want to raise a number of questions pertaining to this issue which merit further investigation and give an outline of how a version of OT, which takes representational issues seriously, might look like, and what it needs to address. Central to this paper are two claims: First, that a stringent theory of representations in GEN may reduce the number of constraints needed, or unify them in a small number of constraint classes, allowing for a more economical CON, second, that there are universals that are not subject to constraint interaction (impossible structures that are not explicable by harmonic bounding alone).

The paper is organized as follows: Section 2 will review the current situation in OT, with its focus on constraint interaction and an aversion against hardwiring universal restrictions in a theory of GEN, although we will show that a strong version of this claim is not supported by the original architecture outlined in Prince and Smolensky (1993). We will rather argue that OT also needs a theory of representations. Section 3 then discusses the state of representations in present-day OT, looking at feature theory and at autosegmental models of segment organization, and reaffirm the need for a stringent theory of representations but also refute the claim that a theory of CON can effectively model and replace autosegmental theories of feature interaction. Section 4 takes a deeper look at restrictions that are potentially better accounted for in a theory of GEN than in a theory of constraint interaction and argue that the scope of representational restrictions might in fact be significant, which would allow for a more streamlined constraint set in turn. Section 5 draws a sketch of a more representation-conscious theory of OT. Section 6 concludes.

2. Are there Restrictions on GEN?

The proposal to put filters on GEN first seems to go against fundamental principles of OT, which sees the locus of grammatical variation in CON and possible rankings thereof. Consequently, Yip holds that restricting the output of GEN is not "fully within the spirit of OT, committed as it is to an unfettered GEN, and free constraint ranking" (Yip 2005:63). McCarthy (2002) assists, arguing that "[t]he explanations for universals should be sought in factorial typology under a particular theory of CON and not in GEN and other 'universal' aspects of OT" (119 f.). A unified theory of universals and their sources thus becomes possible if both universal properties of language and typological variation can be shown to stem from the same source, i.e. CON. In contrast, "hardwiring universals into GEN is inevitably a matter of brute-force stipulation, with no hope of explanation or connection to other matters" (8).

The idea to model universals as resulting from constraint interaction has been highly successful. One example is the typology of syllable structure and universals of syllabification which can be reduced to the interaction of the constraints ONSET and NOCODA with faithfulness constraints. It is thus predicted that there are languages which only allow syllables of the type CV and languages which are more permissive but which still try to maximize the number of open (and onsetful) syllables in syllabification but no languages which have only VC syllables. Epenthetic segments are typically unmarked segments, their choice explicable by the interaction of markedness scales on place and manner of articulation or the sonority scale. The observation that no language chooses [ø] and [x] as default epenthetic segments follows from their relative markedness; candidates with such epenthetic segments are harmonically bounded by candidates with less marked segments, say, schwa or a glottal stop. Implicational relations in segment inventories are modeled similarly. In short, OT offers an explanation for cases where languages that have some property A must also have some other property B, that there are languages that have only B, and no languages that have only A. The universal absence of an additional property C can also be accounted for, if it is shown that the hypothetical presence of C depends on A or B. In this example, C is predicted not to exist if it depends on the presence of A and absence of B (since the presence of A depends on the presence of B).

McCarthy's position on universals is probably uncontested within most of the OT community. Phonological explanation should reside within CON and EVAL. And if this is so, filters on candidate generation would be superfluous since they best duplicate the job that is already taken care of by the constraints. In addition, such filters or restrictions seem to violate Freedom of Analysis, which holds that GEN is free to posit whatever structure in the computation of candidates and prohibits the exclusion of potential output forms from the candidate set. Such a position begs two questions, however. First, is it true that there are really no restrictions on GEN, even under a maximally permissive interpretation of this function? Second, is it true that all universals can be explained by reference to a set of violable constraints and possible rankings thereof? To come back to the above abstract example, can there be a property D which is universally present or absent which cannot be explained by interaction with A, B or C? The following sections will address both these issues.

While denying the possibility of "hardwiring universals into GEN", the opposite, a truly "unfettered GEN", also does not seem to be consensus among OT practitioners. McCarthy (2002:8) concedes that "the freedom [of GEN] is limited only by primitive structural principles essential in every language, perhaps restricting GEN to a specific alphabet of distinctive features". What this restriction means is that candidates must be (well-formed) linguistic objects. While [🐱] is not a potential output candidate for an input /kæt/, so probably are candidates which are specified with non-existing distinctive features (like [+meow]) or with conflicting feature values (say, a segment which is specified as [+voice] and [−voice] simultaneously). The question then is what exactly the "primitive structural principles" referred to by McCarthy are. What are the restrictions on being a well-formed linguistic object, eligible for inclusion in the candidate set generated by GEN?

Little has been said about such restrictions in the OT literature. They seem to be assumed implicitly, and they may differ between scholars with respect to which kinds of restrictions are being assumed. The general consensus seems to be to keep these restrictions as minimal as possible, as suggested also by the above McCarthy quote. Interestingly, however, such a view of GEN seems to be at odds with what the original proposal suggests; in Prince and Smolensky's (1993) manuscript, the set of primitives seems more inclusive. They state that "Gen contains information about the representational primitives and their universally irrevocable relations [...] [and] generates for any given input a large space of candidate analyses by freely exercising the basic structural resources of the representational theory" (5/6). They thus stress the importance of a representational theory, conceding that OT does not make any commitments with respect to a specific representational theory employed, stressing that "different structural assumptions can suggest or force different formal approaches to the way that Optimality theoretic constraints work" (88). Such structural assumptions still figure prominently in their manuscript, so their analysis of Yidiny utilizes insights from Feature Geometry (§9.1.2, p.195ff.), and in their analysis of Shona tone spread they state that "[w]e assume without further comment that a familiar set of constraints are imposed on the candidate sets generated by Gen: e.g., all σs must be associated to tones, association lines do not cross, the OCP"(232). It seems far from clear whether the majority of the OT community today would follow these assumptions (to pick a random example, see Boersma 2003, who views the prohibition against crossed association lines as a violable constraint). The crucial point is, though, that representational issues, which still have a place in early OT work, have received less attention in current research, although it is clear that the choice of representational theory impacts on the OT analysis and thus is part and parcel of any OT analysis. Every discussion about the appropriateness and the explanatory value of an analysis is incomplete without taking the underlying representational assumptions into account as well. The current neglect of representations is probably not warranted.

2.1. Representations and Operations

In the opening paragraphs of their manuscript, Prince and Smolensky (1993:1) briefly touch upon a basic distinction in all theories of grammar. Every theory needs a theory of representations and a theory of operations. A theory of representations specifies what the primitives, the basic structural units are, and in which relations they may stand, while a theory of operations is needed to state how such representations can be manipulated when mapped from an input (underlying form) to an output (surface form). To elaborate on this basic distinction, consider the Sound Pattern of English (SPE; Chomsky and Halle 1968). Representationally, it assumes that words are linear strings of segments, which themselves contain unordered bundles of distinctive features. Underlying forms are mapped to surface forms via sets of rules, which are feature changing or feature filling. Subsequent research concentrated on both representations and operations, although the focus shifted over time. While a theory like Lexical Phonology (e.g. Kiparsky 1982) is primarily concerned with a theory of operations, Autosegmental Phonology (Goldsmith

1976, 1990) focuses on a theory of representations. In fact, research in the 1980s concentrated heavily on representations, with research on segment structure (autosegments and feature geometry, e.g. Clements 1985, 1991; Sagey 1986), on suprasegmentals (syllable structure, metrical structure; for an overview, see also Goldsmith 1990, among others) or on underspecification (e.g. Archangeli 1984 *et seq.*). Especially strong was Autosegmental Phonology, which reduced the role of operations to two basic operations, linking and delinking, shifting the burden of explanation to increasingly complex representations. This development is nicely summed up in McCarthy's (1988:84) hope that "if the representations are right, then the rules will follow".

Within OT, research into representations has become a minor issue, at least in segmental phonology. Besides, much research is not explicit about which theory of representations it assumes. That such a theory must be assumed should be clear from the foregoing discussion. However, both representations and operations are largely outside candidate evaluation and constraint ranking, which is probably why they have been suffering from neglect. They are instead relevant to GEN which builds candidates according to some theory of representations. GEN thus needs two types of restrictions. First, it is constrained by the representational primitives and the structure of representations assumed, because it will only be able to construct candidates which are well-formed with respect to these assumptions (GEN constructs only possible linguistic objects). Second, GEN must also contain information on the kinds of operations that can be performed on an input to yield a licit candidate. Only rarely are these restrictions discussed (but see McCarthy 2004 for a counterexample – his discussion of Span Theory is very explicit about what GEN can and cannot do).

The remainder of this paper will focus on representations. This does not mean that a theory of operations is not a desideratum in OT. In fact, fairly little has been said about it. In classic Containment (Prince and Smolensky 1993), it is assumed that GEN freely applies operations to the input, restricted, however, by the condition that nothing be literally added or removed. Candidate Chain theory (McCarthy 2007) also assumes operations which are performed on the input, although always only one at a time, in a framework of harmonic serialism (McCarthy 2000). In Correspondence Theory (McCarthy and Prince 1995 *et seq.*), it is less clear how the candidate set is generated. Is it still the case that operations are performed on the input, or does GEN simply provide an infinite set of possible output forms which are then linked to the input via an exhaustive set of correspondence relations, whose computation is the only type of operation performed by GEN? While such issues may seem largely technical, a comprehensive grammatical theory should have something to say about them. Approaches which make explicit statements about the theory of operations assumed are still rare (but see van Oostendorp 2007).

3. Representations in OT

Disregarding theories of operations, we want to focus on a theory of representations in OT in this paper and probe more deeply into the question of what the structure of representations in OT is and what the "primitive structural principles" that McCarthy mentions are. A belief that seems to be shared tacitly in large parts of the community is that representations should be kept simple, and that phenomena that used to be explained representationally could receive an alternative explanation rooted in constraint interaction, thus yielding a less abstract and more surface-oriented model of phonology.[1] This is a viable null hypothesis, and many phenomena could be shown to be explicable without stipulations about representations. It is an important issue to find out how much can be explained by constraint interaction alone, without reference to representations. It needs to be shown also, however, what the limits of a purely constraint-based approach are, and it should be suggested how simple representations should be – leaving aside the issue of how the simplicity of a representation could be evaluated meaningfully. Instead, there seems to have been a tacit but never openly motivated shift back to SPE-type representations (while perhaps only a minority maintained more complex representations, e.g. Beckman 1995, 1998, Lombardi 1999). A thorough research program on what the representational residue in a constraint-based framework could and should be has never been embarked upon. If nothing else, this paper is the call for such a research program and a first evaluation of how well the abandonment of representational complexity (assuming for the moment that autosegments or feature geometry are in fact more complex than SPE-type representations) is motivated.

A qualification is in order: Suprasegmentally, there has never been a return to simpler structures. Insights from syllable theory or metrical theory have been readily transferred to OT, and the prosodic hierarchy has never been called into question, despite its high degree of abstractness. Onsets and nuclei, moras and feet have never been seriously called into question. In contrast, much research on suprasegmental issues in OT includes representational suggestions. A similar argument can be made for OT syntax: The representational theory behind it (say, some version of X-bar theory) has never been challenged. No syntactician proposed that the advent of OT provides an opportunity to get rid of all representational baggage and view sentences as linearly ordered strings of words again, whose relations among each other are entirely governed by a universal set of violable constraints (with the notable exception of Gáspár 2005). It is puzzling that such arguments have been forwarded with respect to segmental structure. Consider the two models of segment structure in (1), illustrated by their respective representations of the segment [p]. (a) is a representation in the spirit of the SPE. A segment is associated with a set of binary features, this association is bijective: Every segment is specified only once for each feature, and every feature is associated with exactly one segment. (b) in contrast is a feature-geometric representation, using here the Clements and Hume (1995) model of feature geometry. Note that both laryngeal features and [nasal] are taken to be privative here, hence the segment lacks any laryngeal or nasal specification, except for an empty Laryngeal node.

(1) Segmental specification: representations

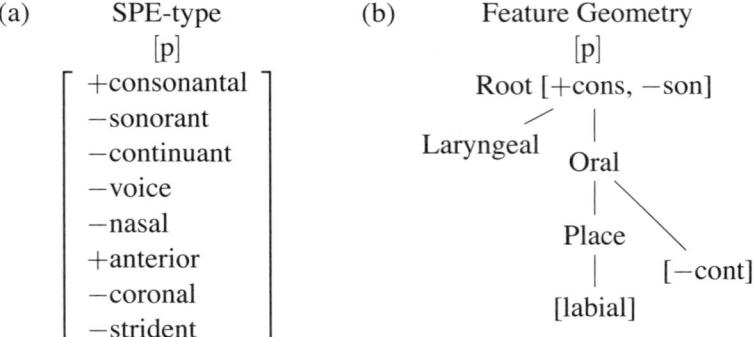

The comparison of the two possible types of segment representations (disregarding other possibilities for the sake of expositional clarity) raises the question of what type of representation one should assume in OT. Here, a major source of disagreement between different approaches seems to exist, although this disagreement is hardly ever being discussed. On the one hand, some researchers continue to assume complex representations as in

(1b), but they hardly discuss the consequences of such an assumption for CON (see e.g. Beckman's 1995, 1998 analyses of Shona height harmony or Lombardi's 1999 treatment of voicing assimilation). On the other hand, an increasing number of scholars has argued explicitly against autosegmental representations (e.g. Baković 1999, Padgett 1995, 2002, Ní Chiosáin and Padgett 1997, 2001; see also the critique of autosegmentalism in McCarthy 2002), trying to capture generalizations from this theory differently (more on that in Section 4 below). The remainder of this section will review two representational issues in greater depth, viz. feature valency, the question of whether to assume binary or privative features – and its impact on OT analyses – and the question of whether autosegmental representations can in fact be superceded by a representationally impoverished but constraint-based model of phonology.

3.1. Feature Theory in OT: Assimilation

Most research on segment interaction in OT seems to assume binary features (for some random examples, see e.g. Baković 1999, 2000, Beckman 1998, Krämer 2003, McCarthy 2003, Uffmann 2005), despite a body of research in the 1990s which proposes privativity at least for laryngeal features and nasality (Itô and Mester 1989, Lombardi 1991, *inter alia*) since only the positive value of each feature seems to be active in alternations and interactions (but cf. Wetzels and Mascaró 2001 who maintain binarity of [voice]). Others have argued that all features should be privative (e.g. in Element Theory, Harris and Lindsey 1995, or more recently the Parallel Structures Model of Feature Geometry, Morén 2003, 2007). Little of this research seems to have translated into OT analyses (with the notable exception of Lombardi 1999, 2001). We remain agnostic here with respect to the question whether features should be binary or as privative but wish to point out that the choice of one of the two alternatives has severe analytic consequences. If OT is about understanding the motivation behind phonological processes, this issue should thus be taken seriously. Different assumptions about the nature of phonological features translate into divergent analyses. True insight into the nature of phonological processes as resulting from constraint interaction is therefore only possible if representational issues (here feature valency) are also taken into account.

Voicing assimilation provides a good example of how different representational assumptions potentially translate into different OT analyses. Many languages (e.g. Catalan, Beckman 1998; Dutch, Grijzenhout and Krämer 2000; Serbo-Croatian, Wetzels and Mascaró 2001; Yiddish, Baković 1999, Lombardi 1999; for an overview, see Lombardi 1999 and Wetzels and Mascaró 2001) have a process where coda obstruents in heterosyllabic clusters assimilate to the following onset with respect to voicing. Consider the Yiddish examples in (2) (taken from Baković 1999):

(2)　Voicing assimilation in Yiddish
　　　vɔg　'weight'　vɔksɔl　'scales'
　　　briv　'letter'　briftrɛgər　'postman'
　　　bak　'cheek'　bagbejn　'cheekbone'
　　　bux　'book'　buɣgəʃəft　'bookstore'
　　　zis　'sweet'　zizvarg　'sweets'

The examples in (2) demonstrate that Yiddish has contrastive coda voicing but that this contrast is neutralized before an onset obstruent. These data have received different analyses.

Most widespread probably is an analysis in terms of voicing agreement, as proposed in Baković (1999). In such an analysis, assimilation is forced by high-ranked AGREE(voice) which demands that adjacent obstruents should agree in voicing, i.e. should have identical feature values for [voice]. The formulation of this constraint makes crucial reference to binary features; hence an analysis of assimilation as agreement also depends on a representational stipulation (anchored in GEN), viz. the binarity of distinctive features.

Lombardi (1999) suggests a similar analysis, also using agreement,[2] but maintaining privative features instead. It might thus appear as if the analysis does not hinge upon the choice of one particular theory of feature valency. By using agreement as the driving force behind assimilation, Lombardi sacrifices the predictions made by privativity, though. She analyzes agreement as agreement between the presence or absence of a feature. But since clusters may also agree in the absence of a feature, her analysis becomes empirically indistinguishable from an analysis which uses binary features; it simply replaces '+/−' values with presence/absence of a feature. The central insight of privativity, that absence of a feature means invisibility, is lost. Privativity can thus not be maintained under an agreement approach to assimilation (see Honeybone 2006 for an elaboration of this argument and the demonstration that pseudo-privative agreement can model unattested behavior, such as assimilation to non-nasality). If true privativity, at least with respect to certain feature classes, like place features or laryngeal features, is to be maintained, agreement cannot be a possible explanation for assimilation. Conversely, if agreement proves a good explanation, then feature binarity follows. Surprisingly, research has hardly addressed this issue (again, cf. Honeybone 2006).

An alternative conceptualization of assimilation which is found in the literature, assimilation as feature economy (Beckman 1998, Uffmann 2005), also works only under the assumption of feature binarity. In this approach, assimilation occurs in order to minimize the number of [±F] autosegments in a domain. Voicing assimilation in heterosyllabic clusters would thus reduce the number of autosegments from two ([+voice] and [−voice]) to one (only [+voice] or [−voice]). Obviously, this take on assimilation again crucially depends upon the assumption that features are binary. If [voice] were a privative feature, nothing would be won by spreading it to an obstruent which is unspecified for this feature, since no feature is removed or deleted. Structural economy has thus no explanatory power if features are privative. To name one more model, Span Theory (McCarthy 2004) also only works under the assumption of binary features, since every segment in a candidate must by definition (as a restriction on GEN) be included in some span for every feature (either '+' or '−'span).

Modeling assimilation in OT with a set of privative features seems to work only with a set of SHARE or SPREAD constraints, autosegmental cousins of AGREE, as Honeybone (2006) points out. What this means for either theories of assimilation in OT or for theories of feature valency will be left for future research. The important point is that OT analyses do crucially hinge upon a theory of representations in GEN. A theory of binary features allows for different analyses of assimilation phenomena than a theory of privative features.

The problem of feature valency combines with issues of segment-internal structure when place features are considered. Place features like [coronal] or [dorsal] are commonly assumed to be privative, which would make it problematic for agreement (or faithfulness, see below) or other theories of assimilation which presuppose binary features. Interestingly, AGREE or IDENT constraints in these cases typically refer to Place. Unless one assumes multivalued features à la de Lacy (2002), an interesting representational proposal in itself, such a constraint would only make sense if a Place node is assumed, agreement or identity being computed over its dependents. Theories of assimilation as autosegmental economy (as in Beckman 1998, Uffmann 2005) have no problem here, since they maintain segment-internal structure. How

AGREE(Place) would work in a non-feature geometric approach which does not subscribe to de Lacy's proposal is unclear to me.

3.2. Feature Theory in OT: Faithfulness

The problem of binarity/privativity of features is not limited to assimilation phenomena. It also affects faithfulness. The standard feature faithfulness constraint IDENT(F) also assumes binary features, a stipulation that has never been called into question. Consider the classic formulation in (3) (from McCarthy and Prince 1995: 264).

(3) IDENT(F) Correspondent segments have identical values for the feature F. If x$\Re$y and x is [γF], then y is [γF].

Several things are worth noticing about this formulation which bear on representational issues. First, by definition features are (at least) binary. But binarity is also a prerequisite in order to allow for a single constraint which assigns a violation mark to any feature change. Suppose we reformulate the constraint to refer to privative features. Then two constraints are essentially necessary, depending on which member of the input-output candidate pair carries the feature which is absent from the other one (separate IO and OI Correspondence, as in MAX and DEP).

Second, the constraint does not evaluate features per se but segments as feature bearers. Nothing is thus said about feature faithfulness proper – a feature which shifts to some other segment will incur two IDENT(F) violations, as would any unmotivated double change of feature values. Research has thus suggested to complement IDENT(F) constraints with MAX(F) and DEP(F) (Lombardi 1998, 2001, Walker 2001), which also seem to be more compatible with privative features. The division of labor between IDENT(F) and MAX/DEP(F) has not been sufficiently addressed yet, though.

Third, and this introduces the following section, the formulation of the IDENT(F) constraint suggests that segments and features stand in a bijective (one-to-one) relationship, as in early generative phonology. Since IDENT(F) evaluates segments rather than features, the constraint works best if features are deprived of their (autosegmental) autonomy. Once we allow feature autonomy, multiple associations, etc., MAX/DEP(F) constraints are additionally needed in order to evaluate whether a feature reassociation at some segment is unfaithful to underlying feature specifications or not, and the evaluatory force of IDENT(F) constraints dwindles rapidly. Only when features are restrictively tied to segments does a segment-targeting evaluation function come to its full potential. The question that this raises, though, is whether autosegments are still a necessity (or a desideratum) in an OT model of phonology. Some recent research suggests that they are not. The following section will therefore review arguments in favor of and against autosegmental representations in OT.

3.3. Autosegmental Representations in OT

Autosegmental Phonology (Goldsmith 1976, 1990) was a representational solution to two problems of phonological theory: the possible independence of segments and features and relativized locality (interaction over a distance). By attributing autosegmental status to features, they no longer stand in a bijective relationship with segments; instead, they may extend over spans larger than one segment (spreading), they may reassociate with other segments (shifting), etc. By segregating autosegments on different tiers, nonlocal interactions can also be explained: Autosegments may interact as long as they are adjacent on their respective tier (although strictly local, root-adjacent interaction is preferred; for a typology of locality effects, see Odden 1994). Feature Geometry (Clements 1985, 1989; Clements and Hume 1995; Sagey 1986) extends the notion of autosegments, originally designed to account for tonal phenomena, to all distinctive features, positing complex subsegmental structure and grouping features into feature classes.

Any theory that wishes to do away with autosegmental representations and tier structure has to be able to account for non-local interactions and the class behavior of features (laryngeal features, place features, etc.). If feature independence is also to be given up (return to bijectivity), then the theory must also be able to account for why a contiguous string of identical feature specifications often behaves as a single unit.

Some models of OT attempt to provide such an alternative account. Most elaborate are models of strict locality, which speak out against complex subsegmental representations (Padgett 1995, 2002; Ní Chiosáin and Padgett 1997, 2001; Gafos 1999), although retaining the idea of feature spreading. Baković's (2000) agreement model of assimilation and harmony additionally disposes of the notion of spreading, replacing it with a model of intersegmental correspondence.[3] Two questions will be briefly addressed now. First, is a model of strictly local segment interaction empirically adequate? Second, does such a model put less restrictions on GEN, allowing for greater analytical freedom?

Ní Chiosáin and Padgett's (1997, 2001) model of strict locality addresses these issues, attempting an autosegment-free model of spreading (for reasons of space we will restrict ourselves to a discussion of this model here). First, the property of segments to form classes which can spread as a whole, is captured set-theoretically in Padgett (1995, 2002); features are coindexed for classhood rather than being associated with a class node. Tiers are abolished, which makes it more difficult to account for non-local interactions. Crucially, Ní Chiosáin and Padgett argue that all spreading is strictly local. Seemingly transparent segments participate; in vowel harmony, consonants therefore also participate. However, the articulatory and acoustic effect of imposing a vowel feature on a consonant is so minor that consonants seem to be transparent (but coarticulatory effects are measurable). This analysis entails a number of additional moves.

First, the model must explain why vowels can propagate across consonants but consonants cannot propagate across vowels. Here, Ní Chiosáin and Padgett invoke the 'Bottleneck Effect', grounded in aerodynamics, which states that consonantal features cannot be superimposed on vowels, because that would deprive them of their vocalicness.[4] This in turn means that place features must all be coindexed for aperture, so the phonology can distinguish at least between a consonantal place feature, which cannot propagate onto a vowel, an approximant place feature, which realizes secondary articulations (palatalization, labialization, etc.), and a vocalic place feature, which has virtually no perceptual effect on a consonant. This extension of place features has an important consequence: Features are no longer necessarily contrastive; a consonant carrying also a vocalic feature is not phonologically distinctive from a consonant without one. In order to explain the non-distinctiveness of such segments, Ní Chiosáin and Padgett must therefore additionally invoke Dispersion Theory (Flemming 1995).

On the formal side, we see that giving up some representational stipulations (autosegments and feature geometry) and hence restrictions on GEN means introducing other stipulations – again, as restrictions on GEN. Representationally, strict locality multiplies the number of place features (by degrees of aperture); the feature inventory becomes less economical. Additionally, the tenet that all spreading is strictly local is of course also a restriction on candidate generation, thus as much a stipulation as claiming that spreading may be non-local. Ní Chiosáin and Padgett must also impose a restriction on possible operations, by implementing the Bottleneck Effect. Dispersion Theory needs an additional mechanism, both in constraint evaluation and in candidate generation, to be able to compare inventory types. In short, giving up autosegments does by no means increase analytic freedom but imposes a number of conditions on candidate generation. It is probably neither possible nor advisable to calculate an evaluation metric which compares such different types of restrictions and assigns them a restrictiveness coefficient, the analyst's task then being to choose the least restrictive version of GEN in order to maximize Freedom of Analysis. There is no conceivable restriction-free version of GEN. Whatever the theory, some basic assumptions about permissible representations and operations are necessary.

This puts decisive weight on the empirical adequacy of different proposals. We want to argue here that the seemingly anti-representational approaches in OT run into severe problems when trying to account for a number of phonological processes. These problems will be discussed only briefly now; a more comprehensive discussion is found in Uffmann (2004).

First, the Bottleneck Effect makes too strong a prediction by stating that consonants may not just not propagate features across vowels but also onto them. There are, however, many counterexamples, involving consonants which spread their place specification onto a vowel, e.g. fronting and lowering in Maltese (Hume 1996), Circassian fronting and backing (Smeets 1984), uvular harmony (on consonants and vowels) in Palestinian Arabic (Vaux in prep.), fronting in Serbian (Morén 2006); for labial attraction in several languages, see Campbell (1974). Epenthetic vowels in loanwords also receive their color frequently from an adjacent consonant (Uffmann 2004, 2006).[5]

A second problem concerns the claim that all spreading is strictly local. While simple vowel harmony systems can perhaps be explained by assuming that consonants participate in this harmony, problems arise with vowel harmony systems with transparent vowels, where harmony apparently skips intervening material (see e.g. Odden 1991, 1994), or with nasal harmony which may skip laryngeals (Walker 1998). Still more serious are instances of true long-distance interaction, such as nasal assimilation in Kikongo (Odden 1994, Rose and Walker 2004), long-distance voicing assimilation in Kera (Ebert 1979, Uffmann 2005), laryngeal spreading in Saanish (Vaux in prep.) or high tone lowering in Arusa (Odden 1994). Especially interesting is back harmony in Karaim (Nevins and Vaux 2003), where all consonants in a word agree in backness without affecting intervening vowels (which do not contrast in backness) – a particularly challenging problem, since spreading is both non-local and in disregard of the bottleneck effect.

Long-distance interaction has been modeled by Rose and Walker (2004) as correspondence between segments in a word, and thus formally distinct from spreading, which might be a potential solution to the problem. However, it does not seem to be clear when which type of assimilation (spreading or correspondence) occurs.[6] There is an additional problem since the notion of spreading in general has already been analyzed as intersegmental correspondence (Baković 2000, Krämer 2003). If all assimilation is correspondence, there is no way of distinguishing between local and non-local types.

Assimilation as correspondence between adjacent segments as a variant of theories of strict locality is additionally problematic since it cannot treat segments which agree in some feature specification as a unit, unlike spreading-based approaches which analyze agreement as the realization of the same feature on different segments. This inability is critical for analyses of tone. In Namwanga, for example (Bickmore 2000), the OCP motivates two different processes on adjacent high tones. Two underlyingly adjacent high tones fuse, but if adjacency occurs as a result of high tone spreading, downstep ensues. Consider [úkú¹lééta] 'to bring' from underlying /ú-ku-léet-a/. Prefix H doubling causes adjacency of the two underlying H, which is repaired via downstep. A correspondence-based approach to tone spreading would be unable to see whether two tones are underlyingly adjacent or not. The form [úkú¹lééta] would be represented as containing four high tones (from two high tones in the input, which then multiply via agreement), and the computation of where downstep applies (according to Bickmore a phonetic process, since it applies automatically whenever two underlyingly non-adjacent high tones clash) would be next to impossible. Note also that all successful analyses of tone in OT so far (e.g. Bickmore 1996, 2000, Yip 2002, Zoll 2003, Morén and Zsiga 2006, *inter alia*) have never called into question the autosegmental nature of tone. By granting tones autosegmental status and denying it to other features, we arrive at an uneconomical system of representations where different types of representations are assumed in different domains of the phonological system. Conversely, if autosegments are independently needed, nothing should speak against their across-the-board implementation (as in classic Autosegmental Phonology).

4. How Complex are Representations?

We conclude that arguments against autosegments in OT are not well-supported. If autosegments are replaced, other restrictions on the nature of representations have to be made, and nothing is won in terms of Freedom of Analysis. Additionally, Autosegmental Phonology has proven very successful in modeling segment interaction, especially in determining which features can interact over which distance (Clements 1991, Odden 1994). We therefore suggest reintegrating autosegments and feature geometry into OT and to re-evaluate advances in these fields, evaluating how they can be combined with a constraint-based model of phonology. This section will outline a research program for a representationally more conscious version of OT. Rather than presenting one such model in detail, we would like to point out some issues that result from taking representations more seriously and spell out some of the consequences of such a model in the following section. This is only the beginning of research into this field, and much still needs to be done.

The central question is which universals are hardwired into representations and thus lie outside constraint evaluation, and also to identify the sources of variation and to investigate how such variation can be understood as resulting from constraint interaction. We would like to suggest to take a more radical approach first and to assume that the central findings of autosegmental and feature-geometric research be incorporated into the model as restrictions on GEN. Hence, the conceptualization of features as autosegments, tier independence (with concomitant locality effects) and the existence of feature classes, expressed geometrically as universal relations between features and their mother nodes, should, as a null hypothesis, be taken over into OT. This section will explore and discuss further potential restrictions on GEN below.

At the same time, we would like to argue that at least the peripheral parts of such geometries are probably subject to parametric variation. Much discussion in the early 1990s revolved around how to represent some of the perhaps more marginal features. While the existence of a class of laryngeal features, subsumable under a Laryngeal node, or the unity of the place features [labial], [coronal], [dorsal] as daughters of a Place node was relatively uncontroversial, manner features in particular were the cause for much disagreement. Yip (2005) discusses the case of [lateral] which in the literature had been variably assumed to be a dependent of either the Coronal node (Blevins 1994) or the Sonorant (or Spontaneous) Voicing node (Rice and Avery 1991). With respect to place features, Clements and Hume (1995) discuss the lack of agreement of where to locate [pharyngeal] in the geometry, as a Place node dependent (Clements 1991) or as a dependent of a Guttural node (McCarthy 1988). Such variable classhood could be expressed – as Yip (2005) does – as effects of feature cooccurrence constraints; features which are not associated with any class but directly to the root node (and perhaps even features which are associated with a class node) can variably also interact with other features under the pressure of cooccurrence constraints. These, however, are variable processes, as opposed to the unity of laryngeal or place features, whose classhood seems undisputed. The problematic status of some features is thus no argument per se against a universal set of representations. In the remainder of this section, I would like to discuss one case that can be made for more complex representations, laryngeal specifications (Kehrein 2002, Golston and Kehrein 2004), argue that the generalizations cannot be captured by constraints, and discuss some of the wider implications of what this means for GEN before outlining a more strongly representation-based model of OT in Section 5.

4.1. Laryngeal Representations (Golston and Kehrein 2004)

Kehrein (2002) and Golston and Kehrein (2004) make a case for reconceptualizing laryngeal specifications on segments. They notice that crosslinguistically, syllable constituents (onsets, nuclei, codas) never bear more than one contrastive laryngeal specification. Thus, there are no languages in which segments in an onset cluster contrast for [voice]; [voice] is only contrastive for entire clusters. This allows clusters /ks, gz/ but not a threefold distinction */ks, kz, gz/ because that would involve contrastive specifications of [voice] on more than one segment in the cluster. Where exactly and how this specification is realized in the cluster is merely a matter of phonetic phasing, not a matter of segmental specification. Hence, underlying /pr$_{\text{[spread glottis]}}$/ may be realized as [p^{h}r,pr̥, p^{h}r̥, ^{h}pr ...], depending on language-specific phonetic implementation; the different possible realizations never contrast, though (no pre- vs. postaspiration contrast, no contrast between aspirated plosive and devoiced sonorant, etc.). Their formalization of this finding, that there may be no contrasting laryngeal specifications in an onset, a nucleus or a coda, is purely representational: They assume that laryngeal specifications are not a property of segments but of syllable constituents. The Laryngeal node is not a dependent of the Root node but of a syllable constituent node like Onset, as shown in (4).

(4) Laryngeal specifications (Kehrein 2002, Golston and Kehrein 2004)

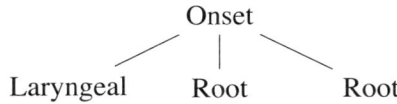

The representation in (4) renders conflicting laryngeal specifications within a syllable constituent formally impossible. Taken over into an OT model as a restriction on GEN (which can only use the structural resources provided by the theory of representations assumed), this means that there are even no candidates with conflicting specifications. Every possible candidate must contain only one set of laryngeal specifications per syllable constituent.[7]

4.2. Constraints on Laryngeals

This restriction cannot be expressed in a standard theory of CON and EVAL. AGREE constraints or their close relatives (like Pulleyblank's 1997 identical cluster constraints) would militate against conflicting laryngeal specifications and enforce identity within the cluster, but are still violable. AGREE(Lar) could account for a tendency towards having identical laryngeal specifications within a cluster but it could never ban non-identity in a cluster (since there is always the option of ranking FAITH above AGREE). The option of assuming that some agreement constraints are universally undominated is in disregard of a central tenet of OT, that constraints be freely rankable. GEN thus seems the best place to put such universal restrictions lest we have to maintain that certain ranking permutations of CON do not exist, for whatever reason.

One anonymous reviewer suggests a different, constraint-based solution to the problem, arguing that a reformulation of IDENT constraints could capture the universal prohibition against conflicting laryngeal specifications in syllable constituents, by defining IDENT to apply to domains. Consider the reformulation in (5) (taken from the reviewer):

(5) $\sum$-IDENT(F)
For every constituent $\sum$, some output segment s in $\sum$ has an input correspondent s' with the same value as s for F.

Defining ∑ to be a syllable constituent for [voice], this reformulation would indeed neutralize voicing contrasts within the domain. Assume a set of input onsets /sp, sb, zp, zb/ and a set of output candidates [sp, sb, zp, zb]. For input /sp/, [sp, sb, zp] would all satisfy IDENT, since some input segment has a faithful output correspondent. The choice between the three candidates would then be down to some markedness constraint, say *[+voice], which would select [sp]. [sp] would emerge as optimal for inputs /sp, sb, zp/; it satisfies both IDENT and *[+voice]. Only for input /zb/, a different output candidate would be optimal because [sp] would violate IDENT. The set of inputs would thus reduce to two optimal output candidates.

Promising as such a reanalysis might seem, it has a few catches. Notice first that the simple interaction of IDENT and *[+voice] predicts that clusters strive to reduce the number of [+voice] segments (barring possible interactions with AGREE). For an input /zb/, [zp] or [sb] would emerge as optimal, since they contain one [+voice] segment less than fully faithful [zb], contrary to what is generally found, that the entire cluster is either voiced or voiceless (as in Italian, Polish or Romanian). More problematic is the potential interaction with other faithfulness constraints which could override the drive to neutralizing cluster contrasts, for example MAX(F). Ranked high, it can force a faithful map of all possible four inputs (for arguments in favor of MAX(F) constraints, see Lombardi 1998, Walker 2001). Similarly, morpheme faithfulness may interact with IDENT if the cluster is heteromorphemic (as the drive to preserve each voicing specification because they are morphologically differently affiliated). Other constraints can thus override the effects of modified IDENT; within-cluster neutralization can be blocked, and Golston and Kehrein's generalization cannot be captured.

Under the representational solution forwarded by Golston and Kehrein, in contrast, only two possible output candidates are computed for the input set /sp, sb, zp, zb/, viz. [sp] and [zb] (disregarding unfaithful maps of other features or segments). GEN simply cannot build the problematic candidates [sb] and [zp]. This is a welcome restriction as we have seen that it is probably impossible for any theory of CON to ensure that these candidates are always harmonically bounded. The representational solution thus shifts a heavy burden away from CON and EVAL, limiting at the same time the set of candidates provided by GEN.

4.3. Representational Universals and Constraints

We conclude that the representational solution is to be preferred because the prohibition against conflicting laryngeal values in syllable constituents can probably not be captured by constraint interaction. How about McCarthy's call for "deriving universals and typology from constraint interaction" (McCarthy 2002: 9) then? Are we not trying to explain universals in GEN rather than in factorial typology, contrary to McCarthy's recommendation? The solution, we believe, lies in the type of universal under investigation. The universals McCarthy discusses are universals subject to parametric variation and implicational universals (see McCarthy 2002: 112 ff. for an elaboration). For example, markedness scales can account for observations of the type that languages which allow A must also allow B, with only a subset of B-type languages also allowing A, and languages allowing neither (e.g. segment inventories). A theory of CON can thus explain why there are no languages which allow only marked structures, but that less marked structures always come for free once the grammar allows also for more marked structures. Universal prohibitions can be explained in CON by the property of harmonic bounding – some candidates are never optimal, under any ranking, because there are always candidates which incur only a proper subset of constraint violations. Again, however, such universals result from constraint interaction, some potential outputs never being favored by the constraints. The universal expressed by Golston and Kehrein is fundamentally different. It expresses a universal prohibition which is never subject to any typological variation (as compared to heterosyllabic cluster agreement, for example). Additionally, it does not seem to interact with other principles and thus cannot be captured by a set of violable constraints. We believe that the best place for such universals is in GEN. There seems to be general (if often implicit) agreement that GEN is constrained by the set of phonological primitives available, and the relations they can enter. Many of these restrictions seem trivial: the set of distinctive features, segments, syllable structure, the prosodic hierarchy. The issue is not so trivial, however, because first, there is no general agreement about the exact shape of these primitives (take feature theory as one example, already discussed above), and second, because the size of the set of primitives and their relation is not clear. We believe that Golston and Kehrein's restriction on laryngeal specifications is one such primitive. It is generally assumed without further comment that segments can only be specified once by each feature (no segment is [+back] and [−back] simultaneously), and few would argue that GEN does emit such structurally ill-formed candidates. The claim that this type of bijectivity holds at the segmental level is mere stipulation, however. The observation that it may hold for domains larger than the segment can improve empirical adequacy without introducing an entirely new type of restriction on GEN; rather, the familiar set of restrictions is redefined and extended, in this case, by arguing that laryngeal features do not associate with segments but with syllable constituents. Statements about how the different phonological elements associate have to be made anyway. The question is how large the set of primitives is, and which relations they can enter. There has been little research into this area, and this paper is a call for reopening the debate about which universals are best captured representationally. Note that research into representations has been kept alive outside OT circles, with intriguing results, e.g. ongoing research into features and contrast by the Toronto School (see e.g. Dresher 2003), or in Government Phonology. For example, Scheer (2004, in press) argues that epenthesis sites are variable (hence subject to constraint interaction) but follow representationally. These are underexplored issues in current OT.

5. Towards a Theory of Representations in OT

In sum, we believe that representations need to be reconsidered more seriously in OT. A theory of representations is needed anyway, and there are universal prohibitions which cannot be modeled as the effect of violable constraints (as instances of harmonic bounding). Such prohibitions are thus best accounted for in a theory of representations which can account for non-occurring structures as being absolutely ill-formed and thus not generated by GEN. This theory of representations is still a desideratum within OT, especially with regard to subsegmental structure. Hence, we will not commit ourselves to one specific model here. Research into feature geometry needs to be reviewed in the light of OT. Earlier proposals have all suffered from their restrictiveness. While the class behavior of core features (Place or Laryngeal, for example) is undisputed, there seems to be more variability in the periphery, and it is this periphery that much of the discussion in the early 1990s centered around. OT is a powerful tool to explain some of the variation or seemingly variable classhood, since this could be captured by feature co-occurrence constraints (as in Yip 2005). Much of the core, however, does not seem to be subject to any variation, and is hence best accounted for in a theory of representations, in GEN.

As long as no such theory has been proposed, let us outline some of the consequences of letting feature geometry into the picture using the Clements/Hume model (Clements 1991, Hume 1996, Clements and Hume 1995) which unifies consonantal and vocalic features and the interaction of which with OT has already been discussed (Uffmann 2004, 2005). Such a move also has an impact on our theory of CON. Trivially so because certain constraints are no longer needed – the constraint set can thus be streamlined. In addition, the reality of representations also entails that constraints should be able to evaluate such representations. A more representation-conscious theory of CON, which is less surface-oriented in a crude sense, is thus needed. Uffmann (2004, 2005, 2006) suggests a set constraints on representations. These constraints express preferences and tendencies that have been noted previously in the literature on autosegments and feature geometry. Let us discuss them briefly to see how they impact on an analysis of segment interactions. Central structural markedness constraints are

(6) *MULTIPLE
Nodes are dominated by only one node exclusively.

(7) *LINK(X,Y)
Features should not be dominated by two different mother nodes.

(8) *SKIP
No material should intervene between interacting segments.

*MULTIPLE militates against spreading, the multiple association of one feature or class node with several mother nodes. *LINK(X,Y) militates against a special type of multiple association, one in which the feature links to two different mother nodes (Hume's 1996 Mother Node Attraction Principle). This constraint is especially relevant for place features, which in the Clements/Hume model of Feature Geometry can link to either a C-Place node or a V-Place node, but might also apply to other features. For example, Bradshaw (1999) argues that voicing and low tone are really the same feature, only that in one case it is linked to the Laryngeal node, in the other to a tone bearing unit (a similar claim can be made for |L| in Element Theory). Finally, *SKIP enforces root-adjacent (strictly local) spreading – but is violable, as non-local feature interactions show (see Odden 1994 for a typology of locality effects). Still, non-locality in spreading has to obey central tenets of Autosegmental Phonology; association lines must not cross, interaction must at least be tier-adjacent, no potential feature bearers can be skipped – these restrictions are taken care of by GEN which will only emit autosegmentally well-formed candidates to EVAL.

This set of constraints allows for a straightforward analysis of assimilatory processes. If a constraint against some feature *[F] ranks above *MULTIPLE, the offending feature may be disposed of via spreading. The palatalization of dorsals in the context of front vowels, for example, can be explained by the ranking of *MULTIPLE below *DORSAL. Then, [coronal] can spread from the vowel, and assimilation to a less marked feature can occur. In addition, this ranking also enforces harmony, since *[F] does not count instantiations of one feature on each segment but the feature as autosegment. Voicing assimilation (see above) reduces the number of [voice] autosegments in a cluster, motivated by ranking *MULTIPLE below *[±voice]. Locality effects are accounted for by *SKIP. High-ranked, it will allow only root-adjacent spreading, but ranked lower it can account for non-local interactions (e.g. long-distance voicing assimilation in Kera; Ebert 1979, Uffmann 2005), always under the condition that non-local linkage is autosegmentally well-formed. Uffmann (2004, 2006) uses the constraints in (6)-(8) to show how the intricate interaction of different spreading processes in vowel epenthesis can be understood, problematic for non-autosegmental accounts. Besides, locality effects in dissimilation can also be modeled by the interaction of *SKIP with OCP constraints (Uffmann 2005). While dissimilation has long been formalized as an OCP-effect in OT, locality issues (for an overview, see Odden 1994) have not yet received a satisfying treatment. Traditional OT accounts cannot predict over what distance dissimilation can occur. Further research is necessary, however, to see whether the set of constraints proposed here can account for the full range of segment interaction phenomena found in the world's languages.

Also promising seems a connection of this model with some of the proposals made in this book. There is an obvious connection to Morén's model of Feature Geometry as a model which lays great emphasis on representations which are composed of a small number of features which combine in various dependencies (parallel consonantal and vocalic structures for place, manner, glottal configuration, partially reusing the same set of features). Particularly promising, however, seems a connection with two other models, van Oostendorp's theory of Colored Containment, which marks a return to early OT's Containment Theory, although on a higher level, and with Revithiadou's reappraisal of Turbidity Theory, as originally proposed in Goldrick (1998, 2000) and Goldrick and Smolensky (1999).

Turbidity Theory (for a more detailed introduction, see Revithiadou 2007) holds that two types of relations hold between phonological elements (elements in a representation), projection and pronunciation. Assume now for segmental phonology (pace the proposal in Goldrick 1998) that segments project features onto autosegmental tiers, building feature-geometric structure, and that these features in turn are pronounced by segments. Such a representational commitment enables us to forward a theory of GEN as well. In this model, GEN builds feature-geometric structure by projecting features which are underlyingly associated with segments. In addition, GEN also establishes pronunciation relations between features and segments, freely employing the set of operations provided by the model – inserting pronunciation lines freely (as long as they do not cross) or inserting features. Freedom of Analysis thus means the computation of an exhaustive (and potentially infinite) set of projection and pronunciation relations. Such a model is also in the spirit of Containment: Faithfulness violations can be read off representations directly as mismatches between projection relations and pronunciation relations, and the input is literally contained in each candidate (as the projection of input material). Markedness constraints can then be formulated with direct reference to representations (as constraints on projection/pronunciation relations, see Goldrick 1998, 2000). Goldrick (2000) and Goldrick and Smolensky (1999) demonstrate how Turbidity can be implemented successfully to account for opacity effects. We wish to argue that it may also provide us with a principled theory of GEN and put a check on the proliferation of CON, e.g. by disposing of correspondence relations and by facilitating a uniform formalization of markedness constraints as constraints on projection/pronunciation relations. Future research will have to show whether this is a viable path towards a more restrictive version of OT in which both operations in GEN and the shape of constraints are formally more clearly defined.

6. Conclusion

This paper has argued that current OT suffers from a lack of representation-consciousness, at least in the domain of segmental phonology, concentrating on the properties of the set of constraints instead. While this has initially been a source of many important observations, it has more recently also led to a plethora of proposals with respect to CON, without coming to a satisfying conclusion. We believe that a more balanced view of both constraints and representations is necessary, not least because constraints evaluate representations. A more explicit theory of GEN is thus needed. GEN is the place where representational restrictions hold, and every theory of constraint interaction also needs a theory of representations in order to ascertain what the objects are which are evaluated. We have also argued for a more stringent theory of representations, refuting claims that all universals can be expressed by violable constraints but defending the idea that some hard universals are best explained representationally, namely restrictions that hold for all languages without being subject to parametric variation or being explicable by harmonic bounding (through the interaction of several constraints), i.e. restrictions that are outside evaluability. Some of them are trivial, e.g. the basic elements of phonological representations (the notion of segments, for example), while some may be more intricate (the lack of multiple laryngeal specifications on tautosyllabic clusters, for example). We need to be clear about what these representational universals are because our theory of representations has repercussions on our theory of constraints. We have argued for a reappraisal of Autosegmental Phonology here. It first restricts the set of possible candidates to those which are autosegmentally well-formed. CON need not worry about ill-formed candidates. Second, it also allows us to formulate constraints on autosegmental representations which may in the end limit the size of CON as well. Both CON and GEN are thus limited by restricting Freedom of Analysis to the generation and evaluation of well-formed linguistic objects. Future research is still needed to ascertain what a well-formed linguistic object is, and this is where research into representations becomes important. The division of labor between constraints and representations still is very much an open issue. We have outlined a research program here and suggested a first sketch for a theory which incorporates both a theory of representations and a theory of constraints on representations.

Notes
* I want to thank participants of the "Freedom of Analysis" workshop in Tromsø, two anonymous reviewers and Laura Downing for comments and suggestions. All remaining errors are my own.
1. To mention a few examples, Padgett's (2002) work on feature classes discusses how class behavior can be modeled without assuming a model of feature geometry. Yip (2005) accounts for class behavior by constraints on feature combinations. Span Theory (McCarthy 2004) tries to capture autosegmental behavior without assuming complex autosegmental representation, through the introduction of feature spans.
2. Note that the formulation of agreement differs between the two approaches. While Lom-

bardi formulates AGREE as a markedness constraint, Bakovic formalizes agreement as intrasegmental correspondence, as does Krämer's (2003) related model of syntagmatic identity.
3. For yet another way of formalizing agreement (in a non-autosegmental model) see Span Theory (McCarthy 2004).
4. In classic Feature Geometry (Clements and Hume 1995), the difference in the spreading abilities of consonants and vowels is explained by linking place features to different mother nodes (C-Place and V-Place, which is a dependent of C-Place; hence, V-Place nodes may spread to the next vocalic node skipping intervening C-Place nodes. This is impossible for C-Place features (since intervening vowels also have a C-Place node).
5. One might argue that consonants are redundantly specified also for vocalic place, which then spreads. This, however, is not only highly stipulative, it also contrasts with secondary approximantal specifications (like in palatalization or labialization) which frequently are different from the major articulation.
6. Rose and Walker (2004) name a few diagnostics, but these are not always helpful. By their measure, vowel harmony for example – a prime example of strictly local spreading according to Ní Chiosáin and Padgett (1997, 2001) – should probably be analyzed as correspondence (non-local interaction of similar segments). For a more detailed critique of their proposal, see Uffmann (2004) and Vaux (in prep.).
7. One reviewer suggests that this prohibition is probably grounded in articulation and perception (difficulty of maintaining enough acoustic cues in a cluster to make different laryngeal specifications perceptible). While I agree with this observation, I do not think that it is an argument against capturing the prohibition representationally; rather, it phonetically grounds the representational proposal.

References

Archangeli, Diana
    1984   Underspecification in Yawelmani phonology and morphology. Ph. D. diss., MIT.
Baković, Eric
    1999   Assimilation to the unmarked. Ms., Rutgers University. ROA 340
    2000   Harmony, Dominance and Control. Ph. D. diss., Rutgers University, New Brunswick NJ. ROA 360
Beckman, Jill
    1995   Shona height harmony. In *Papers in Optimality Theory*, Jill Beckman, Laura Walsh Dickey and Suzanne Urbanczyk (eds.), 53–75. (Massachusetts Occasional Papers in Linguistics 18). Amherst, Mass.: GLSA.
    1998   Positional Faithfulness. Ph. D. diss., University of Massachusetts at Amherst.
Bickmore, Lee
    1996   Bantu tone spreading and displacement as alignment and minimal misalignment. Ms., University of Albany, NY. ROA 161.
    2000   Downstep and fusion in Namwanga. *Phonology* 17: 297–333.
Blevins, Juliette
    1994   A place for lateral in the feature geometry. *Journal of Linguistics* 30, 301-304.

Boersma, Paul
  2003   Nasal harmony in functional phonology. In *The Phonological Spectrum, vol. I: Segmental Structure*, Jeroen van de Weijer, Vincent J. van Heuven and Harry van der Hulst (eds.), 3-35. Amsterdam: Benjamins.
Bradshaw, Mary
  1999   A Crosslinguistic study of consonant-tone interaction. Ph. D. diss., Ohio State University, Columbus, Ohio.
Campbell, Lyle
  1974   Phonological features: Problems and proposals. *Language* 50: 52–65.
Chomsky, Noam and Morris Halle
  1968   *The Sound Pattern of English*. New York: Harper and Row.
Clements, G. N.
  1985   The geometry of phonological features. *Phonology Yearbook* 2: 225–252.
  1991   Place of articulation in consonants and vowels: A unified theory. *Working Papers of the Cornell Phonetics Laboratory* 5, 77–123.
Clements, G. N. and Elizabeth Hume
  1995   'The internal organization of speech sounds'. In *Handbook of Phonological Theory*, John Goldsmith (ed.), 245–306. Oxford: Blackwell.
Dresher, B. Elan
  2004   On the acquisition of phonological contrasts. In *Proceedings of GALA 2003*, Jacqueline van Kampen and Sergio Baauw (eds.), 27–46. Utrecht: LOT.
Ebert, Karen
  1979   *Sprache und Tradition der Kera (Tschad). Teil III: Grammatik*. Berlin: Reimer.
Gafos, Diamandis
  1999   *The Articulatory Base of Locality in Phonology*. New York: Garland.
Gáspár, Miklós
  2005   Coordination in Optimality Theory. Ph. D. diss., Eötvös Loránd University, Budapest. ROA 824
Goldrick, Matthew
  1998   Optimal opacity: Covert structure in phonology. Ms., Johns Hopkins University.
  2000   Turbid output representations and the unity of opacity. In *Proceedings of the 30th Meeting of the North East Linguistic Society*, Masako Hirotani, Andries Coetzee, Nancy Hall, and Ji-yung Kim (eds.), 231–245. University of Massachusetts, Amherst, Mass.: GLSA.
Goldrick, Matt and Paul Smolensky
  1999   Opacity and turbid representations in Optimality Theory. Paper presented at the Annual Meeting of the Chicago Linguistics Society, 22-04-99.
Goldsmith, John
  1976   Autosegmental Phonology. Ph. D. diss., MIT.
  1990   *Autosegmental and Metrical Phonology*. Oxford: Blackwell.
Golston, Chris and Wolfgang Kehrein
  2004   A prosodic theory of laryngeal contrasts. *Phonology* 21: 325–357.
Grijzenhout, Janet and Martin Krämer
  2000   Final devoicing and voicing assimilation in Dutch derivation and cliticisation.

In *Lexicon in Focus*, Barbara Stiebels and Dieter Wunderlich (eds.), 55–82. (Studia Grammatica 45). Berlin: Akademie Verlag.

Harris, John and Geoff Lindsey
    1995   The elements of phonological representation. In *Frontiers of Phonology*, Jacques Durand and Francis Katamba (eds.), 34–79. London: Longman.

Honeybone, Patrick
    2006   Disagreeing with AGREE: Sharing and subsegmental theory. Poster presented at the 3rd Old-world Conference in Phonology, Budapest, 18-01-06.

Hume, Elizabeth
    1996   Coronal consonant, front vowel parallels in Maltese. *Natural Language and Linguistic Theory* 14: 163–203.

Itô, Junko and Armin Mester
    1989   Feature predictability and underspecification: Palatal prosody in Japanese mimetics. *Language* 65: 258–293.

Kehrein, Wolfgang
    2002   *Phonological Representation and Phonetic Phasing : Affricates and Laryngeals*. Tübingen: Niemeyer.

Kiparsky, Paul
    1982   Lexical morphology and phonology. In *Linguistics in the Morning Calm*, In-Seok Yang (ed.), 3–91. Seoul: Hanshin.

Krämer, Martin
    2003   *Vowel Harmony and Correspondence Theory*. Berlin: Mouton de Gruyter.

de Lacy, Paul
    2002   The formal expression of markedness. Ph. D. diss., University of Massachusetts at Amherst. ROA 542

Lombardi, Linda
    1991   Laryngeal features and laryngeal neutralization. Ph. D. diss., University of Massachusetts, Amherst.
    1998   Evidence for MAXFEATURE constraints from Japanese, Ms., University of Maryland. ROA 247
    1999   Positional faithfulness and voicing assimilation in Optimality Theory. *Natural Language and Linguistic Theory* 17, 267-302.
    2001   Why Place and Voice are different: Constraint-specific alternations and Optimality Theory. In *Segmental Phonology in Optimality Theory: Constraints and Representations*, Linda Lombardi (ed.), 13–45. Cambridge: Cambridge University Press.

McCarthy, John J.
    1988   Feature geometry and dependency: A review. *Phonetica* 43, 84-108.
    2000   Harmonic serialism and harmonic prallelism. In *Proceedings of the 30th Meeting of the North East Linguistic Society*, Masako Hirotani, Andries Coetzee, Nancy Hall, and Ji-yung Kim (eds.), 501–524. University of Massachusetts, Amherst, Mass.: GLSA.
    2002   *A Thematic Guide to Optimality Theory*. Cambridge: Cambridge University Press.
    2003   Comparative markedness. *Theoretical Linguistics* 29: 1–51.

2004   Headed spans and autosegmental spreading. Ms., University of Massachusetts at Amherst. ROA 685
2007   *Hidden Generalizations: Phonological Opacity in Optimality Theory*. London: Equinox Publishing.

McCarthy, John J. and Alan S. Prince
1993   Prosodic morphology I: Constraint interaction and satisfaction. Rutgers Technical Report TR-3. New Brunswick, Rutgers University Center for Cognitive Science. ROA 482.
1995   Faithfulness and reduplicative identity. In *Papers in Optimality Theory*, Jill Beckman, Laura Walsh Dickey and Suzanne Urbanczyk (eds.), 249–384. (Massachusetts Occasional Papers in Linguistics 18). Amherst, Mass.: GLSA.

Morén, Bruce
2003   The parallel structures model of feature geometry. *Working Papers of the Cornell Phonetics Laboratory* 15, 194–270.
2006   Consonant-vowel interactions in Serbian: features, representations and constraint interactions. *Lingua* 116: 1198–1244.
2007   The division of labor between segment-internal structure and violable constraints. This volume.

Morén, Bruce and Elizabeth Zsiga
2006   The lexical and post-lexical phonology of Thai tones. Natural Language and Linguistic Theory 24: 113–178.

Nevins, Andrew and Bert Vaux
2003   Consonant harmony in Karaim. In *The Proceedings of the Workshop on Altaic in Formal Linguistics*, Aniko Csirmaz, Youngjoo Lee and MaryAnn Walter (eds.), 175–194. (MIT Working Papers in Linguistics 46). Cambridge, Mass.: MIT.

Ní Chiosáin, Máire and Jaye Padgett
1997   Markedness, segment realisation, and locality in spreading. Ms., University College Dublin and UC Santa Cruz.
2001   Markedness, segment realisation, and locality in spreading. In: *Constraints and Representations: Segmental Phonology in Optimality Theory*, Linda Lombardi (ed.), 118–156. Cambridge University Press.

Odden, David
1991   Vowel geometry. *Phonology* 8: 261–289.
1994   Adjacency parameters in phonology. *Language* 70, 289–330.

van Oostendorp, Marc
2007   Derived Environment Effects and Consistency of Exponence. This volume.

Padgett, Jaye
1995   Feature classes. In *Papers in Optimality Theory*, Jill Beckman, Laura Walsh Dickey and Suzanne Urbanczyk (eds.), 385–420. (Massachusetts Occasional Papers in Linguistics 18). Amherst, Mass.: GLSA.
2002   Feature classes in phonology. *Language* 78, 81–110.

Prince, Alan S., and Paul Smolensky
1993   Optimality theory. Constraint interaction in generative grammar. Technical Report #2, Rutgers University Center for Cognitive Science. ROA 537; Published in 2004 by Blackwell Publishers).

Pulleyblank, Douglas
1997 Optimality Theory and features. In *Optimality Theory: An Overview*, Diana Archangeli and Terence Langendoen (eds.), 59–101. Oxford: Blackwell.
Revithiadou, Anthi
2007 Colored Turbid accents and Containment: A case study from lexical stress. This volume.
Rice, Keren D. and Peter Avery
1991 On the relationship between laterality and coronality In *The Special Status of Coronals*, Carole Paradis and Jean François Prunet (eds.), 1–124. New York: Academic Press.
Rose, Sharon and Rachel Walker
2004 A typology of consonant agreement as correspondence. *Language* 80: 475–531.
Sagey, Elizabeth
1986 The Representation of Features and Relations in Nonlinear Phonology. Ph. D. diss., MIT.
Scheer, Tobias
2004 *A Lateral Theory of Phonology, Vol.1: What is CVCV, and why should it be?* Berlin: Mouton de Gruyter.
in press Syllabic and trapped consonants in (Western) Slavic: different but still the same. In *Investigations into Formal Slavic Linguistics*, Gerhild Zybatow and Luka Szucsich (eds.). Frankfurt/Main: Lang.
Smeets, Rieks
1984 *Studies in West Circassian Phonology and Morphology*. Leiden: Hakuchi.
Uffmann, Christian
2004 Vowel Epenthesis in Loanword Phonology. Ph. D. diss., Philipps-Universität Marburg.
2005 Optimal geometries. In *The Internal Organization of Phonological Segments*, Jeroen van de Weijer and Marc van Oostendorp (eds.), 27–62. Berlin/New York: Mouton de Gruyter.
2006 Epenthetic vowel quality in loanwords: empirical and formal issues. *Lingua* 116: 1079–1111.
Vaux, Bert
in prep. On locality. Ms., University of Wisconsin, Milwaukee.
Walker, Rachel
1998 Nasalization, neutral segments, and opacity effects. Ph. D. diss., University of California at Santa Cruz.
2001 Positional markedness in vowel harmony. In *Proceedings of HILP 5*, Caroline Féry, Antony Dubach Green and Ruben van de Vijver (eds.), 212–232. Universität Potsdam.
Wetzels, Leo and Joan Mascaró
2001 The typology of voicing and devoicing. *Language* 77: 207–244.
Yip, Moira
2002 *Tone*. Cambridge: Cambridge University Press.
2005 Variability in feature affiliations through violable constraints: The case of [lateral]. In *The Internal Organization of Phonological Segments*, Jeroen van

de Weijer and Marc van Oostendorp (eds.), 63–91. Berlin/New York: Mouton de Gruyter.

Zoll, Cheryl
2003   Optimal tone mapping. *Linguistic Inquiry* 34: 225–268.

Chapter 13
The division of labor between segment-internal structure and violable constraints*

Bruce Morén

This paper touches on a range of conceptual and practical issues that are relevant to current discussions regarding the nature of the phonological component of the grammar, including: featural, representational and constraint economy; representation versus evaluation; computation versus competence; the line between phonetics and phonology; categorical perception; full-specification of features versus minimal/contrastive specification; Richness of the Base; the infinite candidate set; universality of constraints; the lexicon; and phonological acquisition. The paper begins with a review of several conceptual issues, highlights some interesting general problems and possible solutions (necessarily abridged due to space considerations), and then moves on to a detailed discussion of how one might model the segment inventory (including phonetic dispersion and variation) of a specific language in Optimality Theory (Prince and Smolensky 1993).

1. Conceptual

1.1. Classic (and not-so-classic) Optimality Theory

The classic Optimality Theory architecture is depicted in (1). OT is basically a Theory of Computation by which an input string is modified by a GEN(erator) function to produce a candidate set of possible outputs. This candidate set is evaluated by a language-particular hierarchy of violable constraints (i.e. the EVAL(uator) function), and the candidate that is most harmonic with respect to the constraint hierarchy is optimal and surfaces as the output string.

Although the classic OT model has been used extensively for over a decade in the field of phonology, and the model itself is fairly simple and elegant, the simplicity of the overall architecture belies many complications lying beneath the surface. Interestingly, although most people claim to be using classic OT, there is actually a range of differences in implementation and assumptions

(1) Classic OT Model (P&S 1993)

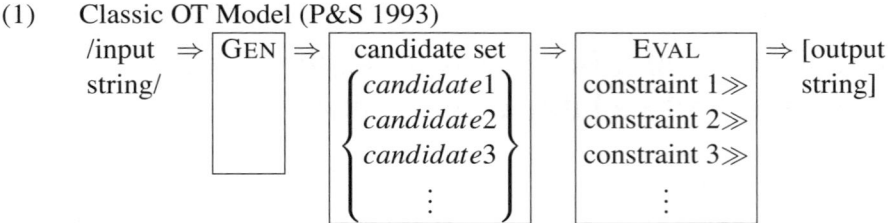

implicit in the published and unpublished literature that are left to the reader to discover for him/herself.

In this paper, I suggest that phonologists need to be more explicit in what they consider the object of phonological research and where the various components of sound (and sign) patterns fit into the overall structure the language faculty. Further, I suggest that it is partially the lack of a concrete set of theories relevant to representations, constraints and the lexicon (and their interactions) that is to blame for some of the confusion in the OT phonological literature and much of the criticism leveled at OT as a model of grammar. In an attempt to help clarify things, I will briefly review select issues with OT phonology and propose a concrete set of possible roads to follow in search of an explicit statement about the nature of the phonological grammar.

Let us begin with an articulated view of "phonology" in the broadest sense and make some claims about what is part of the phonological computational system and what is part of related areas of the conceptual system. This is important because it is often not clear where individual researchers draw the line between these related, but distinct systems.

As the diagram indicates, I suggest that several components commonly implied in the literature as integral parts of phonological computation are not. For example, underlying representations are lexical items that get mapped onto morpho-syntactic constituents and submitted to the phonological computational system for evaluation. They are language-particular representations that are independent of the phonological computation. As we will see below, this view has a significant impact on how one interprets the role of Richness of the Base and Lexicon Optimization (Prince and Smolensky 1993) in evaluating OT as a model of phonological computation. In addition, the "output" of phonological computation is fed to the phonetics-phonology interface where it is mapped to phonetic (articulatory/perceptual) content. The phonological output itself does not include detailed phonetic information. This is contra more functional approaches to phonology (e.g. Flemming 1995,

(2)   A possible model of "phonology"

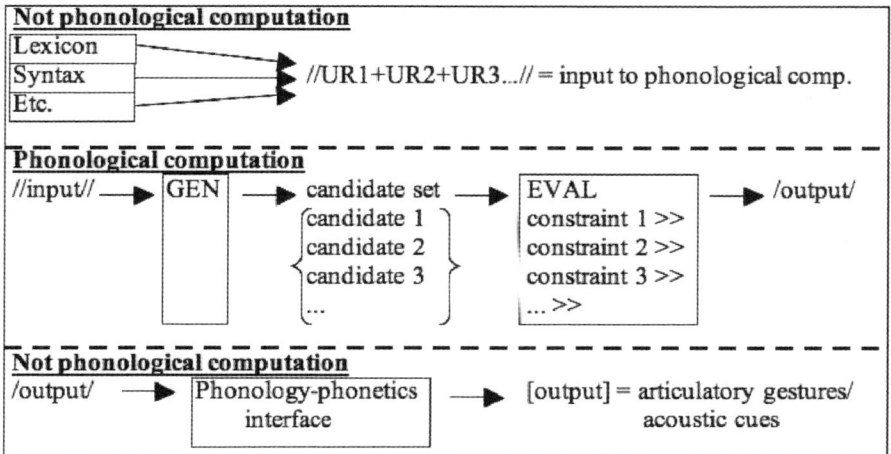

Boersma 1998, Kirchner 1998), but is along the same lines as recent work of Boersma (2006).

Under this view of "phonology", there is a clear distinction between phonological computation and phonological competence (for lack of a better term). Phonological computation is a means of building, manipulating and evaluating abstract representations that are for the most part devoid of lexical and phonetic content. This is similar in flavor to the "substance-free" phonology of Hale and Reiss (2000). In contrast, phonological competence is the result of interactions among the phonological computation, lexicon, morpho-syntax and phonetics.

To aid in disentangling phonological computation and competence, I will briefly review the various parts of classic OT phonology as a Theory of Computation and make some concrete statements about the nature of each part.

1.1.1. Lexicon

What is the lexicon? Although this is not a part of the phonology computation as conceived of in this paper, it plays a role in phonological competence and is often made reference to in the phonological literature (e.g. Hammond 1995, 2005; Russell 1995, 1999; Itô and Mester 1998; Meyer 1999; Harrison and Kaun 2000; Sanders 2003; Ota 2004). I take the common post-Lexicalist position that it is the residing place of stored items that are not composed productively. This includes unpredictable phonological information, morpho-syntactic information and encyclopedic knowledge.[1] Different kinds of information stored in the lexicon are available to different parts of the grammatical/conceptual system, but not all of that information is used by all parts of the system. What is most important for the current paper is that the lexicon does not normally involve online computation (contra the Lexicalist Model (Kiparsky 1982, 1985), its various descendents, and some recent work in OT (e.g. Hammond 1995, 2005; Russell 1995, 1999)).

1.1.2. Syntax

What is syntax? Again, this is not a part of the phonology proper, but it plays a role in phonological competence. Minimally, syntax is a computational system by which morpho-syntactic constituents are built/evaluated. For reasons of space, I have nothing more to say here, other than underlying phonological forms from the lexicon are mapped onto morpho-syntactic constituents and submitted to the phonological computation for evaluation.

1.1.3. Phonological input

What is the phonological input? If we assume the modular approach to phonological competence given in (2), there are at least three ways one might conceive of a "substance-free" input (i.e. not tied to phonetic or lexical implementation). First, it could be a collection of universally available morpho-phonological elements (assuming that the phonology manipulates morpho-phonological material). In which case, we might consider this the Richness of the Base model. Second, it could be a collection of non-redundant/unpredictable morpho-phonological features/structures for which there is overt, positive evidence in the language. We might consider this the language-specific under-specification model. Third, it could be a collection of all surface morpho-phonological structures/features for which there is overt, positive evidence in the language. We might consider this the language-specific full-specification model. Because the first option places no restrictions on the input to the phonological computation other than it use the appropriate symbolic alphabet, it is the strong hypothesis and as such should be the starting assumption. If lexical storage and morpho-syntax are separate from the computational phonology, then the only restriction we can place on the input when addressing phonological computation is that it is morpho-phonological in nature. This is the Richness of the Base hypothesis of Prince and Smolensky (1993). In stepping away from this strong hypothesis, we move into the realm of language-particular phonological competence and require an explicit statement about what we adopt as a *Theory of the Lexicon* and a *Theory of Representation*. Without such a statement, all restrictions placed on inputs to the phonological computation are stipulations.

Note that in modeling morpho-phonological computation (divorced from real language data and other grammatical/conceptual systems), Richness of the Base is vital (as stated above) and Lexicon Optimization is irrelevant. Since Lexicon Optimization is a mechanism by which individual lexical items are stored given language-particular data and a language-particular constraint ranking, it is relevant to phonological competence and *not* phonological computation.

1.1.4. GEN

The GEN(erator) function produces a set of potential outputs known as the candidate set. When asking about the nature of GEN, we are really asking what a candidate is. There are at least three options.[2] First, a candidate could be any collection of universally available phonological elements (e.g. features, segments, moras, syllables) related to one another in all logically possible ways. For example, all of the structures in (3) are candidates in all languages (assuming feature geometry and ignoring supra-segmental structure for simplicity).

(3) a. [root]   b. [cor]   c. [phar]   d. [root]   e. [root]
                                            | |
     f. [root] g. [root] h. [root]   [cor]   [phar]
         | | /   \ | |
       [cor]   [phar] [cor] [phar]   [phar]   [cor]

Second, it could be a language-particular collection of phonological elements related to one another in all logically possible ways. For example, (3c, d, e, g, h) are not candidates in a language that does not make phonological use of the pharynx. Third, it could be a language-particular collection of phonological elements related to one another in a language-particular way. For example, (Xd, e, h) are not candidates in a language where [cor] and [phary] never co-occur within a segment in the output.

The first option is the strong hypothesis and should be assumed as the starting point since it does not have any unstipulated restrictions placed on it. This is the classic OT option. Unless we adopt a specific *Theory of Representation*, we cannot step away from this strong hypothesis without stipulating restrictions on candidate sets. For this reason, work on features and representations is vital to constraining the infinite candidate set of the classic OT phonological computation. I will show that the partial *Theory of Representation* that I use below restricts the output of GEN to only certain language-particular structures.

1.1.5. EVAL *and* CON

EVAL assesses sets of candidates with respect to one another and the input via a hierarchy of ranked, violable constraints. I have little to say about this and simply assume classic OT.

CON is the set of violable constraints. In classic OT, *the* most important question is what the set of constraints is, followed closely by how they are ranked. However, rather than setting up a *Theory of Constraints* guiding their formulation and specifying the means by which they are violated, there has been a tendency to propose constraints to solve a particular language puzzle and not to worry about the conceptual, formal or typological validity of those constraints. While having an adventurous and laissez-faire attitude is a good place to start to explore the range of constraints we might need (particularly in the infancy of a constraint-based theory of grammar), there comes a point when a *Theory of Constraints* is vital to give OT phonology any credibility/explanatory power. Although there has been much insightful work toward a *Theory of Constraints* (e.g. Hayes 1999, McCarthy and Prince 2003, Smith 2004, the attempts to only propose constraints that make reference to established morpho-phonological constituents and the constellation of constraint "families"), there is an astonishing amount of disagreement, and many phonologists using OT simply do not concern themselves with the issue. This is quite surprising given the principal role constraints have in OT.

That said, there are two types of constraints in OT – markedness[3] and faithfulness. Markedness constraints require or penalize configurations of phonological elements (e.g. *[labial], ONSET, FOOTBINARITY), while faithfulness constraints penalize differences between related forms (e.g. input-output). Both faithfulness and markedness constraints can be relativized to different structures, positions, (and perhaps) morphological classes, etc. (e.g. nucleus, prosodic heads, past-tense).

When conceiving of the phonological constraint set, there seem to be at least three directions one might go. First, one could assume that all constraints are universal and only make reference to phonological structures. Second, constraints could be built from universally available phonological primitives, on a language-particular basis, based on overt, positive evidence. Third, constraints might be built from universally available phonological primitives, on a language-particular basis, based on overt, positive evidence; and there is propagation across constraint families once a particular primitive is activated. The first option is the strong hypothesis and that taken by classic OT. Without adopting a specific *Theory of Constraints* or without evidence that the strong hypothesis is incorrect, we are obliged to assume this option. Otherwise, we are merely stipulating sets of language-particular constraints without a mechanism to either derive them or restrict them. That said, I will propose in the second half of this paper part of a *Theory of Constraints* relevant to phonological features and segment-internal structures that is consistent with the third option.

1.1.6. Output

Finally, the output of the phonological computation is not as straightforward as one might expect. There is a dramatic range of structures, morphological information and phonetics encoded in the outputs in many phonology papers. In taking a modular, substance-free approach, I suggest that the output of the phonological computation is a set of abstract structures with a minimum of morphological information and no phonetics encoded. The only morphological information available to the phonological computation is that relevant to productive phonological patterns, e.g. morphological class information is available to the phonological computation of a particular language if that language shows different phonological behaviors for different morphological classes. It is the role of the phonology-phonetics interface to map the abstract phonological structures to articulatory gestures/perceptual cues. Assuming a substance-free output is vital for two main reasons. First, sign languages clearly challenge any theory of universal features that relies on detailed articulatory gestures and/or acoustic cues. Not only does segmental phonology seem to be consistent across modalities despite quite different phonetics, but the range of articulatory combinations allowed in sign languages is greater than those allowed in spoken languages. This suggests that the phonological system is more abstract and combinatory than usually assumed and it is not possible to simply map sign language gestures onto spoken language features. See Morén 2003 for a more detailed discussion. Second, we have known for years (since the Structuralists, at least) that the same phonological representation can have different phonetic realizations 1) in different phonetic contexts within a language (e.g. articulatory overlap), 2) in the same phonetic context within a language (e.g. free variation) and 3) in different languages, and we have also known that the same (or very similar) phonetic realizations can map to different phonological representations depending on the contrastive segment inventory of the language.

To illustrate this point, I present a phonetic and phonological comparison of the Yiddish and Standard Italian vowel systems (ignoring length) in (4). The shaded cells indicate phonetic similarity as indicated by fairly standard transcriptions, while the indices show one possible analysis of phonological identity. What we see here is that while these inventories share only two phonetically similar short vowels, many phonological analyses would assume that they share five phonological short vowels as defined by contrastive phonological features. For example, the Yiddish high front vowel is laxer than the Italian high front vowel, but this laxness/tenseness seems to be a phonetic property, not the result of a phonological feature difference. In contrast, the phonetically similar vowels could be analyzed as being phonologically different in that the Italian mid lax vowels seem to have a feature the non-lax vowels and the Yiddish vowels do not, as indicated by their phonological behavior.

(4) Vowel systems of Yiddish and Italian

Yiddish		Italian	
		i_1	u_2
I_1	$ʊ_2$		
		e_3	o_4
$ɛ_3$	$ɔ_4$	$ɛ$	$ɔ$
	$ɐ_5$		
		a_5	

It is difficult to compare these vowel inventories and assume there is a 1:1 correspondence between phonetic realization and phonological specification – at least if we believe there is some systematicity to phonological feature specifications. Given the usual approach in the OT literature of fully specifying bundles of SPE-like binary features read directly from the phonetics, it is less than obvious what features various researchers would assign to each of these vowels since the decision of how much phonetic information is phonologically full-specified is usually idiosyncratic and rarely discussed.

1.1.7. Summary

Classic OT is a simple and elegant computational system assuming the strongest hypotheses with respect to the input (Richness of the Base), the candidate set (unrestricted) and the constraint set (universal). Any deviation from these strong hypotheses requires a substantive theory of the lexicon, representations and/or constraints. I suggest that many of the criticisms of classic OT currently found in the literature are correct in that they either implicitly or explicitly call for a comprehensive *Theory of the Lexicon*, *Theory of Representation* and/or *Theory of Constraints*. However, these criticisms are fairly empty since they rarely provide viable alternatives/theories of their own and simply advocate abandoning OT – essentially "throwing the baby out with the bathwater."

I suggest that if we only look at the phonological computation system, then the exact nature of underlying representations is irrelevant, Lexicon Optimization is irrelevant, and Richness of the Base is vital. Finally, given an acknowledged lack of parity between phonological structure and phonetic realization, it seems prudent to assume a substance-free phonology and a phonetics-phonology interface component that maps between abstract phonological structures and articulatory gestures/ perceptual cues.

The remainder of this paper will take these points seriously and will suggest part of a *Theory of Representation* and part of a *Theory of Constraints* that impact on phonological competence and a *Theory of the Lexicon*.

1.2. Toward a *Theory of Representation* — the Parallel Structures Model

There are currently many competing feature theories and models of segment-internal representations. Despite differences in detail, however, the general proposals are fairly uniform, each making minor modifications to the feature set of the Sound Patterns of English (Chomsky and Halle 1968) and the geometry of Clements (1985) – with four notable exceptions. First, Clements (1991a) proposed an innovative unification of consonant and vowel place features, which greatly economizes the set of those features and helps to explain C-V place harmony asymmetries and assimilations. Second, Clements (1991b) proposed a set of vowel height features that makes a more direct connection between those features and degrees of vocal tract constriction. Third, Steriade (1993, 1994) proposed that consonant manners are differentiated via different types of root nodes corresponding to different degrees of vocal tract constriction. Fourth, Particle Phonology (Schane 1984), Dependency Phonology (Anderson and Ewen 1987, van der Hulst 1989, 1999) and Element Theory (Harris and Lindsey 1995) differ radically from the SPE feature tradition in a number of ways – most notably, they assume that vowels and consonants make active use of the same set of features/elements.

The Parallel Structures Model of feature geometry (Morén 2003, 2004a, b, 2006) combines insights from each of these lines of research. It extends the mechanism of Clements' place model to other areas of the phonology, unifies Clements' constriction model and Steriade's aperture model, and incorporates some of the segment-internal organization proposed in Particle Phonology, Dependency Phonology and Element Theory. In addition, it makes use of structural and featural economy to the greatest extent possible. The result is a feature theory that eliminates a large number of features from the grammar (including the major class features); provides a unified analysis for consonants, vowels, place and manner; and captures consonant-vowel interactions, alternations and harmony asymmetries in a natural and straightforward way.

According to the Parallel Structures Model, phonological segments are composed of a limited set of identical structures and a limited set of privative features.[4] The form of the basic structure is essentially that proposed by Clements (1991a) and is given in (5). A significant difference between this model and Clements' is that I claim that the same token feature cannot associate with both a C-class node and a V-class node simultaneously.

Minimally, there is a set of place and manner features that associate with identically configured place and manner class nodes, as shown in (6).

(5)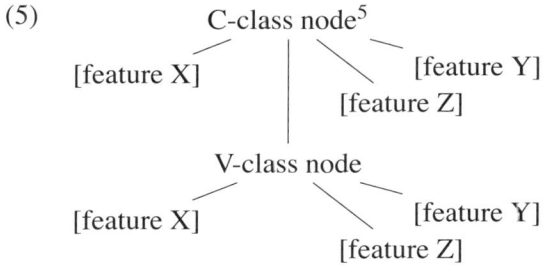

(6)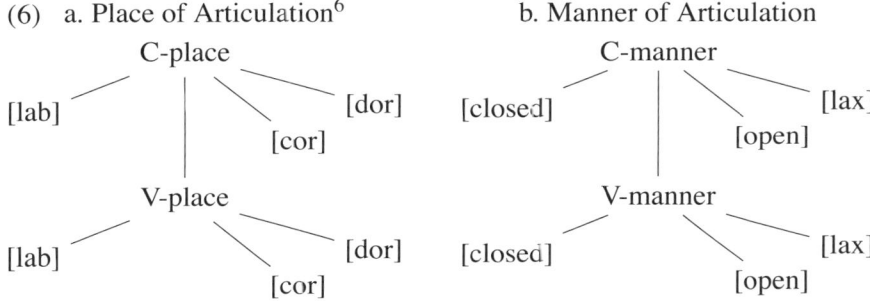

The place features are currently in widespread use and will not be discussed – see Clements (1991a) and Morén (2003). The manner features are based on degrees of constriction and relative articulator rigidity. See Morén (2003) for a general discussion of these features. The manner features [open] and [closed] are demonstrated below.

The Parallel Structures Model also assumes that the grammar is structurally economical and that more complex structures are built from less complex structures. This is in keeping with some of the principles of Particle Phonology, Dependency Phonology and Element Theory, and the Modified Contrastive Specification Model (Dresher and Rice 1993, Dresher *et al.* 2004), as well as other work of Avery and Rice (1989), Rice and Avery (1989) and Rice (1992). One consequence of this is the prediction that languages have simple segments that are featurally minimal – e.g. have only a manner feature or only a place feature.

To demonstrate how the Parallel Structures Model establishes minimal feature specification for a given contrastive inventory, let us assume the following very limited set of segments: [t, ɬ, s, l, ɹ, i, e, a]. This imaginary inventory does not have any place contrasts, but differentiates among stops, lateral fricatives, fricatives, lateral approximants, rhotic approximants, high vowels, mid vowels and low vowels. In other words, it contrasts among three major classes (obstruents, sonorant consonants and vowels), and within each of these major classes, there are manner and height distinctions. In addition, the mapping from a given feature specification to a phonetic realization is determined on a language-by-language basis based on a combination of contrasts and behavior. Therefore, a given phonetic transcription (i.e. IPA symbol) can correspond to different feature specifications in different languages. Using the features in (6b), and building complex feature combinations from simpler feature combinations, we might describe this inventory as in (7).

(7) PSM feature specification for the target segment inventory

		C-manner		V-manner			
		[closed]	[open]	[closed]	[open]		
Stop	[t]	✓					Obstruent
Lateral fric.	[ɬ]	✓		✓		Consonant	
Fricative	[s]		✓				
Lateral approx.	[l]	✓		✓			Sonorant
Rhotic approx.	[ɹ]		✓	✓			
High vowel	[i]			✓		Vowel	
Mid vowel	[e]			✓	✓		
Low vowel	[a]				✓		

Note: shaded cells indicate simple (i.e. single) feature specification.

There are a number of observations that are important here. As discussed in Morén (2003), the major classes are not defined via separate major class features (e.g. [±sonorant]) but can be defined structurally via combinations of C-manner and/or V-manner features, as shown in (7). Consonants have a C-manner feature, while vowels do not, and sonorants have a V-manner feature, while obstruents do not. Sonorant consonants have both a C-manner and a V-manner feature. Second, "lateral" consonants are not defined via a distinct lateral feature, but rather as a combination of a C-manner[closed] and a more open gesture. Third, manner of articulation and vowel height are captured using the same set of articulator-based features distributed across two related class nodes. Fourth, relative markedness relationships among manners and heights can be captured via relative structural complexity. That is, plain stops and plain fricatives are structurally less marked than lateral fricatives because they each have only a single manner feature, whereas the lateral fricative has two. Similarly, high and low vowels are structurally less marked than mid vowels because they each have only a single manner feature, whereas the mid vowels have two. Sonorant consonants are also more structurally marked than either simple obstruents or simple vowels for the same reason.[7]

To summarize, there has been much insightful work done on segmental features and geometry over the past three decades, and we continue to refine the feature sets and representations that we assume to be universal. However, there are still unresolved issues and many important questions to answer. Specifically, what is the full set of universal features, and what are the ways in which they can combine to form all the segments found cross-linguistically? The Parallel Structures Model takes the insights and formalisms of several current feature theories and combines them into a new model using parallel structures and feature sets when possible.

As we will see, the assumptions that more complex structures are built from less complex primitives can be mirrored in the building of more complex feature co-occurrence constraints from less complex primitives. This will then have an impact on the types of segments that are actually categorically perceived by individuals.

1.3. Toward a *Theory of Constraints* – building segment inventories

Most OT analyses in the literature do not explicitly state the mechanism by which the segment inventories of languages are captured using constraints. Nor do they motivate the feature specifications they assume for given segments. Rather, they assume particular (usually fully-specified) bundles of SPE features for given segments and use constraint interaction to account for specific phenomena without questioning the validity of those features and constraints for the rest of the language. While such analyses are certainly interesting and address particular theoretical and empirical questions, it is also important to put analyses within the larger context of the grammar of the language under investigation. Therefore, I suggest that all phonological analyses of languages are obligated to provide a justification for the features and structures assumed for individual segments. This is something that was quite important in the pre-OT literature but has since been largely ignored.

Before providing an OT analysis of the segment inventory of a language (i.e. Hawai'ian), I will state some concrete assumptions. First, I assume that only the representations of the Parallel Structures Model are possible segment-internal structures. Therefore, universally illicit structures are impossible outputs of GEN and are thus absent from the candidate set. This is a statement about the nature of the grammar, in which GEN, not the constraint ranking, ensures that only particular representations are universally available. Thus, I am making a proposal about one aspect of a *Theory of Representation* and an explicit statement about the division of labor between segment-internal representations and constraints. The representations regulate the possible relationships among segment-internal elements while the constraint ranking determines which representations occur in a given context in a specific language. Some examples of possible and impossible sub-structures are given in (8).

(8) Examples of possible and impossible structures

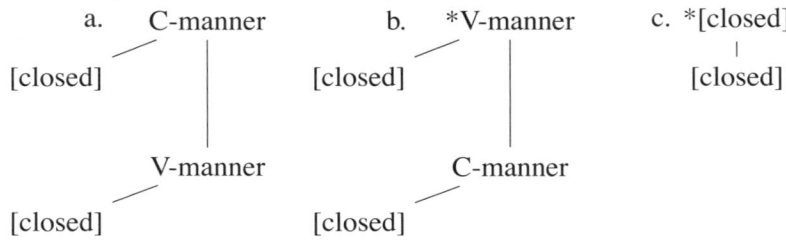

Second, I assume the Correspondence Theory (McCarthy and Prince 1995) version of faithfulness constraints in which features are treated as autosegments, not attributes (Lombardi 1998, 1999). This is compatible with the monovalent features employed by the Parallel Structures Model. Thus, I use MAX and DEP constraints rather than IDENT constraints. Third, the feature markedness and faithfulness constraints make reference to both class node and feature specification, as shown in (9)[8] and (10).

(9) a. *C-MANNER[closed]
       Assign a violation mark for every C-manner[closed].
    b. *V-MANNER[closed]
       Assign a violation mark for every V-manner [closed].

(10) a. MAX C-manner[closed]
        Assign a violation mark for every C-manner[closed] in the input that does not have a correspondent in the output (do not delete).
     b. MAX V-manner[closed]
        Assign a violation mark for every V-manner[closed] in the input that does not have a correspondent in the output (do not delete).

c. DEP C-manner[closed]
Assign a violation mark for every C-manner[closed] in the output that does not have a correspondent in the input (do not epenthesize).

d. DEP V-manner[closed]
Assign a violation mark for every V-manner[closed] in the output that does not have a correspondent in the input (do not epenthesize).

Finally, there are a number of possible ways to formalize constraints against feature co-occurrence. I suggest that the phonological grammar is economical and uses combinations of primitive constraints to form more complex constraints. This could be done using local conjunctions of simple feature markedness constraints in a way that meets the strictest requirements on local conjunction by defining the domain as the root node and only allowing related constraints from the same constraint family to be conjoined (Fukazawa and Miglio 1998). This is an explicit claim that feature co-occurrence constraints are not universally specified and thus a statement about the *Theory of Constraints*.

(11) Local Conjunction (Smolensky 1997)
The local conjunction of C_1 and C_2 in domain D, C_1 & C_2, is violated when there is some domain of type D in which both C_1 and C_2 are violated.

(12) *C-MANNER[closed]&*V-MANNER[closed]
The local conjunction of *C-manner[closed] and *V-manner[closed] is violated when both *C-manner[closed] and *V-manner[closed] are violated by the same segment.

With essential assumptions made, I will now implement this system by providing an analysis of Hawai'ian segmental phonology.

2. Implementation and refinement – Hawai'ian

2.1. Language description (based on Elbert and Pukui 1979)

2.1.1. Consonant inventory, phonetic dispersion and allophony

Hawai'ian has a very small consonant inventory – only 11 surface consonants, phonetically described in (13). Interestingly, some of these consonants (shaded cells) are not contrastive and only appear as allophones - to be discussed. This leaves Hawai'ian with an even smaller and rather unusual contrastive inventory – eight consonants and no "coronal" stop.

(13) Phonetic descriptions of surface consonants

	Bilabial	Dental-alveolar	Alveolar	Velar	Glottal
Stop	[p]	[t]		[k]	[ʔ]
Fricative	[v]				[h]
Nasal	[m]		[n]		
Lateral			[l]		
Rhotic			([ɾ]) [9]		
Glide	[w]				

Note: Shaded segments indicate non-contrastive phonetic variants.

The underlying labial glide varies in the amount of rounding by both speaker and context. Some speakers consistently use [w] or [v] (at least at slower speech rates), while other speakers show phonetic variation based on the quality of the preceding vowel. The more rounded allophone appears after back round vowels [u] and [o], the less rounded allophone appears after front unrounded vowels [i] and [e], and either one may appear word initially or following a low vowel [a]. This variation suggests it is phonetic. The most surprising fact about the Hawai'ian consonant inventory is that there is variation in the realization of what looks to be underlying /k/. Some speakers randomly substitute [t], particularly in fast speech and when following [i]. However, it is clear from the descriptions that the phonetic velar stop is the more general surface segment corresponding to what we might call the phoneme (e.g. it appears in slow, careful speech), while the phonetic alveolar stop is a phonetic variant. This is a very interesting and striking fact (although not unheard of among Polynesian languages) because there is a conspicuous absence of typical coronal obstruents (i.e. dental/alveolar/palatal) from the contrastive inventory – much to the puzzlement of those assuming a [coronal] unmarked place of articulation and a direct relationship between phonological feature specification and phonetic realization.[10]

From a phonetic dispersion perspective, the Hawai'ian inventory is interesting because place of articulation is phonetically disperse in that five places are used for only eight consonants, and three places are used for only one consonant each. In addition, the less-sonorous segments tend to be articulated toward the rear of the vocal tract, while more-sonorous segments tend to be articulated toward the front of the vocal tract. The major questions to answer are what are the phonological features that make up this inventory and how do we explain both the contrasts and the variation?

2.1.2. Consonant phonological processes

Hawai'ian has no documented phonological processes involving consonants, as one might expect from a language without adjacent consonants (i.e. no consonant clusters or codas).

2.1.3. Vowel inventory, phonetic dispersion and allophony

If we ignore vowel length, Hawai'ian has a typical five-vowel system, phonetically described in the following chart:

(14)   Phonetic descriptions of Hawai'ian surface vowels

	Front	Central	Back/Round
High	[i]		[u]
Mid	[e] ~[ɛ]		[o]
Low		[a]	

As one might expect, these vowels are maximally dispersed from a phonetic perspective. The vowels showing a contrast along the front-back dimension use both tongue configuration and lip rounding to maximize their acoustic difference. In contrast, the one low vowel is central in the acoustic space since it is not in contrast along the front-back dimension and being central makes it more perceptually distinct from the non-low non-central vowels, as well as articulatorily more neutral.

330 Bruce Morén

That said, the actual phonetic realization of these vowels changes slightly depending on the prosodic and segmental context. The high and low vowels are slightly lower in unstressed syllables, while the low vowel is realized as slightly higher. The mid front vowel is more centralized when adjacent to a consonant made with an alveolar articulation (i.e. [l] or [n]). Both of these variations are consistent with known cross-linguistic phonetic tendencies and do not seem to be phonological in nature.

2.1.4. Vowel combinations (phonology)

Hawai'ian has no documented segmental processes involving vowels. There are, however, restrictions on the allowable combinations of adjacent vowels within a single syllable (i.e. diphthongs). Importantly, the first vowel of a diphthong must be lower than the second. This results in eight diphthongs, as shown in (15).

(15) Diphthongs

		Second V (unstressed)				
		i	u	e	o	a
First V (stressed)	i	–	–	–	–	–
	u	–	–	–	–	–
	e	ei	eu	–	–	–
	o	oi	ou	–	–	–
	a	ai	au	ae	ao	–

2.2. Phonological analysis (representational)

Given the phonetic and distributional facts, one might expect the Hawai'ian phonological system to use a very limited and economical set of features and structures. The chart in (16) lists the segments and one interpretation of their phonological feature specifications using the Parallel Structures Model. There are only six phonological features used - two place features, two consonant manner features and two vowel manner features.

The fully specified PSM representation used in Hawai'ian is given in (17), and the representations of each segment are given in (18) through (22).

(16) Hawai'ian segments defined by PSM features

			C-place		C-manner		V-manner	
			[lab]	[tongue]	[closed]	[open]	[closed]	[open]
Mannerless	/w/	[w]~[v]	✓					
	/l/	[l]~[ɾ]		✓				
Stop	/ʔ/	[ʔ]			✓			
	/p/	[p]	✓		✓			
	/k/	[k]~[t]		✓	✓			
Stop+ Continuant	/n/	[n]			✓	✓		
	/m/	[m]	✓		✓	✓		
Continuant	/h/	[h]				✓		
High	/i/	[i]					✓	
	/u/	[u]	✓				✓	
High+ Low	/e/	[e]~[ɛ]					✓	✓
	/o/	[o]	✓				✓	✓
Low	/a/	[a]						✓

Note: Shaded cells indicate segments composed of only a single feature.

(17) Hawai'ian PSM Geometry

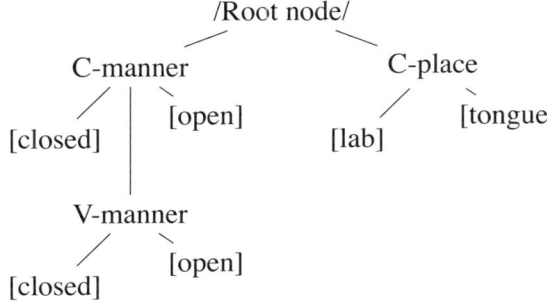

(18) Mannerless simple place segments
 a. [w]~[v]   b. [l]~[ɾ]

```
   /root/        /root/
     |             |
   C-place       C-place
     |             |
   [labial]      [tongue]
```

(19) Placeless simple manner segments

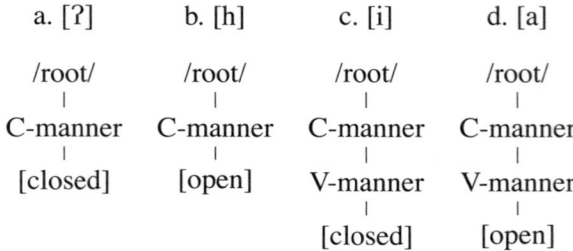

(20) Simple manner with simple place segments

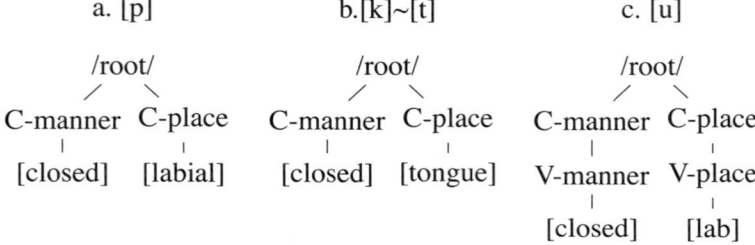

(21) Placeless complex manner segments

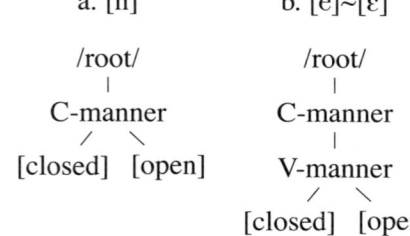

(22) Complex manner and simple place segments

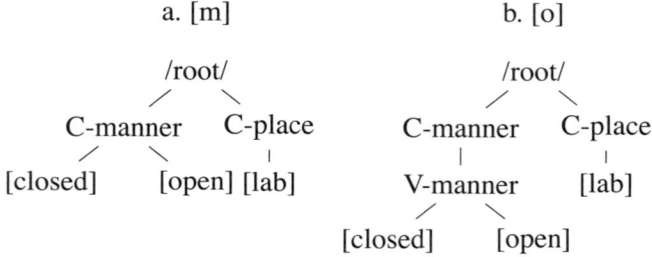

Given these phonological representations, the phonetic variation in the realization of [w]~[v] and [l]~[r] is explained by their lack of manner features. Because they are unspecified for phonological closure, they may vary in their closure realization either by phonetic context or freely. Similarly, the phonetic place variation of the mid front vowel is explained by its lack of a phonologically unspecified place feature – thus it is susceptible to co-articulation effects.[11]

This analysis provides a reason for both the conspicuous absence of contrastive dental/alveolar/palatal obstruents and the free variation (and lack of a contrast in any environment) that is seen between velar stops and alveolar stops in some dialects. Since there are no sub-place distinctions among obstruents using the tongue as an active articulator, then a simple raising of the tongue body to form an obstruent constriction does not have to be specified with respect to the part of the tongue making the constriction. Thus, the tongue dorsum makes as good an active articulator as the tongue blade, and the lack of a 1:1 correspondence between phonological feature specification and phonetic realization (free variation in this case) is due to a combination of an abstract substance-free phonology and a language-particular mapping between phonological features and sensory-motor coordinations.

Among vowels, restrictions on the types of diphthongs allowed (i.e. the first element must be more "open" than the second element) suggest that there are three phonological heights in Hawai'ian. This was shown in (16), where relative vowel height/sonority is defined by V-manner features.

2.3. Summary

The privative features and restrictions on segment-internal complexity of the Parallel Structures Model lead to a simple account of the phonological segment inventory of Hawai'ian. Although the relationship between phonological feature specification and phonetic realization in this analysis seems, at first glance, somewhat opaque since one cannot simply assume a traditional set of phonological features based on static phonetic descriptions (e.g. [k] and [t] are phonologically coronal in a sense), the actual behavior of the segments (both phonetic and phonological) makes that relationship quite straightforward. In fact, the puzzle of the lack of contrastive dental/ alveolar/palatal obstruents and the unusual [k]~[t] free variation is very difficult to account for using theories in which phonological representations are universally mapped to particular phonetic realizations.

2.4. OT Analysis of the Hawai'ian segment inventory

2.4.1. Simple segments, categories and restrictions on GEN

With essential representational assumptions made, we can move on to an OT analysis of Hawai'ian. Recall that Hawai'ian has six segments composed of only a single feature – two segments are mannerless and four segments are placeless. Using the standard OT strategy of ranking markedness constraints below faithfulness constraints to yield a surface contrast, the following constraint rankings yield these first order contrastive segments.

In each of these rankings, the faithfulness constraint against deleting an individual feature is ranked above a markedness constraint against that feature. The result is a set of six surface segments composed of only a single phonological feature.

(23) a. MAXC-place[lab] ≫ *C-place[lab] (i.e. /w/)
b. MAXC-place[tongue] ≫ *C-place[tongue] (i.e. /l/)
c. MAXC-manner[closed] ≫ * C-manner[closed] (i.e. /ʔ/)
d. MAXC-manner[open] ≫ *C-manner[open] (i.e. /h/)
e. MAXV-manner[closed] ≫ *V-manner[closed] (i.e. /i/)
f. MAXV-manner[open] ≫ *V-manner[open] (i.e. /a/)

The tableaux in (24) and (25) demonstrate how this provides the correct results for the fricative and the high front vowel. In both tableaux, feature deletion in candidate (b) is ruled out by the higher-ranked faithfulness constraint.

(24)

//C-manner[open]//	//h//	MAXC-manner[open]	*C-manner[open]
☞ a. C-manner[open]	/h/		*
b. —	/ /	*!	

(25)

//V-manner[closed]//	//i//	MAXV-manner[closed]	*V-manner[closed]
☞ a. V-manner[closed]	/i/		*
b. —	/ /	*!	

In contrast, segments composed of features not used in this language (e.g. C-place[pharyngeal]) are prohibited. However, I propose that this is not because the relevant markedness constraint against these features outranks the related faithfulness constraint, as is usually assumed in the OT literature. Rather, I suggest that children learning the language have had no overt, positive evidence with which to propose an abstract phonological feature that is mapped to a set of phonetic characteristics signifying a pharyngeal place of articulation. Thus, such a feature (and segments making use of that feature) does not exist in the language in the constraint set, candidate set, or even the lexicon. In essence, categorical perception is an emergent quality resulting from a language-particular mapping of abstract phonological features with their phonetic realization. This emergent quality has a direct impact on the candidate and constraint sets. This is the logical consequence of assuming a substance-free phonology. If we assume that the phonology does not make reference to the phonetics directly and that there are no universal mappings between abstract phonological features and sets of phonetic characteristics, then featural constraints must be learned via overt, positive evidence from the environment. This is a major departure from classic OT, which assumes that all constraints are universal. Thus, I am proposing part of a *Theory of Constraints* in which feature markedness constraints are developed as part of the acquisition process. Acoustic/visual signals are mapped onto abstract phonological features thus triggering a set of markedness and faithfulness constraints, which can be ranked in EVAL in the usual way. At some point during the acquisition process, the abstract features based on acoustic/visual signals are mapped onto articulatory coordinations (see also Boersma 1998, 2006). In addition, I suggest that there is simultaneous propagation of the acquired phonological feature across constraints making reference to features.

Developing a *Theory of Constraints* in this way has serious and restricting consequences for GEN and the lexicon as they pertain to phonological competence. Simply put, GEN can only produce a candidate making use of features for which there is positive, overt evidence in the language. This means that candidates not making use of the features of the language should simply not be considered in an OT tableau. This is distinctly different from a classical OT evaluation. However, as stated in section 1, classic OT is a theory of phonological computation, not competence, and what I am advocating here is a competence application of the OT architecture. Thus, this *Theory of Constraints* has a direct relationship to the *Theory of Representation* as instantiated by GEN and the *Theory of the Lexicon* as instantiated by specific underlying forms of morphemes.

2.4.2. Complex segments

As simple features are acquired and made available to the grammar via markedness constraints, they may be combined to form more complex structures. In Hawai'ian, there are only six simple features used in the Parallel Structures Model analysis discussed in section 2.2. These can combine two at a time to yield $6C2 = 6!/(2!(6-2)!) = 720/48 = 15$ second order segments/constraints. This means that there are 15 logically possible segments composed of two features. Of these, only five are actually used in this language.[12] The allowable combinations of two features are the result of the constraint rankings in (26). Tableau (27) demonstrates how the labial stop results from the ranking in (26a).

(26) a. M$_{AX}$C-place[lab], M$_{AX}$C-manner[closed] ≫
       *C-place[lab]&*C-manner[closed]   (i.e. /p/)
    b. M$_{AX}$C-place[tongue], M$_{AX}$C-manner[closed] ≫
       *C-place[tongue]&*C-manner[closed]   (i.e. /k/)
    c. M$_{AX}$C-manner[closed], M$_{AX}$C-manner[open] ≫
       *C-manner[closed]&*C-manner[open]   (i.e. /n/)
    d. M$_{AX}$C-place[lab], M$_{AX}$V-manner[closed] ≫
       *C-place[lab]&*V-manner[closed]   (i.e. /u/)
    e. M$_{AX}$V-manner[closed], M$_{AX}$V-manner[open] ≫
       *V-manner[closed]&*V-manner[open]   (i.e. /e/)

(27)

//C-place[lab] C-manner [closed]//		M$_{AX}$ C-place [lab]	M$_{AX}$ C-manner [closed]	*C-place[lab] &C-manner [closed]	*C-place [lab]	*C-manner [closed]
☞	a. /p/			*	*	*
	b. /w/		*!		*	
	c. /ʔ/	*!				*
	d. //	*!	*!			

Combining three markedness constraints at a time using local conjunction, we get $6C3=6!/3!(6-3)!=720/36=20$ third order constraints. Of these, only two are used in this language. Tableau (29) demonstrates the evaluation of the segment /o/.

(28) a. MAXC-manner[closed], MAXC-manner[open], MAXC-place[lab]
≫
*C-manner[closed]&*C-manner[open]&*C-place[lab] (i.e. /m/)
b. MAXV-manner[closed], MAXV-manner[open], MAXC-place[lab]
≫
*V-manner[closed]&*V-manner[open]&*C-place[lab] (i.e. /o/)

(29)

//V-manner[closed] V-manner[open] C-place[lab]//	MAX V-man [closed]	MAX V-man [open]	MAX C-pl [labial]	*V-manner[closed]& *V-man[open]& *C-place[lab]
☞ a. V-manner[closed]& V-manner[open]& C-place[labial /o/				*
b. V-manner[closed]& V-manner[open]/e/			*!	
c. V-manner[closed]& C-place[labial /u/		*!		
d. V-manner[open]& C-place[labial	*!			
e. / /	*!	*!	*!	

Note that Hawai'ian does not have a contrastive segment composed of just V-manner[open] and C-place[lab] (candidate (d)), so the question of how to represent such a feature combination in the phonological computation remains. There are a number of possibilities, none of which I have space to explore fully here, but several of which I will mention. One possibility is that GEN could not produce such a combination since it is not a linguistic category of the language (similar to the lack of [phar] in a language not making phonological use of the pharynx). In which case, we do not need to consider candidate (d) in Hawai'ian. Another possibility is that GEN could produce such a combination and the constraint ranking rules it out. Given the evaluation in (29) which predicts that such a segment could be optimal, a more sophisticated set of feature co-occurrence constraints would be needed than those presented here. For example, the markedness constraints would have to be evaluated over entire segments, not partial segments. A third possibility is that GEN could produce this candidate and it could be the optimal candidate for some input, but it never appears because there is no surface data in the language that would lead to the required lexical item (see Blevins 2004). This is then a phonological competence explanation, rather than a phonological computation explanation. A fourth possibility is that GEN could produce it and it could be the optimal candidate for some input, but is could not be mapped onto a distinct set of articulatory gestures at the phonology-phonetics interface. This could cause phonological ineffability (i.e. a crash/gap) or it could be phonetically realized as indistinct from another licit category. Again, this would be a competence, rather than computational, explanation. I leave this an unresolved issue and the topic of future research.

To summarize, the constraint ranking necessary to account for the segment inventory of Hawai'ian is given in (30). The feature co-occurrence markedness constraints define the categorical segments of the language, and their ranking relative to other constraints (e.g. faithfulness) determines the surface distribution of those segments.

(30)   Hawai'ian segment inventory constraints and ranking
MAXC-place[lab], MAXC-place[tongue], MAXC-manner[closed],
MAXC-manner[open], MAXV-manner[closed], MAXV-manner[open]
≫
*C-manner[closed]&*C-manner[open]&*C-place[lab],
*V-manner[closed]&*V-manner[open]&*C-place[lab],
*C-place[lab]&*C-manner[closed],
*C-place[tongue]&*C-manner[closed],
*C-place[lab]&*V-manner[closed],
*C-manner[closed]&*C-manner[open],
*V-manner[closed]&*V-manner[open],
*C-place[lab], *C-place[tongue], *C-manner[closed],
*C-manner[open],
*V-manner[closed], *V-manner[open]

2.5. Summary

This section explored the phonetic and phonological sound patterns of Hawai'ian, proposed an economical set of feature specifications for the individual segments, and provided a constraint-based account of the inventory facts.

All in all, we see that the simplicity of the phonological grammar of Hawai'ian makes it perfect for demonstrating the current proposal for marrying a particular model of phonological features with constraint interaction free of complex phonological alternations. In assuming that the phonology is substance-free in not encoding phonetic details, we are forced to conclude that individual abstract phonological features, their combinations and their mappings to phonetics are acquired via overt, positive evidence and are not initially/universally available. This has the effect of forcing us to conclude that constraints making reference to those features are also not initially present. It also has the effect of severely restricting the output of GEN to only those features acquired. What is universally available (minimally) is 1) an abstract phonological alphabet, 2) ways in which they can relate to one another, 3) a computational system that can manipulate them and choose among them, and 4) a means to map them to the physical world.

3. Conclusions

There were two main goals of this paper. The first was conceptual – to review the basic OT architecture, discuss some of the difficulties/uncertainties that arise in trying to use it to model phonology, and suggest answers to some criticisms. I suggested that without a *Theory of the Lexicon*, a *Theory of Representation* and a *Theory of Constraints*, we are forced to assume the classic OT computational model at face value – including Richness of the Base, an unrestricted candidate set and a universal set of constraints. However, I also suggested that the phonology is fairly substance-free and that phonetic details are not universally encoded in phonological features (supported by both work on sign languages, cross-linguistic variation, and phonetic variation). This has serious consequences for a *Theory of Representation* and *Theory of Constraints*, as well as a *Theory of Acquisition*. I proposed that we are endowed with a universal set of abstract phonological feature primitives that can be mapped during the acquisition process to phonetic content. Once features are acquired, they can be combined to form more complex structures and constraints given overt, positive evidence. The presence of acquired features and combinations of features, encoded in markedness constraints and conjunctions of markedness constraints, has the effect of enforcing phonological categories (categorical perspective) and limiting the output of the GEN(erator) function to only those categorical structures.

The second goal of this paper was practical – to show that integrating an economical and highly restrictive model of segment-internal structure into OT is possible. I did this by introducing the Parallel Structures Model, applying it to the segment inventory of Hawai'ian, and incorporating it into an OT analysis of the Hawai'ian inventory.

Notes

* I am grateful to the participants of the Freedom of Analysis? Workshop, Sylvia Blaho and one anonymous reviewer for insightful comments and discussion.
1. Phonetic details may also be stored in the lexicon, as Bybee (2001) and other suggest. I remain agnostic about this.
2. There are, of course, a number of other possibilities, but they are not discussed here for reasons of space.
3. I consider alignment constraints to be markedness constraints, contra suggestions that they are a separate class.
4. The issue of substance-free phonology is important here since the PSM assumes "articulator-based features". In comparing spoken and signed languages, it is clear that both modalities use a set of articulators and degrees of constriction/rigidity (Morén 2003, 2006). Thus, I assume that the abstract phonological grammar makes reference to Place and Manner. It may be possible to reduce these to even more abstract class nodes and encode place and manner aspects in the phonetics-phonology interface, but I do not do so here. The actual features themselves are likely to be abstract and mapped by the phonetics-phonology interface onto sets of articulatory gestures/perceptual cues.
5. The use of "C" and "V" to indicate node type is a mnemonic device more than a statement about the phonological nature of the nodes. That is, vowels can have "C-node" features and consonants can have "V-node" features. In the lack of a contrast, all segments will have "C-node" features. However, if there is overt evidence in the language that consonants and vowels behave differently with respect to a particular feature, then the consonant has the "C-node" feature and the vowel has the "V-node" feature.
6. This is simplified in not including [pharyngeal] and not stating place in a more modality neutral way that could include sign language articulators.
7. It is important to note that this discussion is highly simplified and that phonetically similar segments in different languages have different feature specifications and, in fact, different phonological markedness relations.
8. This is not the only logical possibility, but is assumed here for concreteness and to simplify the remaining discussion. For example, these complex constraints could be formulated as local conjunctions of markedness constraints against individual class nodes and individual features, e.g. *C-manner&*[closed]. More research is needed here.

9. The rhotic is a very limited dialectal variant (Ni'ihau) of the lateral and will not be discussed as it seems solely conditioned by speech rate.
10. There is recent work arguing that the universal phonological unmarkedness of coronal place is a myth and that phonetically labial and dorsal segments are phonologically unmarked for place in some languages (e.g. Avery and Rice 2004, Morén 2006).
11. While phonetic variation *can* indicate of a lack of feature specification along a particular phonological dimension, the lack of feature specification *need not* imply phonetic variation along that dimension. The relationship between phonetic variability and phonological feature un(der)specification is asymmetrical and language particular.
12. The fact that Hawai'ian only uses 5 of 15 possible second order feature combinations is a historical fact, not something that needs to be synchronically justified (see Blevins 2004). It is, however, synchronically explained by the ranking of the relevant markedness constraints above the relevant faithfulness constraints. Without sufficient exposure to the right type of stimulus, children learning Hawai'ian would not be motivated to modify this default ranking.

References

Anderson, John and Colin Ewen
    1987   *Principles of Dependency Phonology*. Cambridge: Cambridge University Press.
Avery, Peter and Keren D. Rice
    1989   Segment structure and coronal underspecification. *Phonology* 6: 179–200.
Blevins, Juliette
    2004   *Evolutionary Phonology: The Emergence of Sound Patterns*. Cambridge: Cambridge University Press.
Boersma, Paul
    1998   Functional Phonology: Formalizing the interactions between articulatory and perceptual drives. Ph.D. dissertation. University of Amsterdam.
    2006   The acquisition and evolution of faithfulness rankings. Presented at the 14th Manchester Phonology Meeting, Manchester, England.
Bybee, Joan
    2001   *Phonology and Language Use*. Cambridge Studies in Linguistics 94. Cambridge: Cambridge University Press.
Chomsky, Noam and Morris Halle
    1968   *The Sound Pattern of English*. New York: Harper and Row.
Clements, G. N.
    1985   The geometry of phonological features. *Phonology* 2: 225–252.
    1991a   Place of articulation in consonants and vowels: A unified theory. In *Working Papers of the Cornell Phonetics Laboratory*, vol. 5. Ithaca: Cornell University.
    1991b   Vowel height assimilation in Bantu languages. In *Working Papers of the Cornell Phonetics Laboratory*, vol. 5. Ithaca: Cornell University.
Dresher, B. Elan and Keren Rice
    1993   Preface: Complexity in phonological representations. In *Toronto Working Papers in Linguistics* 12(2), Carrie Dyck (ed.), i–vi.

Dresher, B. Elan, Glyne Piggott and Keren Rice
    1994   Contrast in Phonology: Overview. In *Toronto Working Papers in Linguistics* 13(1), Carrie Dyck (ed.), iii–xvii.

Elbert, Samuel and Mary Kawena Pukui
    1979   *Hawai'ian Grammar*. Honolulu: University Press of Hawaii.

Flemming, Edward
    1995   *Auditory Representation in Phonology*. Ph.D. dissertation. UCLA. Published in 2002 by Routledge.

Fukazawa, Haruka and Viola Miglio
    1998   Restricting conjunction to constraint families. *Proceedings of the 9th West Coast Conference on Formal Linguistics*, Aaron Halpern (ed.), 102–117. Stanford, Cal.: CSLI

Hale, Mark and Charles Reiss
    2000   "Substance abuse" and "dysfunctionalism": Current trends in phonology. *Linguistic Inquiry* 31(1): 157–169.

Hammond, Michael
    1995   There is no lexicon! Ms.,University of Arizona.
    2005   Gradience, phonotactics, and the lexicon in English phonology. Ms., University of Arizona.

Harris, John and Geoff Lindsey
    1995   The elements of phonological representation. In *Frontiers of Phonology: Atoms, Structures, Derivations*, Jacques Durand and Francis Katamba (eds.), pp. 34–79.

Harrison, K. David and Abigail Kaun
    2000   Pattern-response lexicon optimization. Ms., Yale University.

Hayes, Bruce
    1999   Phonetically-driven phonology: The role of Optimality Theory and inductive grounding. In *Functionalism and formalism in linguistics*, Michael Davell, Edit Moravcsik, Frederick Newmeyer, Michael Noonan, and Kathleen Wheatley (eds.), 243–285. Amsterdam: John Benjamins.

van der Hulst, Harry
    1989   Atoms of segmental structure: Components, gestures and dependency. *Phonology* 6: 439–477.
    1999   Features, segments and syllables in Radical CV Phonology. In John Rennison and Klaus Kühnhammer (eds.) *Phonologica 1996: Syllables!?* The Hague: Holland Academic Press.

Itô, Junko and Armin Mester
    1998   The phonological lexicon. Ms., University of California, Santa Cruz.

Kiparsky, Paul
    1982   From cyclic phonology to lexical phonology. In Harry van der Hulst and Norval Smith (eds.), *The Structure of Phonological Representations*, vol 1. Dordrecht: Foris.
    1985   Some consequences of lexical phonology. *Phonology Yearbook* 2: 85–138

Kirchner, Robert
    1998   An Effort-based approach to consonant lenition. Ph. D. diss., UCLA.

Lombardi, Linda
 1998 Evidence for MAXFEATURE constraints from Japanese. Ms., University of Maryland at College Park.
 1999 Positional faithfulness and voicing assimilation in Optimality Theory. *Natural Language and Linguistic Theory* 17: 267–302
McCarthy, John J. and Alan S. Prince
 1993 Generalized alignment. *Yearbook of Morphology*, 79–153.
 1995 Faithfulness and reduplicative identity. In *Papers in Optimality Theory*, Jill Beckman, Laura Walsh Dickey and Suzanne Urbanczyk (eds.). Amherst, Mass.: GLSA.
Myers, James
 1999 Lexical phonology and the lexicon. Ms., National Chung Cheng University, Taiwan.
Morén, Bruce
 2003 The Parallel Structures Model of Feature Geometry. In *Working Papers of the Cornell Phonetics Laboratory*, vol. 15. Ithaca: Cornell University.
 2004a Accounting for Serbian consonant-vowel interactions and alternations using the Parallel Structures Model of feature geometry. Presented at the 12th Manchester Phonology Meeting, Manchester, England.
 2004b Interactions among phonetics, phonology and morphology in Serbian: Explaining consonant-vowel interactions and alternations. Presented at the Annual Meeting of the Modern Language Association (MLA 2004), Philadelphia, Pennsylvania, USA.
 2006 Consonant-vowel interactions in Serbian: Features, representations and constraint interactions. *Lingua* 116:1198–1244.
Ota, Mitsuhiko
 2004 The learnability of the stratified phonological lexicon. *Journal of Japanese Linguistics* 20:19–40.
Prince, Alan S., and Paul Smolensky
 1993 Optimality theory. Constraint interaction in generative grammar. Technical Report #2, Rutgers University Center for Cognitive Science. ROA 537; published in 2004 by Blackwell Publishers.
Rice, Keren D.
 1992 On deriving sonority: A structural account of sonority relationships. *Phonology* 9:61–99.
Rice, Keren D. and Peter Avery
 1989 On the interaction between sonorancy and voicing. *Toronto Working Papers in Linguistics 10*, Barbara Brunson, Strang Burton, and Tom Wilson (eds.), 65-82.
Russell, Kevin
 1995 Morphemes and candidates in Optimality Theory. Ms., University of Manitoba, Canada.
 1999 MOT: Sketch of an OT approach to morphology. Ms., University of Manitoba, Canada.
Sanders, Nathan
 2003 Opacity and sound change in the Polish lexicon. Ph.D. dissertation. University of California, Santa Cruz.

Schane, Stanford
    1984   The fundamentals of Particle Phonology. *Phonology Yearbook* 1:129–156.
Smith, Jennifer L.
    2004   Making constraints positional: Toward a compositional model of CON. *Lingua* 114 (12): 1433–1464.
Smolensky, Paul
    1997   Constraint interaction in generative grammar II: Local conjunction or random rules in Universal Grammar. Paper presented at the Hopkins Optimality Theory Workshop/Maryland Mayfest '97. Baltimore, Maryland.
Steriade, Donca
    1993   Closure release and nasal contours. In *Nasals, Nasalization and the Velum*, Marie Huffman and Rena Krakow (eds.), 401–470. San Diego: Academic Press.
    1994   Complex onsets as single segments: The Mazateco pattern. In *Perspectives in Phonology*, Jennifer Cole and Charles Kisseberth (eds.), 203–292. Stadford: CSLI.

Chapter 14
Variables in Optimality Theory*

Chris Golston

Optimality Theory (Prince and Smolensky 1993) is a theory of constraint interaction. At its core it is quite simple:

> Universal Grammar provides a set of highly general constraints. These often conflicting constraints are all operative in individual languages. Languages differ primarily in how they resolve the conflicts: in the way they rank these universal constraints in strict domination hierarchies that determine the circumstances under which constraints are violated. A language-particular grammar *is* a means of resolving the conflicts among universal constraints.
> (Prince and Smolensky 1993:3)

All sorts of other ideas can be associated with OT, but we must distinguish those that *follow from* the theory and those that can be *added* to the theory. The theory proper consists of "EVAL-mediated comparisons of candidates by a hierarchy of violable constraints. No matter how the details are executed or in what overall context it is embedded, any model with these indispensable characteristics will express the central claim and insight of OT" (McCarthy 2002:11).

An important add-on to the theory since its inception has been the claim that the set of candidates evaluated by the hierarchy of violable constraints is both universal and infinite. This paper argues that neither property follows from any principle of OT and that theory-neutral considerations put a different set of restrictions on what GEN most likely generates. (§1). I'll also show that the universality and infinity of GEN are needed mostly to prop up an untenable theory of underlying representation carelessly carried over from work in the 1960s that eschewed prosodic structure entirely (Chomsky and Halle 1968). Once we have a better theory of underlying representation that includes a great deal of underlying prosody, the work that GEN must do changes drastically (§2) and the candidate set of surface representations turns out to be finite, indeed quite small (§3).

1. GEN

GEN is what the grammar adds to stored or underlying representations (URs) to make phonetically detailed programs for speech production or surface representations (SRs). Roughly, GEN is what is stripped from SR to make it storable or, what amounts to the same thing, what is added to UR to make it sayable. GEN is SR minus UR. To understand GEN, we therefore need a good understanding of both underyling and surface levels of representation. The more alike they are, the less GEN has to do. The less alike they are, the more it has to do.

Because GEN has no ability to output just the correct form of a given input, the ranked and violable constraints of OT require a set of candidates for EVAL to select from:

(1)   An OT grammar
/kætz/ ⇒ GEN ⇒[kætz] ⇒ EVAL ⇒[kætz]
              [kæts]   ☞ [kæts]
              [kætəz]   [kætəz]
              etc.   etc.

That much follows from the basic tenets of OT. Two additional claims about GEN, however, are theoretical add-ons that require additional support because they do not follow from having ranked and violable constraints. These add-ons are that the set of candidates is *universal* and that the set of candidates is *infinite*.

We'll take these issues one at a time, beginning with the universality of GEN:

> GEN is universal, meaning that the candidate forms emitted by GEN for a given input are the same in every language. These candidates are also very diverse. This property of GEN has been called inclusivity or freedom of a- nalysis. Precisely because GEN is universal, it must at a minimum supply candidates varied enough to fit all of the ways in which languages can differ.
> (McCarthy 2002:8)

The universality of GEN is clearly stipulative. No attempt is made to derive the universality from the theory of OT, presumably because there is no logical connection between the claim that constraints are ranked and violable (OT) and the claim that the candidate set is the same for all languages (universality). Nor is any empirical support offered for it, presumably because there isn't any. I'll argue below that abandoning universality for GEN has no negative consequences for the theory of grammar.

The *infinity* of GEN, on the other hand, is not stipulated, but the arguments for it are fatally flawed. Consider McCarthy's discussion in full:

> If GEN incorporates any recursive or iterative operations, as it surely must, then there is no bound on the size of a candidate and every candidate set, from every input, is infinite. This is perhaps not too surprising in syntax, where the infinity of sentences has long been accepted, but it is also true in phonology. Epenthesis is an iterative procedure of candidate-generation, so the set of candidates derived from input /ba/ must include /bati, batiti, batititi.../. No GEN-imposed bound on the number of epenthesis operations is appropriate. Rather, the economy of epenthesis should and does follow from constraint interaction.
>
> (McCarthy 2002:9)

Note first that the case for iterative epenthesis is purely hypothetical: no language epenthesizes more than a foot in any given spot. Thus the parallel with syntax, where recursive structure really is commonplace, is not compelling. Some types of OT already do without an infinite GEN, including what McCarthy calls *persistent OT* (2007).

So let us narrow down what GEN really has to do. To make things concrete (and thus psychologically plausible) I'll assert what I'm sure my GEN does not generate; the reader is invited to join along with her own GEN to compare, but the conclusions will be pretty similar.

First consider actual physical objects like motorcycles and whales. Since I cannot produce these things with my vocal tract, there is no reason to think that GEN would ever generate them. One could of course devise a grammar to generate them and then filter them out with constraints, but this would serve little purpose, as Reiss has pointed out with respect to a hypothetical constraint NOBANANA:

> Note that the claim intended by the constraint NOBANANA, that no representation of a sentence contains bananas, is probably true for all human languages. However, there are an infinite number of true claims of this type. No language requires speakers to dance a jig to express iterativity, no language has pizza as an element of syntactic trees; etc... We do not want our model of grammar to express every true statement about what structures do not occur, since there are an infinite number of such statements and the grammar must be stable in finite terms if it is to be instantiated in human brains.
>
> (Reiss 2002:2)

As Bruce Morén points out (p.c.) one can readily dismiss such options if one just assumes that the grammar manipulates *linguistic elements*. That will get rid of a lot of garbage in the grammar and has no bad effects on OT as an explanatory theory of how language works. And so we may postulate a reasonable restriction on GEN, which nobody should object to:

(2)   Restriction 1: My GEN only generates linguistic elements.

My own GEN has a lot of additional restrictions that have been there since I reached the age of 10 months or so and lost the ability to discriminate speech sounds and structures that are not part of my native language, English, or the one other language I speak with some degree of fluency, German. I cannot reliably perceive or produce things like [ɦɶ|ɒʋə], [ɘʛɵçɣʎ], or [Өɥ‖ɥʙɴʄ]. My grammar no longer has the capacity to deal with rising-falling tones, linguolabials, voiceless implosives, ejective fricatives, voiceless nasals, or pulmonic ingressives, though it once did. Since I'm not (presently) modeling my grammar at the age of 10 months, I can reasonably add

(3)   Restriction 2: My GEN only generates English and German.

We commonly do construct English OT grammars with constraints against things that no English (or German) speaker would produce or perceive, but these constraints are as pointless as the NOBANANA constraint given the actual abilities of a given adult speaker.

This is not to say that my present grammar isn't plastic to some degree or that I couldn't learn to produce and perceive speech sounds outside of the languages I currently know. But at any given point in time my grammar is pretty much blind to things that aren't found in the languages I speak. Generally, when listeners are presented with sounds or sequences of sounds that are illegal in their native language(s), they tend to assimilate them to form sounds or sequences that *are* legal (Massaro and Cohen 1983; Hallé et al. 1998; Dupoux et al. 1999; Dupoux et al. 2001).

Recall that the universality of GEN is not a necessary part of OT and that no good arguments have been given for it; what serious reason is there to think that my grammar generates and evaluates things I can neither say nor perceive? A useful parallel is the DNA in cells. The grammar of a neonate is like a stem cell that has the ability to become a hair or bone or brain cell but isn't one yet. But an *adult* grammar like the one in your head or mine is like a hair or bone or brain cell that no longer has the ability to become any other type of cell. It no longer has the plasticity of a stem cell and shouldn't be described like one that does. (Whether an infinite GEN is necessary for language acquisition I leave to those who know more about it.)

Returning to the specific limitations of my own GEN, I am quite sure that it does not normally produce things that I don't intend to talk about either: if I'm trying to say *cats* it just doesn't worry about [dɔgz], [ˌsɛ.vn.ti.ˈfaɪv], or [ˌæv.ɪl.lə.ˈvin]. In the event that I do say something along these lines it is a speech error involving lexical access, not the product of my phonology.

(4) Restriction 3: My GEN only generates my message.

If I end up saying *white Anglo-Saxon prostitute* instead of *white Anglo-Saxon Protestant*, this is not because GEN included it as a candidate, but because GEN was misfed something by earlier parts of speech production. The restriction I'm proposing is related, of course, to the classical OT notion of Containment (Prince and Smolensky 1993), which requires that the output include the input. I'm proposing slightly more, that the output *only* include the input. This will be interesting when it comes to things like epenthesis, where I'll need to introduce the notion of variable, familiar enough from basic mathematics.

Finally, there's no reason to think that GEN ever considers morphological monsters like [kæ-ts] or [k-æts] when I'm trying to produce cat-s. GEN doesn't change basic sound-meaning relationships in this way. This is enshrined already in OT as Consistency of Exponence. See Van Oostendorp (2007) for more reasons to think that this is a good restriction to keep:

(5) Restriction 4: My GEN doesn't change morphological affiliation.

We've seen that there are no theoretical or empirical reasons to think that GEN is universal or infinite and that there are perfectly reasonable, theory-neutral restrictions we may put on GEN, including Restrictions 1-4 above. Before we can calculate what GEN actually produces, however, we have to have a clearer understanding of what GEN operates on. And so we turn to underlying representations, the input to GEN.

2. Underlying representations

OT offers no guidelines or insights on either underlying or surface representations: "The core assumptions of OT are pretty general, and so they are compatible with a wide range of representational assumptions." (McCarthy 2002: 243). So we must look elsewhere if we want to know how people actually store things and how those things look once the phonology has processed them. Traditional representation is segmental, so that representations consist of a string of phonemes. For Saussure the phonème "designates what we would today call phonetic segments, considered as (*ultimately unreducible*) units in acts of speaking" (Anderson 1985: 38, my emphasis).

(6) Phonemes (Saussure 1916)

|
/kæt/

Trubetzkoy (1939) brings out the importance of distinctive features in phonological representation, but it is Jakobson (1939) who first makes them central to phonological description, so that features become the atoms of representation in subsequent theory (Jakobson, Fant and Halle 1952; Chomsky and Halle 1968):

(7) Bundled features (Chomsky and Halle 1968)

$$\begin{pmatrix} f_a \\ f_b \\ f_c \\ \vdots \end{pmatrix} \begin{pmatrix} f_r \\ f_s \\ f_t \\ \vdots \end{pmatrix} \begin{pmatrix} f_x \\ f_y \\ f_z \\ \vdots \end{pmatrix}$$

Clements argues that "if we find that certain sets of features consistently behave as a unit with respect to certain types of rules of assimilation or resequencing, we have good reason to suppose that they constitute a unit in phonological representation" and proposes that distinctive features are organized in trees (1985: 226):

(8) Arboreal features (Clements 1985)

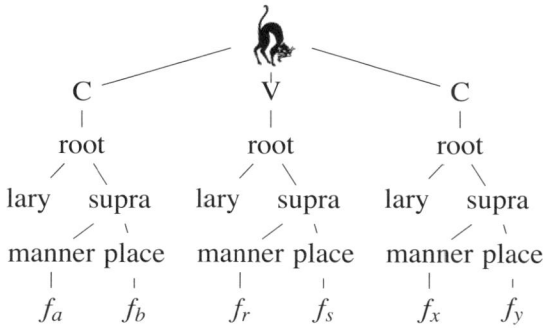

(Note: *lary* = laryngeal node, *supra* = supralaryngeal node.)

Browman and Goldstein (1986, 1990) represent things as gestures organized like musical scores that encode timing relations.

(9) Gestural scores (Browman and Goldstein 1986, 1990)

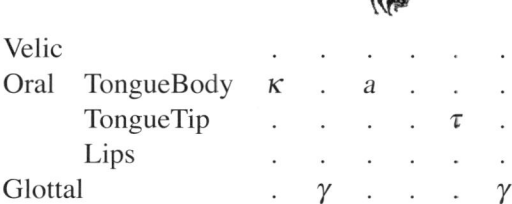

There is no hierarchical structure here at all, but later versions of Articulatory Phonology add it to varying, if conservative, degrees (Browman and Goldstein 1989, 1990, 2000; Byrd 1996; Byrd and Saltzmann 2003).

Padgett (1995) brings us back to a Chomsky and Halle type of representation in which features are just bundled, though the bundles are now rows instead of columns.

(10) Feature classes (Padgett 1995)

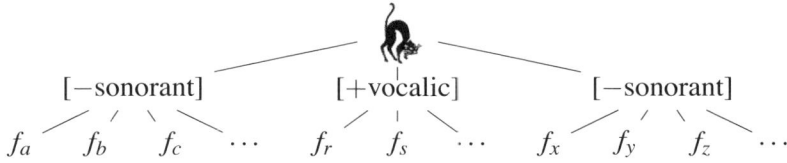

Golston and van der Hulst (1999) propose that underlying representations are organized into syllables rather than segments, based in part on psycholinguistic evidence reviewed below.

(11) Syllables (Golston and van der Hulst 1999)

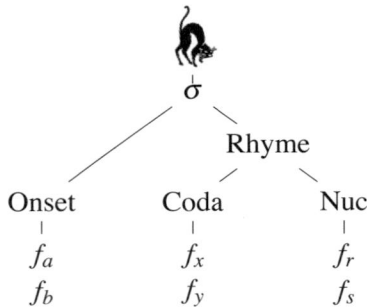

```
              σ
           /  |  \
          /  Rhyme
         /   /   \
      Onset Coda  Nuc
        |    |    |
       fₐ   fₓ   fᵣ
       f_b  f_y  f_s
```

Standard OT is of two minds with respect to representation. Surface representations are usually highly prosodified, with onsets, (no) codas, syllables, feet, and so on playing a very prominent role. Underlying representations, on the other hand, are almost always just strings of segments. No reason is given for this in the literature, and it is generally simply assumed that non-contrastive prosody is added by the grammar and not part of underlying representation. In practice, then, URs are strings of phonemes and the grammar adds structure like syllables and feet. But there are good reasons to think that this is not the case, including facts about long term and working memory.

2.1. Working memory and UR

Underlying representations must be stored in long term memory somehow and they must get into long term memory through working memory, because there's no other way in. Memory limitations put real restrictions on what kind of symbolic information can be memorized and stored and accessed; theories of grammar that do not respect these restrictions are therefore poor models of the human language faculty.

Evidence for how words get into long term memory comes from limits on short term (working) memory, which holds surprisingly few chunks of information (Miller 1956). Recent research suggests that working memory is different for spatial information than it is for verbal/numerical information (Baddeley 1986; Oberauer et al. 2003). Limiting ourselves to the verbal/numerical domain, the number of chunks that can be held in working memory is only 4±1 in young adults, somewhat less in older adults and children (Cowan 2001, 2005; see also Cowan 1995, 1999). Focusing on experimental conditions where chunks can be identified, capacity limits can be observed, and subjects are kept from rehearsing stimuli, Cowan finds a single, central capacity limit averaging about four chunks. His full model of working memory has two embedded levels. The first consists of long-term memory representations for which there is no limit on activation. The second level ('the focus of attention') is capacity limited and holds up to four of the activated representations. (See also Oberauer et al. 2000; Oberauer 2002).

Since morphemes have to get through working memory in order to be stored in long term memory, they must be recognized as no more than four or so chunks that have already been stored. For *cat* these chunks could be one syllable (Golston and van der Hulst), three segments (Saussure), feature-bundles (Chomsky and Halle, Padgett), or feature-trees (Clements), or five gestures (Browman and Goldstein). Happily, all of these fall into the 4±1 range and thus all of these types of representation seem to be plausible *prima facie*. But longer morphemes provide a *faciem secundam*.

Consider a monomorphemic word like *Apalachicola*, a town in Florida's western panhandle. If I say this word to a stranger who hasn't heard it before, they can usually repeat it back to me with no difficulty. But with 12 segments, /æpəlætʃɪkoʊlə/ is too long to learn if I have to get it through working memory one segment at a time, rather like my mother's eleven digit phone number (15053455480), but one unit worse. Like most people I chunk long phone numbers into prefixes, area codes, and so on, each of which is fairly short: 1-505-345-5480. Working memory limitations like this show us that *Apalachicola* does not make it into LTM one segment at a time, so we can reject Saussure's representation outright.

Breaking segments down into feature bundles doesn't help and actually makes things worse. The Chomsky and Halle model still requires us to memorize the linear order of the twelve feature bundles, something which we cannot do. Worse yet, *none* of the feature bundles is learnable, because each feature bundle consists of far more than 4±1 *unordered* features. Real-world limitations on working memory make learning even a single Chomsky and Halle segment impossible, much less an eleven unit long string of such segments. The same applies to more recent unstructured representations like Padgett's.

Clements' feature geometry makes segments learnable because it bundles the features a few at a time into chunks that can be learned. These chunks can themselves be chunked four or so at a time to make bigger chunks, and so on, till segments are learned. So we can learn sounds like [æ], [p], [ə], etc. in chunks. But there's still no way to get long strings of these sounds through working memory without chunking *them* into bigger units.

Trying to get all of this in as a bunch of coordinated gestures is out of the question unless those gestures are bundled into bigger units; so unadorned Articulatory Phonology is not a viable model of phonological representation. Models that incorporate more prosodic organization are another matter, but no explicit models yet exist for this within Articulatory Phonology as far as I am aware.

Syllable-based representation (Golston and van der Hulst) takes arboreal chunking one level higher, making it possible to store even larger chunks of sound. But if one can only store 4 ± 1 chunks and the largest chunks we have are syllables, it is still impossible to squeeze *Apalachicola* through working memory. So it looks like none of the theories of representation phonologists have proposed so far can be the ones humans actually make use of.

But there's a moral here: more structure is better because it makes more things chunkable and thus more things learnable. *Apalachicola* in gestures is unthinkable, in segments impossible, in syllables unlikely, but *better*. The obvious solution is to assume that *feet* (groups of syllables) are the chunking mechanism used for working memory. Feet make *Apalachicola* learnable. Assuming that English feet are moraic trochees, the word can enter working memory in four chunks [æ.pə], [læ.tʃɪ], [koʊ], [lə]. If English feet aren't quantity sensitive, the word can enter in three chunks: [æ.pə], [læ.tʃɪ], [koʊ.lə]. Foot-based representation actually makes a testable prediction: no language should contain a morpheme longer than 5 phonological feet. Longer *words* should be commonplace, as long as they can be chunked roots or stems of 4 ± 1 morphemes, each of which can be 4 ± 1 feet, syllables, sounds, or combinations thereof. (Following Selkirk 1995 I assume that prosodic categories need not be strictly layered, so that a word like English *bereft* might be represented in LTM as a syllable [bə], a foot [rɛf] and a stray sound [t].)

A few studies of the prosodic shapes of roots suggest that natural languages fall well within this upper limit of two feet. Kager (1995), for instance, reports that canonical roots contain at most two feet in five western Australian languages, Yidiɲ (Dixon 1977), Wargamay (Dixon 1981), Mbabaṟam (Dixon 1991), Gumbayŋgir (Eades 1979) and Uradhi (Crowley 1983). The 836 roots of Dixon's (1977) vocabulary of Yidiɲ are typical, falling into the following classes prosodically (L = light syllable, H = heavy):

(12) Roots in Yidiɲ
    LL   590 gala 'spear', gugaɾ 'large guanna'
    LLL   219 /gindanu/ [gindaan] 'moon', /gudaga/ [gudaaga] 'dog'
    LLLL   12 ɟulugunu 'black myrtle tree', yiŋgilibiy 'bee'
    LH   11 durguu 'mopoke owl', giŋaa 'vine species'
    LLLLL 2 /ɟilibugabi/ [ɟilibugaabi] 'next day'
    LHLL 1 waɾaabuga 'white apple tree'
    LLLH 1 galambaɾaa 'march fly'

Most of these root are a single foot (LL), or a foot plus a syllable (LLL, LH); a few are two feet (LLLL), or two plus a syllable (LLLLL, LHLL, LLLH); none is longer than this. Golston and Wiese (1995) report essentially the same facts for roots in German; Lewis and Golston (2005) report essentially the same facts for White Hmong (Heimbach 1966) and Nukuoro (Carrol and Soulik 1973); and I assume this will be found to be the case generally. There is a maximal size for roots across languages, it is comfortably smaller than four feet, and it is due to extragrammatical constraints imposed by working memory.

2.2. Long term memory and UR

Long term memory of words is best probed through studies of lexical access. The two most relevant areas for how the phonological forms of words are stored in the brain are tip-of-the-tongue (TOT) states and malapropisms. The two types of evidence bear directly on the mental representations speakers store and it is significant that they agree with one another point for point in showing that prosodic information is not only available but more prominent than segmental material (Cutler 1986:173; Levelt 1989:355).

An influential study by Brown and McNeill (1966) shows that speakers who cannot think of a word tend to know three things about it: the initial segment or onset, the number of syllables, and the stress pattern. When a speaker is primed for *sextant*, for instance, but cannot remember it, two-syllable (xx) words like *secant* and *sextet* come to mind rather than one-syllable words like *sect* (x) or three-syllable words like *sacrament* (x..). Much subsequent research has confirmed these results (e.g., Koriat and Lieblich 1974; Brown 1991; Meyer and Bock 1992; Miozzo and Caramazza 1997; Vigliocco, Antonini, and Garrett 1997; James and Burke 2000; Abrams, White and Eitel

2003). This strongly suggests that speakers store words as syllables or other prosodic groups and not (just) as strings of segments.

Classifications of speech errors include a category called sound-related substitutions (Fromkin 1973) or malapropisms (Fay and Cutler 1977). These involve mis-selection of a word that is phonologically similar to the intended word but semantically different. Typical cases include ('F' from Fromkin; 'FC' from Fay and Cutler):

(13) Malapropisms

Intended	Spoken	
white Anglo-Saxon Protestant	white Anglo-Saxon prostitute	(F)
a routine proposal	a routine promotion	(F)
the conquest of Peru	the conquest of Purdue	(F)
prohibition against incest	prohibition against insects	(F)
week	work	(FC)
open	over	(FC)
constructed	corrected	(FC)

As these cases illustrate, the overall prosody of the target is matched by the overall prosody of the error, both in terms of overall stress pattern and in terms of syllable count (14).

(14) Stress pattern and syllable count of malapropisms

Intended	Spoken	Stress Pattern	Syllable Count
Protestant	prostitute	(x..)	3
proposal	promotion	(.x.)	3
Peru	Perdue	(.x)	2
incest	insects	(xx)	2
week	work	(x)	1
open	over	(x.)	2
constructed	corrected	(.x.)	3

What we do not generally find in sound-related substitutions are cases like *protester* (xx.) for *Protestant* (x..); *propinquity* (.x..) for *proposal* (.x.); *perdition* (.x.) for *Peru* (.x); or *insecticide* (.x.x) for *insects* (xx) – all forms we would expect if words were stored as segment strings.

The criteria for phonological similarity here are identical to those found in TOT states: same onset, same stress pattern, same number of syllables. Data like this has led researchers like Crompton (1982), Fromkin (1985) and Butterworth (1989) to posit a phonological sub-lexicon within the mental lexicon, i.e., a way of finding and storing morphemes using phonological addresses. *White Anglo-Saxon prostitute* is produced when *prostitute* is mis-selected because of its proximity to *Protestant* in the phonological sub-lexicon, that is, by a similar phonological address in LTM. Recent work by Brown (2004) suggests that sound substitutions in speech errors are governed *solely* by prosody, so that errors involve features in authentic units of prosody (onset, syllable, etc.) but never segments. None of this makes any sense if predictable prosodic information like syllable count and stress pattern is not somehow stored.

It is significant that two quite different sources of evidence converge on the same criteria: word-onsets, stress pattern and number of syllables. Any psychologically real model of grammar must come to terms with this and admitting prosody into underlying representation seems like the necessary first step. Phonologists raised on the 1960s notion that everything predictable is left out of UR should recall that OT presents a new paradigm in which this claim is completely irrelevant.

The proposal is less novel than it first appears. It amounts to saying that URs are simply what SRs have been for decades in phonology: *trees* full of information, not structureless strings of segments. There has never been good reason to ban prosodic structure from underlying representation, and there are no reasons at all to ban it within OT.

All of this suggests an answer to a longstanding question: what is the prosodic organization in natural language for? In a few languages the prosodic organization of an utterance is actually contrastive, as has been shown for Scottish Gaelic, where monosyllabic words contrast minimally with bisyllabic words (Clements 1986b; Bosch 1998; Ladefoged et al. 1998):

(15) Scottish Gaelic
 tu.an 'hook'
 tuan 'song'
 pal^y.ak 'skull'
 pal^{y}ak 'belly'

Brazilian Portuguese has similar contrasts, with minimal pairs like monosyllabic [pais] 'parents' and bisyllabic [pa.is] 'country' (Alice Meyer, p.c.).

But in most languages the prosodic organization of an utterance is not contrastive. In many languages, prosody helps position where stress goes (see

Hayes 1995) but since predictable stress of this sort has no clear function either, locating stresses can hardly be the general goal of prosodic organization. Languages with prosodic organization but no stress make this point especially clear: Japanese, for instance, organizes things into moraic trochees for purposes of morphology and poetic meter but has no stress at all (Poser 1990). All languages have prosodic organization but they don't all use it to the same ends and often don't seem to use it for any ends at all.

So what does it do and why is it there? I propose that *prosody is a data compression device* which allows lots of distinctive features to be compressed into bigger and bigger units that can be memorized; these memorized chunks can then be used to chunk still larger units like *Apalachicola* which would otherwise be unstorable. If this is correct, prosodic structure is used in all languages to shepherd distinctive features through working memory into long-term memory.

To tie this proposal into something that has been proposed on independent grounds, I adopt from Marcus (2001) a neural model of representation involving linked and nested register sets that he and Jackendoff (2002) use to model stored semantic, syntactic, and morphological representations. The underlying representation for *cat* would then be an arboreal graph of a foot (with some abbreviation to make it fit on a page) in (16).

Representations like this are memorizable because you can chunk things from the bottom and store the resulting constituents for later. As successively larger chunks make it into long term memory, the 4 ± 1 limit on working memory allows larger and larger units to get in a few at a time: once I've got *kiss* and *fat* I can parse *cat* with an onset and rhyme I already have stored in LTM. In this way, even the six syllables of *Apalachicola* can make it into LTM by coming in as feet. It would seem that long morphemes like this *must* be stored with foot and syllable structure because there is no way to get all of those segments through working memory.

A reviewer asks 'If storage is limited to four or five items in the horizontal dimension of a representation, why does this not hold for the vertical dimension?' The answer is essentially that the vertical dimension represents what has already been memorized (for other words). A speaker who knows the UR for 'cat' in English has stored its sounds, organized into a syllabe that constitutes a foot. The (vertical) prosodic organization is the means of storage for the (horizontal) distinctive features/gestures.

Returning to Marcus's model, he proposes a computationally tractable model of treelets stored and used in the brain. An empty treelet is something

(16) *cat*

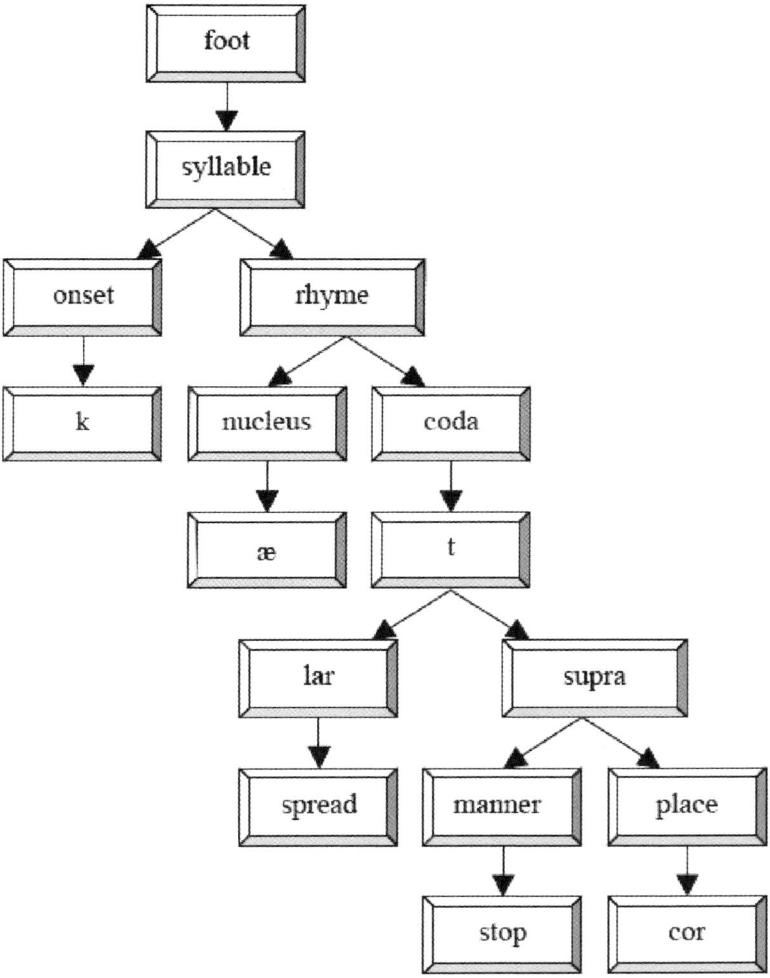

like a stem cell, ready to take on whatever representational configuration is necessary (17).

A filled treelet like in (18) stands for propositions held in LTM. The five digit numbers encode atomic elements already held in LTM.

When the numbers are cashed in for their LTM equivalents you get a representation like the one for *cat* in (16) or the one in (19) for a clause.

Learning a new fact amounts to setting values of the register sets within a treelet.

360 *Chris Golston*

(17) Empty treelet

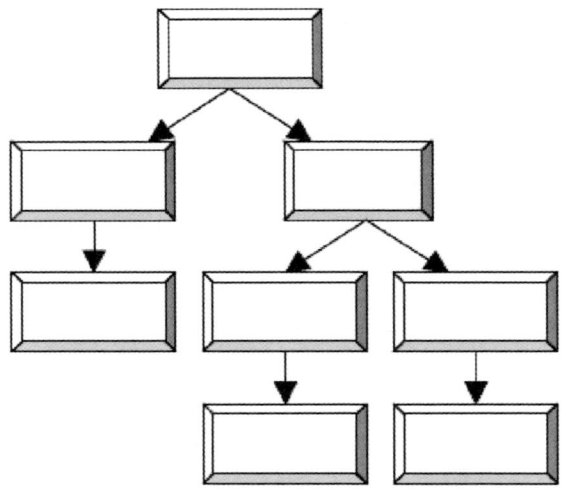

(18) Filled treelet

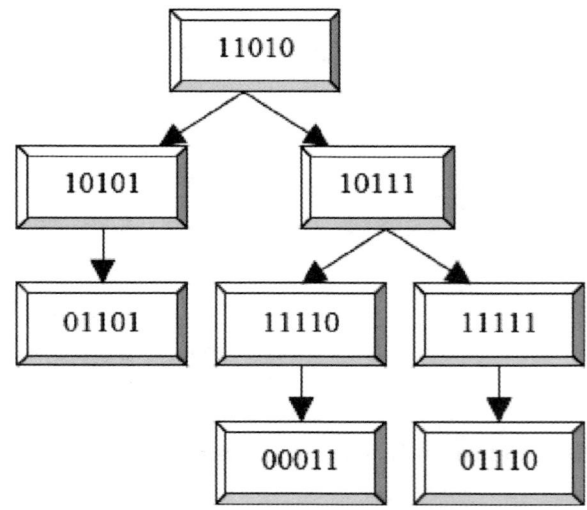

Fundamental to my proposal are the assumptions that the mind has a large stock of empty treelets on hand and that new knowledge can be represented by filling in an empty treelet (that is, by storing values in the register set) or by adjusting the values contained in an existing treelet.

(Marcus 2001, 108)

(19) What the numbers encode

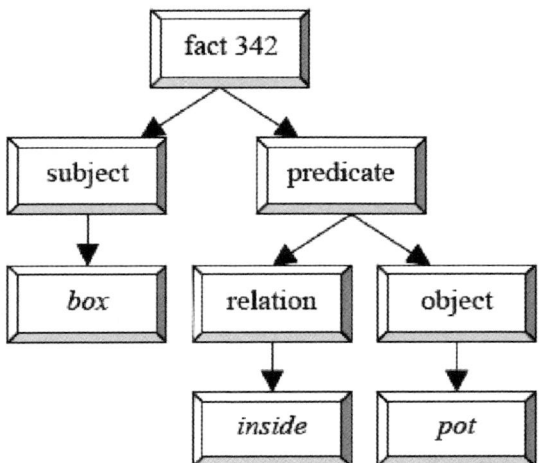

As we have seen, this solves the chunking problem for getting long morphemes though working memory into LTM. If LTM stores treelets that correspond to sounds, syllables, and feet, these stored chunks can be used to pass information through working memory and into LTM in successively larger chunks.

But the treelets are as yet too fixed to handle phonological alternations. For this we need *variables*. A major part of Marcus' proposal is that not all parts of a treelet are filled in – and the empty register sets in a tree represent variables. Jackendoff (2002) proposes a number of linguistic structures that make use of such variables along the following lines. An idiom like *take (x) to task* has a variable position that must be filled by material with material which matches the category type of the variable (NP in this case). The idiomatic reading shows that the whole thing must be stored and the fact that all sorts of things can go in the middle slot shows that the representation must contain a variable of some sort (20).

Moving a step closer to phonology, we can treat suppletion along similar lines but with information prespecified. The root for *carry* in Latin is *fer-* (*fer-o* 'I carry') in the present system, *tul-* (*tul-i* 'I have carried') in the perfect, and *lat-* (*laat-us* 'be carried') in the supine (see Aronoff 1994, 31-59). Treelets with different roots and different aspects handle this otherwise very problematic type of case straightforwardly (21)–(22).

This is compatible with extant treatments of allomorphy in OT (see, for instance, McCarthy 2002:152-156).

(20) *take (x) to task* (Jackendoff 2002: 172)

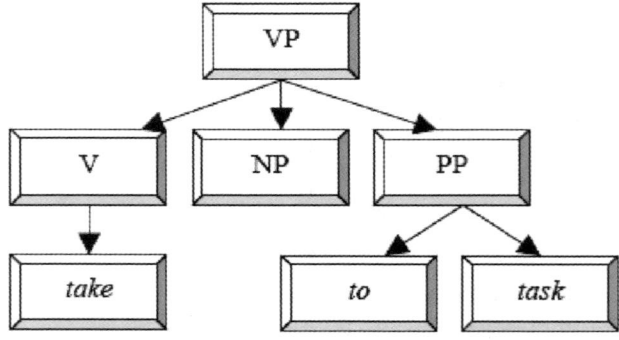

(21) *fer-* 'carry (present)'

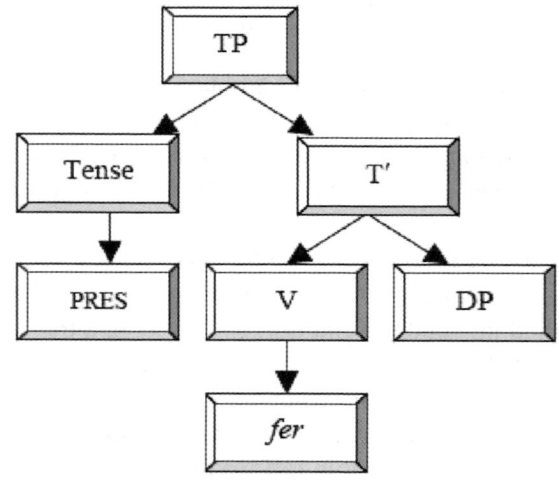

3. Surface representations

If underlying representations are trees with variables, surface representations are trees with those variables solved. This means that GEN has merely to supply the values that the variables stand for. As long as the variables have a finite number of values, the number of surface candidates EVAL has to consider remains finite. Consider how epenthesis and voicing assimilation might work for English plural -*s*.

There are a lot of ways to pluralize nouns in English, including many that

(22) tul- 'carry (perf)'

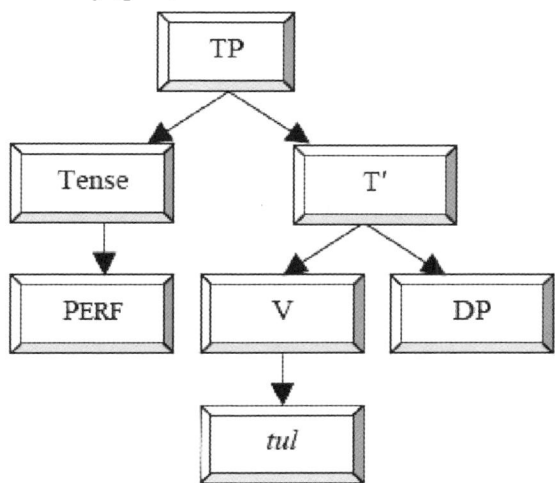

must be listed in the lexicon (*deer:deer, datum:data, locus:loci*) and thus, I assume, stored with the roots they go with in trees like those given above for Latin *fer- tul- laat-* 'carry'. But the common way of pluralizing is to add *-s*. As is familiar, plural *-s* has three shapes depending on the final sound of the stem to which it attaches, [z, əz, s]. The UR for *-s* is then just a tree with variables, along the lines in (23).

The dotted lines connecting Nucleus to Rhyme and [voiced] to the laryngeal node of the coda are realized or not depending on EVAL. This gives us four possible ways of realizing the plural [əs, əz, s, z], one of which [əs] is never used for reasons we'll see below.

A root like *bus* can surface in one of two ways: [bʌs] as in *bus* (with everything in the same syllable) and [bʌ.s] as in *bussing* with the [s] in the onset of the next syllable. The UR for *bus* thus has everything nailed down except the final consonant, which is potentially the coda for the root syllable or the onset for the following suffixal syllable. I represent this with the variable Edge (= Ons/Nuc) in (24).

Given two realizations of the root and four of the suffix there are eight candidates that need to be generated. A few constraints will suffice to pick out the winner as is common in OT (25)–(29).

(23) [z, əz, s] 'PLURAL'

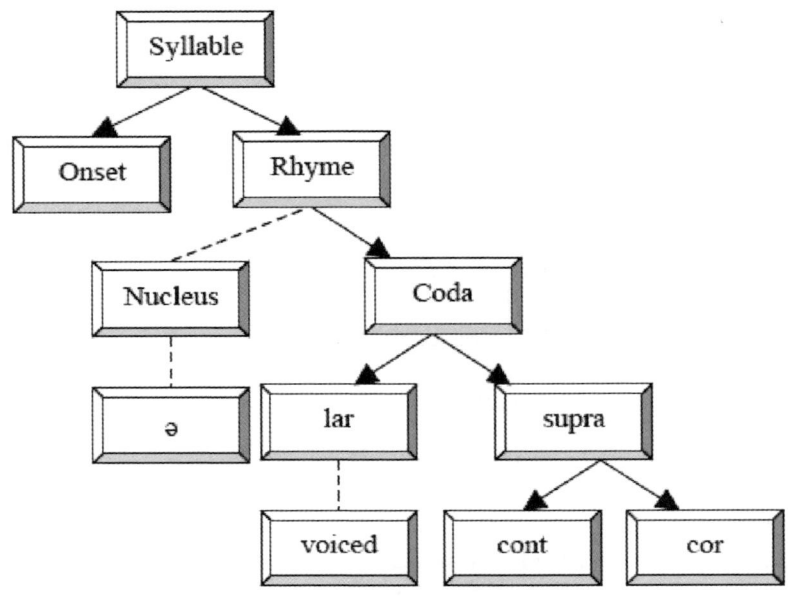

(24) UR for *bus*

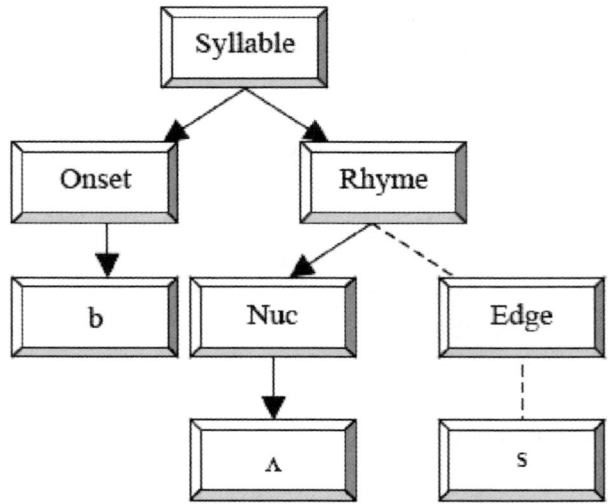

(25) AGLAR
Consonant clusters agree in laryngeal features.

(26) OCP
No sibilants are adjacent.

(27) ONSET
Syllables begin with consonants.

(28) MAXVOI
Underlying voiced is licensed prosodically.

(29) MAXə
Underlying schwa is licensed prosodically.

The tableau in (30) lays out the candidates and how they are evaluated, with most of the surface prosody left out to save space.

(30) *bus-s* [bʌsəz]

	OCP	AGLAR	ONSET	MAXVOI	MAXə
[bʌss]	*!			*	*
[bʌsz]	*!	*			*
[bʌzs]	*!	*		*	*
[bʌzz]	*!				*
[bʌs.əz]			*!		
[bʌs.əs]			*!	*	
[bʌ.səs]				*!	
☞ [bʌ.səz]					

The last candidate violates none of the constraints and bests the rest. The first four candidates fail on the OCP because of the illicit [ss], [zz], etc. clusters; the fifth and sixth fail on ONSET; and the seventh loses because the underlying voicing feature of the suffix isn't realized. Tableaux for *butts* and *buds* should be self-explanatory. The only point of this exercise is to illustrate how few candidates are actually needed to guarantee having the winner show up. *A candidate set that consists of the union of the set of root allomorphs and the set of suffix allomorphs must include the winner.* Other candidates are superfluous.

An anonymous reviewer points out that a generalization is lost here, since it is now coincidental that the epenthetic vowel for 3sg -*s*, possessive -*s*, plural -*s*, and past tense -*t* is always schwa. This can be addressed by replacing schwa with a variable that covers mid vowels, or vowels, or sonorants, or whatever; EVAL will then select the best of these. Here as elsewhere the key to keeping GEN small is to use variables, since a given node can be filled by only a given number of features.

Thus when Jessen and Ringen (2002) analyze German final fortition in words like *bunt* 'colorful' and *Bund* 'club' as the addition of [spread glottis], we need not consider all possible changes to the final consonant, only those that fill in permissible values of the laryngeal node. If we specify the laryngeal node of German /t/ as [spread glottis] and of /d/ as nothing, GEN will fill in [spread glottis], [constricted glottis] or [voice] for each and CON will choose the best one. Fortition processes don't require an infinite GEN if we circumscribe the range of fortition with variables. Similarly for reduction, lenition, assimilation, and so on; everything can be short and finite as long as variables are allowed in underlying representations and GEN just spells out those variables.

Other types of phonological alternation can be handled analogously, as allomorph selection (already necessary in standard OT), as morphemes with floating elements, or as morphemes with elements unspecified. The latter case will cover consonant- and vowel-harmony, where certain nodes in the tree (e.g., rounding or backness) will be empty. As long as a given node in a feature tree is limited to a small number of possibilities (e.g., Labial can dominate [round] or not, but cannot dominate [nasal]) this manner of encoding variables should always result in a finite number of candidates. The standard method of treating variation in OT has been to have GEN produce an infinite set of candidates that includes the faithful candidate and enough nearly faithful candidates to include the winner. Variable notation, familiar from simple algebra, allows a more focused and parsimonious way of handling variation in phonology. The specific treatment of variables borrowed from Marcus and Jackendoff has the additional advantage of applicability across different domains of cognition. As Jackendoff points out, "all combinatorial rules of language – formation rules, derivational rules, and constraints – require typed variables" (2002: 65).

4. Conclusion

A better understanding of the role of prosody in lexical representation undermines a long-held assumption in phonology, that underlying representations are stored without prosodic structure (syllables or feet). This assumption has necessitated a large gulf between underlying and surface forms and has thus required a lot of work for GEN in Optimality Theory. Working memory restrictions, TOT states, and malapropisms strongly suggest that the stored representations we call underlying representations are not stored as beads on a string but as hierarchically organized prosodic structures that may be graphed as trees. Prosodic structure most likely functions as a data compression device that gets large amounts of information (features or gestures) through working memory and into long term memory. Assuming that prosodic trees can include variables, as has been suggested by Marcus and Jackendoff for morphology, syntax, semantics, and long term memory, the difference between underlying and surface representations in phonology reduces to trees with variables and trees with those variables spelled out. This reduces the function of GEN to solving for variables, a finite and fairly well-understood task.

Note

* Thanks to audiences at California State University Fresno and the University of Tromsø for important questions and suggestions for improvement. Special thanks to Jason Brown, Tomas Riad, and two anonymous reviewers for their careful and valuable comments on an earlier draft of this paper. Any remaining shortcomings are of course my responsibility.

References

Abrams, Lisa, Kathryn K. White, and Stacey L. Eitel
    2003   Isolating phonological components that increase tip-of-the-tongue resolution. *Memory & Cognition* 31(8): 1153–1162.

Anderson, Stephen R.
    1985   *Phonology in the Twentieth Century: Theories of Rules and Representations.* Chicago: The University of Chicago Press.

Aronoff, Mark
    1994   *Morphology by Itself: Stems and Inflectional Classes.* Linguistic Inquiry Monograph Series 22. Cambridge: MIT Press.

Baddeley, Alan D.
    1986   *Working Memory.* Oxford: Clarendon Press.

Bosch, Anna
1998 The syllable in Scottish Gaelic dialect studies. *Scottish Gaelic Studies* XVIII: 1–22.

Browman, Catherine P. and Louis Goldstein
1986 Towards an articulatory phonology. *Phonology Yearbook* 3: 219–252.
1989 Articulatory gestures as phonological units. *Phonology* 6: 201–251.
1990 Tiers in articulatory phonology, with some implications for casual speech. In *Papers in Laboratory Phonology: I. Between the Grammar and the Physics of Speech*, John C. Kingston, and Mary. E. Beckman (eds.), 341–376. Cambridge: Cambridge UniversityPress.
2000 Competing constraints on intergestural coordination and self-organization of phonological structures. *Bulletin de la Communication Parlée* 5: 25–34.

Brown, Alan S.
1991 The tip of the tongue experience: A review and evaluation. *Psychological Bulletin* 10: 204-223.

Brown, Jason C.
2004 Eliminating the segment tier: Evidence from speech errors. *Journal of Psycholinguistic Research* 33(2): 97-101.

Brown, Roger and David McNeill
1966 The "tip of the tongue" phenomenon. *Journal of Verbal Learning and Verbal Behavior*, 5: 325-337.

Butterworth, Brian
1989 Lexical access in speech production. In *Lexical Representation and Process*. William Marslen-Wilson (ed.), 108–135. Cambridge, Mass.: MIT Press.

Byrd, Dani
1996 A phase window framework for articulatory timing. *Phonology* 13(2): 139–169.

Byrd, Dani and Elliot Saltzmann
2003 The elastic phrase: Modeling the dynamics of boundary-adjacent lengthening. *Journal of Phonetics* 31: 149–180.

Carrol, Vern and Topias Soulik
1973 *Nukuoro Lexicon*. Honolulu: University Press of Hawaii.

Chomsky, Noam and Morris Halle
1968 *The Sound Pattern of English*. New York: Harper & Row.

Clements, G. N.
1985 The geometry of phonological features. *Phonology Yearbook* 2: 223–250.
1986 Syllabification and epenthesis in the Barra dialect of Gaelic. In *The Phonological Representation of Suprasegmentals*, Koen Bogers, Harry van der Hulst, and Maarten Mous (eds.), 317–336. Dordrecht: Foris.

Cowan, Nelson
1995 *Attention and Memory: An Integrated Framework*. New York: Oxford University Press.
1999 An embedded-process model of working memory. In *Models of Working Memory. Mechanisms of Active Maintenance and Executive Control*, Akira Miyake and Priti Shah (eds.), 62–101. Cambridge, UK: Cambridge University Press.

2001   The magical number 4 in short-term memory: A reconsideration of mental storage capacity. *Behavioral and Brain Sciences* 24(1): 87–114.
2005   *Working Memory Capacity.* New York, NY: Psychology Press.

Crompton, Andrew
1982   Syllables and segments in speech production. In *Slips of the Tongue and Language Production*, Ann Cutler (ed.), 663–716. Berlin/New York: Mouton de Gruyter.

Cutler, Ann
1986   Phonological structure in speech recognition. *Phonology Yearbook* 3: 161–178.

Crowley, Terence
1983   Uradhi. In *Handbook of Australian Languages*, Robert M.W. Dixon and Barry J. Blake (eds.), 307–428. (Volume III.) John Benjamins: Amsterdam.

Dixon, Robert M. W.
1977   *A Grammar of Yidiɲ.* Cambridge University Press, Cambridge.
1981   Wargamay. In Robert M.W. Dixon and Barry J. Blake (eds.), *Handbook of Australian Languages, Volume II*, 1–144, John Benjamins, Amsterdam.
1991   Mbabaṛam. In *The Handbook of Australian Languages, Volume IV*, Robert M. W. Dixon and Barry J. Blake (eds.), 349–402, Oxford University Press, Oxford.

Dupoux, Emmanuel, Kazuhiko Kakehi, Yuki Hirose, Christophe Pallier and Jacques Mehler
1999   Epenthetic vowels in Japanese: A perceptual illusion? *Journal of Experimental Psychology: Human Perception and Performance.* 25(6), 1568–1578.

Dupoux, Emmanuel, Christophe Pallier, Kazuhiko Kakehi and Jacques Mehler
2001   New evidence for prelexical phonological processing in word recognition. *Language and Cognitive Processes* 16(5-6), 491–505.

Eades, Diana
1979   Gumbaynggir. In *Handbook of Australian Languages, Volume I*, Robert M. W. Dixon and Barry J. Blake (eds.), 245–361. John Benjamins: Amsterdam.

Fay, David and Ann Cutler
1977   Malapropisms and the structure of the mental lexicon. *Linguistic Inquiry* 8: 505–520.

Fromkin, Victoria A. (ed.)
1973   *Speech Errors As Linguistic Evidence.* The Hague: Mouton & Co.
1985   Evidence in linguistics. *Linguistics and Linguistic Evidence. The LAGB Silver Jubilee Lectures 1984.*, 18–38. Newcastle: Grevatt & Grevatt.

Golston, Chris and Harry van der Hulst
1999   Stricture is structure. In *The Derivational Residue in Phonological Optimality Theory*, Ben Hermans and Marc van Oostendorp (eds.), 153–174. Amsterdam: Benjamins.

Golston, Chris and Richard Wiese
1998   The structure of the German root. In *Phonology and Morphology of the Germanic Languages*, Wolfgang Kehrein and Richard Wiese (eds.), 165–185. Tübingen: Niemeyer.

Hallé, Pierre, Juan Segui, Uli Frauenfelder and Christine Meunier
1998   Processing of illegal consonant clusters: A case of perceptual assimilation?

Journal of Experimental Psychology: Human Perception and Performance, 24(2), 592–608.

Hayes, Bruce
1995 *Metrical Stress Theory: Principles and Case Studies*. Chicago: The University of Chicago Press.

Heimbach, Ernest E.
1966 *White Hmong-English Dictionary* (Linguistics Series IV). Ithaca, NY: Southeast Asia Program, Data paper: Number 75.

Jackendoff, Ray
2002 *Foundations of Language*. Oxford: Oxford University Press.

Jakobson, Roman
1939 Observations sur le classment phonologique des consonnes. *Proceedings of the 3rd International Congress of Phonetic Sciences*. 34–41.

Jakobson, Roman, Gunnar Fant and Morris Halle
1952 *Preliminaries to Speech Analysis*. Cambridge: MIT Press.

James, Lori E. and Deborah M. Burke
2000 Phonological priming effects on word retrieval and tip-of-the-tongue experiences in young and older adults. *Journal of Experimental Psychology: Learning, Memory and Cognition* 26(6): 1378–1391.

Jessen, Michael and Catherine Ringen
2002 Laryngeal features in German. *Phonology* 19, 189–218.

Kager, René
1995 On foot templates and root template. In *Linguistics in the Netherlands 1995*, Marcel den Dikken and Kees Hengeveld (eds.), 125–138. Amsterdam: John Benjamins.

Koriat, Asher and I. Lieblich
1974 What does a person in a "TOT" state know that a person in a "don't know" state doesn't know? *Memory & Cognition* 2: 647–655.

Ladefoged, Peter, Jenny Ladefoged, Alice Turk, Kevin Hind, St John Skilton
1998 Phonetic structures of Scottish Gaelic. *Journal of the International Phonetic Association* 28: 1–42.

Levelt, Willem J. M.
1989 *Speaking: From Intention to Articulation*. Cambridge, Mass.: MIT Press.

Lewis, Will and Chris Golston
2005 The randomness of the signifier. Paper presented at the Annual Meeting of the Linguistic Society of America. Oakland, Cal.

Marcus, Gary F.
2001 *The Algebraic Mind: Integrating Connectionism and Cognitive Science*. Cambridge, Mass.: MIT Press.

Massaro, Dominic W. and Michael M. Cohen
1983 Phonological constraints in speech perception. *Perception & Psychophysics* 34, 338–348.

McCarthy, John J.
2002 *A Thematic Guide to Optimality Theory*. Cambridge: Cambridge University Press.
2007 Restraint of analysis. This volume.

Meyer, Antje S. and Kathryn Bock
1992   The tip-of-the-tongue phenomenon: Blocking or partial activation? *Memory & Cognition* 20: 715–726.

Miller, George A.
1956   The magical number seven, plur or minus two: Some limits on our capacity for processing information. *Psychological Review* 3: 81–97.

Miozzo, Michelle and Alfonso Caramazza
1997   Retrieval of lexical-syntactic features in tip-of-the-tongue states. *Journal of Experimental Psychology: Learning, Memory, and Cognition* 23: 1410–1423.

Oberauer, Klaus
2002   Access to information in working memory: Exploring the focus of attention. *Journal of Experimental Psychology: Learning, Memory, and Cognition* 28(3): 411–421.

Oberauer, Klaus, Heinz-Martin Süss, Ralf Schulze, Oliver Wilhelm and Werner W. Wittmann
2000   Working memory capacity – facets of a cognitive ability construct. *Personality and Individual Differences*, 29: 1017–1045.

Oberauer, Klaus, Heinz-Martin Süss, Oliver Wilhelm and Werner W. Wittmann
2003   The multiple faces of working memory: Storage, processing, supervision, and coordination. *Intelligence* 31(2): 167–193.

van Oostendorp, Marc
2007   Derived Environment Effects and Consistency of Exponence. This volume.

Padgett, Jaye
1995   Feature classes. In *University of Massachusetts Occasional Papers in Linguistics 18*, Jill Beckman, Laura Walsh Dickey, and Suzanne Urbanczyk (eds.), 385–420. Amherst, MA: GLSA.

Poser, William
1990   Evidence for foot structure in Japanese. *Language* 66: 78–105.

Reiss, Charles
2002   The OCP and NOBANANA. *Carleton University Cognitive Science Technical Report* 2002-03. http://www.carleton.ca/iis/Tech Reports

Prince, Alan S., and Paul Smolensky
1993   Optimality theory. Constraint interaction in generative grammar. Technical Report #2, Rutgers University Center for Cognitive Science. ROA 537; published in 2004 by Blackwell Publishers.

de Saussure, Ferdinand
1959   *Course in General Linguistics*, translated by Wade Baskins. New York: The Philosophical Library.

Selkirk, Elizabeth
1995   The prosodic structure of function words. In *Papers in Optimality Theory*, Jill Beckman, Laura Walsh Dickey, and Suzanne Urbanczyk (eds.), 439–470. Amherst, MA: GLSA Publications. Also in *Signal to Syntax: Bootstrapping from Speech to Grammar in Early Acquisition.*, James L. Morgan and Katherine Demuth (eds.), 187–214. Lawrence Erlbaum Associates.

Trubetzkoy, Nikolai S.
1939   *Grundzüge der Phonologie*. Travaux du cercle linguistique de Prague 7.

Vigliocco, Gabriella, Tiziani Antonini and Merrill F. Garrett
 1997   Grammatical gender is on the tip of Italian tongues. *Psychological Science* 8: 314–317.

Subject index

absolute ungrammaticality, 64
accent, 4, 5
    lexical
        in Greek, 149–154
        in Russian, 149–154
    locality, 150, 151, 155, 157, 162–165, 169
    migration, 150, 151, 153, 156, 159, 160, 162–165, 169
allomorphy, 93–95, 118, 361
    non-optional, 73–80
    phonologically 'optional', 71–73
    suppletive, 3, 63–86, 118
    in Turkish, 94–95
Alternant Optimization, 3, 12–13, 17–18, 25, 28–29, 35–36, *see also* Lexicon Optimization
Alternation Condition, 12, 37
amphibrach, 238–242
anchoring
    opaque, 81, 84
    prosodic, 81
    soft, 82
Anti-Faithfulness, 119
ATR harmony, *see* harmony, ATR
attribute value matrices, 67
auditory system, 265
augmentation
    in Axininca Campa, 211–212
    in Lardil, 209–214
autosegmental flop, 219–222
    in Esimbi, 220–222
Autosegmental Phonology, 293–296
    autosegmental unit, 156, 157, 159
Autosegmental Span Theory, 291

blicket detector task, 38–39, 47–48
Bottleneck Effect, 294–295

candidate set
    finite, 206–208
    infinite, 206
child language, 265
coda, 264, 265, 271, 272
coda devoicing
    in Turkish, 13–16, 38–46, 190
Colored Containment, *see* Coloured Containment
Coloured Containment, 83, 123, 126, 135, 137, 141–145, 151, 159, 304
*COMPLEX CODA, 71–72
*COMPLEX ONSET, 77
CON, 3, 5–7, 9, 63–65, 85, 129, 181, 183, 184, 189, 192–195, 197, 198, 203, 207, 208, 212, 213, 216, 241–242, 246, 247, 249–250, 257–260, 263–264, 271, 274, 281–283, 289, 299–301, 303, 305, 306, 318
Consistency of Exponence, 123–135, 144, 159, 349
constraints
    mirroring, 166
    functionally grounded, 257, 260–261, 265, 268
    indexed, 151, 152, 165, 168, 171
    positional, 267
Containment, 4, 83, 125, 126, 145, 286, 304, 349
Containment Principle, *see* Containment
CONTIGUITY, 79
Continuous Column Constraint, 205–206, 214
CONTROL Theory, 65
CONTROL Theory, *see also* MORPHOLEXICAL CONTROL

Correspondence Theory, 4, 20, 83, 126, 128, 145, 203, 286, 326
crazy rules, 86
culminativity, 154

deneutralization, 38
DEP, 15, 20, 22, 23, 25, 94–96, 98–100, 103, 112, 113, 171, 186, 187, 196, 198, 209–214, 223–225, 267–270, 292, 326, 327
  DEP-link, 156, 162
Dependency Phonology, 322
derived environments, 4, 119, 123, 127, 135–145, 162
diachronic change, 20, 85, 273
  phonological typology and, 275
Dispersion Theory, 294–295
Distinctness Condition, 15–16

Element Theory, 289, 303, 322
Elsewhere Principle, 64, 75
Emergence of the Unmarked, 30, 70
Enriched Input Model, 3, 93–118
epenthesis, 40, 67–69, 82, 83, 97–100, 103, 105, 106, 112–114, 116, 117, 125, 126, 183, 184, 187–189, 197, 206–211, 226, 264, 267–269, 275, 302, 304, 347, 349, 362
  in Yowlumne, 103
  iterated epenthesis, 207
EVAL, 2, 3, 5, 6, 9, 175, 185, 186, 199, 204, 207, 209–212, 216, 222, 225, 226, 281, 284, 299, 300, 304, 313, 314, 318, 335, 345, 346, 362, 363, 366

Feature Geometry, 6, 140, 142, 287–289, 293
  Parallel Structures Model, 289, 322–339
feature theory, 289–293

features
  binary, 289–293
  class behaviour, 293
  privative, 289–293
  unary, *see* features, privative
final devoicing, *see also* coda devoicing
final devoicing
  in German, 366
foot
  degenerate, 239–241
  ternary, 239–241
foot minimality
  in Axininca Campa, 211–212
fortition
  of coronals
    in Korean, 46–47
free ride, 41, 55
Freedom of Analysis, 1–8
functional grounding, *see also* constraints, functionally grounded
functionally grounded, 85

gaps
  in Norwegian imperatives, 67–69
GEN, 2–9, 65, 123–125, 127–130, 134, 135, 143, 145, 159, 160, 175–178, 183–185, 187–198, 203, 204, 206–208, 210, 211, 213, 216, 218, 220, 222, 224–226, 233–236, 238, 241–242, 246, 247, 249–253, 257–264, 268, 271, 272, 274, 275, 283–287, 313, 314, 317, 318, 325, 326, 334, 335, 337–340, 345–349, 362, 366, 367
  restrictions on, 257, 262
    content-based, 258
    representational, 258, 262

glides
   as rimal onglides, 260, 261, 263–265, 268–272, 274, 275
   as true onset, 260, 263–265, 268–271, 273–275
   onset-based restrictions on, 257, 264–271, 273–275
   pre-peak, 260, 264, 268, 269, 271, 273, 274
   sonority of, 264–275
   syllable-initial, see glides, pre-peak
global minimum, 214–225
Government Phonology, 302

harmonic improvement, 204–206, 214–225
harmony, see also vowel harmony
   ATR
      in Yoruba, 17–18
HARMONY, 17
head
   dominance, 166
   of foot, 155
   prosodic, 155, 262, 319
height harmony
   in Shona, 289
hypercorrection, 52–53

idempotency, 207
imperatives
   in Norwegian, 67–69
   in Yowlumne, 104
ineffability, 64, 176, 192, 196, 338
Infinity Problem, 186–188
infixation, 227
   in Kentakbong, 79
   in Leti, 82
   in Nakanai, 79
   in Palauan, 131, 132
   in Tagalog, 82, 227, 259
   in Ulwa, 83
input, 316–317, see also Enriched Input Model

INTEGRITY, 4, 5
Interpretive Loop, 175, 176, 184, 188, 197, 198
invariance, 162, 163, 170
INVARIANCE, 162–165

*LAPSE, 243–247
Lexical Phonology and Morphology, 8
lexical statistics, 37–51
lexicon, 315–316
Lexicon Optimization, 3, 35–37, 55, 314, see also Alternant Optimization
   "pattern-responsive", 47
LINEARITY, 218–219
local conjunction, 327
local minimum, 214–225
locality, 293–296
long-distance spreading, see non-local spreading
long-term memory, 355–361
loop, 5
   between GEN and EVAL, 204
   interpretive, 5
lowering
   in Yowlumne, 104–105

MAX, 15, 20, 22, 23, 25, 29, 71, 72, 76, 94–96, 98–100, 103, 182, 183, 187, 198, 215–217, 292, 300, 326, 334, 336–338, 365
MAX-link, 156, 162
metathesis, 126, 176, 182–184, 218–219, 227
   double, 218
   in Kui, 82
   in Lokaa, 181
   long-distance, 218–219
metrical theory, 235–238
MIRROR-HEAD, 166
mirroring, 166, 167, 169, see also constraints, mirroring

Modified Contrastive Specification Model, 323, *see also* contrast
morpheme
   accentless, 152, 153, 168, 171
   post-accenting, 149, 151, 153–158, 162, 164, 168, 169
   pre-accenting, 150, 153–157, 164, 169, 171
Morpheme Realization Theory, 208
morpho-accentual processes, 149, 156, 167–169
morpholexical constraints, 3
MORPHOLEXICAL CONTROL, 65–67
morphological recoverability, 166
MPARSE, 70–71, 75

neutralization
   of rhotics
      in Spanish, 50–51
NOCODA, 71–72, 74, 76, 80
non-local spreading, 296, 303
null parse, 3, 70, 196

ONSET, 80
opacity, 3, 4, 93–118, 144, 157, 170, 196, 226, 281, 305
   in Tiberian Hebrew, 195
   opaque anchoring, *see* anchoring
   opaque selection, 83
      in Turkish, 95, 97–99
      in Yowlumne, 99–103
Optimality Theory, 234–235
   classical, 1
   Classical OT, 313–314, 345–347
   parallelist, *see* classical
   Persistent OT, 6, 203–226, 347
      language typology, 212–225
      ranking arguments, 208–212
orthographic knowledge, 53–58
OT, *see* Optimality Theory

Particle Phonology, 322
polysystematicity, 86

projection (turbid relation), 150, 157–163, 166, 170
pronunciation (turbid relation), 150, 157–162, 164, 166, 170, 171
prosodic anchoring, *see* anchoring

r-insertion
   in Easter Massachussets English, 55
RECIPROCITY, 161, 162, 166, 170
representational complexity, 257, 259, 261, 274, 297–302, 324
representations, 7, 8, 281–307
   laryngeal, 298–300
   orthographic, 37
   SPE, 287, 288
   underlying, 35–58
restrictions on GEN
   content-based, 258
Richness of the Base, 1–3, 9, 11, 12, 23, 24, 29, 30, 74, 248, 250, 252, 313, 314, 316, 317, 321
rimal onglide position, 273
rime, 260–264, 271–273, 275
rising diphthongs, 270, 273

scope, 162–164
segmental frequency, 37, 50
short-term memory, 8
shortening
   in Yowlumne, 105
sonority, 27, 28, 67, 184, 257, 260, 261, 264–275, 333
   sonority scale, 265, 267, 268, 275, 283
*SONSEQ, 67
sound-related substitutions, *see* speech errors, malapropism
Span Theory, 286, *see* Autosegmental Span Theory
speech errors
   malapropism, 355
   tip-of-the-tongue states, 355

spelling, *see* orthographic knowledge
spirantization
    in Polish, 135, 137, 140–144
stop nasalization
    in Vimeu Picard, 223–225
stress, 7, 54–56, 73, 79, 86, 179, 180, 184, 190, 240, 243, 244, 246, 272, 273, 355–358
    default, 153, 168
    in Cayuvava, 236–244
    shift, 54, 204, 205, 226
    ternary, 238, 241, 250
stress shift
    in English, 214
subcategorization, 63, 66, 171
Successive Division Algorithm, 30
suppletion, *see* allomorphy, suppletive
surface representations, 362–366
syntax, 316

ternary rhythm, 233–253
Toronto School, 302, *see aslo* contrast
Transderivational Anti-Faithfulness, 4, 167–169, 208
transparency
    input-output, 37
truncation, 215–218
Turbidity Theory, 141, 150, 157, 304, 305

underlying representations, 350–361, *see* representations, underlying
underspecification, 11–30
uninterpretability, 177–184
    contradictory, 175, 178, 179, 181, 183, 194
    harmonic bounding of, 176, 179, 180, 182, 183, 186, 191, 197
    in Pasiego Montañes vowel harmony, 179–186
    interpretatively incomplete candidate, 175, 178, 179, 183, 184, 190, 194, 198

voicing assimilation, 3, 18–30, 289–292
    in Yiddish, 290
vowel harmony
    in Turkish, 127, 135–137, 143, 144
    in Yowlumne, 104
    Pasiego Montañes Spanish, 179–186
vowel reduction
    in European Portuguese, 55–57

weak local parsing, 242–250
working memory, 352–355

Language index

Akkadian, 131
Antillean creole, *see* Haitian
Anxiang, *see* Chinese
Arusa, 295
Axininca Campa, 78, 188, 212, 226
    augmentation, 211–212
    foot minimality, 211–212

Berber, 203
Burushaski, 77, 83

Catalan, 290
Cayuvava
    stress, 236–244
Chinese
    Anxiang, 130
    Mandarin
        Pingding dialect, 82
Cupeño, 156, 170
Czech, 12, 18, 29, 30
    voicing assimilation, 18–29

Djabugay, 71–72
Dutch, 42–46, 127, 129, 290
Dyirbal, 73–75

Emakhuwa, 222
English, 47, 52–55, 196, 260, 346, 348, 354, 358, 362
    Eastern Massachussets
        r-insertion, 55
    stress shift, 205–206, 214
Esimbi, 220–222
    autosegmental flop, 220–222

Finnish
    Helsinki, 135–137, 139
French, 51, 57, 260, 262

German, 55, 129, 223
    final devoicing, 348, 355, 366

Greek, 155, 158, 163–166, 169, 171
    lexical accents, 149–154
Guugu Yimidhirr, 266

Haitian, 80
Hawai'ian, 325, 327–341
Hebrew
    Tiberian, 195
Hungarian, 31

Italian, 32, 77, 273, 320

Japanese, 273
Jingulu, 193

Kaititj, 79
Karaim, 295
Kentakbong
    infixation, 79
Kera, 295, 304
Kikongo, 295
Kimatuumbi, 78
Korean, 46, 47, 77, 135, 138
    coronal fortition, 46–47
    Seoul, 266
Kui
    metathesis, 82
Kuman, 266

Lardil
    augmentation, 209–214
Latin, 361, 363
Leti
    infixation, 82
Lezgian, 41
Lokaa, 181, 182, 186

Mbabaram, 266, 269
Mongolian, 266

Nakanai
    infixation, 79
Namwanga, 296
Ndyuka, 77
Nez Perce, 31
Norwegian, 67–69
Nukuoro, 355

Palauan, 131–134
Pasiego, see Spanish
Pingding, see Chinese, Mandarin, Pingding
    dialect
Pitta-Pitta, 266
Polish
    spirantization, 135, 137, 140–144
Portuguese, 57
    European
        vowel reduction, 55–57

Russian, 164, 166, 168–171
    lexical accents, 149–154

Saanish, 295
Sanskrit, 170
Sardinian
    Campidanian
        Iglesias, 266–271, 273, 275
        Sestu, 266, 267, 269–271, 275
Shona, 285
    height harmony, 289
Slave, 188
Slovak, 260
Spanish, 50, 51, 84, 260, 262, 272, 273
    neutralization of rhotics, 50–51
    Pasiego Montañes, 179–181, 183, 185–187, 193
        vowel harmony, 179–186
        vowel uninterpretability, 179–186

Tagalog, 82, 227, 259
Turkana, 78

Turkish, 12, 17, 18, 20, 23, 30, 36, 38–40, 42–46, 48
    coda devoicing, 13–16, 38–41, 43–46, 190
    opaque selection, 95, 97–99
    suppletive allomorphy, 94–95
    vowel harmony, 127, 135–137, 143, 144

Udihe, 72
Ulwa
    infixation, 81, 83

Vai, 87
Vimeu Picard, 223–225
    stop nasalization, 223–225

White Hmong, 355

Yiddish, 32, 290, 320
    voicing assimilation, 290
Yoruba
    ATR harmony, 17–18
Yowlumne, 93, 99–117
    epenthesis, 103
    lowering, 104–105
    opacity, 99–118
    opaque selection, 99–103
    shortening, 105
    vowel harmony, 104
Yupik, 119

Zuni, 79

Author index

Abbott, Barbara, 119
Abrams, Lisa, 355
Ahn, Sang-Cheol, 46
Akinlabi, Akinbiyi, 181, 182, 190
Albright, Adam, 47
Alderete, John, 5, 119, 154, 156, 167–171, 208
Anderson, John, 322
Anderson, Stephen R., 350
Antonini, Tiziani, 355
Anttila, Arto, 135, 136, 139, 144, 146, 151
Apoussidou, Diana, 168
Archangeli, Diana, 99, 100, 103, 105, 108, 114, 115
Archangeli, Diana, 31, 119, 223, 286
Aronoff, Mark, 361
Auger, Julie, 223
Avery, Peter, 28, 297, 323, 341

Baayen, Harald, 42–44, 46
Bach, Emmon, 86
Baddeley, Alan D., 352
Baertsch, Karen, 273
Baković, Eric, 31, 119, 289, 290, 293, 296
Barlow, Jessica, 265
Beaver, David, 199
Beckman, Jill, 287, 289–291
Berger, Hermann, 77, 83
Bermúdez-Otero, Ricardo, 84
Berry, Lynn, 252
Bickmore, Lee, 296
Bird, Steven, 96, 178
Black, H. Andrew, 203
Blaho, Sylvia, 12, 31, 145
Blake, Barry J., 266
Blevins, Juliette, 9, 85, 252, 261, 266, 297, 338, 341, see also Levin, Juliette

Bock, Kathryn, 355
Boersma, Paul, 6, 30, 32, 85, 178, 285, 315, 335
Bolognesi, Roberto, 266, 270
Booij, Geert, 63, 70, 71, 134
Bosch, Anna, 357
Bradshaw, Mary, 303
Breen, Gavan, 266
Broselow, Ellen, 262
Browman, Catherine P., 351, 353
Brown, Alan S., 355
Brown, Jason C., 357
Brown, Roger, 355
Burke, Deborah M., 355
Butterworth, Brian, 357
Bybee, Joan, 340
Bye, Patrik, 12, 145, 196
Byrd, Dani, 351

Campbell, Lyle, 295
Caramazza, Alfonso, 355
Carleton, Troi, 165
Carpenter, Angela, 219
Carrol, Vern, 355
Cassimjee, Farida, 222
Chéreau, Céline, 57
Charles-Luce, Jan, 52
Chen, Su-I, 262
Cheng, P. W., 39
Chomsky, Noam, 175, 191, 208, 285, 322, 345, 350, 351, 353
Clements, G. N., 6, 67, 97, 220, 286, 288, 293, 297, 298, 303, 307, 322, 323, 350, 351, 353, 357
Coetzee, Andries, 185, 198, 199
Cohen, Michael M., 348
Cole, Jennifer S., 99, 110, 223
Cowan, Nelson, 353
Crompton, Andrew, 356
Crosswhite, Katherine, 262

Crowhurst, Megan, 194
Crowley, Terence, 354
Cutler, Ann, 355, 356

d'Andrade, Ernesto, 55
Davis, Stuart, 260, 273
Delgutte, Bertrand, 265
Dell, François, 265, 272
Dimmendaal, Gerrit J., 78
Dixon, Robert M. W., 73, 266, 269, 354
Downing, Laura J., 226
Dresher, B. Elan, 30, 31, 237, 252, 253, 302, 323
Dupoux, Emmanuel, 348

Eades, Diana, 354
Eisner, Jason, 242
Eitel, Stacey L., 355
Elbert, Samuel, 328
Elenbaas, Nine, 242, 244–248, 250, 252
Ellison, Mark, 96
Elmedlaoui, Mohamed, 265, 272
Ernestus, Miriam, 42–44, 46
Everett, Daniel L., 252
Ewen, Colin, 322

Féry, Caroline, 196
Fanselow, Gisbert, 196
Fant, Gunnar, 350
Fay, David, 356
Feng, Bella, 129, 130, 135, 160
Firth, John Rupert, 86
Flack, Kathryn, 268, 269
Fleischhacker, Heidi, 85
Flemming, Edward, 314
Frauenfelder, Uri, 348
Frazier, Melissa, 262
Fromkin, Viktoria A., 356
Fukazawa, Haruka, 170, 327

Gáspár, Miklós, 288

Gafos, Adamantios, 215, 227
Gafos, Diamandis, 293
Gallistel, Randy, 47, 49
Garrett, Merrill F., 355
Gnanadesikan, Amalia, 265
Goldrick, Matthew, 141, 150, 157, 158, 170, 196, 304, 305
Goldsmith, John, 115, 220, 285, 286, 293
Goldstein, Louis, 351, 353
Golston, Chris, 126, 133, 298–301, 352–355
Gopnik, Alison, 39, 47, 48
Gordon, Matthew, 243, 252, 261, 265
Gouskova, Maria, 208
Green, Antonio, 70
Green, Thomas, 243, 252
Grijzenhout, Janet, 290
Grimshaw, Jane, 208

Hale, Kenneth, 81, 175, 181, 195, 209
Hale, Mark, 85, 315
Hall, Daniel Currie, 12, 20, 26, 31, 32
Hall, Nancy, 275
Hallé, Pierre, 57, 348
Halle, Morris, 15, 85, 153, 170, 175, 236, 238, 252, 285, 322, 345, 350, 351, 353
Hammond, Michael, 170, 178, 252, 260, 262, 315, 316
Hansson, Gunnar, 99
Harms, Robert, 86
Harris, James, 50, 140, 260, 272
Harris, John, 289, 322
Harrison, K. David, 47, 315
Harrison, Sheldon P., 252
Haviland, John, 266
Hayes, Bruce, 85, 187, 237, 239, 242, 248, 252, 260–262, 272, 318, 358
Heim, Irene, 195
Heimbach, Ernest E., 355
Hewitt, Mark, 252

Hind, Kevin, 357
Hirose, Yuki, 348
Hoeksema, Jack, 166
Honeybone, Patrick, 290, 291
Horwood, Graham, 227
Houghton, Paula, 252
Huffman, Marie, 262
van der Hulst, Harry, 237, 252, 253, 322, 352–354
Hume, Elizabeth, 6, 219, 227, 288, 293, 295, 297, 303, 307
Huttar, George L., 77
Hyde, Brett, 252
Hyman, Larry, 220, 273

Idsardi, William, 47, 85, 170
Inkelas, Sharon, 3, 12–18, 20, 31, 35, 36, 44, 45, 48, 119, 151, 155, 190
Ishii, Toru, 243, 252
Itô, Junko, 31, 32, 170, 215, 221, 264, 289, 315
Iverson, Gregory, 46, 135

Jackendoff, Ray, 358, 361, 362, 366, 367
Jakobson, Roman, 350
James, Lori E., 355
Janda, Richard D., 166
Jespersen, Otto, 55
Jessen, Michael, 366
Johnson, Raymond Leslie, 79
José, Brian, 223
Jun, Jongho, 196

Kager, René, 71, 94, 242–248, 250, 252, 258, 354
Kaisse, Ellen M., 260, 272
Kakehi, Kazuhiko, 348
Kang, Yoonjung, 46
Kaun, Abigail, 47, 315
Kaye, Jonathan, 166, 260
Keating, Patricia, 177

Kehrein, Wolfgang, 298–301
Kenstowicz, Michael, 135, 252
Key, Harold H., 236
Keyser, Samuel J., 195
Kilimangalam, Ashtamurty, 55
Kim-Renaud, Young-Key, 266
Kingston, John, 198
Kiparsky, Paul, 8, 12, 37, 41, 50, 135, 157, 170, 196, 285, 316
Kirchner, Robert, 223, 315
Kisseberth, Charles, 99, 135, 222, 223
Kitahara, Mafuyu, 170
Klein, Ewan, 178
Klokeid, Terry, 209
Koch, Harold J., 79
Koriat, Asher, 355
Krämer, Martin, 20, 31, 54, 289, 290, 296, 307
Kratzer, Angelika, 195
Kučera, Henry, 26
Kubozono, Haruo, 273
Kurisu, Kazutaka, 208

Lacayo Blanco, Abanel, 81
de Lacy, Paul, 177, 183, 194, 198, 275, 291, 292
Ladefoged, Jenny, 357
Ladefoged, Peter, 357
Lahiri, Aditi, 30, 237, 252
Lakoff, George, 99
Lee, Hanjung, 199
Lee, Young-Sook C., 77
Leer, Jeff, 240, 252
Lepschy Giulio, 77
Lepschy, Anna Laura, 77
Levelt, Willem J. M., 355
Levelt, Willem J. M., 87
Levi, Susannah, 264
Levin, Juliette, 236, 252, *see also* Blevins, Juliette
Lewis, Geoffrey, 40, 95
Lewis, Will, 355
Lieber, Rochelle, 64

Lieblich, I., 355
Lindsey, Geoff, 289, 322
Lombardi, Linda, 223, 287, 289, 290, 292, 300, 307, 326
Lowenstamm, Jean, 260
Luce, Paul, 45, 52
Lynch, John, 266
Łubowicz, Anna, 129, 131, 132, 134, 135, 137, 140, 142, 146, 188

Mackenzie, Sara, 31
Manganaro, Linda, 273
Marcus, Gary F., 358, 360, 361, 366, 367
Martin, Samuel E., 77
Masayesva Jeanne, LaVerne, 175, 181
Mascaró, Joan, 70, 140
Mascarenhas, Salvador, 55
Massaro, Dominic W., 348
Mateus, Maria Helena, 55
McCarthy, John J., 1, 3–6, 9, 41, 47, 55, 63, 70, 73, 74, 79, 81–84, 99, 101, 109–111, 119, 123, 125, 127, 129, 142, 143, 145, 155, 159, 165, 167, 170, 175, 179, 182, 190, 195, 196, 203, 204, 211, 212, 215, 217, 218, 223, 226, 234, 235, 239, 242, 251, 252, 258, 259, 261, 262, 264, 265, 267, 281, 283, 284, 286, 287, 289, 291, 292, 298, 301, 306, 307, 318, 326, 345–347, 350, 361
McLennan, Conor, 52
Mehler, Jacques, 348
Melvold, Janis Leanne, 153, 170
Mester, Armin, 31, 32, 170, 221, 289, 315
Meunier, Christine, 348
Meyer, Antje S., 355, 357
Michaels, David, 53–55, 58
Miglio, Viola, 327
Miller, George A., 352

Miozzo, Michelle, 355
Morén, Bruce, 32, 289, 295, 296, 304, 320, 322–324, 340, 341
Moreton, Elliott, 29, 207
Myers, Scott, 165, 182, 273, 275

Ní Chiosáin, Máire, 227, 289, 293, 294, 307
Napoli, Donna Jo, 273
Nevins, Andrew, 38, 55, 295
Newman, Stanley, 99, 100, 119
Nikolaeva, Irina, 72
Norton, Russell J., 203
Noske, Roland, 100, 145

Oberauer, Klaus, 352, 353
Odden, David, 78, 293, 295, 297, 303, 304
Ogden, Richard, 86
Ohala, John J., 265
Omar, Asmah Haji, 79
van Oostendorp, Marc, 83, 124–126, 151, 159, 166, 170, 287, 304, 349
Orgun, Cemil Orhan, 13, 14, 16, 20, 65, 69, 119, 190
Ota, Mitsuhiko, 170, 315

Padgett, Jaye, 25, 31, 32, 140, 227, 259, 289, 293, 294, 306, 307, 351, 353
Palková, Zdena, 26
Pallier, Christophe, 348
Parker, Steve, 275
Paster, Mary, 63, 78, 79
Pater, Joe, 218
Patz, Elizabeth, 71
Payne, David L., 78, 188, 211
Pensalfini, Rob, 193
Peperkamp, Sharon, 188
Piggott, Glyne, 323
Pisoni, David, 45
Platero, Paul, 175, 181

Polgárdi, Krisztina, 135
Poppe, Nikolaus, 266
Poser, William, 219, 358
Prince, Alan S., 1–6, 11, 12, 27, 63, 70, 73, 81–83, 93, 101, 119, 123, 125, 127, 129, 133, 145, 149, 159, 165, 167, 170, 175, 182, 185, 186, 196, 199, 203–206, 209, 211, 212, 215, 217, 218, 226, 233, 234, 238, 239, 242, 251, 252, 257, 259, 261, 262, 264, 265, 267, 272, 275, 281, 282, 284–286, 292, 313, 314, 317, 318, 326, 345, 349
Prince, Alan S., 35
Pukui, Mary Kawena, 328
Pulleyblank, Douglas, 31, 223
Pycha, Anne, 44, 45

Raffelsiefen, Renate, 65
Ramsey, S. Robert, 266
Reetz, Henning, 30
Regh, Ken, 87
Reiss, Charles, 31, 85, 315, 347
Revithiadou, Anthi, 138, 141, 165, 166, 170, 304, 305
Reynolds, George S., 49
Rhee, Sang Jik, 135
Rice, Curt, 64, 67, 237, 240, 252, 253
Rice, Keren D., 28, 188, 297, 323, 341
Rifkin, Jay I., 252
Riggle, Jason, 197
Ringen, Catherine, 366
Rose, Sharon, 227, 295, 296, 307
Rosenthall, Sam, 272
Rubach, Jerzy, 63, 70, 71, 134, 137, 140, 260
Russell, Kevin, 315, 316

Sagey, Elizabeth, 178, 286, 293
Saltzmann, Elliot, 351
Samek-Lodovici, Vieri, 196
Sanders, Nathan, 315

Sapir, Edward, 53
de Saussure, Ferdinand, 350, 353
Schane, Stanford, 322
Scheer, Tobias, 302
Schulze, Ralf, 353
Scobbie, James M., 65
Segui, Juan, 57, 348
Seidenberg, M. S., 57
Selkirk, Elisabeth, 261, 262
Selkirk, Elizabeth, 188, 194, 243, 354
Sezer, Engin, 97, 119
Skelton, St John, 357
Skousen, Royal, 46
Smeets, Rieks, 295
Smith, Jennifer L., 128, 261, 266, 275, 276, 318
Smolensky, Paul, 1, 2, 4–6, 11, 12, 27, 29, 35, 63, 93, 125, 133, 145, 149, 159, 175, 185, 189, 196, 199, 203, 204, 206, 209, 223, 226, 233, 234, 238, 239, 252, 257, 265, 272, 281, 282, 284–286, 304, 305, 313, 314, 317, 327, 345, 349
Sobel, David, 39, 47, 48
Sohn, Ho-Min, 266
Sohn, Hyang-Sook, 46
Soulik, Topias, 355
Spring, Cari, 211
Sprouse, Ronald, 44, 45, 65, 69, 99
Stallcup, Kenneth L., 220
Stanley, Richard, 31
Steriade, Donca, 177, 265, 322
Stevens, Kenneth N., 265
Stump, Gregory T., 66
Süss, Heinz-Martin, 352, 353
Suzuki, Keiichiro, 99, 105, 114, 119

Tanenhaus M. K., 57
Tenenbaum, Joshua, 39, 47, 48
Tesar, Bruce, 189, 208, 226
Tolskaya, Marina, 72
Trefry, David, 266

Trigo, Lauren, 110
Trubetzkoy, Nikolai S., 350
Turk, Alice, 357

Uffmann, Christian, 289, 291, 295, 303, 304, 307

Vaux, Bert, 295, 307
Vergnaud, Jean-Roger, 170, 236, 238, 252
Vigliocco, Gabriella, 355
van de Vijver, Ruben, 252

Walker, Rachel, 129, 130, 135, 160, 220, 221, 227, 292, 295, 296, 300, 307
Warner, Natasha L., 265
Wedel, Andrew, 44, 45
Weenink, David, 32
Welmers, William Evert, 87
Wheeler, Deirdre, 170
Wiese, Richard, 215, 355
Wilhelm, Oliver, 352, 353
Wilkinson, Karina, 209
Wilson, Colin, 6, 223
Winfield, W. W., 82
Wittmann, Werner M., 352, 353
Wolf, Matthew, 3, 64, 70, 74, 84
Wright, Richard, 265, 276

Yip, Moira, 119, 283, 296–298, 306
Yolcu-Kamali, Beste, 38
Yu, Alan, 41, 79, 82

Zec, Draga, 215, 272
Zhang, Jie, 261
Zimmer, Karl, 119
Zoll, Cheryl, 16, 99, 100, 109, 151, 190, 221, 296
Zsiga, Elizabeth, 296
Zuraw, Kie, 85
Zwicky, Arnold, 58

Contributors

Sylvia Blaho
University of Tromsø

Faculty of Humanities
Center for Advanced Study
in Theoretical Linguistics
Breivika
N-9037 Norway

sylvia.blaho@hum.uit.no

Paul de Lacy
Rutgers University

Linguistics Department
18 Seminary Place
NJ 08901-1184
USA

delacy@rutgers.edu

Daniel Currie Hall
University of Toronto

Department of Linguistics
130 St. George Street
Toronto, Ont. M5S 3H1
Canada

daniel.hall@utoronto.ca

John J. McCarthy
University of Massachusetts, Amherst

Department of Linguistics
226 South College
150 Hicks Way
Amherst, MA 01003-9274
USA

jmccarthy@linguist.umass.edu

Patrik Bye
University of Tromsø

Faculty of Humanities
Institute of Linguistics/CASTL
Breivika
N-9037 Norway

patrik.bye@hum.uit.no

Chris Golston
California State University, Fresno

Department of Linguistics
5245 North Backer Avenue
Fresno, CA 93740-8001
USA

chrisg@csufresno.edu

Martin Krämer
University of Tromsø

Faculty of Humanities
Institute of Linguistics/CASTL
Breivika
N-9037 Norway

martin.kramer@hum.uit.no

Bruce Morén
University of Tromsø

Faculty of Humanities
Center for Advanced Study
in Theoretical Linguistics
Breivika
N-9037 Norway

bruce.moren@hum.uit.no

Andrew Nevins
Harvard University

Department of Linguistics
317 Boylston Hall
Cambridge, MA 02138
USA

nevins@fas.harvard.edu

Orhan Orgun
University of California, Davis

Department of Linguistics
108 Sproul Hall
1 Shields Avenue
Davis, CA 95616
USA

ocorgun@ucdavis.edu

Curt Rice
University of Tromsø

Faculty of Humanities
Center for Advanced Study
in Theoretical Linguistics
Breivika
N-9037 Norway

curt.rice@hum.uit.no

Jennifer L. Smith
University of North Carolina

Department of Linguistics
322 Dey Hall, CB 3155
Chapel Hill, NC 27599-3155
USA

jlsmith@email.unc.edu

Bert Vaux
University of Cambridge

Department of Linguistics
Faculty of Modern and Medieval Languages
Sidgwick Avenue
Cambridge, CB3 9DA
England

bv230@cam.ac.uk

Marc van Oostendorp
Meertens Instituut

Joan Muyskenweg 25
1096 CJ Amsterdam

Postbus 94264
1090 GG Amsterdam

marc.van.oostendorp@meertens.knaw.nl

Anthi Revithiadou
University of the Aegean

Department of Mediterranean Studies
1 Demokratias Avenue
85100 Rhodes
Greece

revithiadou@rhodes.aegean.gr

Ronald Sprouse
University of California, Berkeley

Department of Linguistics
1203 Dwinelle Hall
Berkeley, CA 94720-2650
USA

ronald@uclink.berkeley.edu

Christian Uffmann
University of Tromsø

Faculty of Humanities
Center for Advanced Study
in Theoretical Linguistics
Breivika
N-9037 Norway

christian.uffmann@hum.uit.no